Strategic Market Creation

Strategic Market Creation

A New Perspective on Marketing and Innovation Management

Edited by:

Karin Tollin
and
Antonella Carù

WILEY

John Wiley & Sons, Ltd

Email (for orders and customer service enquiries): cs-books@wiley.co.uk
Visit our Home Page on www.wiley.com

Other Wiley Editorial Offices
John Wiley & Sons Inc., 111 River Street, Hoboken, NJ 07030, USA
Jossey-Bass, 989 Market Street, San Francisco, CA 94103-1741, USA
Wiley-VCH Verlag GmbH, Boschstr. 12, D-69469 Weinheim, Germany
John Wiley & Sons Australia Ltd, 42 McDougall Street, Milton, Queensland 4064, Australia
John Wiley & Sons (Asia) Pte Ltd, 2 Clementi Loop #02-01, Jin Xing Distripark, Singapore 129809
John Wiley & Sons Canada Ltd, 6045 Freemont Blvd, Mississauga, ONT, L5R 4J3

Wiley also publishes its books in a variety of electronic formats. Some content that appears in print may not be available in electronic books.

Library of Congress Cataloging-in-Publication Data

Strategic market creation : a new perspective on marketing and innovation management / edited by Karin Tollin & Antonella Carù.
     p. cm.
  Includes bibliographical references and index.
  ISBN 978-0-470-72509-2 (cloth) – ISBN 978-0-470-69427-5 (pbk.)
 1. Marketing–Management.   2.   Product management.   I. Tollin, Karin.   II. Carù, Antonella.
  HF5415.13.S8774 2008
  658.8'02–dc22

                                                                    2008016872

A catalogue record for this book is available from the British Library

ISBN 978 0 470 72509 2 (hbk)
ISBN 978 0 470 69427 5 (pbk)

Typeset by Thomson Digital, India
Printed and bound in Great Britain by CPI Antony Rowe, Chippenham, Wiltshire

Contents

About the Authors

Henrik Andersen is director of Andersen & Partners Management Consulting. He has been in global consultancy for almost 20 years, serving leading global firms. Until he founded his own business 5 years ago, he was partner with PricewaterhouseCoopers. His main interests are business strategy, customer relationship management, and customer segmentation. He has contributed to various books on customer relations management and customer strategy.

Mogens Bjerre is associate professor of Marketing at Copenhagen Business School, where he is associate dean of the Executive MBA and Executive Certificates. His research interests are focused on retail and service marketing and on the relationships between buyers and sellers in related industries. He has also worked on various research projects in e-commerce and sales management. He has published on these topics in various national and international journals and books.

Stefania Borghini is assistant professor of Marketing at Università Bocconi. Her research interests are focused on symbolic consumption read through the perspective of consumer culture theory. She applies ethnographic methods in research projects developed in business market contexts, where she investigates the role of industrial branding and buyer behaviour. Her works have been published in various international books and journals.

Bruno Busacca is professor of Marketing at Università Bocconi and director of the Corporate Executive Education Division – Custom Programmes at the SDA Bocconi School of Management. His research interests are focused on consumer behaviour, strategic brand management, customer value management, and market-based assets. He has published on these topics in various national and international journals and books.

Antonella Carù is professor of Marketing at Università Bocconi, where she is director of the MSc in Marketing Management. Her research interests are focused on services marketing and on the experiential perspective in consumption and marketing. She has also worked on various research projects in the arts and cultural marketing field. She has published on these topics in various national and international journals and books.

Bo T. Christensen is assistant professor in the Department of Marketing, Copenhagen Business School, and trained as a cognitive psychologist. His research interests focus on creative cognitive processes and he is currently conducting research relating to design cognition, the subjective evaluation of creativity, and user-centred innovation. In his research he combines ethnographic studies of designers at work, using video-recordings and verbal protocol studies, with traditional experimental studies conducted in the psychological lab.

John K. Christiansen is professor of Management of Projects and Innovation at Copenhagen Business School, where he is currently acting head of the Department of Operations Management. His research is directed towards the use of management technologies in ambiguous, loosely coupled situations. He has published research on implementation of management systems, perspectives on management, and management of innovation and product development. He is a member of the organizing committee for the International Product Development Management Conference.

Paola Cillo is an assistant professor of Management at Università Bocconi. Her research and teaching interests focus on creativity and innovation in symbol-intensive industries. She is author of different publications in Italian and international journals.

Bernard Cova is professor of Marketing at Euromed Marseilles – School of Management and a visiting professor at Università Bocconi, Milan. A pioneer in the consumer tribes field since the early 1990s, his internationally influential research has emphasized what he calls "the Mediterranean approach" of tribal marketing. He is also known for his groundbreaking research in B2B marketing, especially in the field of project marketing. His work on this topic has been published in various national and international journals and books.

Francesca Golfetto is professor of Marketing at Università Bocconi. She is co-director of CERMES – Università Bocconi Centre of Researches on Markets and

Industries – and director of MIMEC – Master in Marketing and Communication. Her research interests focus on value creation and marketing communications in industrial markets. Previous works have been published in various international journals.

Tilde Heding has an MSc in Design and Communication Management from Copenhagen Business School and runs the brand consultancy company heding & knudtzen in partnership with Charlotte Knudtzen. heding & knudtzen believes firmly in a vision of making brand management more scientific. This vision is reflected in its business consultancy and teaching, and in its publication of articles and textbooks about brand management.

Juliana Hsuan-Mikkola is associate professor of Operations Management at Copenhagen Business School. She was an automotive electrical design engineer as well as an executive trainee (with Motorola in the USA) before joining academia. Her teaching and research interests include operations management, modularization, innovation management, and portfolio management of R&D projects. Her research has been published in various international journals and books.

Richard Jones is associate professor of Marketing at the Department of Marketing, Copenhagen Business School, and programme director of the MSc programme Marketing Communications Management. His main areas of research are brand management, stakeholder relations, and public relations, and works by him have been published in various international journals. His most recent research looks at safeguarding brand value and issues around the implementation of branding strategies at a managerial level.

Charlotte Knudtzen has an MSc in International Marketing and Management from Copenhagen Business School. She is a partner in the brand consultancy company heding & knudtzen. heding & knudtzen specializes in researching and developing brand management for business areas of all kinds. heding & knudtzen also publishes articles and textbooks about brand management and Charlotte teaches Strategic Brand Management at Copenhagen Business School.

Niels Kornum is associate professor of Marketing at Copenhagen Business School. His research interests have been focused on market creation in consumer e-commerce, especially grocery e-commerce. Recently he has combined this perspective with interests in firm-initiated consumer communities and stakeholder responsibility and Fair Trade market creation.

Anne Sofie Lefèvre has an MSc in Communication and Design Management from Copenhagen Business School. She has specialized in how different market conceptions influence the choice of user involvement strategies in the innovation process. At the moment she is working in a Copenhagen-located design company, 1508, participating in project management, (user) research, and concept development within the areas of corporate branding and service design.

David Mazursky received his PhD in marketing from the Graduate School of Business Administration at New York University. A professor at the Hebrew University of Jerusalem, School of Business Administration, and adjunct professor at Università Bocconi, Milan, he served as the director of the Business Administration Department, the head of the PhD Committee, and the director of The Kmart Centre for Retailing and International Marketing. His theories and research have been widely published in leading journals.

Stefano Pace is assistant professor in Marketing at Università Bocconi, where he earned his PhD in Business Administration and Management. His current research interests include brand communities and services marketing. He was a visiting PhD student at the Sol C. Snider Centre (Wharton Business School, Philadelphia, USA). He has published in various national and international journals.

Stefano Podestà is a full professor at Università Bocconi. He is the editor of *Finanza, Marketing e Produzione,* one of the leading management journals in Italy. His research interests are competition and market evolution, as well as consumer behaviour. He is also involved in the postmodern debate about the new challenges of marketing.

Emanuela Prandelli is an associate professor of Management at Università Bocconi and senior lecturer at SDA Bocconi School of Management. Her research focuses on collaborative marketing, virtual communities of consumption, the study of e-business, and the process of innovation. She has published several international articles in leading international journals.

Diego Rinallo is assistant professor of Marketing at Università Bocconi. He is a senior analyst at CERMES – Università Bocconi Centre of Researches on Markets and Industries. His research interests include the culture-producing role of marketers and consumers and the role of collective events in the social construction and evolution of markets, industries, occupations, and communities of consumers. His work has been published in various international books and journals.

Thomas Ritter is professor of Marketing at the Copenhagen Business School, where he is also the research director at the Centre of Business Marketing and Purchasing. His main research interests are in business relationship and interfirm network management, collaborative value creation, and customer segmentation. His work has been widely published in leading marketing journals.

Karin Tollin is associate professor of Marketing at the Department of Marketing, Copenhagen Business School, and programme director of the MSc programme Strategic Market Creation. Her main research falls in the areas of product innovation and knowledge and brand management, with a special focus on top managers' mindsets for innovation and on marketing's role for firms' innovation capability. She has published on these issues in international books and journals.

Gabriele Troilo is professor of Marketing at Università Bocconi and SDA Bocconi School of Management. He is also vice-president of the European Marketing Academy (EMAC). His main research interests are marketing strategy, marketing in creative industries, and marketing knowledge management. On these topics he has published several books and papers in national and international journals.

Mads Vangkilde is a PhD student at Copenhagen Business School. His research revolves around timing strategies, innovation, and sustainability of competitive advantages. This research is tested on the e-grocery sector in Denmark. Moreover, he works as online sales manager at Sonofon A/S, the second largest telecommunications company in Denmark.

Claus J. Varnes is associate professor at the Department of Operations Management, Copenhagen Business School. His research focuses on the use of formal management methods and approaches in innovation, decision-making, and performance management. He teaches Management of Product Development and Performance Management in Sales and Marketing at graduate level. He has published on these topics in international journals.

Gianmario Verona is associate professor of Management at Università Bocconi, where he is associate director of the PhD in Business Administration and

Management. His research and teaching activity is focused on technology and product innovation, with special emphasis on the role of organizational competences and exploration processes. He has published several articles in both leading academic journals and practitioner-oriented outlets.

Salvio Vicari is professor of Innovation Management and head of the Department of Management at Università Bocconi. His research and teaching focus on product innovation, creativity, organizational learning, and strategic marketing. He is author and editor of numerous works on marketing, technology and innovation management, creativity, and knowledge management.

Luca M. Visconti is professor of Marketing at Università Bocconi, where he is director of the Master in Marketing and Communication (MiMeC). His research activities deal with consumer marketing as read through the perspective of consumer culture theory. In particular, he investigates the topic of marginal consumers, social movements, and Mediterranean marketing. He has published on these topics in both national and international journals and books.

Astrid S. Wolf has an MSc in Communication and Design Management from Copenhagen Business School. She has specialized in how different market conceptions will influence the choice of user involvement strategies in the innovation process. At the moment she is working in the Department of Advertising at Peoplegroup, a communication agency located in Copenhagen.

Fabrizio Zerbini is assistant professor of Marketing and director of the Master in Event and Experiential Marketing at Università Bocconi. His research interests are focused on business markets, and especially on business services, value creation strategy, and the multiplicity of market relationships. Prior research has been published in various international journals.

Introduction and Overview of Strategic Market Creation

For a long time, new product, service, and/or brand innovation within some industries and companies has been regarded as a core business process and a capability that has to be "in place" in order to prosper or even to survive. During the last decade, however, it has become evident that this strategy has attracted interest and even been adopted within industries and by companies that, until now, have never or only occasionally been described as creative, entrepreneurial, or innovative. In short, the issue of how to realize new business opportunities by creating new meaningful value experiences in new or already existing markets has come to be very central in the business world and in academia. As for other strategies and during other time periods, success depends on values, processes, knowledge, relationships, etc., expressing the qualities of the particular context and period of time. The purpose of this book is to address the latter and our notion that the present era calls, in many respects, for new ideas, perspectives, insights, and practices to address and to deal with radical innovation of a firm's market offerings. Behind this proposition, as will be made clear in the book, stand many insightful contributions by researchers from different academic fields and parts of the world. In this book, some of these contributions are referred to, discussed, and/or presented with the aim of encouraging the reader to take part in creating new knowledge about marketing and innovation management.

As indicated by the title of the book, we have chosen "strategic market creation" as a signifier of the composition, and implicitly as a description of what issues the book is dealing with. One reason for this combination of words is to express two more or less established ideas, or, more correctly, propositions, in the contemporary literature on marketing and innovation management. According to these ideas, radical innovation of a firm's market offering not only presupposes but also often gives rise to considerations of resources, processes, and capabilities of a corporate and long-term character and significance. Furthermore, a successful realization of new product, service, and/or brand innovation depends on having the needed structures and processes in place to make co-creation of meaningful experiences with customers become a reality.

The idea to produce this book was born two years ago in response to a successful launch of a new Master Programme in Marketing at Copenhagen Business School (CBS), "Strategic Market Creation" (SMC), and to the creation of a double-degree agreement between the Copenhagen SMC programme and the Master of Science in Marketing Management of Bocconi University in Milan. The agreement and the book were made possible by common thoughts and ideas about the directions in which marketing as a field of knowledge is developing in research and in the business world, and consequently has to develop in marketing education. The book is structured around the above-mentioned two ideas or propositions. This means that the book begins with contributions dealing with "Knowledge, Processes, and Capabilities for Market Creation", followed by contributions concerned with "Co-creation of Meaningful Experiences with Customers".

A key issue when dealing with innovation of a firm's market offerings is how to detect new viable business ideas. Owing to the features of this process, it has come to be called the fuzzy front end, or phase, in an innovation process. Thus, this is the phase within which evolving and new technologies and/or latent customers' needs and values are identified and evaluated as to their originality and ability to be converted into a physical product or service with a possibility of becoming a business opportunity. In the literature, a prevalent view, grounded on numerous example cases from the business world, is that radical innovation emanates from new knowledge and/or new combinations of existing knowledge about product and process technology, above all, and consequently from a capability to detect, develop, and deploy knowledge about technology. In contrast to this view, the stance taken in the marketing literature, and based on numerous studies, is that successful product and service innovation (incremental as well as radical) is the result of insights and ideas about and from customers. Notwithstanding this experience and stance within the two fields, the question of what other perspectives and knowledge areas may be of value in creating original and productive ideas has begun to be asked. In the first part of the book there are three chapters (Chapters 1, 3, and 7) that explicitly deal with arguments and approaches concerning the integration of different perspectives in the fuzzy front end. In Chapter 1 it is product and market knowledge that stands in focus, whereas in Chapter 3 it is creativity studies and consumer insights emanating from a marketing perspective. And in Chapter 7, arguments for linking technology management with a supply chain perspective are made.

The issue of how to detect, or more correctly "where" to create, new business opportunities is also discussed in Chapters 5, 8, 9, and 11. In Chapters 8 and 11 it is suggested that a company look for growth and prosperity within its already existing markets, i.e. within its group of customers and the social and economic arrangement. Chapter 9, on the other hand, encourages companies to approach and create new markets by keeping an eye on the unexpected phenomena that take place within existing markets. Furthermore, in Chapter 5, the role of trade shows as collective initiatives to realize ideas for renewing industries is discussed. From the viewpoint that new product and service innovation follows a linear sequence of disparate processes and fields of knowledge, starting with idea detection and ending with branding and market entry considerations, among other things, it appears – according to Chapters 2 and 10 – that the possibilities of a successful market launch could be a matter for debate. In Chapter 10, questions relating to the market entry of a new product or service idea are addressed. And, with the contributions in Part II and the presentation in Chapter 2 of ideas and practices about brand management, it becomes clear that the contemporary or recent approaches to branding are not limited to the market launch phase.

A need to discuss how to perceive and manage innovation as a process (incremental as well as radical product and service innovation) is highlighted throughout the book. In Chapters 4 and 6, however, two common issues are focused upon, namely the characteristics of the innovation process and the organization of product, service, and brand innovation processes. Chapter 4 presents a critical reflection on the two existing and dominating views of innovation management. And in Chapter 6, the need to take a critical reflective view of marketing's role (as a particular field of knowledge, set of activities, or function) in the innovation economy is discussed.

Co-creation with customers has been extensively debated in work on product innovation, and the boundaries of innovation have been extended beyond the company to include customers with their resources and skills as an active part of the creative process aimed at creating meaningful individual and collective experiences. The question of co-creation is a common aspect of the contributions in the second part of the book, which considers numerous points of view and addresses different topics. Considering the various roles that companies and customers can play in the creation of consumption experiences, some contributions look in detail at the role of consumer agency in innovation processes (Chapter 12), which at times can produce social transformations (Chapter 17). Other chapters focus to a greater extent on the role and means by which companies seek to manage user involvement in innovation (Chapter 13), and in Chapter 16 the analysis is extended to the role of communities. Furthermore, communities are addressed as creative subjects that act independently or even in opposition to companies (Chapter 14), or even as subjects that companies can create directly (Chapter 15).

The contributions on the topic of co-creation are rich and varied. Without any claim to completeness, we indicate here some of the most important issues. The first question is certainly that of the fundamental role played by the Internet in creating the conditions for a significant involvement of customers in co-creation processes. The issue, which is well argued in Chapters 14 and 16, highlights the power of the Internet, which on the one hand enhances the opportunities for companies to involve customers and on the other hand creates the environment to aggregate consumers in active communities. A second aspect is the change in customer participation, which now extends beyond the role of "prosumer" that was found to be typical of service contexts some time ago. The consumer agency plays an important role in innovation and market creation. It goes well beyond reference to aspects of interaction tied to the production process and the use of products and services to involve the emotions and significances at both an individual (Chapter 12) and social level (Chapters 17 and 14).

A third element concerns the various environments in which co-creation can occur. The most typical context is the new product development process (Chapters 13 and 16), but innovation might also affect other areas more under the control of consumers, such as in the processes of co-creation of their own solutions and experiences (Chapter 12). Finally, there is the role of companies. Some contributions explicitly assume the company point of view, e.g. Chapters 13 and 15. In general, however, all the studies consider the managerial implications that co-creation processes may have for companies with a view to helping understand the changes under way in consumption processes, and assessing these changes in terms of new opportunities for companies to look at innovation from a market creation perspective.

Part I: Knowledge, Processes, and Capabilities for Market Creation

During the last decade it has become opportune in the marketing literature to acknowledge that customer knowledge alone may not always provide the one and only optimal input in the idea generation phase. In Chapter 1, written by Bruno Busacca, Paola Cillo, and David Mazursky, the creativity template approach for retrieving and making use of product knowledge is presented, alongside cases that provide the practical meaning and rationale of the approach. The chapter also contains a discussion about how to enhance the integration of tacit customer knowledge in product innovation by adopting an ethnographic approach in consumer studies.

When looking into the grand and classical models of buyer behaviour, it is evident that some of the most successful new brands of the last decades have been created from another mindset about brands, consumer behaviour, and brand management. Chapter 2, written by Mogens Bjerre, Tilde Heding, and Charlotte Knudtzen, deals with this issue in terms of the evolution of ideas and practices about brand management. The key contribution of the chapter lies in the presentation of a methodology, the dynamic funnel approach, to analyse and to make sense of the evolution of the brand management concept over the last 20 years.

From a marketing point of view, either in academia or in the business world, it is certain that some new perspectives and capabilities for knowledge creation and innovation have to be entered into fully – if opting for an influential position in a business area that has come to be called "the innovation economy". Furthermore, it is certain that creativity studies and practices represent one of these "must-have" perspectives. However, as discussed in Chapter 3, written by Bo T. Christensen, it is clear that marketing has something to build on, namely a mindset and a set of tools and skills for communicating with "the audience" when it comes to knowledge development about creativity – and implicitly to the contribution of creativity studies.

For a long time there have existed two very different views on how to conceive the process of innovation management. In Chapter 4, written by John K. Christiansen and Claus J. Varnes, the two views are carefully investigated. There are many reasons behind this investigation. One reason is that both views are on the one hand applauded and on the other hand criticized for their basic assumptions, distinctive features, and managerial implications. Another reason discussed in the chapter concerns the situation when one view appears to be obsolete, because of various factors. The challenges then facing managers are highlighted in the chapter by an example case.

Chapter 5, written by Francesca Golfetto and Diego Rinallo, deals with a role of trade shows that until now has received only little attention in the marketing literature, namely the implementation of collective market-shaping strategies. Thus, besides representing an important promotional tool for an individual company or groups of companies, the chapter demonstrates that trade shows are to be regarded as an influential force in the adoption of new technologies and product innovations in an industry. The presentation of this role comes from the authors having perceived trade shows as constituting field-configuring events, and having conducted a longitudinal study of the European clothing industry's most important trade shows. Thus, the chapter contains rich data about the unique features and historical developments of major trade shows in the European fashion industry.

In Chapter 6, written by Richard Jones and Karin Tollin, it is proposed that marketing's role and contribution (as a discipline, set of activities, or organizational unit) for firms' innovation capability still needs further exploration. The basis to this relates to the findings from an investigation of chief marketing executives' mindsets and an analysis of how marketing's role has been dealt with in the marketing literature until now. Two other and related propositions put forward are that marketing's contribution depends on its ability to treat "creating" and "sustaining" as two distinct and unique fields of capabilities, and to make use of corporate branding as a strategic tool in order to realize a continuous and ambidextrous innovation strategy.

Whether one's project concerns the development of theory about innovation management or the implementation of an innovation strategy in the business world, it is certain that a multidisciplinary perspective on knowledge for innovation is needed. In Chapter 7, written by Juliana Hsuan-Mikkola, two fields of knowledge and their relationships are presented: technological innovation and supply chain management. Through a presentation of key topics dealt with within these two fields, a framework is outlined for managing technological product innovations. In doing this, the chapter points to some fundamental considerations and competencies concerning portfolio management, outsourcing, and mass customization, among other things.

In Chapter 8, written by Henrik Andersen and Thomas Ritter, two interpretations of the market creation concept are presented and reflected upon after the authors have defined what a market is. The underlying proposition put forward in the chapter is that the most promising opportunities for market creation are to be found within already existing markets. It is, among existing buyers and sellers, the social arrangement that defines the frame for their exchange. A tool to realize this strategy, and implicitly to understand variations in social arrangements in markets and their causes and consequences in terms of new competitive arenas, is presented.

Successful market creation stories repeatedly tell us that nobody could foresee the point of time, the magnitude, or the speed of development of consumers' interest in an innovative new product, service, or market channel. In Chapter 9, written by Gabriele Troilo and Salvio Vicari, an explanation of this is presented through the concepts of "unexpected market events" (UMEs) and "market structural holes", among other things. Furthermore, a number of successful market creation stories and three major types of UME are presented. Finally, the important issue of how to make a UME become a market creation strategy and a business opportunity is discussed.

The chapter presentations above indicate that a number of important "what", "why", and "how" issues are prevalent for firms' top managers in relation to the detection, evaluation, and realization of new business opportunities within or outside existing markets. In Chapter 10, written by Mads Vangkilde, an additional issue stands at the centre, namely the issue of "when", or, alternatively, the issue of whether or not to adopt the first-mover role. A model is presented, derived from the literature on pioneering and sustainability of advantages, for analysing the causality of order entry and the effect on competitive advantage. In relation to this, a list of "must issues" for top managers, when the vision is market creation in a highly competitive and fast-moving area, is presented.

Within the service management literature dealing with product (goods) innovation, a recurrent and quite recent theme has been the issue of the combination of innovations (concept, interface, support, and/or delivery) that provides customers with maximum value. In Chapter 11, written by Fabrizio Zerbini, new and important insights are presented regarding the role that radical innovation of a service concept might have within the value-supplying process in B2B markets. In addition to this, the chapter contains empirical insight into the meaning of adopting a process view on solution selling, and new evidence on the importance of both parties perceiving the service offering as an ongoing and continual process.

Part II: Co-creation of Meaningful Experiences with Customers

Co-creation is a central argument in many debates on the role of companies and consumers. Consumers' resources and skills are applied creatively and spontaneously in a continuous process, regenerating consumer identity and product meanings. In this new light, the boundaries of innovation are extended well beyond the company to include the customers and their cultural resources and skills as an active part of the creative process. This topic is addressed in Chapter 12 by Stefania Borghini and Antonella Carù with the aim of contributing to the development of theory on the ways this co-creation may occur – from the consumer agency in the construction of solutions and experiences to the production of meanings through material resources provided by the market.

Moving attention to the company perspective, the analysis by John K. Christiansen, Anne Sofie Lefèvre, Claus J. Varnes, and Astrid S. Wolf in Chapter 13 looks into the relationship between companies' market perception and how they deal with the users during product development, and how the knowledge (potential or actual) obtained is utilized for market creation. According to the authors, the choice of strategy for user interaction will be influenced by the company's perception of the market and its relation to the company. Each perspective has implications for how companies interact with their customers and users in innovation processes and how they exploit knowledge from users. The study reports an empirical analysis of four companies and their use of various approaches, highlighting the relationship between companies' market perception and their approach to user involvement.

The debate in the literature on the fact that consumers do not act in isolation but within social relations has given considerable emphasis to the topic of communities. Marketing and consumer behaviour researchers already explicitly recognize the importance of considering communities as subjects acting in the market and playing a role in many important processes for companies. This involvement certainly includes innovation at various levels, e.g. the creation of the commercial offer and the means of market communication/dialogue. The role of communities in the innovation process is the topic addressed by Bernard Cova and Stefano Pace in Chapter 14. The contribution starts from the observation that marketing expertise is no longer a tool exclusively in the hands of companies.

Sometimes, companies that are directly involved in the creation of communities tied to the products and brands address the questions on how best to manage and use these structures. Niels Kornum considers the issue of the initiation and maintenance of online communities and the extent to which they support the company's market creation efforts. In Chapter 15 the author focuses on company-initiated or company-related online communities, and in particular on the corporate social responsibility community, in which ethical considerations are crucial, and a direct connection to brand and product pushing will be, at least, counterproductive and, at worst, devastating for the trust between the community members and the host company.

While customer interaction has always been important in new product development, the widespread deployment of information and communication technologies (ICTs) has greatly enhanced companies' ability to engage with customers in the product innovation process. This is the question addressed in Chapter 16, written by Emanuela Prandelli and Gianmario Verona, who argue that the Internet increases the opportunities to engage customers in collaborative innovation in various ways. Companies can transform episodic and one-way customer interactions into a continuous dialogue. Companies can use a variety of mechanisms to facilitate collaborative innovation in virtual environments. However, mechanisms differ in terms of the stage of the development process in which they are most useful and the nature of the customer interactions they enable.

A good deal of attention in recent literature has been paid to the question of minorities and their relationship with the market. Considering the heterosexual mainstream and the gay minority, in Chapter 17, Stefano Podestà and Luca M. Visconti suggest that market transformation can also be originated by the market and social cross-talk at the consumer level. In particular, the chapter shows how gay consumers can symbolically appropriate certain brands and products and transform them into gay icons. Similarly, the chapter also documents the opposite path by which gay icons are transferred into the heterosexual realm by means of imitation and straight contestation. These findings show that company strategies of strategic market creation can be further investigated by studying what markets do and how people use them and are used in them.

Karin Tollin   **Antonella Carù**
Copenhagen Business School,   *Bocconi University,*
Copenhagen, Denmark   *Milan, Italy*

PART I

Knowledge, Processes, and Capabilities for Market Creation

1

From Market Research to Creativity Templates: Leveraging Tacit Knowledge for Ideation

Bruno Busacca, Paola Cillo, & David Mazursky

Introduction

In several industries, the dynamics of competition has recently shifted the focus of sustainability of competitive advantage to the ability to manage innovation and change (Tushman & O'Really III, 1997; Prahalad & Ramaswamy, 2004). Product innovation is not new to the management field, as contributions from several disciplines have set the foundation for the understanding of the phenomenon of innovation since the late 1960s. In this respect, most of the current findings on continuous innovation are focused on knowledge that is drawn from science and technology (Brown & Eisenhardt, 1997; Verona & Ravasi, 2003; Chesbrough, 2004).

While the fundamental role of basic and applied research in spurring continuous innovation at the industrial and organizational levels cannot be ignored, it is at the same time the case that the knowledge that comes from the broad market base (customers, distributors, competitors, and so on) might play a fundamental role not simply in the management of the individual innovation projects but also in managing the continuity of innovation over time. In particular, of major interest may be the understanding of how consumer tastes, needs, and habits evolve over time. In addition to that, more recent research has emphasized the role that the product itself may play as a main source of ideas for new products (Goldenberg, Mazursky, & Solomon, 1999; Goldenberg, Lehmann, & Mazursky, 2001).

In this chapter we focus on customer knowledge and product-embodied knowledge as the two main determinants of new product success. This choice is coherent with the indications provided by the recent Marketing Science Institute report identifying innovation and customers as the key research priorities (MSI, 2008). In particular, innovation is presented as the primary engine of customer growth, and customers as those playing the most relevant role in shaping innovation strategies and implementation.

The first group of determinants – market-based determinants – recognizes the centrality customers have assumed over the past years in influencing the direction of companies' innovation strategy. This is related to the opportunities opened up by new technologies in enabling customers' integration in innovation practices. Specifically, we focus our attention on the techniques used by companies to create a thoughtful understanding of customer needs and preferences. The second group of determinants – product-based determinants – relates to existing product-embodied knowledge as a source of new product ideas. The product itself has been neglected as a potential source of new product ideas, because the essence of a product has always been considered the technology that is embodied in it. Yet, more recent research on the topic has highlighted a neglected aspect of products – their inherent capacity to code the evolution of market needs. Indeed, new products responding to market needs survive over time, and those that are not appreciated on the market do not leave any trace. Thus, information embodied in the product provides interesting directions for product innovation. We focus on the operators (Goldenberg, Mazursky, & Solomon, 1999) that can be used to manipulate the product in order to generate new ideas, by leveraging the information set contained in the product itself.

This chapter is organized as follows. In the next section we present the framework we use to introduce the techniques useful in the process of ideation. We then describe emerging techniques that leverage customers' tacit knowledge for ideation. Finally, we present the creativity template approach to show how to manipulate an existing product for generating ideas about future products. We conclude by highlighting key issues and caveats when using these techniques for ideation.

A framework for leveraging product and market knowledge in new product ideation

In analysing the techniques companies may potentially use to leverage market-related knowledge on the one hand and product-embodied knowledge on the other, we offer a framework emphasizing the dimensions of knowledge (tacitness and locus) to be used for the understanding of the types of technique that need to be adopted. In particular, we draw a distinction between the different potential sources of new product ideas by leveraging two dimensions: the main source of knowledge for ideation, which can be either related to existing products or to consumers'/customers' knowledge, and the type of knowledge that can be leveraged in product ideation (see Figure 1.1).

We posit that the type of knowledge that needs to be selected represents the key driver in explaining why some techniques are more effective than others when used in new ideas and concept development. In this respect we use a well-established distinction between tacit and explicit knowledge. The relevance of

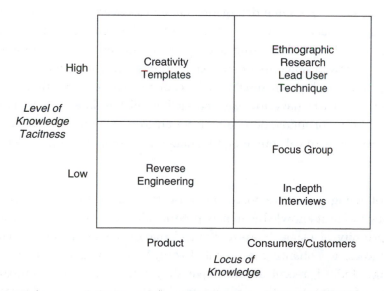

Figure 1.1 A framework for leveraging product and market knowledge in new product ideation

tacit knowledge lies in the fact that humans know more than they are aware of (Leonard & Sensiper, 1998) and can tell (Polany, 1966). This epistemological dimension of knowledge is not necessarily a dichotomy, but may be more effectively interpreted as a continuum that ranges from the tacit to the explicit (Nonaka & Takeuchi, 1995). At one end of the spectrum, this knowledge is almost completely tacit; at the other end it is explicit and, most importantly for our argument, it is accessible to people other than those originating it. The level of codification is therefore a fundamental property of knowledge: it refers to the fact that knowledge may be organized into a set of identifiable rules and relationships that can be easily communicated (Kogut & Zander, 1992). Tacit knowledge does not necessarily mean that it cannot be codified. Individuals and firms can under-take processes of socialization and externalization that might help codify tacit knowledge. However, some knowledge is unlikely ever to be codified because it might be embedded in individual or organization cognition and abilities (Leonard & Sensiper, 1998; Prahalad & Ramaswamy, 2004). In this sense, the quantity and quality of knowledge that can be transmitted and used depend very much on the ability and procedures a company develops to extract this knowledge.

It is clear that companies may want to exploit the power of tacit knowledge when ideating a new product, because it is that kind of knowledge that is difficult to capture and therefore that might represent a source of sustainable advantage. A company active in the home detergents market discovered that consumers were not looking so much for better and more powerful detergents as for solutions enabling them to avoid creating a dirty environment. So, for example, most persons interviewed stated that they were putting some aluminium paper close to the stove in the kitchen when using it for cooking. This enabled them to remove the paper and not to have to clean the kitchen all the times it was used. Most interesting ideas for innovation come from customers' hidden needs, and those needs represent a critical source of advantage for companies able to detect those needs.

In the following pages we focus on those techniques that best leverage the contribution of tacit knowledge in new product ideation. In particular, we discuss the opportunity of using "non-traditional" market research, such as ethnogra-phical studies, to enhance the potential contribution of unconscious customer knowledge. Indeed, recent studies have shown that successful companies are those that, among other things, tend to experiment with new approaches to gathering insights about consumers (see Box 1.1).

Box 1.1 Winning through new approaches for generating customer insights

A recent study presented in *The McKinsey Quarterly* (Crawford, Gordon, & Mulder, 2007) – aimed at understanding how consumer goods marketers are coping with the rapid pace of change in actual contexts – has shown how leading marketers use practices that are not common in non-leading marketers. The distinction between leading and non-leading companies has been developed by using different performance measures of the companies involved in the survey in four different areas – brand management, brand portfolio, innovation, and customer insights. The results of the study show that those companies identified in the study as high performers:

- tend to perceive insights as central to their culture;
- invest more in non-traditional approaches, such as the use of "cool hunters" to identify new trends in the field or "buzz" networks creating emotion around a specific product.

In particular, high-performing companies (HPCs), compared with the other companies (OCs) in the sample, use ethnography – defined as research based on observation of behaviour – with a percentage of 100% compared with 33% of OCs. In addition, HPCs use web-based panels with a percentage of 80% versus a percentage of 67% for OCs, and they employ cool hunters – defined as people who observe cultural trends and social behaviour among the general public and identify emerging trends in the marketplace – with a percentage of 40% compared with a usage from the OCs that is equal to 20% (Crawford, Gordon, & Mulder, 2007).

We present some examples of companies that have fruitfully used ethnographical research and have been able to manage customer insights to create new product ideas. We then explore the creativity template approach (see Goldenberg, Mazursky, & Solomon, 1999) as a structured way to generate new concepts within the product historic path and the company's existing competences.

Leveraging customers' knowledge for ideation

In dealing with new product ideation companies can leverage differences among consumers in their *expertise* regarding a specific product, in the *interest* they manifest in contributing to new product ideation, and in their *ability to anticipate* market evolutionary trends. These variables greatly affect the actual contribution customers can provide to firms engaged in the innovation process. The role of consumers' expertise has been particularly emphasized in literature on innovation (e.g. von Hippel, 1986).

Expertise affects the extensiveness of the analytic process because of consumers' ability to engage in such a process. Expertise makes consumers' cognitive structures more complex, which increases the consumers' ability to differentiate among competing alternatives, and prompts finer discriminations with greater reliability (Alba & Hutchinson, 1987). As expertise affects cognitive differentiation, experts use more attributes and varied attribute levels to differentiate between objects in a domain. Not only are they better equipped to understand the meaning of the offers, but they also need a lower amount of cognitive efforts for any specific level of comprehension. Owing to these double effects on comprehension and cognitive efforts, expertise is likely to affect the extent to which consumers search for and process information prior to making a purchase decision (Mitchel & Dacin, 1996). In addition, experts may engage in a more complex problem-solving activity simply because they are aware of a greater amount of relevant aspects to be kept informed about (Brucks, 1985) or because they are more capable of formulating specific questions about a larger number of attributes. For these reasons, the contribution that expert customers may provide to companies for the ideation and development of a new product becomes critical.

Lead users, trendsetters, and creative consumers: different sources of new product ideas

Eric von Hippel (1986), in his seminal research, has shown how in business-to-business contexts the collaboration a firm is able to create with selected customers – namely lead users – represents one of the most important determinants of a new product success. In focusing on customers in *business-to-business* contexts, he defines lead users as those customers whose current strong needs will become general in the marketplace months or years in the future. More specifically, a lead user is a customer who (1) uses a novel or enhanced product, (2) senses needs that will become prevalent in the marketplace, and faces them much in advance with respect to the rest of the market, and (3) can benefit significantly from obtaining a solution (von Hippel, 1986, 2005).

Similar to lead users are those consumers who are defined as trendsetters in business-to-consumer contexts. They usually share with lead users the fact that they are able to anticipate trends that will spread over the market months or years later. Yet, differently from lead users, they are not interested in benefiting from the new product, because they are not directly involved in the usage of the product a company is trying to enhance. Usually, trendsetters are those consumers who are not particularly loyal to any specific product and for this reason do not have any specific economic interest in supporting the development of one product over another. Yet, they may orient the new product ideation process in a profitable direction, because of their peculiar sensitivity towards emerging market trends. The main difference between lead users and trendsetters is related to the fact that lead users are those who adopt and use novel or enhanced products, while trendsetters – acting mainly in consumer markets – are not involved in product use. Actually, trendsetters are not users at all of the products they contribute to creating: they represent a source of inspiration for new trend discovery from consumer market companies. Diesel – an Italian company in casual wear – provides an example of how to exploit the power of trendsetters while setting the themes and ideas for a new collection (Cillo, 2004). Diesel has stood out in the fashion industry through its disruptive and provocative behaviour. In particular, the kind of products it makes, the means of communication and distribution it uses, and the way it interacts with consumers are highly unorthodox. The company has grown considerably during the past 10 years – with a fourfold increase in its revenues and employees. In spite of the considerable increase in the company's size, Diesel has continued to maintain its focus on innovation by defining a fine-grained structure for its innovation processes. The most relevant innovation process is the one related to the creation of the two collections every year: the spring–summer and autumn–winter ones. The new collection development process aims at developing products that are on the fringes of fashion, and abandoning a trend as soon as it is adopted by the vast majority of the industry players. To put this philosophy into practice, Diesel developed a fine-tuned procedure for sensing market trends, understanding their evolutionary pattern, and using this knowledge to maintain continuous innovation. Among other things, Diesel especially relies on the ability of its designers to interact with non-mainstream customers who can be defined as trendsetters. The managers view the target market as a pyramid, with the trendsetters, who are capable of sensing the market trends before anyone else, at the top. The second layer of the pyramid is made up of opinion leaders, responsible for spreading the trend. They play a key role once Diesel incorporates the ideas of the trendsetters in new products. The third layer is made up of the bulk of the market – namely either consumers who want to follow the trend or functionally oriented consumers who simply buy a product just because it is useful and/or comfortable. Trendsetters are considered as one of the most reliable sources of insights into market trends because they are not influenced by what others are wearing and tend to abandon a trend as soon as it becomes popular. As Renzo Rosso, founder and current CEO of Diesel, said: "They are the people who have to look inside the jacket to find out the brand they are wearing, and that usually buy in second-hand shops so they can mix and match different pieces they like". At Diesel, the most important mechanism to interact with non-mainstream customers is represented by the trips each group of designers makes every year to different parts of the world, with a specific budget allocated to the acquisition of tangible memories. These artefacts will allow the designers to retrieve what they experienced when travelling. In addition, Diesel has created many different events in the shops, specifically designed to involve the consumers, who provide valuable input in formulating company fashion trends. Even the Internet has become a primary source of data collection in the virtual community that the company has created for the most interactive target customers. In the offline and online events, the company tries to challenge customers on specific topics – for example, by running a competition on the best design for a specific piece of the collection or by giving consumers the opportunity to see their designs reproduced and sold in their stores.

Finally, and more recently, some researchers have introduced the concept of the *creative consumer* as an "individual or group who adapts, modifies, and trans-forms a proprietary offering, such as a product or a service" (Berthon *et al.*, 2007, p. 40). In particular, these authors emphasize the difference between lead users and creative consumers. Indeed, creative consumers (1) work with all types of offering, not just with novel or enhanced products, (2) face needs that will not necessarily surface – they often work towards achieving personal interests, and (3) do not benefit directly from their innovations, but more through an increase in their social capital. In this last respect, for example, some companies tend to reward the contribution of these consumers by inviting them regularly into their premises or by providing them with experimental and still unknown versions of the product. Very often, though, the reward is not really what these consumers are looking for. Indeed, most often the opportunity to work on their preferred product or to feel part of a group or community emerges around the brand that represents the actual reward they expect. The movement around open-source software provides ample evidence in this regard. Lastly (4), while lead users are usually "discovered" by the companies, creative consumers tend spontaneously to embrace a project related to a product owing to their involvement with the product, or the brand. Based on this distinction, it is also possible to use the concept of creative consumer as one of the proxy variables defining the concept of lead user. Indeed, usually those customers acting as leaders in specific markets tend to be very proactive in manipulating the product and in adapting it to their specific needs. For this reason, the identification of creative customers – defined as those who adapt, transform, and modify proprietary offerings – may lead to a first screening potentially useful for identifying lead users.

Traditional market research techniques, such as focus groups, are mostly useful when companies want to interact with customers to leverage the knowledge customers are aware of. It is, indeed, very useful to use these kinds of technique when testing the concept or a prototype of a new product. When facing a discussion topic in a non-familiar place and in a group that has been created for research reasons, customers usually do not feel at ease and tend not to expose themselves. This behavioural dynamic, while not compromising the potential contribution of consumers when directly confronted with a concept or a product, may instead inhibit their actual contribution when it is related to their personal experiences, attitudes, and emotions. Similarly, in-depth interviews, although more useful to catch individuals' experience, represent nonetheless an ex post rationalization that might be less reliable because of memory failure, unconscious experiences, and difficulties in knowledge articulation.

Involving end-users in consumer markets: the role of ethnography

These problems can be overcome by using observation of actual behaviours through techniques referring to the ethnographical method rather than on consumers' direct interviews. These techniques – named also "corporate ethno-graphy" or "ethnographic-style research" (Fulton & Gibbs, 2006) – are based on observation of people in a particular context. Consumer ethnography "aims to produce generative insights from the application of a broad and deep understanding of how cultures are organized, careful attention to the details of how culture plays out in everyday life, and disciplined curiosity about what people are up to" (Arnould & Price, 2006, p. 251). Indeed, focusing just on consumer wording leaves out a lot of the experience that ethnography attempts to capture. In particular, ethnographical research aims at uncovering tacit knowledge that is often difficult to articulate and exists in routines, silences, postures, and gestures, as well as in statements about the values and beliefs a person has. Traditionally developed within services contexts – such as point of sales – this set of methodologies has been more recently applied also to explore the use that consumers make of the products in their own premises. In the context of innovation, the purpose of ethnography is to use customers' observation to produce insights that can then be leveraged to create new product concepts. An insight, indeed, represents the underlying motivation or explanation of a specific behaviour (Fetterman, 1998). By exploring this deep motivation behind consumer behaviour, companies are then able to explore new conceptual platforms that yield new product ideas.

Ethnography in consumer markets: an example from a leading Italian pasta producer

PastaMaker[1] is a leading Italian company in the packaged food industry that is famous worldwide because of its capacity continuously to innovate. For example, it has introduced new products and new subbrand lines that specialize in the production and distribution of bakery products.

PastaMaker has always considered innovation a key strategic factor in sustaining its competitive advantage over time. In all the in-company innovation processes, a key role is given to the internal structure – called Insight – created almost 10 years ago to keep track of emerging market trends. This internal structure carries out all the market analyses needed to develop new ideas or pretest new products or advertising campaigns. However, the most innovative activity is the one carried out by PastaMaker's House of Pasta. This is the name of a laboratory that continuously monitors customer trends and changing habits by directly involving consumers in PastaMaker's innovation processes. House of Pasta is the name of an old mansion located at the PastaMaker headquarters in Italy. The building is rather unusual, consisting of six modern kitchens, which allow the consumers

---

[1] The name PastaMaker is used to avoid disclosing the actual company name for confidentiality reasons.

brought to House of Pasta to feel completely at home. In this way, the company can collect data on consumer behaviour by observing how their products and those of their competitors are used. These data are subsequently used by Pasta-Maker to define new concepts for its products.

House of Pasta represents a repository of market knowledge, as it has made it possible to gather information directly from customers over a long period of time (for example, while consumers prepare lunch or dinner in one of House of Pasta's kitchens). This approach has allowed PastaMaker to keep up with the changing trends in consumer tastes and to create innovations tailor made to satisfy consumers. This is exemplified by a new line of products using traditional recipes, reflecting a growing consumer preference for natural food and the traditional way of preparing food.

Insight – and especially House of Pasta – can be considered to be the most sophisticated type of internal market knowledge broker (Cillo, 2005). Insight generates knowledge about customers, but also integrates knowledge of customers that is subsequently used by different business units in the company. It acts as a knowledge broker because it transfers ad hoc knowledge developed in one project – for example, a new line of biscuits – to be used in other innovations – for example, a new type of pasta. Market knowledge produced in one context is then repackaged and used to meet the objectives of a different project. It acts as a solution provider by creating the "right" package of market knowledge that is needed in one specific innovation project and by leveraging the knowledge developed by other innovation teams for different purposes.

To sum up, the main advantage of having an internal structure devoted to interacting with customers and aimed at developing a sound understanding of market trends is twofold. Firstly, it gives the company an opportunity to develop its own methodology to understand consumers and their own knowledge to track the trends in consumer tastes over time. Secondly, this structure promotes the process of cross-fertilization between different business units and different functions in the company – such as between marketing and R&D. This would be impossible if the market knowledge were produced by an external market research company for each specific innovation process. This cross-fertilization occurs because market knowledge is diffused and dispersed in House of Pasta and the people who work there know how to manage this knowledge and make it useful for different purposes.

Lead user methodology for customer involvement in new product ideation

Lead user analysis is one of the techniques that companies may use to leverage the power of tacit knowledge for ideation. It has been developed and used in different industrial contexts but also applied in low-tech contexts, where the detection of a trend is critical to explore new venues for innovation. The methodology suggested by Urban and von Hippel (1988, pp. 570–571) comprises four steps:

1. *Specify lead user indicators*
   (a) Find market or technological trends and related measures. Lead users are defined as those customers who are ahead of the market on a critical dimension that is changing over time. For this reason, it is important to select the trend one wants to focus on before selecting the lead users to be involved in the process of ideation.
   (b) Define measures of potential benefit. The second identifying characteristic for lead users is that of being "positioned to benefit significantly by obtaining a solution to those needs" (Urban & von Hippel, 1988, p. 569). Measures of potential benefits for lead users are related to indicators of the attitude and ability of customers in adapting the products to their specific needs (that is what we have referred to before as an attitude typical of creative consumers). Additional potential measures may be related to user dissatisfaction towards existing solutions, speed of adoption of innovation, and consumer innovativeness (Hirschman, 1980).

2. *Identify lead user groups*
   To identify lead user groups, usually a survey via a questionnaire built around the identified measures for lead users may be used in order to identify target groups of users to be involved in the concept development phase. This survey supports the process of identification and description of user subgroups based on the different characteristics and on differential levels of involvement.

3. *Generate concept (product) with lead users*
   This step is based on a direct interaction of the company with lead users in order to generate modifications of existing products or to work and elaborate on products already modified by lead users to meet their specific and direct needs.

4. *Test lead user concept*
   The final stage is extremely relevant because the needs of lead users do not very often coincide with those of more traditional users within the market.

Therefore, the process of testing is even more critical than for products emerging from more traditional market research techniques, usually targeted to a larger segment of customers and leading to concepts addressing more general needs.

The lead user technique has been incrementally modified to address issues emerging in low-tech contexts and in business-to-consumer environments, but it still represents a very fruitful approach to the identification and development of new concepts (Herstatt & von Hippel, 1992).

Leveraging product knowledge for ideation: the creativity template approach

We have so far viewed the key role of the customer and the relevance of techniques aimed at collecting and using customer knowledge, especially through the support of non-traditional techniques.

As far as considering the product itself as a potential source of knowledge for new product ideation is concerned, a technique with a long-standing history of application is reverse engineering. Reverse engineering is a process that derives the technological principles of a device, a product, or a system through the analysis of its structure, function, and operation. Although useful especially to speed up the process of ideation and development of a new product, reverse engineering is nonetheless an approach leading to incremental innovations that mostly leverage the contribution of knowledge developed by third parties, with severe limitations in potential applications.

A more recent approach leveraging the stock of knowledge inside the product has been developed by starting from a very simple consideration obtained by analyzing the evolution of products – those that survive and those that are extinguished. This approach may be important in predicting the development of future products. A product that does not fulfil a vital need disappears, just as a living creature unable to compete for basic needs dies out. Analogous to Darwin's theory of natural selection, this reasoning states that, given the changing needs of the marketplace over time, the products that will survive are those that adapt to the changing environments through alterations in their own features. Thus, over time, the market needs are "mapped" or "encoded" into a product, which accumulates properties that enable it to be competitive. The product becomes a physical representation of the market benefits and it contains the information about the evolution of its needs.

Just as market researchers attempt to identify trends in the marketplace on which to base a newly generated product, we can identify market trends by analysing the product itself in predicting the basic features of a new product. Goldenberg, Mazursky, and Solomon (1999) identified a well-defined sequence of operators that manipulate the product-based information, termed "creativity templates". The evidence showed that 70% of successful new products can be related to one of five templates.

Accordingly, creativity templates depict discernible, measurable, and learnable regularities or patterns in innovation and novelty emergence. They enable us to understand general mechanisms of past product alterations, as well as to foresee the next alteration in the series.

The creativity template approach does not contradict any current marketing theory. It does, however, add another perspective to the process of product innovation by drawing on the primacy of the idea itself as a driving force towards new product success. Creativity templates are derived by inferring patterns in the evolution of products, such as those that can be inferred from the following illustrations.

The rationale behind the creativity template approach: the Edison and Compaq examples

One legend about Thomas Alva Edison, one of the outstanding geniuses in the history of technology, tells that Edison's guests were always complaining that the gate to his house opened with great difficulty, and they were required to exert great force in order to open it. Jokes were rampant about the obstinate gate and the clever inventor who could not find a way to fix it. At the end of his days, Edison was finally willing to explain: the gate was connected to a water pump, and anyone who opened the gate unknowingly pumped up water to fill Edison's private swimming pool.

Can anything be learned about creativity and innovation from this amusing story? Would information about the form of Edison's brain, his modes of thinking, or his lifestyle aid us to be more creative?

We have no information about the form of Edison's brain, but this, in any case, would not help us much. Scientists have recently found that one part of Einstein's brain (the inferior parietal region) was indeed physically extraordinary – but how can such information be useful to us in the search for ideation methods?

Studying Edison's modes of thinking will also not be of much use. Some of his own words about the creative process include "Good fortune is what happens when opportunity meets with preparation", and "The three things that are essential to achievement are: hard work, stick-to-it-evenness, and common sense". Neither from these words nor from other sources can we explain his success. It seems that it is not from Edison's biography that we may learn about creativity. In fact, by reviewing another example, we may infer some similarity in the overall structural form, even though the content is very different.

Compaq Computer Corporation is a Fortune Global 100 company, the second largest computer company in the world and the largest global supplier of personal computers. In mid-1999, the Compaq Corporation announced a new innovation: a Notebook computer whose battery is recharged by typing on the keyboard. The ingenuity of this invention lies in the fact that the very activity that discharges the battery serves also to recharge it. The target population for this computer is businessmen on the move. Its benefits are obvious: its weight is reduced by eliminating the need to carry a spare battery and by reducing the size of the main battery (Goldenberg & Mazursky, 2002).

Can you see any difference in the basic structure of the above two illustrations (Edison's gate and the new configuration of the Compaq computer)? In both cases the innovators harnessed an energy source from the immediate environment (Edison's guests or Compaq end-users) in order to fulfil a necessary function (water pumping and battery recharging). This similarity may point to certain regularities or patterns (or, as we call them, creativity templates).

The creativity template approach precludes the need to enter the brains and the thought processes of innovators such as Edison and the Compaq engineers, and to discover the regularities underlying creative ideas or products. These regularities can be conceived as codes embedded in the product itself and are revealed by observing the pattern in product evolution.

The replacement and attribute dependency templates: examples from Wire Free and Volkswagen Polo Harlequin

Can such patterns (or creativity templates) be applied to problems other than those involving energy sources? Let us illustrate further a brilliant innovation in the category of extended cellular phone microphones installed in cars. The R&D team of Wire Free Ltd, a company that specializes in such microphones, has noticed an interesting contradiction: the barrier to the quality of the sound is the miniature loudspeaker, which is one of the most expensive parts in this product (Goldenberg & Mazursky, 2002). Normally, we expect that improvement in the quality of a product entails higher costs and consequently a more expensive product. Relying on the pattern in idea emergence that was identified above (Edison's gate and the Compaq computer), we may expect an idea that will break this vicious circle.

But first, let us generalize further the template structure underlying this type of idea. An internal component that performs a certain function (Edison himself, computer battery) is drawn from the system's configuration. In order to fulfil the function, an external resource (energy from the guests in the case of the gate, and energy from the user in the case of the computer) is called to replace the internal component that was drawn out. This replacement is designed in such a way that the new resource bears the same function as that of the removed component. Let us examine the extended microphone in view of this rule. It is quite obvious that, in order to eliminate the size problem, the loudspeaker has to be removed. The remaining question is whether there is a resource in the vicinity of the system (car) that can carry the function of the removed loudspeaker. A perfect candidate would probably be the loudspeaker of the stereo system in the car itself.

The invention introduced in 1999 by Wire Free was to assign the function of the loudspeaker to the stereo system, enabling major cost savings and, at the same time, a substantial improvement in the sound.

It is interesting to note that the firm reused this template in implementing the connection between the microphone and the radio system. Instead of producing a connector for each radio system, the appliance transmits the signals (in FM) to the radio. It turns off the radio while the telephone is activated.

One abstract template surfaces from all of the above ideas, based on a code underlying them – harnessing resources from the immediate environment to replace a component that fulfils a needed function of the product. We can therefore generalize:

> **Replacement template:** the utilization of resources available in the environment of the product so that it may fulfil a needed function.

This is but one code of innovation emergence that characterizes product evolution. It signifies a certain rule in evolutionary processes. Clearly, it is not the only one. Another template may be extracted from the following illustrations.

In 1995, Volkswagen Motor Co. launched a new model of the Polo car, named "Polo Harlequin". The Polo, marketed until then as a solid, dependable car, acquired a new attribute: each part of the car was painted a different colour. This configuration gave the car an original, mischievous look that appealed to a sizeable market share. A short time after its launching, the Harlequin could be found all over Europe. The only detail changed in the production process was the order of assembly: instead of feeding the robot assembling the car with parts of the same colour, it was fed with multicoloured parts (Goldenberg, Mazursky, & Solomon, 1999).

A curious detail about this story is that this model was originally intended as an April Fool's Day joke. Although this joke was coordinated with the PR Department of the firm, which distributed multicoloured posters to go with the launching (including details of two models produced in this configuration), the company did not intend to implement this concept and launch such an odd product in the market.

To Volkswagen's great surprise, the idea captivated many customers, and a great uproar arose the next day. Orders for this (non-existent) car started piling up in the sales department, and interest kept growing. The next step was obvious: the model was to be offered on the suddenly awakened market.

In a conventional car there is no connection between the type of outer body component of the car (e.g. doors, engine cover, top, etc.) and its colour – all of the components are of the same colour. The Harlequin has the characteristic of a new connection between the type of component and its colour: different components have different colours.

Is this procedure unique to the development of the Polo Harlequin, or is there a recurrent pattern here that we may use in other, different, and seemingly remote cases? From the realm of automobile-industry products, we will move to an illustration from the realm of food-industry services.

Basically, there is no difference between products and services. Let us examine the same template manifestation in a famous service – pizza deliveries.

Domino's Pizza is a world leader in pizza delivery. Its success is partially due to the introduction of a novel idea: a promise to reduce the price of the pizza whenever delivery takes longer than 30 minutes. This new and original promise has caused a boom in Domino's business. In addition to the firm's obligation to fast service, there is an interesting gamble in ordering a pizza: the customer may hope that the delivery will be late and the price reduced (Goldenberg, Mazursky, & Solomon, 1999).

Free deliveries, even a promise of fast delivery, and tasty pizzas existed before Domino's Pizza appeared on the scene. Once again, an innovation can be formulated (graphically) in the same transition from a constant (straight-line) to a step function.

In this illustration, a new dependency was created by a step function between two previously independent variables: price and time. A similar dependency could be created between two other independent variables, e.g. price and temperature. A promise would be given to deliver the pizza to the customer while hot; otherwise the price would be reduced.

Surprisingly enough, this case is exactly the same as that for the Polo Harlequin. What does this mean? Is there a common superstructure behind these ideas that may be extracted and generalized?

> **Attribute dependency template:** finding two independent variables and establishing dependency between them.

Templates of creative thinking taken from the past can be used for accelerating thinking about new ideas in the present. Practically, we don't have to search for creativity templates in ancient Egypt or Greece. Our argument is that some templates have survived over history, and have preserved their structure even though the context has been changed. As in every evolutionary process, "the fittest survives". Adaptable historical templates – those more successful and effective – have survived well, and the information embedded in them may be used in the framework of creative thinking. Therefore, it suffices to locate templates embedded in creative ideas that survived in the twentieth century, in which acceleration of innovative processes has been witnessed and documented. The realm of new products has undergone a genuine revolution in the past 50 years, characterized by an avalanche of innovative ideas and providing evidence for the existence of templates and possibilities for using the information embedded in them.

The component control template: an example from 3M Post-it Notes

A third template is the component connection template. To examine it, let us consider the example of Post-it Notes (Goldenberg & Mazursky, 2002). The development of that product shows that the idea of the "weak glue" on the notes emerged from the process of development of glue. However, the brilliance of the idea is not in the glue itself but in its connection to a coloured memo slip, of the type one lays on an office desk with memos for work.

Such small slips on which notes and memos may be written existed before the development of Post-it Notes – in fact, that was the basic product from which the sticky notes were developed. However, the original product was characterized by a somewhat problematic connection with the surface on which it was placed: it could blow away with every light wind and disappear.

The change in the configuration of the product that was to solve the problem between the product and the external component was based on an extra connection introduced between the surface and the note. In the original configuration the surface placed the note at a certain height, while in the new product an extra connection was formed between note and surface by the introduction of a new internal component in the configuration – glue. The desk now keeps the note at the horizontal level as well, preventing it from sliding along the surface.

Another example of the use of the component connection template is a radiation-filtering computer screen. This screen was developed on the basis of a problem that arose through the continuous use of the computer: the radiation emanating from the computer caused user headaches, eyestrain and dizziness.

The external component in the configuration of the computer is the electromagnetic radiation emanating from it. This environmental component is not controlled by the deliverer of the service but comes in direct contact with the user of the product. In the original state there was a negative connection between the component and the configuration, as described above. The solution for this connection is to include in the configuration a component limiting the amount of emanating radiation.

The division and displacement templates: an example from the shampoo and washing powder markets

The fourth template is division. Let's take an example. All the various soap products available today spawn from a single, multipurpose soap. Early in this process, conditioners were added to soap to soften its harshness, both on the objects to be washed and on the hands of those doing the washing. So it was that the earliest shampoos already included conditioners.

At some point down the road, however, shampoo was split into shampoo and conditioner. Thus, today we buy separate shampoos and conditioners.

Ironically, some consumer-goods companies have made a hit in the last few years by reuniting these long-separated features. Wash-and-go shampoos with conditioners inside are back.

The division template operates in the component space. It involves splitting one component into several components. The split components then either contribute individually to the accomplishment of the function or become responsible for different subfunctions.

In the above example, shampoo was split via the splitting operator into two components – the cleaning agent and the conditioning agent. The new components were linked via the linking operator into either the old product configuration – the shampoo – or a brand-new product configuration – the conditioner. Another example of this template is additives in washing powders. A component (in this case, the active cleaning ingredient) is split into two components, each responsible for a different function – one a delicate cleaning agent, the other a highly active agent. The delicate cleaning agent continues to be an ingredient of ordinary washing powder, and the stronger agents are selectively used as additives depending upon the needs of a particular type of laundry.

The fifth and last template is displacement. The displacement template states that a component may be eliminated from the configuration of a system along with its functions, and thus a new product will be created, addressing a new market.

In the early 1970s, after a lengthy marketing war, the efforts to introduce into the American market food products based on a powder for quick home preparation (among them, of course, instant coffee and various soup mixes) finally met with success. Among the products flooding the market, one of the manufacturers of instant food introduced a cake mix for home baking: the customer buys the special powder, mixes it with water, pours it into a baking pan and puts it in the oven. Expectations of success were great, both because the product seemed to suit a large market share and because all the tests gave its taste a high grade. To the manufacturer's great surprise, the marketing efforts failed.

Extensive market research discovered that, although American customers wish to save time in food preparation, they are interested in adding their personal touch to the cakes they bake, to give the cake a special "home-made" taste. In order to meet this need, it was suggested that a bit of the product's efficiency be "eliminated". After much consideration it was decided to remove the eggs from the mix and instruct the amateur bakers to add them themselves, thus overcoming the recoil from a factory-made cake. Now that the customers had to make an effort, sales of the cake mix rose markedly.

The vacuum package is based on a simple principle: removing the air from the packed product. Thus, the freshness of food products such as meat, natural juices, and others is preserved. Keeping the packed products from coming into contact with the air affords them a longer shelf life, and makes it easier to store and use them.

Another successful product developed by removing a component from an existing product is Motorola's wireless telephone, known as "Mango" (Goldenberg & Mazursky, 2002). In this instrument, the possibility of an outgoing call was removed, markedly reducing both the price of the instrument and the telephone bills, and broadening the target population of cellular communication.

The replacement template introduced us to the idea of excluding internal components, without elimination of their functions. However, the displacement template demonstrated in the above examples is characterized by the exclusion of a component without replacing its function with another component.

> **Displacement template:** removing a component from the configuration, including its functions, in a way that causes a qualitative change in the configuration.

Conclusion

A key challenge that companies have to face in current competitive landscapes is related to the identification and exploitation of new potential sources of knowledge that can be leveraged in new product ideation. To this end, different techniques may be integrated and explored together to succeed in new product ideation. In this chapter, in particular, we have explored the power of product-embodied knowledge and customer tacit knowledge as a major source of new product ideation.

Although product-embodied knowledge has been neglected for a long time as an actual source of new product ideas, it may offer relevant insights when one looks at the evolutionary path of a product and uses the knowledge entrenched in this path to predict the success of future products. In particular, the creativity template approach presented in the previous pages represents a structured approach for the ideation of new concepts departing from the identification of failure and success of products.

On the other hand, non-traditional market research techniques – such as ethnographical studies and lead user analysis – may instead drive the understanding of the motivation behind a customer behaviour and as such provide insights for the development of new concepts. In particular, these methodologies have the advantage of focusing the attention on knowledge that is difficult to elicit, providing a potential source of differential advantage for companies that want to become champions of innovation.

The techniques presented in this chapter represent just a selection of methodologies that companies may use to support the ideation process in innovation. We think, first of all, that a single-method approach is not as fruitful as an integrated one that leverages the upsides of all the methodologies. For example, with respect to the techniques we have considered in this chapter, we think that the creativity template approach may turn out to be even more productive whenever the direction it takes is supported by evidence collected, for example, through direct observation of customers when using a product. Indeed, the application of the template approach provides new avenues for identifying potentially unexplored new product configurations that may address hidden customer needs. Yet, without thoughtful use of advanced research methodologies for customer understanding, the direction the innovation may take might not address customers' expectations.

The theme of product/market knowledge is still critical also from the organizational point of view. Indeed, as long as companies have started to develop units responsible for the development of product/market knowledge, the issue of ownership of this knowledge is important. Many companies have created functions or units named "consumer insights" involving a relatively small and isolated group that concentrates on research and analysis. This process has subtracted knowledge from the product and brand managers in order to centralize it into customer-centric knowledge repositories. Yet, most organizations are still fighting to find a reasonable equilibrium and to be able to integrate product knowledge, usually within the marketing and R&D functions, and customer knowledge, usually into this customer insights unit, to be exploited for innovation.

References

Alba, J. W. & Hutchinson, J. W. (1987) "Dimensions of consumer expertise". *Journal of Consumer Research*, vol. 13, no. 4, pp. 411–454.

Arnould, E. J. & Price, L. L. (2006) "Market-oriented ethnography revisited". *Journal of Advertising Research*, September, pp. 251–262.

Berthon, P. R., Pitt, L. F., McCarthy, I., & Kates, S. M. (2007) "When customers get clever: Managerial approaches to dealing with creative consumers". *Business Horizons*, vol. 50, no. 1, January/February, pp. 39–47.

Brown, S. & Eisenhardt, K. M. (1997) "The art of continuous change: Linking complexity theory and time-paced evolution in relentlessly shifting organizations". *Administrative Science Quarterly*, vol. 42, pp. 1–34.

Brucks, M. (1985) "The effects of product class knowledge on information search behaviour". *Journal of Consumer Research*, vol. 12, pp. 1–16.

Chesbrough, H. (2004) *Open Innovation*. Harvard Business School Press, Boston, MA.

Cillo, P. (2004) *Innovazione e Mercato*. Carocci, Rome.

Cillo, P. (2005). "Fostering Market Knowledge Use in Innovation: The Role of Internal Brokers" *European Management Journal*, vol. 23, No. 4: 404–412.

Crawford, B., Gordon, J. W., & Mulder, S. R. (2007) "How consumer goods companies are coping with complexity". *The McKinsey Quarterly*, May, pp. 1–13.

Fetterman, D. M. (1998) *Ethnography: Step by Step*. Sage, Thousand Oaks, CA.

Fulton, S. J. & Gibbs, H. S. (2006) "Going deeper, seeing further: enhancing ethnographic interpretations to reveal more meaningful opportunities for design". *Journal of Advertising Research*, September, pp. 246–250.

Goldenberg, J., Lehmann, D., & Mazursky, D. (2001) "The idea itself and the circumstances of its emergence as predictors of new product success". *Management Science*, vol. 47, no. 1, pp. 69–84.

Goldenberg, J. & Mazursky, D. (2002) *Creativity in Product Innovation*. Cambridge University Press, Cambridge, UK.

Goldenberg, J., Mazursky, D., & Solomon, S. (1999) "Toward identifying the inventive templates of new products: A channeled ideation approach". *Journal of Marketing Research*, vol. XXXVI, May, pp. 200–210.

Herstatt, C. & von Hippel, E. (1992) "Developing new product concepts via the lead user method: a case study in a 'low-tech' field". *Journal of Product Innovation Management*, vol. 9, no. 3, pp. 213–221.

Hirschman, E. (1980) "Innovativeness, novelty seeking, and consumer creativity". *Journal of Consumer Research*, vol. 7, no. 3, pp. 283–295.

Kogut, B. & Zander, U. (1992) "Knowledge of the firm, combinative capabilities, and the replication of technology". *Organization Science*, vol. 3, pp. 383–397.

Leonard, D. & Sensiper, S. (1998) "The role of tacit knowledge in group innovation". *California Management Review*, vol. 40, pp. 112–132.

Mitchel, A. A. & Dacin, P. A. (1996) "The assessment of alternative measures of consumer expertise". *Journal of Consumer Research*, vol. 23, no. 3, pp. 219–239.

MSI (2008) Research priority report 2006–2007, Marketing Science Institute, Cambridge, MA.

Nonaka, I. & Takeuchi, H. (1995) *The Knowledge-creating Company*. Oxford University Press, Oxford, UK.

Polany, M. (1966) *The Tacit Dimension*. Anchor Day Books, New York, NY.

Prahalad, C. K. & Ramaswamy, V. (2004) *The Future of Competition: Co-creating Unique Value with Customers*. Harvard Business School Press, Boston, MA.

Tushman, M. L. & O'Really III, C. (1997) *Winning through Innovation*. Harvard Business School Press, Cambridge, MA.

Urban, G. & von Hippel, E. (1988) "Lead users analyses for the development of new industrial products". *Management Science*, vol. 3, no. 5, pp. 569–582.

Verona, G. & Ravasi, D. (2003) "Unbundling dynamic capabilities: An exploratory analysis of continuous product innovation". *Industrial and Corporate Change*, vol. 12, no. 3, pp. 577–606.

von Hippel, E. (1986) "Lead users: A source of novel product concepts". *Management Science*, vol. 32, no. 7, pp. 791–805.

von Hippel, E. (2005) *Democratizing Innovation*. The MIT Press, Cambridge, MA.

2

Using the Dynamic Paradigm Funnel to Analyse Brand Management

Mogens Bjerre, Tilde Heding, & Charlotte Knudtzen

Introduction

In order to be innovative, one might be able to benefit from past insight. Scientific knowledge evolves over time in a systematic fashion, and understanding this process not only provides a thorough understanding of the accumulated theory and research of the past but will also enable the creation of well-substantiated theoretical prospects. We set out to provide an analysis in the vast field of brand management, and will in the following show how brand management paradigms and perspectives have evolved.

As an emerging field of research, many different approaches have been introduced to describe, analyse, manage, and understand brands and their nature. The field of brand management, i.e. the way in which practitioners benefit from this research, has also evolved rapidly and seemingly in many directions at the same time. Thus, we have had no overview of this area, and we have had no idea as to how the various contributions were positioned vis-à-vis one other, how they were interlinked – if they were, or how they were related to one another.

Using Kuhn's original philosophy of the evolution of science as a framework for analysis of accumulated theory and research can add new dimensions to the understanding of existing theory. Researchers Berthon, Nairn, and Money (2003) developed the conceptual tool known as the *paradigm funnel*, a methodology for literature analysis that can provide a snapshot of the distribution of research in a given timeframe and help clarify the underlying assumptions of the research effort. The *dynamic paradigm funnel* expands that snapshot to an overview of how a theoretical field has developed over time by incorporating central Kuhnian notions of normal science, anomalies, crises, and scientific revolutions. This chapter demonstrates how the dynamic paradigm funnel can be used in practice. It guides the reader through all steps of such a literature analysis using the analysis of 20 years of brand management as an illustration of how the dynamic paradigm funnel works in practice.

The result of the analysis is an accurate overview of how brand management has evolved over the past 20 years. The methodology has enabled us to categorize the literature into seven "clusters", representing seven different approaches to brand management:

- **The economic approach** – *the brand as part of the traditional marketing mix*
- **The identity approach** – *the brand as linked to corporate identity*
- **The consumer-based approach** – *the brand as linked to consumer associations*
- **The personality approach** – *the brand as a human-like character*
- **The relational approach** – *the brand as a viable relationship partner*
- **The community approach** – *the brand as the pivotal point of social interaction*
- **The cultural approach** – *the brand as part of the broader cultural fabric*

These seven "schools of thought" represent fundamentally different perceptions of the brand, the nature of the brand–consumer exchange, and how brand equity is created and managed. The differences cover real-life managerial implications, scientific concerns regarding methods and validity, and philosophical issues as different perceptions of people (as consumers).

This chapter provides insight into the academic challenges the paradigm-related analysis was able to meet (brand management confusion), the central notions of the philosophy of science by Thomas Kuhn, the methodology of the *paradigm funnel*, its elaborated version – the *dynamic paradigm funnel*, and the main results of the analysis of brand management. The chapter will be finished off with some thoughts on the contributions of the dynamic paradigm funnel as methodology and the results that it has provided when applied to the field of brand management.

The starting point – brand management confusion!

Brand management was faced with three problems at the beginning of the millennium:

- an overwhelming body of literature and theoretical frameworks;
- a variety of frameworks, each developed in its own right;
- a body of literature and different perspectives in brand management insufficiently related to each other in existing categorizations of frameworks.

Branding is the talk of the town. Corporations spend millions of euros planning and implementing brand activities. New research is published and frameworks are developed on a daily basis in an attempt to find the holy grail of brand management (BM). Since the mid-1980s, in particular, researchers and practitioners alike have explored the domain, scope, and potential of the brand. Many different concepts, theoretical frameworks, and ideas have seen the light of day, and, as a result, a wide spectrum of different perspectives on how a brand ought to be conceptualized and managed have been introduced. Because of this overwhelming body of literature and multiple perspectives, it is an overwhelming task to obtain an overview of the field of brand management.

Paradigm thinking – and the evolution of knowledge

The term paradigm is often used indiscriminately. Since the dynamic paradigm funnel is based on a deeper understanding of the paradigm and the interconnected theory of "scientific revolution", a short introduction to these concepts is outlined here.

Thomas S. Kuhn (1922–1996) is one of the most influential philosophers of science. Kuhn was occupied with the explanation of how (scientific) knowledge evolves and how this knowledge affects the surrounding world, and vice versa. His principal work is *The Structure of Scientific Revolutions* (1962). The methodology of the dynamic paradigm funnel is based on the theories of scientific evolution put forward in this work (the 1996 edition) (Kuhn, 1996).

A paradigm is an expression of a set of deep assumptions characterizing an academic field or theoretical approach. It guides the selection of problems, concepts, hypotheses, and methods. Paradigms are " . . . universally recognized scientific achievements that for a time provide model problems and solutions to a community of practitioners" (Kuhn, 1996, p. x in the Preface). Paradigms are usually taken for granted by scientists working under them as the natural "way of the world", and (normal scientific) studies are conducted in accordance with the paradigm: " . . . 'normal science' means research firmly based upon one or more past scientific achievements that some particular scientific community acknowledges for a time as supplying the foundation for its further practice" (Kuhn, 1996, p. 10).

A paradigm consists of four levels: assumptions, theories, methods, and data. These four levels are perceived to be context dependent (linked to changes in the environment); paradigms are hence not stable and change over the course of time (Andersen, 1994). The way a paradigm changes over time follows a certain cyclical pattern. The evolution of, or shift in, a paradigm (a scientific revolution) is instigated the moment facts observed in the environment do not accord with the theories and assumptions describing that environment, or put differently: "The dynamics of a paradigm are a result of ongoing interplay between deep assumptions and surface facts" (Berthon, Nairn, & Money, 2003, p. 56). When a scientist observes "something" in the environment (nature) that cannot be explained by the concepts, hypotheses, theories, and methods provided by the paradigm (in the Kuhnian terminology this "something" is an "anomaly"), the paradigmatic foundation needs to be questioned and a re-evaluation of old assumptions is provoked. Kuhn expresses this process as follows: " . . . to desert the paradigm is to cease practising the science it defines . . . such desertions do occur. They are the pivots about which scientific revolutions turn" (Kuhn, 1996, p. 34).

After some battle between old and new "ways of the world", a new paradigm is established (Kuhn, 1996). A scientific revolution has taken place: "The extra-ordinary episodes in which that shift of professional commitments occurs are the ones known . . . as scientific revolutions. They are the tradition-shattering complements to the tradition-bound activity of normal science" (Kuhn, 1996, p. 6).

New ways of perceiving and understanding the environment and phenomena will emerge; thereby a new or several new paradigms can be developed. A process then takes place where facts are compared with the assumptions and theories of both the old and the new paradigm. This can be described as a process

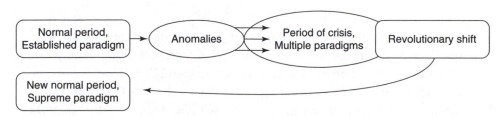

Figure 2.1 A scientific revolution, adapted from Andersen (1994). Reproduced by permission of Samfunslitteratur

of evaluating each paradigm's ability to research and explain the environment (nature) (see Figure 2.1). The paradigm that instrumentally is best at explaining nature at the given point of time "wins". Thereby, a complete scientific revolution and hence "the reconciliation between the observed and the assumed" (Kuhn, 1996) have taken place. After this reconciliation, the scientific community is ready to conduct science under the "umbrella" of the new paradigm: "Led by a new paradigm, scientists adopt new instruments and look in new places" (Kuhn, 1996, p. 111), and new empirical studies, approaches to phenomena, methodologies, and theoretical discussions are carried out.

The paradigm funnel – background and getting started

Understanding the concept of paradigms and scientific evolution is hence fundamental for the understanding of scientific disciplines. But how can one use the Kuhnian notions of paradigms and the evolution of scientific knowledge in real life?

Researchers Berthon, Nairn, and Money (2003) have put forward a conceptual tool for paradigm-related literature analysis, building on the four "layers" of a paradigm (assumptions, theories, methods, and data). When conducting an inquiry using the *paradigm funnel*, one defines: a subject of interest, a time span, and a selection of the most relevant publications within the field of the subject.

Box 2.1 Adopting the paradigm funnel technique: the case of brand management – background

For us, a frustrating work phase began when we tried to find literature about the paradigmatic development of brand management, from around the year 1985 until 2006. Reading through stacks of books and loads of research papers on the subject did not cast sufficient light on present paradigms in brand management. However, stumbling upon the paper *The Paradigm Funnel: A Conceptual Tool for Literature Analysis* (Berthon, Nairn, & Money, 2003) gave us an idea. Maybe we could conduct the analysis ourselves?!

After having embedded ourselves into the Kuhnian way of thinking in a paradigmatic analysis of brand management, we found that "paradigm thinking" does not need to be elusive. Paradigms *can* be analysed in a tangible way, and using the paradigm funnel to analyse an academic field can provide a very tangible overview of the subject of analysis as well. A paradigm-bound analysis can capture many of the "blurry" concepts of management and marketing, and facilitate an understanding of them that is varied and yet precise. An analysis of this sort can anchor a "shallow" and rather unprecise discipline such as brand management in an accurate scientific context and, at the same time, cast light on the theories' congruence with empirical observations of the surrounding environment.

As explained above, a paradigm is "the entire constellation of beliefs, values, and techniques, and so on, shared by the members of a community" (Kuhn, 1996, p. 175). The articles published in the most influential journals within a theoretical field hence play a significant part in the establishment of the research that in time will be perceived as valid and legitimate (Hult, Neese, & Bashaw, 1997; Baumgartner & Pieters, 2002). The ongoing dynamics of paradigmatic develop-ment within a scientific field can thus be observed in academic journals. Using research articles as empirical data is one of the pillars of the paradigm funnel.

Box 2.2   Adopting the paradigm funnel technique: defining data

The "community" of our inquiry was the academic approach to the field of brand management. In brand management, the community's "beliefs, values, and techniques" are shared in academic marketing journals. "The brand" is the subject of interest, the time span is 1985–2006, and the academic publications are: *Journal of Marketing, Journal of Consumer Research,*

Journal of Marketing Research, and *European Journal of Marketing.*[1] Searching these publications for research articles with the brand and brand management as the key topic provided 250+ articles. Hence, the communication of research (the articles) is used as the empirical material. These articles are then analysed quantitatively as well as qualitatively through an empirical-theoretical analysis of the paradigmatic development in brand management from January 1985 to December 2006, focusing on the most influential research conducted in this discipline. The choice of 1985 as the starting point of this inquiry is due to the emergence of brand equity as a management priority in the mid-1980s (Aaker & Biel, 1993; Kapferer, 1997), and it ends in 2006 owing to editorial limitations.

Adopting the paradigm funnel technique – data

The other basic notion of the paradigm funnel is the fact that scientific work under a paradigm has different foci, and that the articles can be sorted in four different levels according to the focus they represent:

1. Empirical observations.
2. Methodologies.
3. Theoretical discussions.
4. Deep assumptions.

The four levels hence represent different paradigmatic levels of research. The dataset is sorted in these four different "piles", each pile reflecting a paradigmatic "level" (reflecting the focus of scientific work). The sorting mechanism of the paradigm funnel is illustrated in Figure 2.2 which also includes the guiding questions one needs to identify in the research articles when identifying which layer the articles represent.[2]

This is the logic of the paradigm funnel (Figure 2.2), reflecting how the four levels relate to each other, and at the same time expresses how knowledge within a scientific field evolves. According to the principles of the paradigm funnel, the

---

[1] The first three being the three most influential marketing journals (Hult, Neese, & Bashaw, 1997; Hackley, 2001), and the fourth to add a European perspective to the analysis.
[2] Examples of the different articles can be found in Berthon, Nairn, and Money (2003).

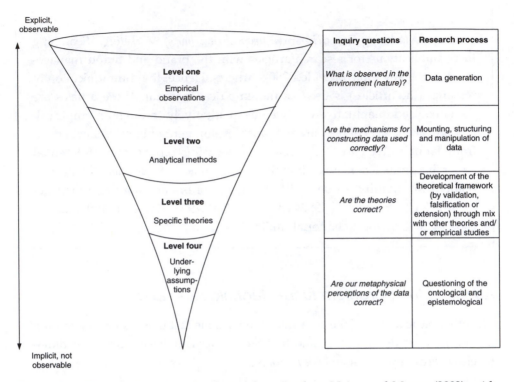

Figure 2.2 The paradigm funnel, adapted from Berthon, Nairn, and Money (2003), with the appropriate research questions and description of research processes corresponding to each level. Reproduced by permission of CRC Press

articles are hence sorted in four different "piles" reflecting different foci of scientific work as illustrated in Figure 2.2:

- *"Level-one" articles: research with an emphasis on empirical observations.* A large amount of level-one articles characterize periods of paradigmatic stability. The environment is observed and presented without questioning existing theory, methods, or deep assumptions. "Empirical articles are those that primarily deal with the description or analyses of phenomena" (Tellis, Chandy, & Ackerman, 1999, p. 129). Here, the focus for scientific work is to examine, explain, and determine significant facts in "nature".

- *"Level-two" articles: research with an emphasis on methodological considerations.* These articles challenge or develop methodological frameworks. A level-two article is hence one that has the primary focus of developing or questioning procedures for gathering data or conducting research. These articles display some degree of paradigmatic turbulence – methodology-wise.

- *"Level-three" articles: research articles preoccupied with theoretical discussions.* Existing theory is either challenged or validated through empirical observations or mere theorizing. The degree of turbulence is increasingly greater in level-three articles. In level-three articles, the scientific focus is to investigate how significant facts match with theory. Level-three articles hence focus on research that develops, challenges, or validates theory. In a period of crisis, more paradigms coexist and anomalies are present; hence, there is a high degree of paradigmatic turbulence because many articles question existing theories. The function of level-three articles is twofold in such a period of paradigmatic turbulence: they either challenge existing theory or validate new theory. In the challenging articles, "anomalies" are pointed out, pinpointing inadequacies of the existing theories' accordance with "nature". These articles are the majority of level three. A smaller number of articles that can be labelled "level three" do the opposite. After the birth of a new approach – a groundbreaking theory – the theory is validated in a number of articles at this level, consolidating the approach.

- *"Level-four" articles: rare articles introducing groundbreaking new thoughts and altering the underlying assumptions.* Here, the deeper assumptions are challenged and the possibility of the birth of new and groundbreaking theory is present: " . . . the questioning of deep ontological, methodological, and axiological assumptions" (Berthon, Nairn, & Money, 2003, p. 60). In our experience, a level-four article often introduces what we call an approach (but not an entire shift in paradigm). This will be explained later. Level-four articles are indicators – or parts – of a revolutionary transition, but one swallow does not (in our experience) make a summer.

Adopting the paradigm funnel technique – analysis

Analysing the content of these four piles of academic articles brings out a precise understanding of the paradigmatic content of a scientific discipline. Sorting the articles and analysing the content of the four paradigmatic levels is suitable for a deep, but static, analysis of a body of literature and is excellent for gaining insight into the content – and eventually pinpointing discrepancies – of a ruling paradigm:

> *The logic is as follows. If facts do not accord with a specific theory, recourse is made to questioning how the data are structured or analysed. If solutions are*

not found at this level, the specific theory that generated the empirical hypotheses may be questioned. Finally, communities of specific theories may be questioned, which may lead to the questioning of deep assumptions and the eventual gestalt flip to a new paradigm. In summary, anomalies on one level of the funnel can potentially be resolved by recourse to a deeper level. Thus, data anomalies may be solved by different data manipulation techniques. If this fails, one has to resort to rethinking theory and ultimately the deep assumptions underpinning a theory. (Berthon, Nairn, & Money, 2003, p. 56. Reproduced by permission of CRC Press.)

Box 2.3   Adopting the paradigm funnel technique – analysing the paradigmatic distribution of research

At this point in time, the dataset is retrieved according to the description in Box 2.2 and the categorization process is about to begin. The following steps are the "hands-on" guidelines on how to do it:

- print all research articles;
- look at one article at a time;
- focus on categorizing the article according to the focus of the research level – what is the research process and the research question (1, 2, 3, or 4) (Figure 2.2) – do not worry about the actual content of the article until later;
- write the number reflecting the research level on the front page of the article (1, 2, 3, or 4);
- write the year of publication on the front page as well.

If the analysis concerns research from a limited number of years, now go through the following steps:

- divide all the research articles into four piles reflecting the research levels;
- conduct a qualitative analysis of each pile;
- now compare the findings from each pile.

You will now have a clear picture of the paradigmatic content of the scientific discipline in question. Which assumptions underlie the empirical studies in pile 1 (assumptions are rarely mentioned, but are revealed in the focus of research, the methods applied, and so on; look for the "taken-for-granted" stuff)? Are the available methods questioned in the articles in pile 2? Are the dominant theoretical frameworks questioned, and how, in the level-three articles? Are the underlying assumptions of the discipline questioned in the level-four pile (if there is one)?

Besides gaining a varied, yet accurate, picture of the paradigmatic *content* of the discipline, you will also be able to detect *discrepancies*. Discrepancies in the scientific discipline will be revealed through a wide gap between "top" and "bottom" of the research articles. If the taken-for-granted assumptions of the empirical studies of level one are fiercely questioned and challenged in the articles of the other levels, the need for a revolutionary transition is present.

It is important to notice that all four levels contribute to the understanding of a paradigmatic development. The level-four articles represent paradigmatic "peaks", where new scientific "puzzles" are added to the discipline, but it is the level-one articles that reveal the most about the underlying assumption of the dominant paradigm because they conduct studies according to the "assumed". Deconstructing the methods, data, and focus of these articles therefore reveals much about the agreed-upon paradigm behind the research. Levels two and three are also important, as they point out the shortcomings of the existing theoretical and paradigmatic framework as well as help integrate new approaches. Hence, the drivers of the continuous paradigmatic development of a scientific field can be found in these piles. Merely sorting the articles and analysing the content of the four paradigmatic levels hence provides a deep, but static, analysis of a body of literature.

The dynamic paradigm funnel

The logic of the paradigm funnel helped us tremendously in our efforts to deconstruct brand management, and it is compelling in its ability to "highlight the way in which research effort is distributed at a point of time" (Berthon, Nairn, & Money, 2003, p. 65). However, a scientific field is under constant development, and the paradigm concept is imperatively linked to the logic of scientific revolutions. Since our dataset consisted of 20+ years of research, we wanted more emphasis on the dynamic and chronological aspects of a paradigmatic development. We also believed that Kuhn's fundamental notions of normal science, anomalies, crises, and scientific revolutions could be incorporated further, and thereby add insight about the *chronological* and *dynamic* evolution of scientific discipline to the results of the analysis. These ideas inspired us to create the *dynamic paradigm funnel*. This elaboration on the existing methodology captures the paradigmatic development over time by calculating how the levels of "paradigmatic turbulence" in the dataset have evolved and changed over time. Paradigmatic *turbulence* versus *stability* are keywords in the dynamic paradigm funnel.

Elaborating on the methodology, it became clear to us that the stable and turbulent periods could be given a numeric value, or rather that each year of an inquiry has a number reflecting its "stability versus turbulence level".

**Box 2.4   Taking it one step further: the dynamic paradigm funnel –
how to add dynamics?**

All the research articles are categorized according to the principles in the paradigm funnel (see "Adopting the paradigm funnel technique – analysing the paradigmatic distribution of research"). Thereby, each article has a number (1, 2, 3, or 4) and a year of publication on the front page. Now go through the following steps:

- Make new piles, one for each year of the whole time span of the analysis (21 piles in our analysis).
- Now calculate the "turbulence level" of each year: all articles published in, say, 1985 are in one pile. In our dataset, three articles on the subject of brand management were published in 1985. Two articles communicated a scientific focus of empirical observations (level one), while the third article discussed and challenged an existing theoretical framework (and hence was a level-three article). Now add the numbers 1 + 1 + 3, equalling 5, and then divide this by the number of articles, i.e. 3. This

provides us with a "turbulence level" of 1.67 being the numeric value expressing the level of paradigmatic turbulence in 1985.

- Repeat the process for each year in the dataset, and you will be able to draw a diagram (like Figure 2.3) illustrating the chronological, paradigmatic development of the discipline.

After having deducted the turbulence levels quantitatively, the data can be analysed qualitatively by looking into what have been the drivers of the evolution. In periods of high turbulence levels, the pattern of evolution of knowledge is that publications initially question existing theory, followed by the introduction of new conceptualizations. Understanding this process requires that the content of each level-two/three/four article is carefully analysed by identifying the elements of existing methods, theoretical frameworks, and methods that are challenged and why. After having identified what is challenged, the articles introducing new theory and new assumptions

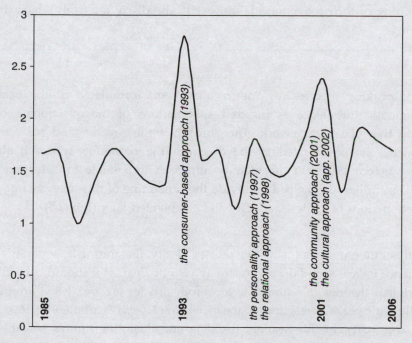

Figure 2.3 The paradigmatic turbulence in brand management 1985–2006

can provide insights into the constructs and assumptions that replace the theories that were challenged in the first place.

The identification of the elements of older theory that are discussed and challenged, followed by an introduction of new theory, hence supplements the quantitative analysis by providing insights into what changes in assumptions, methodology, theory, and practice have driven the evolution of knowledge and how the new theories build on an aim to eliminate the shortcomings of existing theory.

Hence, by adding dynamics to the analysis, one is able to monitor the changes in the scientific discipline as well as identify the shortcomings or changes in environment that are the drivers of change and lay the basis for the evolution of knowledge. The identification of new approaches or other profound changes becomes possible not only because it becomes very clear exactly when groundbreaking new perspectives are born but also because, by understanding them in context, one obtains an under-standing of their interconnectedness with the discipline from which they spring.

Groundbreaking theories (or "approaches") are formulated at the peaks of paradigmatic turbulence as inspired sublimations of the questioning of the existing theoretical framework. The "birth" of the seven brand management approaches is incorporated in the diagram (the economic approach already existing before 1985 and the identity approach impossible to date precisely). The diagram has also helped us divide the timeframe of our analysis into three separate periods of analysis, which will be explained later (Box 2.5).

This illustration provided us with a needed clarity, illustrating how paradigmatic turbulence increases and decreases slowly year by year, as it should, according to the original theories of Kuhn. The level-four articles are published around the paradigmatic peaks as reactions to the increasing levels of turbulence (1993, 1997/1998, and 2001). In this fashion, the diagram illustrates Kuhn's statement on discoveries and paradigmatic development: "not (being) isolated events but extended episodes with a regularly recurrent structure" (Kuhn, 1996, p. 52). During

Box 2.5 Adopting the dynamic paradigm funnel technique: the case of brand management – scientific revolution

The two peaks in brand management reflect profound changes. To structure our dataset further, we divided the period of analysis according to these two peaks – one period before the first, one period in between the first and the second, and finally a period after the second peak of paradigmatic turbulence. The three periods of separate analysis are 1985–1992, 1993–1999 and 2000–2005, which facilitated the further qualitative analysis of the different approaches present in the academic brand management literature and the shifting paradigm, which will be explained below.

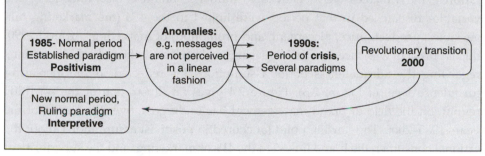

our analysis of the dataset, it became clear that the content of the field changed profoundly around 1993 and then again around the millennium, which is reflected in the two highest peaks.

The logic of scientific evolution is hence found in the continuous interaction between normal science (conducted in accordance with the ruling paradigm), as primarily expressed in level-one articles, anomalies (pointed out in level-two and level-three articles), and groundbreaking theories in level-four articles – pushing a revolutionary transition.

Findings: evolution and revolution in brand management

Having conducted an extended literature review using the methodology of the dynamic paradigm funnel, we were able to establish the following main points: the evolution of the field could be divided into three periods of analysis, and a scientific revolution had taken place during the 1990s. The battle between a positivist paradigm and an interpretive one had been won by the interpretive studies (but the positivist studies are still present in the milieu). Another important result is the identification of seven different brand management approaches ("schools of thought" or "clusters") present in the literature.

The three periods of analysis proved to be markedly different. In 1985, the research of the brand and brand management was inspired by marketing and anchored in a positivist paradigm. The consumer was perceived as being mainly rational, the variables were believed to influence brand choice, and hence the variables researched in that period were linked to the 4Ps (the marketing mix variables: product, price, placement, and promotion) of marketing. Around 1990, this approach was faced with increasing criticism and theoretical discussions regarding the adequateness of its assumptions (as reflected in the increasing turbulence level of Figure 2.3). Figure 2.4 gives an illustration of the scientific revolution the field of brand management has undergone over the course of the years 1985–2006. The starting point (anchored in positivist assumptions about the rational consumer, the brand linked to the 4Ps of marketing, and the superiority of

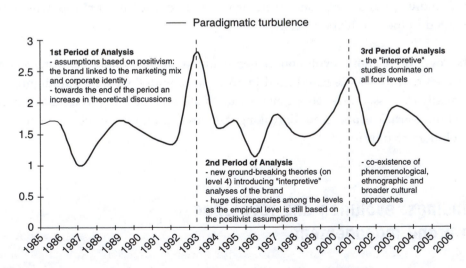

Figure 2.4 The scientific revolution in brand management 1985–2006

quantitative data) was faced with increasing criticism and theoretical discussions regarding the adequateness of its assumptions around 1990. The 1990s were characterized by the presence of a considerable number of groundbreaking theories introducing new scientific approaches to the study of the brand, while the empirical studies (the level-one articles) were still anchored in the positivist paradigm. Hence, the 1990s was a decade of paradigmatic crisis lacking agreement between "the assumed and the observed". Around the millennium, things shifted. The "interpretive", qualitative studies put forward in the new theories of the 1990s now seemed to have "won" the paradigmatic battle, as the majority of empirical studies had adopted the qualitative approaches. It will again be noted that research studies were still – and are still – being conducted under the umbrella of the positivist paradigm, but in an inferior number compared with the qualitative, interpretive studies.

Seven approaches and two paradigms in brand management

As depicted in Figure 2.3, seven brand management approaches were identified and defined during the time span of this literature analysis. These seven approaches are smaller parts of the paradigmatic cloth and fit the term "scientific puzzle" well. Science performed in accordance with the accepted paradigm is labelled "normal science". Kuhn sees this concept as "puzzle-solving", and this metaphor is useful for understanding how one scientific tradition consists of fragments of one specific world view – or, as Kuhn expresses it: " . . . this strong network of commitments – conceptual, theoretical, instrumental, and methodological – is a principal source of the metaphor that relates normal science to puzzle-solving" (Kuhn, 1996, p. 42). Under the umbrella of one paradigm, the concept of "normal science" occurs; it is science performed in accordance with the accepted paradigm.

The seven approaches identified in the scientific field of brand management 1985–2006 are all anchored in different scientific and philosophical traditions and therefore represent different conceptual, theoretical, instrumental, and methodological pieces of their scientific set-up. In our understanding, an approach is *not* a paradigm but a "milestone" in the paradigmatic development. A scientific revolution is a massive undertaking and should be traceable on all four paradigmatic levels.

Arguably, there are two paradigms present in the period of choice. Seven approaches are identified; they are distinctly different, but still able to coexist under the umbrellas of the two overriding paradigms.

Box 2.6 Adopting the dynamic paradigm funnel technique – findings: two paradigms and seven approaches

From 1985 to 2006, two overriding paradigms have been present in the academic world of brand management: one with a positivistic point of departure and one of a constructivist or interpretive nature. The positivistic stance implies a notion of the brand being "owned" by the marketer, who controls the communication to a passive recipient/consumer. Brand equity is being created by the marketer. The interpretive paradigm reflects on the nature of the brand and the value of brand equity as something created in the interaction between marketer and an active consumer. Under the umbrella of each paradigm, different "approaches" coexist.

Being a breakaway discipline from the broad scope of marketing, brand management starts out with a research environment under the influence of traditional marketing theory (as the 4Ps), the brand value under investigation focusing on changes in, for example, distribution channels. The perspective on the consumer in this "economic approach" is based on "the rational man", and laboratory settings and scanner data are illustrative of the methodologies and (always quantitative) data. In a European context, an "identity approach" is also influential during the first years of this inquiry. Focusing on corporate identity, the brand is also primarily perceived as an entity "owned" by the marketer. Integration of the brand on all organizational levels is key. These two approaches form the basis of the discipline of brand management. Hence, in contrast to the five approaches coexisting under the umbrella of the interpretive paradigm, a time of birth and a "founding article" cannot be pointed out.

In 1993, "the consumer-based approach" was founded by Kevin Lane Keller (Keller, 1993). Here, a radical new take on brand equity was presented as accumulated associations in the minds of consumers. In 1997, research into consumers' tendency to perceive brands as human-like personalities was published, establishing "the personality approach". The year after, Fournier presented a study into the human-like relationships with brands experienced by consumers, giving birth to "the relational approach" (Fournier, 1998). The personality approach stems from human personality psychology, while the relational approach borrows from existentialism/phenomenology. Characteristics from anthropology/ethnography were added to the picture when researchers Muñiz and O'Guinn published an article that came to serve as the constitution of "the community approach" in 2001 (Muñiz & O'Guinn, 2001). A "cultural approach" also came into existence around the millennium; here, the brand was being examined as part of the broader cultural fabric, and it was the relationship between the marketer and consumer culture that was the focal point (Heding, Knudtzen, & Bjerre, 2008).

Conclusion

There are many benefits from adopting the techniques of the paradigm funnel and the dynamic paradigm funnel. The establishment of predetermined fixed points for the analysis facilitates the researchers gaining these benefits. This requires the researcher or student to have a general overview of the subject field before undertaking the analysis. The data from this kind of analysis can be immense and overwhelming, which is why a very structured approach to the analysis is essential to avoid getting lost in minor details and maintain perspective on the overall development.

The benefits of using the dynamic paradigm funnel are, however, compelling in our experience. Not only does this analysis enable the scholar to establish and gain a systematic and scientifically viable overview of the exact chronology: paradigms, approaches, and key researchers of the academic field in question. It also enriches the scholar with a "hands-on" experience of the nature of scientific evolution and hence a much better understanding of how scientific revolutions take place as well as a varied insight into the nature of a paradigm. This knowledge also implies an overview of the environmental as well as academic drivers behind the central theories and concepts.

The methodology is very well suited for research of marketing disciplines, because marketing disciplines are relatively young and therefore often suffer from a lack of explicit scientific clarification.

Conducting the 20-year analysis of brand management has been an eye-opening experience, both in terms of Kuhn's philosophy of science and in terms of the specific subject of analysis. The dataset requested for an analysis of this kind is huge, and the sorting mechanism can seem difficult to grasp. When we started out sorting more than 250 research articles according to the principles of the paradigm funnel, we felt quite puzzled. If confusion is the state you are left in at this point of reading, we can only encourage you to go ahead! Learn by doing! The logic *will* appear as you go along.

References

Aaker, D. A. & Biel, A. L. (1993) *Brand Equity and Advertising – Advertising's Role in Building Strong Brands*. Lawrence Erlbaum Associates, Hillsdale, NJ.

Andersen, H. (1994) *Videnskabsteori og Metodelære*. Samfundslitteratur, Copenhagen, Denmark.

Baumgartner, H. & Pieters, R. (2002) "Who talks to whom? Intra- and interdisciplinary communication of economic journals". *Journal of Economic Literature*, vol. 40, no. 2, pp. 483–510.

Berthon, P., Nairn, A., & Money, A. (2003) "Through the paradigm funnel: conceptual tool for literature analysis". *Marketing Education Review*, vol. 13, no. 2, pp. 55–66.

Fournier, S. M. (1998) "Consumers and their brands: developing relationship theory in consumer research". *Journal of Consumer Research*, March, pp. 343–375.

Hackley, C. (2001) *Marketing and Social Construction*. Routledge, London, UK.

Heding, T., Knudtzen, C. F., & Bjerre, M. (2008) Approaches in *Brand Management: Research, Theory and Practice*. Routledge, London, UK.

Hult, G. T. M., Neese, W. T., & Bashaw, E. R. (1997) "Faculty perceptions of marketing journals". *Journal of Marketing Education*, vol. 19, no. 1, pp. 37–52.

Kapferer, J. (1997) *Strategic Brand Management: Creating and Sustaining Brand Equity Long Term*. Kogan Page, London, UK.

Keller, K. L. (1993) "Conceptualizing, measuring and managing customer-based brand equity". *Journal of Marketing*, vol. 57, January, pp. 1–22.

Kuhn, T. S. (1996) *The Structure of Scientific Revolutions.* University of Chicago Press, Chicago, IL.

Muñiz Jr, A. M. & O'Guinn, T. C. (2001) "Brand community". *Journal of Consumer Research,* vol. 27, March, pp. 412–433.

Tellis, G. J., Chandy, R. K., & Ackerman, D. S. (1999) "In search of diversity: the record of major marketing journals". *Journal of Marketing Research,* vol. XXXVI, February, pp. 120–131.

3

Creativity, Cognition, and the Market

Bo T. Christensen

Introduction

What do marketing and markets have to do with creativity? Given the popular conception that marketers and advertisers are some of the most creative professionals out there, the link would intuitively seem to be quite strong. Marketers and advertisers tend to view themselves as highly creative professionals, competing, for example, in the generation of original, expressive, exciting, and provocative advertising that they consider to be creativity par excellence.

However, in most creativity research, marketing is not a creativity stronghold. In fact, when the creativity research literature is examined, marketing is rarely even mentioned as a creative domain. While advertisers and marketers may consider themselves to be highly creative, creativity researchers appear not to share that viewpoint given that the domains of choice when studying creativity are anything but marketing-related domains. To illustrate this, a quick count from the citation database PsychInfo was conducted. Three of the major creativity journals (*Creativity Research Journal*, *Journal of Creative Behavior*, and *Creativity and Innovation Management*) were examined for articles related to creativity in various domains.

The count showed that the prototypical domain is unquestionably the domain of art, with hundreds of references just in these three creativity journals. The subdomains of painting, music, literature and poetry, and movies each have manifold more references than the whole of the marketing domain. Perhaps not surprisingly, the same is the case with product development or invention. A bit more surprising may be the fact that even science is far ahead of marketing, with over fivefold more references than marketing and advertising combined. The domain of education and teaching, too, appears to be much more creative than marketing. And even politics supersedes marketing as a creativity domain! In fact, marketing and advertising are ranked close to the bottom in this simple count of creativity, with only 18 references, placing them only just above journalism and sports. Of course, such citation counts are not proof of the quality or type of article contribution, but they do indicate that marketing is not considered remotely as central a creativity domain as art, science, or invention. Conversely, marketing research does not seem too preoccupied with studying creative processes either.

As such, we have a paradox – marketers and advertisers consider themselves to be involved in a creative domain par excellence. But, in creativity research, marketing appears to be unwanted, and marketing research seems to be neglecting creative processes, too, as a research area. Why is that? Why is hardly anyone studying the creativity–marketing link? In the present chapter we will look at possible reasons for this paradox, and try to make arguments as to why marketing and creative studies could benefit from more interaction than they do today. We will start by looking towards two classical models of what the domains of creativity and marketing respectively are about, to find overlap in focus or skills involved. Then we will develop creativity theory by asking new research questions that may ensure that market creation skills are placed centrally in creative studies. And finally, a few new directions for market creation creativity will be explored.

Two 4P models

Both creativity research and marketing research can be seen as having a number of dimensions to their respective fields. This has been captured in two classical models of the content of these dimensions. Incidentally, in both fields, one of the most classical models for these respective dimensions was developed in the early 1960s, and in looking at these models it would appear that both creativity and marketing have a lot to do with Ps. Both models were called the "4P model"! The models are outlined below, to illustrate potential overlap between marketing and creativity research.

The 4Ps of creativity

The domain of creativity research can be described as being composed of four parts or strands. Rhodes (1961) and Mooney (1963) were the first to describe creativity as consisting of the creative **person**, creative **process**, creative **product**, and creative **press**/environmental factors. Each part or strand identifies one way of looking at creativity, with differing theoretical assumptions, models, and conceptions and with varying means of measuring creativity. We will briefly outline each P here, and produce examples of the theoretical models involved in each P.

Theories looking at the creative **person** focus on the characteristics or attributes of people, notably individual differences in traits, types, motivation, and styles of creativity. Much of the early work in creativity research dealt with individual differences in creativity, such as divergent and convergent thinking (Guilford, 1950). Moreover, throughout the history of creativity research, a focus on what separates the creative genius from the average Joe has received much research attention (see, for example, Simonton, 1999). Studies of the creative person have examined both levels of creativity (e.g. Torrance, 1974) and styles of creativity (e.g. Kirton, 1989). Finally, studies of personality traits have found that creative people tend to be open to new experiences, less conventional, less conscientious, and more self-confident, self-accepting, driven, ambitious, dominant, hostile, and impulsive (Feist, 1999). The traits that distinguish creative children and adolescents tend to be the ones that distinguish creative adults, and the creative personality tends to be rather stable over time.

The theories of the creative **process** focus on mechanisms or stages of the creative thinking process. Based on anecdotal accounts of creative processes by inventors, scientists, and artists, Wallas (1926) suggested the creative process has four stages: preparation, incubation, illumination, and verification. This procedural description has had a large impact on creative studies, possibly because of its face validity, where long periods of intellectual drought or impasses sometimes end in insight and breakthroughs. Theorists in the tradition of creative problem-solving have tried to systematize the creative process into a number of stages, where divergent and convergent thinking takes place in each stage (e.g. Osborn, 1963). Cognitive psychologists have been trying to explain some of the mechanisms involved in creative thinking, such as thinking by analogy, simulation, association, and so on (e.g. Finke, Ward, & Smith, 1992).

Theories of the creative **product** look at the qualities and perceptions of creative outcomes. What characterizes the creative ideas, inventions, advertisements, theories, and pieces of art produced? O'Quin and Besemer (1989) noted three characteristics: novelty (its originality), resolution or usefulness (whether the product met the challenges it was meant to overcome), and synthesis (whether it was carried to a final completion).

And finally the creative **press** (or environmental factors) assesses the context or climate of creativity. Traditionally, the climate debate has primarily concerned organizational or team/group contexts. For example, Ekvall (1996) identified 10 dimensions of the organizational climate that promote or hinder creativity, including such aspects as playfulness and humour, idea time, trust and openness, freedom, and risk-taking. Recently, the discussion of the creative class (Florida, 2004) has led to the argument that the "place" is important for creativity. Florida argues that talent, technology, and tolerance all contribute to making a place (whether a city, a region, or a country) creative.

Each of these four paradigmatic approaches focuses on one aspect of creativity. And each will have different assumptions and different approaches to the theoretical models developed and the empirical tests used. While each P focuses on a particular aspect of creativity, what is perhaps more interesting in this regard is which Ps are missing or not currently being studied. We will now turn to the 4P model in marketing to try to identify any potential overlap between the two models.

The 4Ps of marketing

In marketing, early research pointed towards the business executive as an "artist" mixing ingredients such as advertising, product planning, pricing, promotions, branding, channels of distribution, display, servicing, packaging, fact finding and analysis, physical handling, and personal selling (Borden, 1964). Borden coined the phrase "the marketing mix" to denote important elements that may comprise the marketing programme. The elements in the marketing mix were later regrouped into four elements (product, price, placement, and promotion), thus leading to the memorable and enduring 4P model (McCarthy, 1965). McCarthy defined the term as "a combination of all the factors at a marketing manager's command to satisfy the target market". The product represented a collection of features and benefits that could lead to customer satisfaction. The price was thought to be the revenue-generating element in terms of added value (including customer perception). Promotion covered all types of communicating with markets (advertising, sales promotion, word of mouth, etc.). And placement referred to the distribution channels, location, and logistics. The marketing mix 4P model has frequently been challenged for neglecting or overemphasizing certain issues, leading to frequent suggestions of adding additional Ps to the model (e.g. Booms & Bitnmer, 1981; see also Groucutt, 2005, for a long list of suggested Ps in the marketing literature). One frequently voiced criticism of the 4P model is that the customer is not kept front and centre in the mix. Another criticism that can be made of the marketing mix is that it seems to relate primarily to existing markets: ways of segmenting, communicating, and distributing to markets already out there. However, in strategic market creation it is not enough to have tools for sampling, segmenting, and dealing with existing markets. Markets are not static entities to be explored and optimized – they are created (Kim & Mauborgne, 2005). The marketing mix in this case should thus try to expand the toolbox to include tools that aim at changing or evolving markets and innovations. The traditional marketing mix relates back to marketing as a way of optimizing the sales of new products on existing markets through segmenting, communicating, etc. That may be fine for incremental-type innovations, but, in dealing with radical innovations that create or revolutionize markets, such skills will not suffice. In market creation, however, it is realized that markets and products are codependent, and innovation necessarily involves not just creating products but importantly creating the right product–market match. As such, marketing and innovation become fused, and that fusion implies novel tools in the marketing kit.

In examining these two models of 4Ps, it becomes evident that the focus of the models is not exactly the same. While the creativity 4P model looks at the paradigmatic approaches to creative studies, the marketing mix describes the content of the marketer's toolbox. However, the focus on the marketing toolbox apparently comes at the expense of examining how those skills play out as processes. What do marketers actually do when diving into their toolbox? What processes and mechanisms are at stake and being used by marketers in their allegedly creative everyday tasks? Marketing research has been overwhelmingly focused on the outcome product, at the expense of focusing on marketing processes. The creativity 4P model highlights the fact that there are other paradigmatic goggles to wear, besides the product view. In looking at marketing through a process lens, marketers will become able to examine not just what marketers are supposed to be doing (in terms of applying the 4P toolbox to marketing problems), but what they are actually doing when working creatively. Later in this chapter we will take a look at a few suggestions as to what such a process view on creative marketing could look like when market creation processes are explored by cognitive psychology methods.

In spite of the differences between the 4P models, one thing seems evident: what creativity and marketing seem to share is a common focus on the product. The overlap between creativity and marketing can be found in looking towards the good or product – whereas the other aspects of marketing do not seem to be included in creative studies. Skills involving communication, distribution, and pricing are apparently thought to be unrelated to creativity in the 4P model of creativity at the moment.

Furthermore, the emphasis on the creative product extends to definitions of creativity. Although multiple definitions of creativity have been put forward over the years, the current mainstay definition is that "creativity occurs when someone creates an original and useful product" (Mayer, 1999). While the naming of the product characteristics varies somewhat, it does appear that two product criteria are necessary in the definition: the product needs to be original (or novel, new, or variable) and useful (or appropriate, adaptive, or valuable). This definition has been repeated time and again in the psychological creativity literature, and seems to be the closest to a current definitional consensus (Mayer, 1999). The definition of creativity is sometimes separated from the definition of innovation by stating that, whereas creativity ends in the creation of a novel and useful product, innovation also involves the implementation or launch of that product (Amabile, 1988; Levitt, 1963).

What is apparent from such a definition of creativity is that it creates a narrow focus on the generation of the creative product itself as the criterion for when creativity occurs. But what seems to be missing in the definition is a focus on the receiver or user or customer or evaluator of the creative product. While the user may be implicitly present in the definition in the inclusion of a "usefulness" criterion (whereby the product apparently must be useful to somebody), there is no explicit mention of who is to evaluate creativity.

Perhaps here we have a potential explanation for why marketing is not the domain of choice when studying creativity. Creative studies have identified themselves closely with the generation of products, and, while the focus on products is in part shared by the marketing mix, the other marketing mix skills are apparently distinct from and separate to creative skills. If creativity merely produces products with certain qualities (novelty and usefulness), then we need not bother to examine how those products are communicated, distributed, or priced – this seems to be the argument. Those skills are presently not considered creative. Implied in such a way of thinking is a strict separation of the market from the product. However, as mentioned, when it comes to market creation, that argument appears to break down, as markets and products are shaped and created together. Here, a strict and narrow focus on the creative product will not suffice. Creative studies thus need to take seriously the "audience" of creative products, and learn from marketing.

Who is to evaluate creativity?

Although a consensual definition of creativity exists, the creativity literature is not in agreement about the follow-up question: who is to evaluate creativity, and to whom is creativity supposed to be useful and novel? Such questions relate to discussions of which "level" of creativity we are dealing with. Both novelty and usefulness can occur at various levels. Novelty can be novel for a particular person, for a group of people, for a society, or for the entire population of the world (see, for example, Johannessen, Olsen, & Lumpkin, 2001). Similarly, the creative product can spread simply in the frequency of use of the product by the creator (within the future action of a single person), spread between individuals in a group of peers, or spread between individuals in entire societies or domains, thus highlighting differences in degrees of usefulness. So what are we to call creative? Is it the child's doodling on paper, or is it Einstein's theory of relativity we are talking about? Many creativity researchers have given thought to this subject, and taken sides, or tried to describe the levels of creativity.

On the one hand, there are theories such as creative cognition that argue for creativity being ascribed to all levels, including so-called "mundane" creativity

(Ward, Smith, & Vaid, 1997). Here we also find Boden (1990), who argues that psychology should concern itself only with mundane creativity that is novel to the individual (she calls it P-creativity, for "psychological"), rather than creativity that is novel for the entire world (called H-creativity, for "historical"). Anything H-creative will also always be P-creative, and, argues Boden, studying historical creativity is beyond the scope of a psychological theory. Further still, Weisberg (2006) is yet another theorist with a cognitive bent who has argued for the exclusion of the "usefulness" aspect of creativity, as including usefulness would in his opinion place the creative realm perhaps outside the scope of individual psychology, while moving into social and societal explanations. These three cognitive approaches appear to be arguing that real creativity is of the mundane kind (novel and useful to the individual). On the other hand, we have Simonton (e.g. 1999) arguing for creativity being ascribed to people making products that change societies or domains – the so-called "creative genius" approach. Here, creativity is only creative if the product in fact makes a large impact on domains and traditions, as evaluated by either objective measures of impact or external expert evaluators. Finally, some researchers have tried to classify the levels between the two extremes (see, for example, Cohen, 1989).

But who is to evaluate the novelty and usefulness of such creative products? The ideal implied by some of the above-mentioned psychological approaches to creativity appears to be an objective and neutral view-from-nowhere evaluation of creativity. And notably an objective evaluation that takes place a priori, that is, prior to the product "hitting the market". The "neutral and objective view-from-nowhere evaluation" ideal thus disregards the fact that creativity is always novel and useful to *somebody*, and implies *a somebody* making the evaluation. Indeed, especially the usefulness concept implies a somebody using the product for some purpose, and the outcome being considered by that person to be of value. As such, a "view-from-nowhere" approach will find it notoriously difficult to evaluate usefulness in any domain.

Cognitive approaches to creativity have tried hard to disregard the "somebody" in creative evaluations, by either arguing that the creators themselves make the evaluation of what is creative to them (P-creativity) (Boden, 1990) or by arguing that the subjective "usefulness evaluation" is unnecessary, so that we may regard only the more easily objectified and neutral "originality" evaluation in creativity (Weisberg, 2006). Both approaches aim at throwing the third-party creativity evaluator out of the creative evaluation equation. However, the first attempt fails to account for the evaluative distinctions between so-called "mundane" creativity and historical creativity – making this kind of evaluation practically irrelevant to creativity and innovation scholars look at higher levels of creativity (although it may be suitable for "within-subject learning activities"). In art, science, and invention, such low levels of creativity do not account for evaluative variances at the higher and, arguably, more interesting levels. The second evaluation approach (Weisberg) fails to account for distinctions between what is original and valuable, and what is simply weird and different. The standard argument here is that the delusional or schizophrenic patient may produce a multitude of original ramblings or doodles – but, unless they are also useful to a domain, we would not call them creative. Both cognitive approaches tried to argue for an approach to creative evaluation that disregards societal or market concerns, thus limiting creative evaluation to a strictly psychological level. Or put in other words: in the mainstay psychological explanation of creativity, the market is simply not part of the theoretical model. However, attempts to disregard markets and societal categories in creative evaluations have, in my opinion, so far failed for the above reasons. Below we will thus take the "who is to evaluate" discussion seriously, and look at two alternative approaches to how creativity may be evaluated by third parties: either through gatekeepers or markets.

Two approaches to the evaluation of creativity

In all but the most mundane of creative products, it is necessary to include external evaluators in the creativity model. In these historical creativity cases, creativity is not measured from a view-from-nowhere, nor by the creator himself. Rather, in these historical cases, external evaluators make the judgements necessary. These external evaluators are part of the creativity judgement, in that they set the criteria for originality and usefulness at given points in time. Such criteria and external evaluators may be changing over time, but they cannot be written out of the creativity evaluation equation. It is possible to point to at least two different kinds of external evaluator in creativity judgements. The first concerns the gatekeeper concept, while the second views the market as the evaluator. We will look at both approaches to evaluation below.

Gatekeepers

The gatekeeper is a person, institution, or other social system that decides what shall pass through each gate section. One of the first to use the term "gatekeeping" was Kurt Lewin during World War II (Lewin, 1947) to denote a mother or wife as the decider of which foods end up on the family dinner table. This was an important research task during World War II, as much domestic meat was being shipped overseas to feed soldiers and allies, resulting in the fear that a lengthy war would have the United States starved unless a protein substitute could be found (Wansink, 2002). The challenge became to introduce organ meats (hearts, kidneys, intestines, etc.) to the US dinner tables. But how? Lewin used the gatekeeping concept to describe how certain people control food through different channels (the garden channel, the store channel) and play a central role in deciding which foods end up on the dinner table and are eventually eaten – sometimes even in spite of the preferences of the remaining family. As such, changing US eating habits became a matter of targeting the gatekeeper – the cook who selects, prepares, and serves the food – not the husband or children of the family. By studying the cognition, motivation, and conflicts of gatekeepers, it was possible to incur change in the ecology that led housewives to adopt different habits. Lewin also considered the gatekeeper process in communication, with news items passing though gates – a concept later made famous by White (1961) in journalism.

The idea of applying the gatekeeper concept to creativity evaluation is not new. Morris Stein, working in the marketing domain, applied the concept to, for example, patrons who provide emotional and financial support and transmission agents who disseminate the work to the general public, such as gallery owners, salesmen, advertising agencies, publishers, bookstores, and opinion leaders (Sawyer, 2006). Stein stressed the importance of communicating results to others as an inherent aspect of creativity. In creativity, communication with the self was insufficient, but rather consensual validation was needed in creativity evaluations (Amabile, 1983; Stein, 1953).

Some theories, taking the external evaluator seriously in creativity evaluations, have come up with sociological models of creativity (e.g. Becker, 1982; Csikszentmihalyi, 1988, 1990, 1999). In an elaborate model, Csikszentmihalyi (1990) argued that creativity is not an attribute of individuals but of social systems making judgements about individuals. In a theory of cultural evolution he hypothesized two salient environmental aspects related to evaluation: the field and the domain. The field is a group of gatekeepers (such as critics, teachers, museum curators, etc.) with the authority or ability to sanction new ideas entitled to be included in the domain. The field thus makes up the social organization of a domain. A culture is made up of domains with existing representations and rules (such as mathematics, music, synchronized swimming, etc.), and it is within such domains that new innovations are constructed and evaluated. Domains are necessary in the creativity evaluations because, without reference to "old" or existing patterns, it is impossible to make original contributions. Without rules there cannot be exceptions. Creativity thus occurs when a person makes a change in a domain, a change that will be transmitted through time, making the process similar to the mechanisms of natural evolution, with each part in the creativity model being primarily responsible for one element: variation (by the person), selection (by the field), retention (by the domain).

Market impact

Another approach to creativity evaluation concerns market impact estimates. Here, market impact is basically measured by looking at how much the creative product has spread or diffused onto the market. Depending on the nature of the creative product, such spread measures may concern the number of copies sold, the number of peer-reviewed journal article quotes, the number of times a web page is displayed, the number of search results in Google, the number of tickets sold at the box office, and so on. All these measures are attempts at estimating domain impact through quantitative estimates of product diffusion. In comparison with the gatekeeper approach, the quantitative market estimate is a democratic estimate of spread – basically, every vote counts.

The theory of diffusion of innovation (Rogers, 1995) will be well known to marketers in this regard. Diffusion is defined as a "process in which an innovation is communicated through certain channels over time among the members of a social system. It is a special kind of communication, in that the messages are concerned with new ideas" (Rogers, 1995, p. 5). Through an understanding of the four basic elements in the definition (the innovation itself, communication channels, time, and the social system), diffusion theory examines the factors that determine whether a product will diffuse or spread widely into society. Interestingly, diffusion theory has hardly made any impact on creativity research, even though diffusion theory has discovered several factors concerning both product and audience fostering or hindering product diffusion. Again, perhaps, one could speculate that this may be due to the heavy emphasis on products in creativity research, and underscores the sharp divide that has existed between creativity research and marketing research.

Other approaches to measure creative market impact include Richard Dawkins' notion of memes (Dawkins, 1976). "Examples of memes are tunes, ideas, catch-phrases, clothes fashions, ways of making pots or of building arches. Just as genes leap from body to body via sperm or eggs, so memes propagate themselves in the meme pool by leaping from brain to brain via a process which, in a broad sense, can be called imitation. . . . If the idea catches on, it can be said to propagate itself, spreading from brain to brain" (Dawkins, 1976, p. 192). Memes operate by the same basic principles as genes. The same three qualities that ensure gene survival (fecundity, longevity, and copying fidelity) could ensure meme survival. For example, while one idea may become extinct, other ideas will survive, spread, and mutate through modification. Finally, Simonton (2004) has made numerous studies using creative impact measures on various domains, such as peer-review quotation counts, to pose his argument that creativity involves a great deal of chance.

Creativity estimates or evaluations of the non-mundane kind of creative products are typically carried out by either gatekeepers or markets. As such, the evaluation is not faceless, or done from an objective view from nowhere. Actual people are making these estimates. In most domains, both types of creativity evaluator are in operation. For example, the creativity of technical gadgets may be estimated through market impact (in terms of sold copies), but also through the expert reviews carried out by independent organizations (such as magazine reviews or consumer-protection agencies). The same can be said of creativity in films, where both success at the box office and the Oscars count towards movie creativity. And in science, the Nobel prize and citation counts operate as two different attempts to evaluate creativity of authors and articles.

This may seem straightforward. Creativity evaluation is basically a social or societal process, with people (either on markets or in the form of gatekeepers) making judgements through word or action. What is less straightforward is perhaps the argument that, if this is the case, if creativity judgements are done by people taking a view from somewhere, then including these individuals in models of creativity seems warranted. It is not possible to exclude the external creative evaluator from the evaluation, and nor would you want to. Including an audience in the creativity model is warranted, thereby making the model more sociological than it has been hitherto.

If it is accepted that creativity judgements in this manner include and incorporate external judges, then psychological models of creativity need to address how that affects the skills involved in creative work. And this is where marketing enters the scene. Because arguing for the necessity of including external evaluators in creativity models opens the way for new types of creativity skill not readily acknowledged by traditional psychological product-focused models of creativity. And many of these new creativity skills can be broadly characterized as being based either on the marketing mix or on the new market creation paradigm. In sociological creativity models, the creativity skill toolbox will suddenly find itself full of marketing tools.

Communication is one example: communicating with the audience (whether gatekeepers or markets) involves a host of skills that usually fall under the marketing heading but that become part of an extended creativity model with an audience. Depending on the type of audience (gatekeepers versus markets), different types of communication skill may be central, but, in all cases and domains, communication will play a role for creativity estimates. In an extended creativity model it becomes central to direct information in appropriate ways, through appropriate channels, to the targeted market, in order to ensure that the audience learns about the new product and is persuaded to adopt it. Such marketing basics have not previously been thought to concern creativity in psychological models focusing on products. The same can be argued for distribution and price; again, having an audience leads to considerations about the proper price and distribution channels for creative products. And these considerations can be considered part of (not separate to) creative skills when external evaluators (gatekeepers and markets) are made part of the creativity model.

Furthermore, in creativity, audiences are not just being targeted. They are also to some extent created. The old-fashioned view of creativity involved filling the needs of not-yet or unsatisfied customers. However, audiences (gatekeepers and markets) are not static. In part they are made, and they evolve over time. In constructing blue oceans (Kim & Mauborgne, 2005), innovators do not merely locate unmet needs. They may in fact discover new needs, or create them. Creativity can be market driven – but, more often than not, radical creativity is market changing. Society did not *need* TV or the iPod, or Guernica, or Marxism, or MySpace, or many of the other revolutionary products from the last century. Rather, the products changed their respective domains and markets. The creator of creative products is thus not only writing the play, the play is written for an audience. And selecting the right audience will in part decide the creativity of the product. Sometimes the audience will not take front and centre stage in the generative processes – the author may not always make explicit decisions about who the book is targeting – but the point here is that implicit decisions about the target audience are always made. And finding the right product/audience match is an inherent creativity skill. As such, while evaluators are external to the product they are evaluating, they are not necessarily independent of the decisions of the creator. The decision to create and launch a product in certain ways to certain markets will have implications for the impact of the product on the market. As such, it should be clear that separating the technical/functional aspects of creativity from marketing issues such as communication, the target audience, pricing, etc., is unsound in both marketing and the study of creativity. The creation of products implies creating an audience who will evaluate. Creativity skills are partly about finding the right match between a generated audience and a generated product. And the notion of the audiences (whether found or made) has been a neglected research topic in creativity research.

When it is realized that it is unsound to separate the creative product from its audience, then perhaps it can also be argued that it is unsound to separate them into different organizational functions: an R&D unit and a marketing department respectively. That is not necessarily the argument presented here. But what can be argued is that, if they are separated, then the marketing skills involved in creativity should not merely be an "add-on" to product development, where product developers hand over a finalized product to marketing. Rather, the product should evolve in co-creation of market and product, with close cooperation between product development skills and marketing skills. The cooperation may be ensured both through cross-functional teams or through integrated knowledge and understanding of both audience and product in each individual in the organization. As an example of the latter approach, some companies attempt to bring customers into product development both to generate and evaluate novelty. Usability studies (Rubin, 1994), user involvement in product development (Kujala, 2003), and user-driven innovation (von Hippel, 2005) are all examples of this. As such, there may be many ways to ensure that markets and products coevolve. But, whatever approach is taken, the way forward is not an "over-the-wall" approach where products and audiences are considered separately in the process. Rather, marketing skills contribute actively to all stages of product development by shaping products and users alike. The overall conclusion to be drawn from this is that, regardless of whether creative individuals consider themselves to be doing "marketing", creativity in any domain in essence involves carrying out tasks from the marketing mix. It is time that the social marketing skills in creativity received research attention, rather than being excluded from creative research owing to some mistaken argument that marketing is something completely different from creativity and product development.

Should creativity researchers be saddened by the fact that it now seems inappropriate or impossible to maintain that creativity can be studied merely as a psychological concept? In my opinion psychologists should not be saddened by this. Even though psychologists may lose their property rights for the creativity concept, what they will gain instead is an extended creativity concept for them to explore. As such, as already argued, the extended sociological model will open the way for new kinds of creativity skill currently overlooked in the literature. And these skills can also be studied using psychological theory and methods. Marketing skills from the marketing mix and market creation concepts will make up part of such newly added focus areas for psychological creativity research. As such, psychologists will have lots to say and study about the extended model.

But the pendulum swings both ways, and marketing research should find such a focus area equally exciting, by allowing for new psychological approaches to studying creative marketing processes. By focusing on creative marketing processes through psychological or cognitive methods, marketers may find out what it is creative marketers actually do, and locate cognitive mechanisms and processes involved in market creation. This is currently not something that can be looked up in the typical marketing textbook – here the "psychology" section typically deals strictly with the psychology of the end-user, customer, or decision-maker, ironically without any emphasis on the psychology of the marketers themselves. Below I will take a look at just a few concepts that the extended creativity model allows psychologists and marketers to study. I have chosen to exemplify this with how and on what a *cognitive* approach to creative marketing may begin to focus.

Innovative cognition and market creation

Like the rest of creative studies, the creative cognition approach has been preoccupied with examining how creative products are generated (Finke, Ward, & Smith, 1992), at the expense of looking into audiences and product–market matches. Typical areas of study have been descriptions of how categorization works in producing novel exemplars (Ward, 1994), whether randomness of elements enhances creativity in invention (Finke, 1990), or how fixating elements may keep you from reaching creative solutions (Smith, 1995). While creative cognition has a lot to say about product development and the realization of novel products, the marketing researchers would be at a loss in finding studies looking into central marketing-related creative skills and thinking processes, such as how marketers think about customers and segments and their relation to innovations, how marketers reason creatively about price and availability issues, and so on. Such creative thinking skills have simply not been examined. The same may be said of marketing research: hardly anyone seems to have focused on such marketing-related creativity skills at the process level. In order to differentiate the approach taken here from the past creative cognition product-oriented approach, I will call the present approach "innovative cognition" to highlight that here we are dealing with cognition with a broader focus. Innovative cognition deals with thinking processes involved in market creation, such as thinking and reasoning about audiences and product–market matches, about communicating or distributing to markets, etc. Examples of generative processes could involve analogizing between markets and differentiation from competition. Exploratory processes could involve simulating market segments and user preferences, contextual shifting of product use, functional inference for different segments, and the like. Further, communication, persuasion, and distribution considerations would be an inherent part of innovative cognition. We will now take a look at a few of these examples in a bit more detail.

Randomness and paradox

In creative cognition, randomness and paradox have been linked to increased levels of creativity. For example, Finke (1990) showed how asking people to generate new creative products using random elements or random categories led to increased numbers of creative and highly creative products (although a slight decrease in terms of product usefulness was also detected). In market creation it may be possible to utilize some of the same elements to enhance innovative thinking of markets. For example, creatively analysing or brainstorming how you might diffuse an innovation to current non-customers may lead to insight. Kim and Mauborgne (2005) divided non-customers into three tiers: the first tier on the edge of the market, the second tier who have refused the current offerings from your industry, and the third tier who have never thought about your market's offerings as an option. The third tier is the farthest from your market. By brainstorming "how might we sell product X to third-tier non-customer Y", it may be possible to pinpoint unexpected and lucrative product–market matches using randomness and paradox. The randomness and paradox may be introduced by randomly selecting the non-customer segment to brainstorm, and the paradox may be introduced by selecting segments where it intuitively seems inappropriate or impossible to sell your company's offerings. For example, brainstorming "how might we sell Barbie dolls to young adult males" could lead to surprising results. (Incidentally, a Barbie doll look-a-like is now being sold in UK stores to young adult males. The concept is a gadget involving a sexy doll, a stripper's pole, and PC connectedness. Basically, the gadget allows you to upload your favourite song to the gadget, after which the doll will dance to your tune.) Possibly similar brainstorms led the banking industry to adopt new approaches to banking in order to satisfy the Muslim community's religious beliefs that paying interest on loans or deposits is against the Koran. Islam also forbids certain kinds of risk-taking, including gambling. Islamic finance banks have circumvented this paradox by, for example, seeking to avoid charging interest by sharing profits and risk with the customer, making the bank more of an equity partner. The resulting ways of banking have been hugely successful in capturing previous non-customers. As such, brainstorming paradoxical product–market matches may lead to surprising results, and innovative cognition could study whether, as in creative cognition, paradox and randomness do indeed lead to more creative outcomes.

Mental models of individuals and markets

A mental model is a representation of some domain or situation that supports understanding, reasoning, and prediction based on long-term domain knowledge or theories (Gentner, 2002). In the mental model tradition the focus has been on mechanical reasoning and reasoning about physical systems (Hegarty, 1992; Schwartz & Black, 1996). Causal mental models rely on qualitative relationships, such as signs and ordinal relationships, and relative positions, speed, or mass (e.g. Forbus & Gentner, 1997). When running mental models, people do not estimate exact values or quantities or carry out mathematical calculations in predicting system behaviour. Still, in spite of their lack of detailed quantifications, these qualitative reasoning strategies can be quite powerful, and have the tremendous advantage of allowing reasoning with partial knowledge. Some of the disadvantages of mental models include their inaccuracy and imprecision (Gentner, 2002). Mental model runs allow quick and cheap ways of testing possible alternatives.

Although previous mental models have primarily concerned physical systems ("products"), it is possible in innovative cognition to study mental models involving individuals or markets. For example, as Csikszentmihalyi (1990) argued, creative individuals will attempt to internalize the evaluative criteria of the field, and use that (mental model) internalization as a basis for judging their own creative ideas. Mental models of the evaluative criteria of the field thus constitute and attempt to forecast whether the field will eventually judge the new idea to be creative. Csikszentmihalyi argued that practically all creative individuals say that one advantage they have is that they are confident that they can tell which of their own ideas are bad, thus forecasting the potential verdict of the field, and eliminate those bad ideas without investing time and energy in them. Nobel Prize winner Linus Pauling is a case in point. When asked how he was able to come up with so many groundbreaking ideas, he replied that it was easy – you think of a lot of ideas, and throw away the bad ones. This, however, requires mental models of the evaluative criteria of the field, and the ability successfully to simulate which ideas will pass such evaluations, later to become accepted as grand novelty.

Another type of mental model concerns simulations of markets. Non-static markets and radical novelty make for a tough combination when creators wish to simulate or forecast markets. None the less, creators do simulate and attempt to forecast, by, for example, extrapolating knowledge of individual decision-makers to estimate market impact. Innovative cognition should study how mental models of markets are constructed and used on non-static markets, in order to understand the factors involved. It may be possible, for example, to pinpoint under what circumstances it is appropriate to extrapolate individual decision-making in the model, and when other representations may be more appropriate.

Research questions linking mental models to market creation could involve asking how market creators mentally represent information about the end-user, the field, and the market. What level of representation is involved (individual/group/market), and how does that influence the simulation outcomes? And how can mental models of individuals and markets be enhanced and utilized optimally in market creation?

Analogical reasoning of markets

Analogy involves accessing and transferring elements from familiar categories to use them in constructing a novel idea, e.g. in an attempt to solve a problem or explain a concept (Gentner, 1998). Analogical reasoning is assumed to be a general human capacity (Holyoak & Thagard, 1995) involved in most domains, although, perhaps, notably creative problem-solving domains such as science, innovation, and art. Anecdotes of famous scientists or inventors solving creative problems using analogy abound in the creativity literature. One of the most famous is George de Mestral developing Velcro after examining the seeds of the burdock root that had attached themselves to his dog. He discovered that the burdock root has tiny hooks that attach themselves to the loops in hair or fabric, and he used that discovery to develop Velcro. Like most other creative study concepts, analogical reasoning has primarily been used to illustrate how creative products are generated.

However, analogical reasoning may also be applied to accessing and transferring elements between markets. Like products, markets have a relational structure, and, in trying to find the right product–market match, it may be possible to use analogies of previous product–market matches to come up with new matches. The study of market analogizing may take several forms. For one thing, mapping and transferring innovations to novel hypothesized markets may lead to the discovery of new unrealized market potential. By utilizing knowledge of the nature of markets or segments with which the market creators have past knowledge, market creators can make analogies with future market–product matches by transferring elements. Further, by utilizing knowledge of how past markets were changed or evolved, it may be possible to transfer such knowledge of how markets may change to create future markets for innovations. As such, analogies in market creation will serve the purpose not only of producing novel and useful products but also of exploring and creating novel and useful product–market matches. Research questions could address whether market creators actually use market or product–market match analogies. Further, the types and functions of analogies in this regard would be interesting to pursue.

Conclusion

While creative studies have had four paradigmatic approaches to the study of creativity, marketers seem to have neglected process studies of what it actually is that they do, at the expense of focusing on the marketing mix. Further, the skills involved in the 4P marketing mix model are aimed mainly at exploring and optimizing existing markets, and are not capturing skills involving the creation of more radical novelty in blue ocean strategies. As such, marketing research could benefit from applying psychological process methods from creativity research in order to examine what it is marketers do in market creation, in order to learn how such processes can be taught and improved.

On the other hand, the study of creativity has so far been preoccupied with the study of the generation of novel and useful products. Research questions focusing narrowly on the product have tended to ignore the question as to who is to evaluate creativity. Rather, an objective view-from-nowhere evaluation of creativity has been the norm, in attempts to make the creativity concept one that may be examined and explained purely in psychological terms. However, although that may work for lower "learning-type" kinds of creativity, in non-mundane types of creativity it is necessary to take the "who is to evaluate" question seriously. In non-mundane creativity, evaluators are external and take the form of gatekeepers and markets. As such, it is impossible to ignore the fact that creativity evaluation needs a model involving sociological concepts and explanations. It is time that creative studies received an "audience", and took that audience seriously as evaluators of creativity. Taking the audience seriously carries implications for what may be studied under the creativity headline. For one thing, marketing-related skills of communication, distribution, and pricing and concepts related to market creation become part of the creativity toolbox. This does not mean, however, that creativity is forever lost for psychology. Rather, psychologists should find that loosening the strains of the narrow product focus will lead to new research topics involving, for example, product–market matches. Hopefully, such an expanded creativity model can help ensure that creative studies will recognize the creativity involved in many marketing and market creation activities, and ensure that they receive research attention.

Thus, creative research and marketing research could benefit from fusing their efforts by focusing on the common thread of market creation. An added interaction between marketing and creative studies will thus be beneficial for both research streams. Creative research will gain an expanded creativity model involving added marketing skills, while marketing research will gain from methods and focus on the processes involved in doing market creation. Three suggestions were put forward here for this new field of study: the use of randomization and paradox in market–product matches; the use of mental models in thinking creatively about individuals and markets; and analogizing between markets. However, many more research suggestions can be developed that utilize and develop both fields. Hopefully, such added interactions will help create new markets for both creativity and marketing research.

References

Amabile, T. M. (1983) "The social psychology of creativity: a componential conceptualiza-
tion". *Journal of Personality and Social Psychology*, vol. 45, pp. 357–376.
Amabile, T. M. (1988) "From individual creativity to organizational innovation", in
Innovation: a Cross-disciplinary Perspective, edited by Gronhaug, K. & Kaufmann, G.
Norwegian University Press, Oslo, Norway, pp. 139–166.
Becker, H. S. (1982) *Art Worlds*. University of California Press, Berkeley, CA.
Boden, M. A. (1990) *The Creative Mind: Myths and Mechanisms*. Basic Books, New York,
NY.
Booms, B. H. & Bitnmer, M. J. (1981) "Marketing strategies and organizational structures for
service firms", in *Marketing of Services*, edited by Donnely, J. H. & George, W. R. AMA,
Chicago, IL.
Borden, N. H. (1964) "The concept of the marketing mix". *Journal of Advertising Research*, vol.
4, June, pp. 2–7.
Cohen, L. M. (1989) "A continuum of adaptive creative behaviors". *Creativity Research
Journal*, vol. 2, no. 3, pp. 169–183.
Csikszentmihalyi, M. (1988) "Society, culture, and person: a systems view of creativity", in
The Nature of Creativity: Contemporary Psychological Perspectives, edited by Sternberg, R. J.
Cambridge University Press, New York, NY, pp. 325–339.
Csikszentmihalyi, M. (1990) "The domain of creativity", in *Theories of Creativity*, edited
by Runco, M. A. & Albert, R. S. Sage Publications Inc., Newbury Park, CA, pp. 190–
212.
Csikszentmihalyi, M. (1999) "Implications of a systems perspective for the study of
creativity", in *Handbook of Creativity*, edited by Sternberg, R. J. Cambridge University
Press, New York, NY, pp. 313–335.
Dawkins, R. (1976) *The Selfish Gene*. Oxford University Press, Oxford, UK.
Ekvall, G. (1996) "Organizational climate for creativity and innovation". *European Journal of
Work and Organizational Psychology*, vol. 5, no. 1, pp. 105–123.
Feist, G. J. (1999) "The influence of personality on artistic and scientific creativity", in
Handbook of Creativity, edited by Sternberg, R. J. Cambridge University Press, New York,
NY, pp. 273–296.
Finke, R. A. (1990) *Creative Imagery: Discoveries and Inventions in Visualization*. Lawrence
Erlbaum Associates, Publ., Hillsdale, NJ.
Finke, R. A., Ward, T. B., & Smith, S. M. (1992) *Creative Cognition: Theory, Research, and
Applications*. The MIT Press, Cambridge, MA.
Florida, R. (2004) *The Rise of the Creative Class*. Basic Books, New York, NY.
Forbus, K. D. & Gentner, D. (1997) "Qualitative mental models: simulations or memories?".
Paper presented at the 11th International Workshop on Qualitative Reasoning, Cortona,
Siena, Italy, June 1997.
Gentner, D. (1998) "Analogy", in *A Companion to Cognitive Science*, edited by Bechtel, W. &
Graham, G. Blackwell Publ., Malden, MA, pp. 107–113.
Gentner, D. (2002) "Psychology of mental models", in *International Encyclopedia of the Social
and Behavioral Sciences*, edited by Smelser, N. J. & Bates, P. B. Elsevier, Amsterdam, The
Netherlands, pp. 9683–9687.
Groucutt, J. (2005) *Foundations of Marketing*. Palgrave, New York, NY.
Guilford, J. P. (1950) "Creativity". *American Psychologist*, vol. 5, pp. 444–454.

Hegarty, M. (1992) "Mental animation: inferring motion from static displays of mechanical systems". *Journal of Experimental Psychology: Learning, Memory, and Cognition*, vol. 18, no. 5, pp. 1084–1102.

Holyoak, K. J. & Thagard, P. (1995) *Mental Leaps: Analogy in Creative Thought*. The MIT Press, Cambridge, MA.

Johannessen, J.-A., Olsen, B., & Lumpkin, G. T. (2001) "Innovation as newness: what is new, how new, and new to whom?". *European Journal of Innovation Management*, vol. 4, no. 1, pp. 20–31.

Kim, W. C. & Mauborgne, R. (2005) *Blue Ocean Strategy*. Harvard Business School Press, Boston, MA.

Kirton, M. J. (1989) "Adaptors and innovators at work", in *Adaptors and Innovators. Styles of Creativity and Problem Solving*, edited by Kirton, M. J. Routledge, London, UK, pp. 51–71.

Kujala, S. (2003) "User involvement: a review of the benefits and challenges". *Behaviour and Information Technology*, vol. 22, no. 1, pp. 1–16.

Levitt, T. (1963) "Creativity is not enough". *Harvard Business Review*, vol. 8, no. 3, pp. 72–83.

Lewin, K. (1947) "Frontiers in group dynamics". *Human Relations*, vol. 1, no. 2, pp. 145–153.

Mayer, R. E. (1999) "Fifty years of creativity research", in *Handbook of Creativity*, edited by Sternberg, R. J. Cambridge University Press, Cambridge, UK, pp. 449–460.

McCarthy, E. J. (1965) *Basic Marketing*. Irwin, Homewood, IL.

Mooney, R. L. (1963) "A conceptual model for integrating four approaches to the identification of creative talent", in *Scientific Creativity: its Recognition and Development*, edited by Taylor, C. T. & Barron, F. Wiley, New York, NY, pp. 331–340.

O'Quin, K. & Besemer, S. (1989) "The development, reliability, and validity of the revised creative product semantic scale". *Creativity Research Journal*, vol. 2, pp. 267–278.

Osborn, A. F. (1963) *Applied Imagination*, 3rd revised edition. Charles Scribner's Sons, New York, NY.

Rhodes, M. (1961) "An analysis of creativity". *Phi Delta Kappan*, vol. 42, pp. 305–310.

Rogers, E. M. (1995) *Diffusion of Innovation*, 5th edition. The Free Press, New York, NY.

Rubin, J. (1994) *Handbook of Usability Testing: How to Plan, Design, and Conduct Effective Tests*. John Wiley & Sons Inc., New York, NY.

Sawyer, K. (2006) *Explaining Creativity. The Science of Human Innovation*. Oxford University Press, Oxford, UK.

Schwartz, D. L. & Black, J. B. (1996) "Analog imagery in mental model reasoning: depictive models". *Cognitive Psychology*, vol. 30, pp. 154–219.

Simonton, D. K. (1999) *Origins of Genius: Darwinian Perspectives on Creativity*. Oxford University Press, New York, NY.

Simonton, D. K. (2004) "Creativity as a constrained stochastic process", in *Creativity: from Potential to Realization*, edited by Sternberg, R. J. & Grigorenko, E. L. American Psychological Association, Washington, DC, pp. 83–101.

Smith, S. M. (1995) "Getting into and out of mental ruts: a theory of fixation, incubation, and insight", in *The Nature of Insight*, edited by Sternberg, R. J. & Davidson, J. E. The MIT Press, Cambridge, MA, pp. 229–251.

Stein, M. I. (1953) "Creativity and culture". *Journal of Psychology*, vol. 36, pp. 311–322.

Torrance, E. P. (1974) *Torrance Test of Creative Thinking. Directions Manual and Scoring Guide*. Personnel Press, Lexington, MA.

von Hippel, E. (2005) *Democratizing Innovation*. The MIT Press, Cambridge, MA.

Wallas, G. (1926) *The Art of Thought*. Jonathan Cape, London, UK.

Wansink, B. (2002) "Changing eating habits on the home front: lost lessons from World War II research". *Journal of Public Policy and Marketing*, vol. 21, no. 1, pp. 90–99.

Ward, T. B. (1994) "Structured imagination: the role of category structure in exemplar generation". *Cognitive Psychology*, vol. 27, pp. 1–40.

Ward, T. B., Smith, S. M., & Vaid, J. (1997) "Conceptual structures and processes in creative thought", in *Creative Thought: an Investigation of Conceptual Structures and Processes*, edited by Ward, T. B., Smith, S. M., & Vaid, J. American Psychological Association, Washington, DC, pp. 1–27.

Weisberg, R. W. (2006) *Creativity. Understanding Innovation in Problem Solving, Science, Invention, and the Arts.* John Wiley & Sons, Hoboken, NJ.

White, D. M. 1961, " 'The gatekeeper': a case study in the selection of news", in *People, Society, and Mass Communications*, edited by Dexter, L. A. & White, D. A. Collier-Macmillan, London, UK, pp. 160–172.

4

Management of Innovation and Product Development: a Linear Versus a Process Perspective

John K. Christiansen & Claus J. Varnes

Introduction

This chapter introduces two perspectives on the management of innovation and product development – a linear perspective and a network process perspective – and discusses the differences and implications of these perspectives for innovation management. Our goal is to stimulate reflection on the management of innovation and to increase awareness of the available choices that can be made, as the two perspectives also represent great differences in relevant management technologies. Thus, these represent more than two perspectives, they lay two very different claims on how innovation happens and how innovation should or could be managed.

The linear perspective on management of innovation has emerged from studies on structured approaches to management of projects and innovation and was later supplemented with (especially survey) studies of critical factors in innovation and product development – rather popular with many consultancy companies. The network process perspective has grown out of case-based studies, longitudinal studies, and sociological and ethnographic studies. The process perspective attempts to understand how innovation happens from inside, focusing less on how managers can structure and manage innovation from a distance. Until recently it focused less on demonstrating what the network process perspective offered in terms of understanding managing innovation. This work present a network process perspective in an attempt to promote the perspective more actively.

Some scholars relate innovation processes to project management methods that deliver appropriate quality outputs on time and within cost targets. Basically, the linear perspective regards innovation as a series of discrete and sequential events that can be managed by informed decision-makers through analytical approaches and rational decision-making. The most prominent linear perspective is the phase/decision method with its "working" phases and decision points (Johnson & Jones, 1957). This approach involves high-level decision-makers managing innovative projects, making informed choices based on codified knowledge about projects and their relationships to technology, markets, customers, competitors, production, and the company portfolio.

Until now, research that has tried to understand innovation processes through a network process optic has been limited, but some examples are found in case-based studies on innovation (Kidder, 1981; Van de Ven *et al.*, 1999; Callon, 1986). Hence, we have derived a network process perspective (NPP) (Christiansen & Varnes, 2007) inspired by recent writings in actor network theory and ethnographic and process-oriented empirical studies on innovation practices.

The two perspectives on innovation and managerial technologies presented here are based on more than 25 years of studies on management of innovative projects, innovation, and management of product development, and include many case studies and interactions with companies at all levels, as well as studies of past and recent published research, as reported in this chapter.

The introduction of the two perspectives raises at least three questions. Firstly, how do the two perspectives differ with respect to their basic assumptions, focus, and perspective on knowledge creation, and what are the managerial implications of these differences, i.e. what are the technologies for managing they offer or present as relevant? Secondly, is the linear model obsolete – as it is based on a desire to present models and approaches that seem to reflect an image of innovation that is far from the detailed ethnographic studies? Or, is the linear model needed as a management technology that may not make it possible to manage innovation at a distance but gives the impression that some people – i.e. the managers – are in control? Or, is the linear perspective and its focus on calculations and stages the only way that managers can try to control some of the processes, e.g. by allocating resources according to expected net present value and strategic fits? Thirdly, how do the two perspectives fit with different notions of what innovation can be, e.g. more or less radical or incremental? Is there a relationship between the choice of perspective and the type of innovation with which a company is engaged? Can a company make a shift from one perspective to another, and what are the challenges in doing so? What does practice of innovation look like when we have such different perspectives, and what are the forces that shape the everyday practice in innovation teams and companies?

These issues will be discussed in the following manner. Firstly, the linear perspective and then the network process perspective are introduced. Secondly, a short case from an international company in the healthcare sector, illustrating how a company introduces a more open network process-oriented approach, is used to present some of the challenges when trying to modify existing management practices. Finally, we discuss the decisions and forces that influence the practice of management approaches to innovation and the implications for theory and managers.

The linear perspective

This first part of the chapter outlines the linear process perspective on innovation management. For illustration purposes, we investigate gate models, the most widely used tools to manage the product development process (Griffin, 1997). We outline how this approach works and discuss the issues of linearity in product development and innovation, and begin by examining its history.

Historically, innovation has been regarded as the responsibility of the entrepreneur in economic theory. In the Schumpeterian sense of the word, the entrepreneur is the individual innovator, constantly scanning the surroundings for ways to make novel, often discontinuous, combinations that enable the introduction of new goods to the market (circumventing the competition), making a new production method, opening up a new market, and so on (Schumpeter, 2000). Companies that sought to gain new ground and break or even destroy the competition naturally considered these entrepreneurial skills desirable. Businesses sought a method that would combine the skills unique to the entrepreneur, such as boldness, quick reactions to change, and new perspectives, with the manageability of the company's normal processes, which consisted of systematizing innovation and making it repeatable and therefore economically profitable and less risky. Companies have historically aspired to organize, control, and measure a process that is inherently difficult to manage owing to ambiguity (March, 1994), because the challenge with innovation is that it deals with something that has been compared to a journey into the unknown (Van de Ven *et al.*, 1999).

To handle the challenges of product development and innovation, companies in the late 1950s and early 1960s began to develop methods and models that could manage innovation and product development activities from idea to final product launch. In 1957, the wax manufacturer S. C. Johnson & Son, Inc., based in the USA, reported on its management approach which included organizational structures (responsibility), the information and control procedures (management systems), and decision-making in product development. The proposed method included a sequential, linear process by setting up "decision points" and "phases of evolution" from early phases of exploration to the commercialization of the final product (Johnson & Jones, 1957). These authors also state that: "If a steady stream of new products is the key to continued success, then specialized organization is the answer to the question of how to make the most of them". They claim that the administrative problems concern three areas: classification, coordination, and new knowledge (Johnson & Jones, 1957, p. 51). The first is to identify the type of product proposal and its appropriate handling. The second is to assure continuity and cooperation throughout the phases. The third concerns the challenge of collecting information on (new) products with which the company has no prior experience. This early formulation of a linear approach and its challenges still appears relevant today within its own world-view.

In the 1960s, the National Aeronautics and Space Agency (NASA) in the USA developed the first generation of what would later become known as the gate or phase models (Cooper, 1990; Ulrich & Eppinger, 1995). NASA's phased project planning (PPP) approach was a planning tool to manage cooperation between

NASA and its contractors and suppliers. The PPP approach divided development into phases with review points ensuring a high level of control and measurement, making sure that the project proceeded according to plan and would finish on time (Griffin *et al.*, 1997; Cooper, 1994). The PPP method focused on the technical aspects and was applicable to the physical design and development of projects. It did not include business disciplines such as marketing or customers. Later versions of gate approaches have emphasized the business aspects, and these have now become an integral part of gate models. Many variations of gate models are implemented as each company adopts them to fit specific needs. One significant change from the PPP model is the focus on cross-functionality in the process, which ensures that different functional areas within the firm are involved in each stage. Another important modification from the PPP method is the integration of marketing and manufacturing across the product development process, including the early stages. Finally, the gate approaches assume not only a review of the individual project at a specific gate but also assessment of the portfolio of innovation projects within the company, thus ideally linking projects to the overall company strategy (Cooper, 1994, 2001; Christiansen & Varnes, 2007). The reviews at gates are based on various types of qualitative and quantitative information such as market information, technical and economic calculations, and assessments of strategic considerations, etc.

These are important changes because the gate approach is now perceived as a management tool for product development and for realizing new products, not just a method for controlling and measuring project development. Informing management and allowing them to manage innovation from a distance is a change from the engineer-driven PPP methods.

The gate approach

The gate approach can be seen as an installation of linear thinking on the innovation process, including three fundamental mechanisms to achieve the objective of managing innovation (Varnes, 2005). Firstly, it reduces risk by focusing on decision-making as a gradual allocation of resources and an increase in information on the project. This implies that the product development process is seen as a gradual process where projects will be ended or reworked if the possibility for their commercial success is not evident or high enough. Secondly, as the outcome of a given product development process is uncertain from the onset of the project, information gathered throughout the process should be made

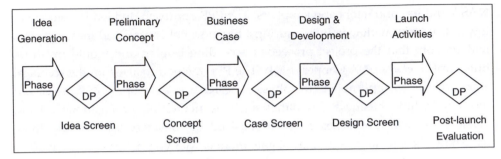

Figure 4.1 A generic linear model for management of innovation with phases and decision points (DPs)

available to the decision gates to inform decision-makers. Thirdly, the performance of a number of mandatory activities is defined as the means to ensure that the quality of decisions is not compromised by a lack of information. This principle is applied particularly to marketing activities where Cooper identified a number of shortcomings that could negatively influence project performance (Cooper, 1990).

We present a generic gate model to describe the different phases of the linear approach to innovation in Figure 4.1. This specific variant has five phases and five (gate) meetings; however, the number of stages and gates is different from one company to the next – some companies use up to 10 stages (Philips *et al.*, 1999). High-level decision-makers are supposed to make decisions that can take one of the following four forms (Cooper, 2001): allow projects to continue into the next stage, stop the project, ask for more information (place on hold or a conditional go), or decide to stop the project in its present form and recycle it into another project.

The five phases span the entire innovation sequence from ideation to launch activities and subsequent post-launch evaluation. Two main differences between the model in Figure 4.1 and other gate models are firstly that the ideation phase is incorporated *into* the model itself – in many linear models the ideation phase is situated *outside* the model, and secondly that a *post-launch evaluation* is integrated into the model, functioning as a feedback loop of information from the market back into the company, whereas other models incorporate *learning*.

Phase 1, decision point 1, phase 2, decision point 2, phase 3, and decision point 3 constitute the predevelopment phases. The ideation phase is the earliest phase of product development where different techniques for idea development can be used, such as user-centred knowledge gathering, e.g. empathic design (Leonard &

Rayport, 1997), focus groups, and the like. Creativity techniques can also be applied, such as methods for divergent thinking, e.g. brainstorming or brainwriting sessions followed by convergent thinking to narrow the scope of ideas and identify an idea that is feasible for further development. Phase 2 develops the idea further through desktop research, technological feasibility projections, and financial "sanity checks". These assessments are then developed into a business case in phase 3 where market and user needs are studied in further detail, and competition as well as positioning are analysed. Technical assessments and financial analyses are made. Decision points have until now been focused on Go/Kill recommendations for the project. The final point of decisions prior to development is decision point 3, which is the last point where the company can terminate the project without costs increasing significantly. In phase 4, product prototypes are developed, and this phase often emphasizes technical work. However, marketing proceeds simultaneously to finalize the launch plan and continuously to test the product.

The product is validated again at decision point 4, the design screen, and then moves into the post-development phase. In the design screen, the product's attractiveness is reviewed again. Development activities are reviewed to ensure that the product is consistent with the original definition specified in phase 4. The product is launched in the market in phase 5 where full production commences and market results are monitored. After a set number of months, a post-launch evaluation point is reached. Here, market learning will be fed back into the company to enable it to answer questions such as the following: How has the product reached the market? Are we satisfied with the result? What can we learn from this product development process? Should we improve a particular phase? Such knowledge and learning processes improve the efficiency of companies for the next product development process.

The stage activities undertaken are summarized in Table 4.1. All these activities can be categorized within the following four main activity areas: market, technical, financial and project planning.

Debate on the linear perspective

The structured linear phase models for managing innovation have become widespread in nearly all types of industry – except maybe the service industry – and empirical studies consistently demonstrate their popularity. In an international benchmarking study, Roberts found that 56% of European firms and 59% of

Table 4.1 Phase activities grouped into four types of activity, developed from Cooper (2001), Schilling (2005), and Varnes (2005)

	Phase 1 Idea generation	Phase 2 Preliminary concept development	Phase 3 Business case	Phase 4 Design and development	Phase 5 Launch activities
Market	• Market trends drive ideation	• Quick scoping: desktop research	• User needs and wants studied • Competition analysed	• Testing customer preferences • Developing marketing plans	• Market launch and rollout
Technical	• Technology trends drive ideation	• Conceptual assessment of technical feasibility	• Detailed technical assessment • Researching intellectual property	• Extensive in-house testing • Production trials	• Full production • Continued optimization
Financial	• Financial analyses drive ideation	• "Sanity check", ROI* outline	• Financial/business analysis • Strategic fit • NPV† analysis	• Investigating possible PLC‡ • Target costing	• Selling begins • Results monitoring
Project plans	• Recommendation for further idea development • Project plan for phase 2	• Recommendation for project Go/Kill • Project plan for phase 3	• Recommendation for project Go/Kill • Project plan for phase 4	• Recommendation for project Go/Kill • Post-launch plans formulated	• Preparing for post-launch evaluation

*Return on Investment (ROI), †Net Present Value (NPV), ‡Products Liability Check (PLC)

Japanese firms use a structured linear approach to product development, while 74% of North American firms apply it (Roberts, 2001). Studies claim that a critical factor for explaining success in product development processes is the application of linear and structured models (Ernst, 2002; Brown, Schmied, & Tarondeau, 2002). Griffin reports that at least five out of 11 best-practice studies list the use of some type of structured linear approach as being critical (Griffin, 1997; Griffin *et al.*, 1997). These results have been confirmed in the 2004 survey by the Product Development Management Association (Adams, 2004) which reports the widespread use of linear structured approaches across industries in the United States, and also claims that the more successful companies have more developed approaches than those that do not perform so well.

Some potential issues regarding the linear perspective have been raised in the past:

- *Idea generation.* The original phase models did not include idea generation, but now an increasing number of companies are becoming more concerned about how to stimulate creativity. Thus, more attention is being paid to idea generation and trying to include ideas in structured phase models.
- *Conformity.* Linear phase models can become too rigid or complex. Recent research has shown how structured phase models become complex systems of rules, with new rules constantly being added to manage innovation, as companies and managers try to handle the problems of the past. On the other side, managers and companies have been seen actively to use linear phase models to influence the mindset of employees, e.g. by stressing that certain types of information and calculation were important for all projects that should pass decision points.
- *The division of the innovation process into stages.* A structure with working phases and decision meetings means that no project can continue into the next phase without formal approval at a decision meeting. If a project has to wait for formal approval, employees in the project are left with nothing to do. They have to wait for the formal meeting, making the phase model a time-consuming device. One workaround is to allow projects to have over-lapping phases, thus introducing a less linear structured model in practice.

The network process perspective

In the linear perspective on innovation and product development it has been argued that it is possible to identify three basic assumptions regarding the role of knowledge (Kreiner, 2002). Firstly, the linear perspective views the process as a matter of implementation after the initial analysis has been carried out. Secondly, knowledge management becomes an issue of providing the relevant information according to specifications. Thirdly, the processes leading to successful new launches are viewed as a matter of organizing and managing explicitly identifiable activities in a certain order. In a network process perspective (NPP), the view of knowledge changes to being a matter of understanding the innovation process as a learning process. Secondly, knowledge management is about mobilization of knowledge, as it is not possible a priori to know what is needed in innovation processes. Thirdly, as innovation processes might seldom be ordered or structured in practice, the view in the network process perspective changes to understanding activities as emerging and influenced by struggles, negotiations, interessement, and spokespersons who advocate their ideas, where the model changes from a sequential step-by-step model into a whirlwind model.

Recent research on product development has acknowledged the need for alternative perspectives. Cunha and Gomes (2003) introduce five different product development processes ranging from a linear, sequential, model to what they refer to as the improvisational model – a non-linear approach to product development that facilitates innovation management under constantly shifting and fluent conditions. In their view, the idea of an organization is changing from a traditional perspective where people are information processors, the surroundings are stable, and the organization's basis for action lies in planning. Instead, Cunha and Gomes state that people are information or knowledge creators, the basis for action is discovery, and the surroundings are dynamic. The focus is on organizing rather than organization, on how self-organizing groups form to innovate rather than how the organization should decide on and outline the path towards innovation. McCarthy *et al.* (2006) present three perspectives on product development: a linear, a recursive, and a complex adaptive system, which in turn is made up of non-linearity, self-organization, and emergence. These perspectives are all interconnected in their view. Both McCarthy *et al.* (2006) and Cunha and Gomes (2003) claim that their new perspectives are complementary to the linear perspective, and they both address the question of finding the "right" approach, contingent on the environment or organizational characteristics.

Many cases and longitudinal studies on innovation based on detailed ethnographic studies (Christiansen & Varnes, 2007; Kidder, 1981) and studies on knowledge management (Kreiner, 2002), technology and innovation (Akrich, Callon, & Latour, 2002a, 2002b; Callon, 1986; Van de Ven *et al.*, 1999), sociology (Kreiner & Tryggestad, 2002; Tryggestad, 2005), and recently marketing (Araujo, 2007) provide strong evidence for the need for and relevance of a network process-oriented view on how innovation happens in practice. We propose a constructivistic network process perspective derived from recent research, as indicated above, not as a supplement, but as an alternative to the linear view.

Innovation as emerging processes

One popular image of innovation is the image of the lonely, brilliant – more or less mad – professor in a confined laboratory who gets a great idea and then nearly instantly becomes world famous. This image has many shortcomings, among them firstly the notion of the swift transfer from idea to a new product or service and to the customer, secondly the notion that ideas occur spontaneously to an individual, and thirdly the notion that the process can be managed well and without any resistance from other actors. Recent studies on innovation have repeatedly demonstrated how innovation mostly emerges through not-so-orderly processes involving multiple actors and is best described as a social process, rather than a technical one (Eisenhart in Hargadon, 2003, p. viii) with many struggles to overcome. The process from idea to innovation is constructed by establishing networks and alliances between human and non-human actors (Christiansen & Varnes, 2007; Kidder, 1981; Kreiner, 2002; Kreiner & Tryggestad, 2002; Akrich, Callon, & Latour, 2002a, 2002b; Tryggestad, 2005; Araujo, 2007; Callon, 1986; Van de Ven *et al.*, 1999; Takeuchi & Nonaka, 1986). Quinn (1985) introduced the concept of innovation management as a matter of controlled chaos. Takeuchi and Nonaka (1986) reported from data of a number of successful companies that the dominant model was not one with sequential stages but one with overlapping ones, and, using a sports metaphor, they argued for "Stop the relay race. Take up rugby", which, among other things, indicates that a team working together finds its own way during the processes. They found that six characteristics dominated the successful teams they studied: built-in instability (with little formalization); self-organizing project teams; overlapping development phases; multilearning in the team and between team and environment; subtle control and transfer of learning (to the rest of the company). The subtle control includes the creation of an open-minded work environment, interaction with customers, debate on evaluation and reward criteria for project and team, the ability to handle diversity, and the acceptance of risk-taking and failures.

Hargadon (2003) found that innovation often is a matter of bringing knowledge from one area to another by what is called "technology brokering". Technology brokering is "a strategy for exploiting the networked nature of the innovation process. Rather than producing fundamentally novel advances in any one technology or dominating any one industry, technology brokering involves combining existing objects, ideas, and people in ways that, nevertheless, spark technological revolutions" (Hargadon, 2003, p. 12). This can be illustrated by a description of how the famous Thomas Edison worked (1847–1931). Thomas Alva Edison, inventor of the incandescent light bulb and the phonograph player, is often described as the "inventor", but he was, in fact, an example of a technology broker and network builder. He depended heavily on the close collaboration of about 15 other people in his own Menlo Park lab. The importance of this lab collective can best be gauged by the fact that the genius of Edison vanished when the lab ceased to exist. Not only do research and development activities in companies work in this way, but professional consultant companies in design and innovation also utilize this approach (Hargadon, 2003, p. 200), such as the world-famous innovation company IDEO (www.ideo.com). Others have suggested that innovation is dependent on various forms of networks, as "the locus of innovation is found in networks of learning, rather than in individual firms" (Powel, 1998). Subsequently, an open innovation paradigm has been proposed to describe how "a company commercializes both its own ideas as well as innovations from other firms and seeks ways to bring its in-house ideas to market by deploying pathways outside its current businesses" (Chesbrough, 2003). Open innovation considers the boundary between the company and its surrounding environment as porous, which enables ideas, concepts, knowledge, and other resources to move easily between the two. Thus, this paradigm is not as radical as our proposed network process perspective presented here.

Struggles, accusations, negotiations, interessement

A theoretical perspective that can embrace the dynamics of innovation includes a change of world-view where one recognizes that innovations are constructed by relations, and that an "idea" is brought into being as it relates to many human and non-human actors (Callon, 1986). Thus, ideas can travel in many directions, meet other actors, and be modified, and are moulded and changed with the relation-ships that are established. As networks are made up of human and non-human actors, understanding innovation in this perspective becomes a question of understanding how actors are able to relate, maintain, and negotiate networks that will ultimately materialize into fact – into a new product, service, or innovation. These relationships and the subsequent networks are created by a process of interessement – which has been described as the process of convincing more and more actors to become part of the developing network (Akrich, Callon, & Latour, 2002a). In innovation and development terms, the process of interesse-ment will both develop the innovation and ultimately ensure its success through adaptation because the recruited actors become allies and construct a network that speaks on both the products' and others' behalf (Akrich, Callon, & Latour, 2002b).

Innovation is constantly in search of allies; if no users of a product – or an idea – adopt it, advocate it to others, develop the network, and create channels for diffusion, the innovation will never take off. The processes include the involve-ment of actors in an ever-expanding or collapsing network – engaging in a "dialogue" between all types of actors. Innovation is the relations *in* the network – constructed in a dialogue, a constant iteration, between human and non-human actors.

According to Akrich, Callon, and Latour (2002b), the company seeking to innovate must learn to work with the forces of interessement and carry out a sociotechnical analysis to understand where innovation is to be found. A socio-technical understanding highlights the middle ground where technology and the social environment are shaping each other. The theory presented does not mean that innovation is being selected by its environment, but that the environment is being produced at the same time as the innovation; the constant sociotechnical compromises and the negotiations allow the mutual adaptation of the innovation, and will ultimately explain its adoption (Araujo, 2007; Kreiner & Tryggestad, 2002).

Decision-making in the non-linear network process perspective thus becomes different from that of the linear perspective. There are no singular points where decisions on "how to" and "where to" can be identified; instead, heterogeneous microdecisions span the ever-growing network of human and non-human actors (Christiansen & Varnes, 2007). The project cannot be managed by careful preparations and well-made plans as in the linear perspective. The outcome of the project depends solely on the network that is established during the process – the alliances it has made and the interest it has created. Innovation management, therefore, is the art of interesting a number of allies who in turn will make you stronger or weaker. Innovation is the art of understanding the effects of inter-essement.

Spokespersons and project visions

The network process perspective assumes that things are more or less loosely coupled (March, 1994), that relations and networks have to be established, and that one important driver to implement this is the ambition to do something that has not been done before, and to be ambitious in the pursuit of success. Being ambitious includes accusations, as pointed out by Akrich, Callon, and Latour (2002b), and setting targets includes the use of visions to formulate the future (Collins & Porras, 1996) and how the proposed or expected innovation fits into this vision. This mobilization and articulation of an envisioned future resembles the process by which designers have worked with projections of possibilities to drive processes forward (Schön, 1983). Projections are part of the methods that spokespersons for innovations can use to get other actors enrolled into the network that constitutes the innovation and makes it stable. Empirical research has demonstrated the value of project visioning in product development projects, especially for evolutionary (having high market or technical uncer-tainty) and radical innovations (Lynn & Akgün, 2001). As projections and visions throw the process forward and engage and interest more and more actors in the network, there is less focus on risk but more on opportunity scouting, trying to stimulate learning, and establishing many relations. The focus on creating networks does not exclude the fact that actors might engage in some form of risk evaluation, but often the establishment of trust involves several steps over time, based on reputation and evaluation of experiences (Christiansen & Vendelø, 2003). Opportunistic behaviour is always a threat, as networks are never stable, but, as pointed out by Powel (1998), the risk of that is often small in many networks, as such behaviour in most cases will exclude one from future collaborative efforts. However, if possible gains by entering alternative networks are expected to be higher than at present, such behaviour is one of the forces that make networks unstable. The spokesperson is engaged in constant arguments, debates, and interessement processes trying to establish and maintain the networks.

Whirlwind innovation processes

In the network process perspective, innovation basically happens everywhere in constant iteration, and with multiple parallel processes taking place simultaneously, based on vivid visions, as illustrated by the design of the famous Macintosh (Guteri, 1984). Based on an idea from an engineer that Apple should develop a cheap, easy-to-use computer, they developed the assembly factory alongside the development of the very computer it was constructed to assemble. The team undertaking the development of the computer was closely knit – they were as compact as the computer they set out to develop. Marketing is engaged at the very beginning of the process, something very different from the linear model. This mix of different skills – working, shaping material, and imposing technical choices – is successful interessement. In this schema, innovation is continuously transformed in accordance with the trials to which it is submitted, that is, each interaction can be both a contribution to the network and an opportunity for change and modification of the network. Each new equilibrium materializes in the form of a prototype, which tests the feasibility of each new imagined compromise. The first prototype created is rarely convincing and usually takes several passes. The process can be described using the metaphor of a whirlwind: at every such loop the innovation is transformed, redefining itself as well as its public (Akrich, Callon, & Latour, 2002b, p. 213). Likewise Eastman set out to devise a camera and products destined for professional photographers. However, he found himself confronting opposition and refusal. Instead of insisting on following a strategy that seemed difficult to follow, he redirected his investigations and, through a series of drifts, defined a whole new product – the easy-to-use camera, and a whole new social category – the amateur photographer.

The manifestation of the whirlwind approach and the network process perspective has not been extensively researched so far. However, we have identified a whirlwind approach in Bang & Olufsen, used among others by the designer Jacob Jensen and the senior management group in the 1980s, as shown in Figure 4.2.

The innovator must be prepared to cast an idea into several successive passes, but without turning such a principle into a tangible rule. The whirlwind model is a formula that excludes nothing and does not set down steadfast rules; in certain strategic phases, the linear model can even be applied, but a clear focus must always be on a no-dogma attitude towards performance. The whirlwind model

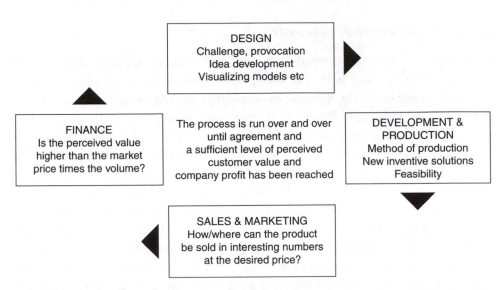

Figure 4.2 A whirlwind process in product development from Bang & Olufsen: the process in the idea group – with senior managers from design, product development and production, sales and marketing, and finance

and its sociotechnical transformations establish the art of compromise and the capacity to adapt as cardinal virtues. The process itself takes numerous turns, where ideas, concepts, and prototypes are challenged and confronted with managerial, technical, and economic demands that constantly challenge the stability of the network that eventually creates the innovation.

Debate on the network process perspective

As the NPP is based on recent works coming from different sources and observations, it is still emerging and growing as this is written. It is not conceptualized into detailed prescriptions or PowerPoint presentations – yet. The most developed part of the NPP is the basic ideas, or assumptions, which have been presented in a rough overview above. The NPP offers a perspective, but little direct advice on what models to draw, or what slides to prepare. It is rather a different state of mind that focuses on a number of issues that are still new to many. However, the authors and their associates are still working to expand and further develop this perspective and explore the possibilities – and limitations. A major limitation for many is that the whole notion of sequentiality fits ideally into the human desire for order and predictability, especially in the Western world (March, 1994).

Case: modifying a linear management approach

Coloplast was founded in 1957 and listed on the Copenhagen Stock Exchange in 1983. The company develops, manufactures, and markets medical devices and services to improve the quality of life of the users of its products. The company has a tradition of practising user-driven innovation. The company employed more than 6 000 people in the fiscal year 2005/2006 and had a revenue of €970 million, and spent €35 million on research and development in that year. Coloplast has three product areas. Firstly, urology and continence-care products for people with problems in their urinary system. Secondly, ostomy products for people whose intestinal outlet has been surgically rerouted through the abdominal wall. Thirdly, dressings for the care of chronic wounds and skincare products for prevention and treatment. Products are manufactured and distributed by the global operations unit which has 3 100 employees at 12 factories and 22 distribution sites all over the world.

The company operates globally, and mainly in niche markets with a few large suppliers. The healthcare authorities reimburse most of the products. Coloplast has in-depth knowledge of the healthcare systems of the countries in which it operates, and is represented by sales subsidiaries in the most important markets. The products are supplied to hospitals, institutions, wholesalers, and retailers. In certain markets, Coloplast directly supplies to users and is thus able to provide optimum advice to them.

In 2006, the executive board and management set very ambitious goals for the company for the next 5 years, which included doubling the revenue and improving profitability. Several initiatives were launched to reach that goal; in 2007, a project in the urology and continence care business unit was set up to examine the existing innovation approach and identify areas to increase not only the speed of innovation but also the number and quality of innovations. The VP of R&D headed a series of workshops that would identify possible options and actions on how to make innovation more global and open process oriented, which should stimulate breakthrough innovation. Presently, Coloplast strictly follows a linear gate model in all innovation projects, except for explorative technology projects, which are run outside that model. The VP of R&D has identified a need for a more open and globally oriented approach towards innovation, based on the following observations:

- Globalization increases, with local differences and cultures to remain.
- Knowledge and competencies within the areas of interest for Coloplast can and will emerge in many places.
- Knowledge is to be found globally where smart people outside the company might provide interesting ideas and solutions.
- Increased innovation require new types of input to the processes.

The discussions resulted in a proposal to establish a globally oriented approach towards the whole innovation process in the area, and identified possible benefits from such a global process-oriented approach, as shown in Figure 4.3.

The process of analysis and discussion of possible actions involved many managers at different levels in the company and the business unit, which also participated in the identification of possible actions to implement this global open innovation approach. The group identified some actions that could facilitate an expansion of the network activities around innovation and another set of actions that could facilitate the changes regarding modifications and development of

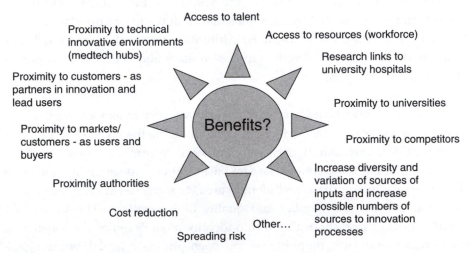

Figure 4.3 Identified benefits from a globally oriented process approach towards innovation

organizational structures and processes. The first set of solutions included an increased international presence to access talents and increase diversity, an increased ability to obtain access to new knowledge by proximity to technology hubs and other competence centres (e.g. universities and hospitals), and improved idea generation and support of new ideas. The identified organizational actions focused on stimulating experiments by allowing different approaches to innovation processes, developing and testing new approaches to stimulate radical innovation, and developing and using a non-linear process for fast-track and strategic innovations, and a human resource policy that supports increased focus on innovation.

These – and other – possible identified options were debated, and the management of the business unit decided to allow the use of different innovation models for different innovation processes, and to experiment with other approaches towards innovation. Some concerns were raised from other functions in the company about the possible deviation from the current linear gate model. The legal department pointed out the need to address the requirements of healthcare authorities, while others were concerned about abandoning a well-known linear model that made it easy to communicate about innovation.

To summarize, we are not able here to reveal in detail all the suggestions and the actions taken, as the process is ongoing. The debate in Coloplast concerned multiple suggestions for introducing a more open process-oriented innovation approach, but various concerns raised in the company made it evident that it was not easy – for different reasons – to break away from the existing approach to manage innovation. Furthermore, the existing structured approach to management of innovation seemed to be much more than a management model, as it also influenced the whole mindset on how to think about innovation. And such a mindset is not easy to change in the short run. However, by initiating a number of smaller experiments, the company tried to test out the opportunities for different ways to manage innovation and think about innovation.

Innovation perspectives and practice

The two perspectives presented offer very different views on what constitutes an innovation process, what it means to manage it, and what management should or could be. A summary of the linear model and the network process perspective is

Table 4.2 Summarizing two perspectives on innovation

	The linear perspective	The network process perspective
Innovation process	A linear process with sequential steps, rational assessment of markets and risks, and planning of process	Human and non-human actors need to be enrolled into strong networks through interessement facilitated by visions and spokespersons
Metaphors	Prepared plans in stages. A relay race	Networks and whirlwind processes. A rugby team effort
Decision-making	An output of rational analytical processes	A number of heterogeneous decisions with some or no direct relationship, which can only be evaluated at the end of the process
Locus of decision-making	Official meetings – expected to make tough decisions	Heterogeneous microprocesses and obligatory passage points
Critical management processes	Analysis of costs and risk and profit evaluation, providing information for rational decision-making	Visions, spokespersons, interessement processes, and creating and maintaining relationships

shown in Table 4.2, based on our past research and published research, as discussed above.

In practice, companies tend to develop extensive and elaborate guidelines, models, and rules for how to manage innovation from a linear perspective. This is seen in the Product Development Management Association survey, which reports that between 80 and 90% of companies use a type of structured approach and others have found that these rules are often very elaborate and constantly growing (Christiansen & Varnes, 2009). However, actual practice may be different from the linear view – even with official linear structured approaches (Christiansen & Varnes, 2007). The actual practice in innovation can thus be seen as the outcome of a process with at least four types of pressure trying to influence the actions. These four forces struggle to define or control how management of innovation takes places in practice, as indicated in Figure 4.4.

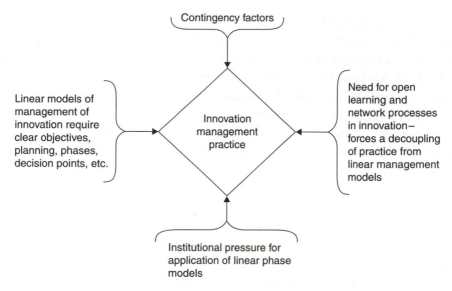

Figure 4.4 Multiple sources of influence on practice for management of innovation and product development. Adapted from Christensen and Kreiner (1991). Reproduced by permission of Økonomforbundets Forlag, Copenhagen, Denmark

Firstly, institutional pressures for linear models are rooted in culture. The linear model represents some values highly desired by many, including explicit desires to be analytical, to prepare plans, and to be on-top-of-the-world, that is, to have control, or take control, and manage innovation. As management and rational decision-making is a virtue in the modern world (March, 1994), the linear model fits well into that frame, while the network process perspective is less orderly and more difficult to communicate to company stakeholders.

Secondly, the linear approaches direct attention towards establishing systems and procedures. The desire to coordinate, integrate, and manage actions and human and non-human actors favours the design and implementation of all types of structures, systems, and rules that collect information for decision-makers.

Thirdly, there are contingencies. Some define innovation as having a creative (fuzzy) front end followed by implementation, as "All innovation begins with creative ideas. . . . We define innovation as the successful implementation of creative ideas within an organization" (Amabile *et al.*, 1996). Thus, creative ideas are not enough, and, according to Flynn and Chatman (2004, p. 235), innovation could be defined as the combination of two processes: (1) creativity or the generation (or finding) of new ideas; (2) implementation, or the actual introduction of the change. We might add that the innovation should lead to the creation of increased value (Kim & Mauborgne, 1999). Accepting different phases with different characteristics opens up a contingency view on the choice of processes based on the type of projects and phase (MacCormack & Verganti, 2003). Some suggest different approaches for different types of innovation project, risk assessment, or similar, e.g. based on more or less uncertainty on either the market or technology dimension (MacMillan & McGrath, 2002) or the need for more or less autonomy from the functional organization (Wheelwright & Clark, 1992).

Lorsch and Lawrence (1965) introduced contingency theory on organization for innovation, and mapped how different units in companies had different orientations and patterns of specializations towards time, other units, and the environment and how companies might handle the need for integration between the different units. In 1967 they presented their findings of six companies in the same industry, which showed, among other things, that organizations must balance differentiation and integration to be successful. Those companies that manage to achieve high subunit differentiation and yet maintain high integration between subunits seem to be best equipped to adapt to environmental changes. Units that are organized to perform simpler, more certain tasks (e.g. production groups) usually have more formal structures than groups focusing on more uncertain tasks (e.g. research and development) (Lawrence & Lorsch, 1967). Thus, organizations might need different types of structure and value system and degree of formalization for different tasks, and some have suggested the use of an ambidextrous organization to solve this dilemma (Duncan, 1976). Pursuing both long-term exploration and short-term exploitation (March, 1991) might be difficult or even impossible with the same organizational structure, so the solution requires companies to accommodate dual orientations at the same time, e.g. by allowing for multiple ways to organize and different norms and values in different parts of the organization, instead of trying to acquire uniformity.

Cunha and Gomes (2003) advocate that, for more radical types of innovation, new approaches like the "improvisational model" are necessary, whereas sequential or linear models are applicable for incremental innovation. Virtues such as planning, information gathering, and the ability to comply with approved schedules are rewarded in the linear approach, but it might not be those norms or values that stimulate activities that lead to new breakthrough products or services. Past research on innovation indicates that disorder, chaos, ambiguity, and complex conditions are related to bringing innovation forward (Quinn, 1985). Recent studies on the influence of management control systems on product development also indicate that management systems can be considered facilitators for incremental product development but not for more radical innovation (Bisbe & Otley, 2004). Adams (2004) reports that between 90 and 95% of all innovations in companies are incremental, and hence might be managed by linear models.

Fourthly, a need for an open network approach focusing on learning. As everyday practices of innovation often seem to be better described with a network process view, the practices might often be seen to be decoupled from linear structured approaches. In several instances we have observed that companies that might be very strict on following some formal structured approach for product development projects redirect more explorative and high-risk activities to run outside the linear models, e.g. they define those as technology projects, research projects, and not-yet-defined projects (Christiansen & Varnes, 2009). Thus, the structured linear approaches might in practice be reserved for rather well-defined and low-risk projects, as one project manager explained: "When the projects are first allowed into the linear gate model, the top management expect that we deliver the results on time to the market". This might also explain how a number of reports and surveys over the last decade seem to indicate improved management of product innovation activities, measured as successful projects launched in the market (Griffin, 1997; Adams, 2004).

Conclusion

Two very different perspectives on the management of innovation and some reflections on why the linear perspective seems to dominate thinking and research on innovation have been presented. Many studies have demonstrated that a network process perspective might better describe how innovation happens in practice. The linear structured perspective represents a "managerial view" that is rather popular, as the focus is on analysis, planning, and risk avoidance. The network process perspective is rather complicated to grasp, as it does not offer many simple tools, but merely a richer understanding of how innovation takes place and the important processes that we need to understand if we really want to manage innovation based on a richer understanding. Different forces influence how companies and organizations in practice try to manage innovation, and we have identified four important pressures. The two perspectives, views, or models can coexist in practice, as the activities in innovation might become decoupled from the managerial models exercised at top management level, and companies might apply different perspectives on different types of innovation. However, if innovation is understood as emerging dynamic microprocesses in a constructivistic network process perspective, management practice in the linear perspective only becomes one among many non-human actors in the complex processes.

References

Adams, M. (2004) PDMA Foundation new product development report of initial findings: summary of responses from 2004 CPAS.

Akrich, M., Callon, M., & Latour, B. (2002a) "The key to success in innovation part I: the art of interessement". *International Journal of Innovation Management*, vol. 6, no. 2, pp. 187–206.

Akrich, M., Callon, M., & Latour, B. (2002b) "The key to success in innovation part II: the art of choosing good spokespersons". *International Journal of Innovation Management*, vol. 6, no. 2, pp. 207–225.

Amabile, T. M., Conti, R., Coon, H., *et al.* (1996) "Assessing the work environment for creativity". *The Academy of Management Journal*, vol. 39, no. 5, October, pp. 1154–1184.

Araujo, L. (2007) "Markets, market-making and marketing". *Marketing Theory*, vol. 7, no. 3, pp. 211–226.

Bisbe, J. & Otley, D. (2004) "The effects of the interactive use of management control systems on product innovation". *Accounting, Organizations and Society*, vol. 29, no. 8, pp. 709–737.

Brown, K., Schmied, H., & Tarondeau, J.-C. (2002) "Success factors in R&D: a meta-analysis of the empirical literature and derived implications for design management". *Design Management Journal*, vol. 2, pp. 72–87.

Callon, M. (1986) "The sociology of an actor-network: the case of the electric vehicle", in *Mapping the Dynamics of Science and Technology*, edited by Callon, M., Law, J., & Rip, A. Macmillan, Basingstoke, UK, pp. 19–34.

Chesbrough, H. W. (2003) "The era of open innovation". *MIT Sloan Management Review*, vol. 44, no. 3, pp. 35–41.

Christensen, S. & Kreiner, K. (1991) *Projektledelse i Løst Koblede Systemer: Ledelse og Læring i en Ufuldkommen Verden*. Jurist-og Økonomforbundets Forlag, Copenhagen, Denmark.

Christiansen, J. K. & Varnes, C. J. (2007) "Making decisions on innovation: meetings or networks?". *Creativity and Innovation Management*, vol. 16, no. 3, pp. 282–298.

Christiansen, J. K. & Varnes, C. J. (2009) "Formal rules in product development. An explorative study of sensemaking of structured approaches". *Journal of Product Innovation Management*, vol. 26.

Christiansen, J. K. & Vendelø, M. T. (2003) "The role of reputation building in international R&D project collaboration". *Corporate Reputation Review*, vol. 5, no. 4, pp. 304–329.

Collins, J. & Porras, J. I. (1996) "Building your company's vision". *Harvard Business Review*, September–October, pp. 65–77.

Cooper, R. G. (1990) "Stage-gate systems: a new tool for managing new products". *Business Horizons*, vol. 33, no. 3, pp. 44–55.

Cooper, R. G. (1994) "Perspective: third-generation new product processes". *Journal of Product Innovation Management*, vol. 11, pp. 3–14.

Cooper, R. G. (2001) *Winning at New Products.* Perseus Books, Cambridge, MA.

Cunha, M. P. & Gomes, J. F. S. (2003) "Order and disorder in product innovation models". *Creativity and Innovation Management*, vol. 12, no. 3, pp. 174–187.

Duncan, R. (1976) "The ambidextrous organization: designing dual structures for innovation", in *The Management of Organizational Design*, edited by Kilman, R. & Pondy, L. North Holland, New York, NY, pp. 167–188.

Ernst, H. (2002) "Success factors of new product development: a review of the empirical literature". *International Journal of Management Reviews*, vol. 4, no. 1. pp. 1–40.

Flynn, F. J. & Chatman, J. A. (2004) "Strong cultures and innovation: oxymoron or opportunity?", in *Managing Strategic Innovation and Change*, edited by Tushman M. L. & Anderson, P. Oxford University Press, Oxford, UK.

Griffin, A. (1997) "PDMA research on new product development practices: updating trends and benchmarking best practices". *Journal of Product Innovation Management*, vol. 14, pp. 429–458.

Griffin, A., Belliveau, P., Markham, S., *et al.* (1997) Drivers of NPD success: the 1997 PDMA report, Product Development & Management Association, Chicago, IL.

Guteri, F. (1984) "Design case history: Apple's Macintosh". *IEEE Spectrum*, December.

Hargadon, A. (2003) *How Breakthroughs Happen. The Surprising Truth about how Companies Innovate.* Harvard Business School Press, Boston, MA.

Johnson, S. C. & Jones, C. (1957) "How to organize for new products". *Harvard Business Review*, vol. 35, no. 3, pp. 49–62.

Kidder, T. (1981) *The Soul of a New Machine.* First Avon Books, New York, NY.

Kim, W. C. & Mauborgne, R. (1999) "Strategy, value innovation and the knowledge economy". *MIT Sloan Management Review*, vol. 40, no. 3, Spring, pp. 41–54.

Kreiner, K. (2002) "Tacit knowledge management: the role of artifacts". *Journal of Knowledge Management*, vol. 6, no. 2, pp. 112–123.

Kreiner, K. & Tryggestad, K. (2002) "The co-production of chip and society: unpacking packaged knowledge". *Scandinavian Journal of Management*, vol. 18, pp. 421–449.

Lawrence, P. & Lorsch, J. (1967) "Differentiation and integration in complex organizations". *Administrative Science Quarterly*, vol. 12, pp. 1–30.

Leonard, D. & Rayport, J. (1997) "Spark innovation through empathic design". *Harvard Business Review*, vol. 75, no. 6, pp. 102–113.

Lorsch, J. W. & Lawrence, P. R. (1965) "Organizing for product innovation". *Harvard Business Review*, January–February, pp. 109–120.

Lynn, G. & Akgün, A. E. (2001) "Project visioning: its components and impact on new product success". *Journal of Product Innovation Management*, vol. 18, pp. 374–387.

MacCormack, A. & Verganti R. (2003) "Managing the sources of uncertainty: matching process and context in software development". *Journal of Product Innovation Management*, vol. 20, May, pp. 217–232.

MacMillan, I. C. & McGrath, R. G. (2002) "Crafting R&D project portfolios". *Research Technology Management*, vol. 45, no. 5, pp. 48–59.

March, J. G. (1991) "Exploration and exploitation in organizational learning". *Organization Science*, vol. 2, pp. 71–87.

March, J. G. (1994) *A Primer on Decision Making. How Decisions Happen*, 1st edition. The Free Press, New York, NY.

McCarthy, I. P., Tsinopoulos, C., Allen, P., & Rose-Anderssen, C. (2006) "New product development as a complex adaptive system of decisions". *Journal of Product Innovation Management*, vol. 23, pp. 437–456.

Philips, R., Neailey, K., & Broughton, T. (1999) "A comparative study of six stage-gate approaches to product development". *Integrated Manufacturing Systems*, vol. 10, no. 5, pp. 289–297.

Powel, W. W. (1998) "Learning from collaboration. Knowledge and networks in the biotechnology and pharmaceutical industries". *California Management Review*, vol. 40, no. 3, pp. 228–240.

Quinn, J. B. (1985) "Managing innovation: controlled chaos". *Harvard Business Review*, May–June, pp. 73–84.

Roberts, E. (2001) "Benchmarking global strategic management of technology". *Research Technology Management*, March–April, pp. 25–36.

Schilling, M. A. (2005) *Strategic Management of Technological Innovation*, McGraw-Hill Education – Europe, 2005.

Schön, D. A. (1983) *The Reflective Practitioner – How Professionals Think in Action*. Basic Books, New York, NY.

Schumpeter, J. A. (2000) "Entrepreneurship as innovation" (originally 1934), in *Entrepreneurship: The Social Science View*, edited by Swedberg, R. Oxford University Press, Delhi, 2000, pp. 51–75.

Takeuchi, H. & Nonaka, I. (1986) "The new new product development game". *Harvard Business Review*, vol. 64, no. 1, January–February, pp. 137–146.

Tryggestad, K. (2005) "Natural and political markets: organizing the transfer of technology and knowledge". *Economy and Society*, vol. 34, no. 4, pp. 589–611.

Ulrich, K. T. & Eppinger, S. D. (1995) *Product Design and Development*. McGraw-Hill, Inc., International Editions, New York, NY.

Van de Ven, A. H., Polley, D. E., Garud, R., and Venkataraman, S. (1999) *The Innovation Journey*. Oxford University Press, New York, NY.

Varnes, C. J. (2005) Managing product innovation through rules – the role of formal and structured methods in product development, PhD, CBS/Copenhagen Business School, School of Technologies of Managing.

Wheelwright, S. C. & Clark, K. B. (1992) *Revolutionizing Product Development: Quantum Leaps in Speed, Efficiency and Quality*. The Free Press, New York, NY.

5

Reshaping Markets through Collective Marketing Strategies: Lesson from the Textile Industry

Francesca Golfetto & Diego Rinallo

Introduction

Many scholars have suggested that major business undertakings like the affirmation of radical innovations are inherently social endeavours that entail the collective pursuing of a new vision of the future. As no firm is an island, the support of relevant partners is of utmost importance to those firms that intend to create new markets or reshape existing ones. Studies of technological change have shown that competing firms or business networks often try to shape the market concurrently by proposing alternative trajectories of innovations (Abernathy & Utterback, 1978; Tushman & Rosenkopf, 1992). In such circumstances, the dominant solution is not necessarily the "best" alternative from a purely technical point of view, but rather the one that successfully gathers the support of key players in the industry (e.g. users, suppliers, competitors, producers of collateral products) through the early involvement of some of them and effective communication strategies to all the others until consensus is reached (Arthur, 1994; Lee *et al.*, 1995). In this chapter, we suggest that trade shows may provide an instrument to obtain the early support of key actors in the industry and to effectively communicate to others a desired state of the future until a critical mass is obtained and that image becomes a reality.

Collective events such as trade shows, professional conferences, technology contests, and public business ceremonies play an important role in the social construction of new markets and industries and in the adoption of new technologies and product innovations. Examples that come prominently to mind include the fashion weeks in the European fashion capitals, the Oscar nights and Grammy Awards for the movie and music industries in the United States, and the most important trade shows devoted to technologies and industrial goods in various countries. For a limited duration, these events bring together in the same location all the leading actors in a field and, through interaction and collective sense-making among participants, exercise major impacts on the fields in which they are embedded. In spite of this importance, however, we still know little of the role these events play in the shaping of markets. Only recently have scholars started to explore these events as a distinct topic of study and research (e.g. Anand & Watson, 2004) and proposed the term "field-configuring events" (Meyer, 2003) as a tribute to their ability to affect the origination and evolution of new technologies, industries, and markets. In this chapter, we contribute to this emerging stream of research by highlighting its strategic implications for firms – and particularly those engaged in strategic market creation.

More specifically, we report a case study of how coalitions of firms in the European clothing fabric industry strategically employ professional trade shows to manage to their advantage the trajectories of innovation in their underlying industries. Marketing literature traditionally considers trade shows as mere promotional instruments and is almost silent on the important role of these events in the shaping of markets. By looking at trade shows from a field-configuring perspective, in this chapter we suggest that these events may be employed as collective marketing initiatives by temporary networks of firms that strategize together to obtain sustainable competitive advantages. These events are particularly important in fragmented industries characterized by myriad small and medium enterprises – a common situation in many European manufacturing sectors. In this sense, national entrepreneurial associations have long organized trade shows to promote the export of their member firms (CERMES, 2006) and support "country-of-origin" image effects – that is, collective "made in" brands. Competitive wars among trade shows – like those we explore in this paper – may thus be seen as the reflection of the underlying competition among national groups of firms. However, in spite of their relevance, research is silent on the dynamics of these competitive wars. The study here reported aims to fill this gap and to shed light on how trade shows may enable collective marketing strategies.

This chapter is structured as follows. Firstly, we briefly review the emerging literature on field-configuring events and the most established marketing scholarship on trade shows. We then describe our empirical setting, the clothing fabric industry and its major trade shows, and provide methodological details of our data sources and analytical procedures. After reporting our research findings, we conclude by discussing the theoretical and managerial implications of our research.

Shaping markets through trade shows: a conceptual framework

Trade shows are recurring events that "bring together, in a single location, a group of suppliers who set up physical exhibits of their products and services from a given industry" (Black, 1986, p. 10). These events are among the most important marketing instruments for firms operating in business markets. It is estimated that 80–90% of firms in Europe's traditional manufacturing industries employ trade shows to build and maintain relationships with their customers, with a share of their total promotional business-to-business budget ranging between 40 and 70% – depending on the firm's size, export orientation, and specific business sector (Golfetto, 2004). In such industries, which are extremely fragmented and mostly constituted of firms lacking a foreign sales force, the decision to exhibit at a specific event is based on that trade show's capability to attract visitors-buyers from the most distant geographical markets – inside and outside Europe. As a consequence, very large trade shows are usually located in proximity to those, among the most accessible European cities, that are centred on the largest areas of demand and/or supply. Such major trade shows, which are at the top of the hierarchy of the numerous events that are usually organized each year in every industry, assemble together in the same location up to 3 000–4 000 exhibitors-manufacturers and even 100 000–150 000 visitors-buyers from the entire world. These events are characterized by a heightened competitive atmosphere, as they give rhythm to the industry's innovation cycle and are the places where each firm tries to build its reputation vis-à-vis competitors. At the same time, top trade shows are also the places where the industry's professional communities meet and interact, and the entire field rallies around common problems. The events' media visibility broadens their influence.

Industrial and collective marketing strategies at trade shows

Trade shows are conceptualized in different manners by current marketing scholarship. The dominant perspective is focused on exhibitors and their need to manage trade show participations profitably. The first contributions on the topic were published in the 1960s – including in prestigious journals such as the *Harvard Business Review* and the *California Management Review* (Bonoma, 1983; Carman, 1968) – and were followed in the 1970s by the first of a long series of empirical studies (e.g. Banting & Blenkhorn, 1974; Cavanaugh, 1976). According to recent reviews (e.g. Hansen, 1996; Munuera & Ruiz, 1999), extant marketing literature provides exhibitors with guidance on three basic managerial challenges: (i) how to select the "right" trade show among the tens or hundreds of alternatives currently available; (ii) how to manage trade show participations effectively; (iii) how to measure trade show performance and returns on investments. However, the dominant perspective conceives trade shows as "zero-sum games" where exhibitors fight amongst each other to win industrial buyers' preferences and thus market shares. Moreover, it is assumed that trade shows just reflect their underlying supply and demand markets rather than having an active role in shaping them. In spite of these prevailing views, over the years a few contributions have adopted different approaches to trade shows that highlight the broader role these events play in the evolution of their underlying industries.

Researchers have long analysed the composition of trade show audiences and noted a significant presence of visitors not involved in purchasing processes (e.g. Bello, 1992; Hansen, 1996). More recently, Borghini, Golfetto, and Rinallo (2006) suggested that the presence of these "atypical" visitors (exhibitors' suppliers, competitors, producers of related products, media workers, and experts), who may even represent 50% and more of total visitors, is motivated by the role trade shows play as providers of "informational externalities" in supply chains. In Europe, the structure of the manufacturing industry and related supply chains is highly fragmented (i.e. there are numerous firms smaller than their American counterparts) and geographically dispersed across several countries, particularly in the age of globalization. Consequently, by attending trade shows in different countries and different phases of their supply chains, these firms are able to anticipate the impact of market trends and technological innovation on their activities. The behaviour of a multitude of actors can thus become aligned. This view of trade shows resonates with an earlier contribution by Rosson and Seringhaus (1995, p. 87) who conceptualized these events as "microcosms of the industries they represent, with a multitude of buyers and sellers, service providers, partners, industry, and regulatory bodies all gathered in one place" and interacting with each other. Trade shows may thus be viewed as complex events where a plurality of actors converge with several objectives in mind. Under this perspective, atypical visitors are not merely a distraction or annoyance to exhibitors (as suggested by some marketing studies), but are rather key constituents whose presence is fundamental to the complex function trade shows play in economic systems.

Another criticizable aspect of the dominant marketing perspective on trade shows is the assumption that these events are just mirrors or representations of underlying supply and demand markets. Most contributions conceive visitors as rational information processors engaged in the evaluation of alternatives in terms of solutions, products, and suppliers (Gopalakrishna & Lilien, 1995) – an approach that reflects Bettman's (1979) influential information processing theory of consumer choice. In other words, during trade shows, marketers from disperse locations reduce buyers' search costs by spatially concentrating information on purchase alternatives for a limited duration of time. With this view, the more a trade show is representative in terms of product variety of the population of companies in the underlying supply market, the greater the completeness of the information available to visitors will be. As mere representations, trade shows are not conceptualized as having the capability to shape underlying industries and markets.

Only a few studies have adopted different paradigmatic lenses. Peñaloza (2000, 2001) investigated exhibitor and visitor coproduction of meaning in the context of a consumer show. Borghini, Golfetto and Rinallo (2006) studied industrial buyer behaviour in the context of professional trade shows and showed how these events create liminal spaces where artefacts and lived experiences enable visitors and exhibitors to make sense of the world along common frames. Although these contributions adopt a social constructive view of trade shows and the fields in which they are embedded, they view collective sense-making as a spontaneous process, not governed by any particular agent. The intentional use of these events to shape industries is absent from these conceptualizations. A recent contribution by Rinallo and Golfetto (2006) suggests, however, that trade shows are sometimes strategically employed by national entrepreneurial associations for the enactment[1] of a favourable environment. In other words, those companies employ trade shows strategically, as collective marketing initiatives, to drive the evolution of innovation in their industry and represent themselves as innovators, leaving competitors in the position of imitators.

To sum up, marketing scholarship has long investigated trade shows, albeit from a perspective that stresses their competitive function as individual marketing instruments. Only a few contributions have highlighted the fact that trade shows may also enable collective marketing initiatives among competitors owing to their market-shaping functions. Moving outside marketing literature, the emerging literature on field-configuring in our view does more justice to the important role of trade shows as contexts where different actors aggregate to enact their environment.

Trade shows as field-configuring events

"Field-configuring events" (FCEs) is the term recently coined (Meyer, 2003) to refer to a broad set of collective events that include professional conferences, trade shows, public business ceremonies, technology contests, and governmental hearings. By bringing together all relevant actors, these events provide participants with a rich context for interaction and collective sense-making.[2] When speaking of the field, these scholars refer to one of the key concepts in organizational theory, i.e. the "organizational field" consisting of "those organizations that, in the aggregate, constitute a recognized area of institutional life: key suppliers, resource and product consumers, regulatory agencies, and other organizations that produce similar services or products" (DiMaggio & Powell, 1983, p. 148).[3] The

---

[1] The term "enactment" was proposed (Daft & Weick, 1984; Smircich & Stubbart, 1985) in the context of theories of social psychology of organizations. According to this perspective, the environment is socially constructed through the interaction between an organization and other relevant actors. By interpreting the environment, organizations may affect it. The primary role of strategic managers is therefore the management of meaning, i.e. the creation of systems of shared meaning that facilitate organized action.

[2] Sense-making is a process of "meaning construction and reconstruction by the involved parties" as they attempt "to develop a meaningful framework for understanding the nature" of a given situation (Gioia & Chittipeddi, 1991, p. 442).

[3] Field, industry, and market are not equivalent terms. Industry is a notion most often employed by strategic management and industrial organization scholars, and refers to sets of competing or related producers. On the other hand, the notion of markets, which is central in macroeconomics and marketing, refers to the idea of the meeting of supply and demand.

qualification "field-configuring" thus implies that these events may play a direct or indirect role in the social construction and evolution of inter-organizational fields.

To date, empirical research on FCEs is limited. The first contributions on the subject examined the role of product or firm contests in legitimating organizations, generating status orderings, and creating favourable reputations (Rao, 1994). Anand and Watson (2004) identified four mechanisms by which award-giving ceremonies, such as the Grammy Awards, influence the development of organization fields: (i) the distribution of prestige between the various players; (ii) the staging of highly charged ceremonial forms designed to attract collective attention; (iii) the surfacing and resolution of conflicts between the various players; (iv) the constitution of interdependence bonds between different subjects. More recently, Garud (2007) has shown that conferences can be occasions to shape emerging organizational fields and enact shared innovation trajectories. Similarly, Lampel (2001) has employed historical case studies to show how creators of radical innovations employ highly spectacularized product demonstrations to attract the attention and support of financiers, key customers, and, more in general, public opinion.

Although the processes identified by these contributions can be generally applied to other typologies of events, trade shows have so far not been explicitly investigated from an FCE perspective. However, in our view this perspective helps make sense of the important functions trade shows play in the life of industries. In this chapter, we contribute to the emerging literature on FCEs by explicitly focusing on trade shows and the mechanisms through which these events may configure the organizational fields in which they are embedded. More specifically, the case study we report in this chapter exemplifies the fact that: (i) there is competition between different trade shows in the same industry, each affecting its own representation and configuration of the reference field; (ii) the influence of trade shows on the development of sectors, markets, and industrial innovation is not necessarily spontaneous but may be guided by the activities of the event organizers; (iii) trade shows may be employed by networks of firms for strategic reasons, for example by exploiting the shows' substantial communicative and relational reach to compete against other business networks.

The clothing fabric industry and its top trade shows

To exemplify how coalitions of firms may strategically employ trade shows to shape their market, we report a case of the European clothing fabric industry and its most important trade shows. Textile manufacture is one of the oldest industries in economic development, but in the last 20 years it has been greatly affected by the phenomenon of globalization. European countries are – or used to be – important producers of textile products, but at the same time they are also (together with the United States) the most attractive market for exporting countries, many of which are situated in South-East Asia. Many developing countries have become very competitive in textile production, as they combine low wage costs with high-quality equipment and know-how imported from more industrialized countries. Moreover, in the period 1995–2005, the process of trade liberation guided by the World Trade Organization (WTO) removed the import barriers set up by the previous GATT (General Agreement on Tariffs and Trade) Multifibre Arrangement, which from 1974 to 1994 protected the EU with a quota system.

In the clothing fabric industry, the most important trade shows are located in European cities with intercontinental accessibility (e.g. Frankfurt, Paris) or centred upon the largest areas of supply (e.g. Milan). Almost all European clothing fabric firms employ these trade shows as their most important sales and market relationship event, and allocate to them the majority of their promotional budgets. These events take place biannually, as fabric collections are renewed every 6 months to follow the fashion cycle and its two seasons (spring–summer and autumn–winter). Clothing fabric trade shows thus give rhythm to the life and innovation-based competition among the firms in the industry, in a highly symbolic context where a sort of collective evaluation is expressed on whether each firm is an innovator or an imitator.

Our investigation tracked the evolution of the most important western European trade shows between 1986 and 2006. While other events exist in the textile industry, our investigation was necessarily selective and did not consider minor events in the clothing fabric industry nor trade shows dedicated to yarns or technical textiles. In this chapter, we focus on the two largest and most inter-nationalized trade shows at the beginning of our observation period: *Interstoff*, based in Frankfurt, and *Première Vision*, based in Paris. As we will see, these two events exemplify two different approaches to the management of trade shows that have important implications in terms of field-configuring capability.

Our data comes from three main sources. We obtained comparable statistical data on key trade show indicators (i.e. space hired, number and origin of exhibitors, number and origin of visitors) from official national control bodies, e.g. FKM (Society for the Voluntary Control of Fair and Exhibition Statistics) for *Interstoff* and OJS (Office de Justification Statistique) for *Première Vision*. Space hired and number of exhibitors are directly proportional to trade show turnover. These indicators can thus be considered as a proxy for a trade show's financial success. Data on the number and the origin of visitors are a proxy for the volume and quality of the audience to which exhibitors pay to have access. Taken together, these statistical figures assess the "health" of trade shows. For example, a prolonged decrease in the number of visitors, even when exhibitors and space hired remain stable, is an early predictor of a show's loss of attractiveness. Similarly, an increase in the number of exhibitors, particularly from abroad, is a sign that the competitive positioning of the show is improving.

We analysed the evolution of the numerical data with the help of articles taken from trade publications covering the clothing fabric industry in the UK, Germany, Italy, and the USA in the period investigated. These articles were selected by searching the Factiva database using the names of the trade in our sample as keywords. Overall, we retrieved 2 332 articles of varying length and level of interest for the purpose of the present study. Additional data sources were obtained from the organizers themselves (e.g. catalogues, press releases, web documentation) on a less structured basis. We analysed our dataset of news articles by content assessment, a procedure first proposed by historical researchers in journalism and consisting of "extensive reading of great quantities of [publications], using the historian's method of reading, sifting, weighing, comparing, and analysing the evidence in order to tell the story" (Marzolf, 1978, p. 15). As our purpose was to discover key facts rather than quantify previously identified themes, we deemed the approach more appropriate than the more quantitative-oriented content analysis.

By integrating our quantitative dataset of statistical indicators of trade show performance with our journalistic dataset reporting hard facts and timely expert opinions from journalists and their sources, we were able to obtain a more robust interpretation of the history of the two trade shows. Moreover, to shed light on the ambiguities of the written sources and the occasional omission of relevant facts, we also conducted confirmatory interviews with 44 informants from the clothing fabric industry. The result of the extended period of immersion in our dataset was an informed interpretation of the history of the *Interstoff* and *Première Vision* shows over our given period of investigation.

Competing to become the top event in the clothing fabric industry: history of a war

Textile is an important part of the European manufacturing sector and consists of a large number of small and medium-sized enterprises, often geographically concentrated in industrial districts (European Communities, 2001). These conditions create a demand for trade shows: the more the supply is fragmented, the greater the demand for trade shows will be, as buyers need to evaluate a large variety of product alternatives. Germany, France, the UK, and Italy are the countries with the largest number of textile companies in Europe and constitute the centre of significant import and export flows throughout the period we investigated. Unsurprisingly, at the beginning of our observation period, these countries hosted many trade shows dedicated to the clothing fabric industry (see Table 5.1), all of which fought to attract foreign buyers from North America and other European countries. As the fashion cycle is biannual, these events took place twice a year (i.e. spring/summer and autumn/winter editions).

British trade shows were located in London and specialized mainly in fabrics for men's fashion. Events were small and, before the end of the 1990s, were terminated as a consequence of the restructuring of Britain's manufacturing system, when many firms closed down, merged, or were acquired, or operations were relocated overseas. Italy had different international trade shows. Three were small and located in the specialized textile industrial districts of Como (*Ideacomo*), Biella (*Ideabiella*), and Prato (*Prato Expo*), while a larger event took place in Milan (*Moda In*). However, the industry was dominated by its largest, most internationalized, and oldest event, *Interstoff* in Frankfurt, whose supremacy would in time be contested by the French *Première Vision*.

1959–1979: the undisputed leadership of Interstoff

Interstoff was started at the end of 1959, when Messe Frankfurt GmbH, the owner of Frankfurt's trade fair venue, launched a new event completely dedicated to textile producers. At the time, trade shows displayed products from a broad range of industries and attracted mixed audiences comprising both businesspeople and consumers. The new event was triggered by a rise in the demand for exhibition space by textile producers. With 60 exhibitors and 2 600 visitors at its first edition, *Interstoff* soon started to grow and attract significant foreign attendance. While

Table 5.1 Top European apparel fabric trade fairs in the 1959–2006 period: an overview

	Organizer	Product range	Origin of exhibitors	Key indicators		
					1986*	1996*	2006*
Interstoff Frankfurt (1959–1999)	Messe Frankfurt GmbH – owned by local territorial stakeholders	Wide	Worldwide	– Square metres – Exhibitors (foreign) – Visitors (foreign)	–40 512 –1 044 (78%) –23 248 (45%)	–4 216 –147 (69%) –5 034 (38%)	//
Première Vision Paris (from 1979)	Première Vision le Salon s.a. – launched by French textile industry associations	Top-quality and innovative companies	Mostly Western Europe	– Square metres – Exhibitors (foreign) – Visitors (foreign)	–17 851 –471 (55%) –27 609 (57%)	–40 180 –821 (71%) –71 410 (74%)	–38 493 (2005) –736 (82%) –30 176 (80%)
Texworld Paris (from 1998)	Messe Frankfurt France s.a.s – acquired in December 2001	Wide. Low prices	Worldwide	– Square metres – Exhibitors (foreign) – Visitors (foreign)	// 	// 	–13 284 –690 (100%) –13 175 (85%)
Moda In Milan (1984–2005)	S.I.Tex s.p.a. – founded by Italian textile associations	Top-quality and innovating companies	Italy and Western Europe. Companies from the rest of the world not allowed	– Square metres – Exhibitors (foreign) – Visitors (foreign)	–10 680 –279 (25%) –13 525 (16%)	–16 562 –454 (23%) –22 437 (25%)	***
Ideacomo Cernobbio, Como (1975–2005)	E.F. Ideacomo, founded by a group of silk producers in the Como area	Mostly silken fabrics. Mid-upper market range	Mostly Italy	– Square metres – Exhibitors (foreign) – Visitors (foreign)	–9 550 –90 (18%) –3 871 (31%)	–4 700 –77 (16%) –2 238 (38%)	***
Ideabiella Cernobbio, Como (1978–2005)	Associazione Ideabiella – founded by medium/fine manufacturers from the Biella area	Fine and medium/fine fabrics, mostly woollen	Northern Italy	– Square metres – Exhibitors (foreign) – Visitors (foreign)	–6 110 –50 (0%) –2 150 (60%)	–5 080 –58 (0%) –810 (74%)	***

(*Continued*)

Table 5.1 Continued

Organizer	Product range	Origin of exhibitors	Key indicators		
				1986*	1996*	2006*
Prato Expo Florence (1979–2005): Pratotrade – initiative of the Industrial Association of Prato	Fine and medium/fine fabrics, mostly woollen	Tuscany (Italy)	– Square metres – Exhibitors (foreign)– Visitors (foreign)	n. a.	–6 650 ** –111 (1%) ** –6 117 (38%) **	***
Milano Unica Milan (from 2005): S.I.Tex + E.F. Ideacomo + Associazione Ideabiella + Pratotrade + Silk Avenue	Selected top-quality and innovating companies	Italy and Western Europe	– Square metres – Exhibitors (foreign) // – Visitors (foreign)	//	//	–27 800 –691 (22%) –35 765 (35%)

Source: elaborations on FKM, OJS, Italian Ministry of Productive Activities, and organizer data.
*Data refer to the trade show's spring/summer editions; ** Data refer to 1998; *** In 2006, Italian trade shows (*Moda In, Ideacomo, Ideabiella, Prato Expo, Shirt Avenue*) constituted *Milano Unica*.

securing the support of the German textile industry's associations, Messe Frankfurt never adopted a protectionist attitude in the management of *Interstoff* and welcomed exhibitors from all over the world. Being owned by local public authorities that evaluated its performance on the basis of the economic impact activated on the host area by exhibitor and visitor expenditure, Messe Frankfurt's strategy was to create large events that would be meeting places also for non-German operators.

For more than two decades, the strategy worked. *Interstoff* was the largest and most representative textile trade show in the world in terms of product quality (high to low), material range (e.g. cotton, silk, wool, linen), market destination (e.g. menswear, women's wear), and visitors attracted (clothing producers from all over the world). Moreover, *Interstoff* was the sole trade show that admitted non-European exhibitors, i.e. fabric suppliers from North America and Asian and South Mediterranean developing countries. Up to the mid-1980s, *Interstoff* maintained its leadership and was considered by operators in the fabric industry as the most important event worldwide. With 900–1 000 exhibitors on a net surface of 40 000–45 000 square metres, each edition of the event showed the widest offer of clothing fabrics, attracting twice a year more than 20 000 visitors from clothing manufacturers across the world. The variety of producers and products created value for visitors who could compare purchase alternatives in terms of products and suppliers and choose those that best suited their needs.

In spite of being its greatest strength, the trade show's size created some difficulties for visitors in their search for new fabrics and fashion trends. To obtain full information, visitors were compelled to undertake a physically fatiguing and mentally overwhelming experience. The layout of the exhibition, which was arranged according to no apparent criteria, did not help visitors to make sense of the trends emerging from the hundreds of collections presented: What were the colours of the season? What were the new ideas in terms of materials and finishing? Who were the most innovative suppliers? For buyers, these questions were not easy to answer after visiting *Interstoff*. This latent dissatisfaction was probably one of the reasons behind *Première Vision*'s success.

1979–1999: the irresistible ascent of Première Vision

Première Vision's origins date back to 1973, when 15 weavers from Lyon undertook a joint promotion. Instead of exhibiting at *Interstoff* where, they believed, their fine fabrics and superior design would have passed unnoticed, they decided to present their collections together at the International Textile Centre in Paris. With the first edition of *Première Vision* in 1977, other associations from the French fabric industry were invited to join the promotional undertaking. To improve the event's visibility, access to the show was opened to carefully selected exhibitors from Western Europe in 1980. The right to exhibit at *Première Vision* was granted on the basis of product quality, creativity, and financial health. As it was owned by the French textile entrepreneurial association, the show's profit orientation was tempered by a desire to promote the image of French and other European producers. While under continuous pressure for access from candidate exhibitors, officials at *Première Vision* maintained their screening policy. Only in 2002 did the trade show open its doors to a few non-European producers that were strictly selected from among the most innovative firms.

Première Vision's performances were immediately outstanding. By 1981, with 249 exhibitors on a surface of slightly less than 6000 square metres, the show attracted the same number of visitors as *Interstoff*, i.e. about 20000. In the years that followed (see Figures 5.1 to 5.3), *Première Vision* challenged *Interstoff*'s

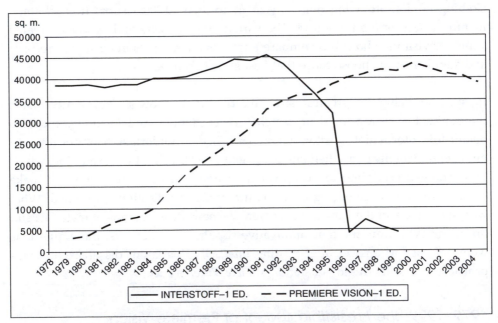

Figure 5.1 *Interstoff* and *Première Vision*: space hired (square metres, 1978–2004) (*Source*: elaborations on FKM and OJS data; data refer to the trade show's spring/summer editions; data for the autumn/winter editions are similar in size and trend)

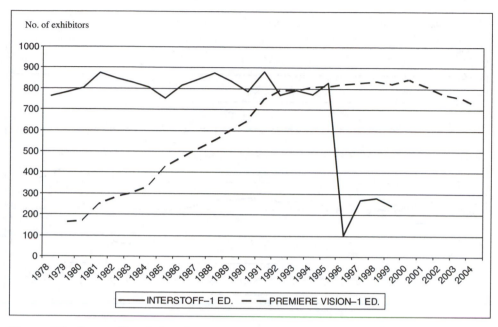

Figure 5.2 *Interstoff* and *Première Vision*: number of exhibitors (1978–2004) (*Source*: elaborations on FKM and OJS data; data refer to the trade show's spring/summer editions; data for the autumn/winter editions are similar in size and trend)

hegemony in the industry and eventually surpassed its German competitor also in the number of exhibitors and in the space hired. How could that happen? *Première Vision's* triumph is to a great extent attributable to a powerful organizational innovation that changed the clothing fabric supply chain forever. It all began when the original 15 Lyon weavers decided "to meet together before the Salon to propose a synthesis of seasonal colour and fabric trends, paving the way for a coherence in the textile offer" (*Première Vision*, 2007, p. 1), a process they called "trend concertation".

In the textile-apparel value chain, the fabric sector is a central locus of innovation. As fabric is a core component of clothing, the stylistic innovation of fabric producers has a direct impact on the stylistic innovation of clothing manu-facturers. When designing their biannual collections, fabric producers have to make decisions in terms of a number of creative variables: colour (e.g. ruby or clay furrow), structure (e.g. jacquard, satin, chiffon), aspect (e.g. structured, light, washed-out, opaque), touch (e.g. soft, warm, fluid, compact), decoration (e.g. arabesque, cashmere, irregular stripes), and treatment (e.g. burnt-out, washed, rubber-coated). Moreover, given the length and fragmentation of the industry's

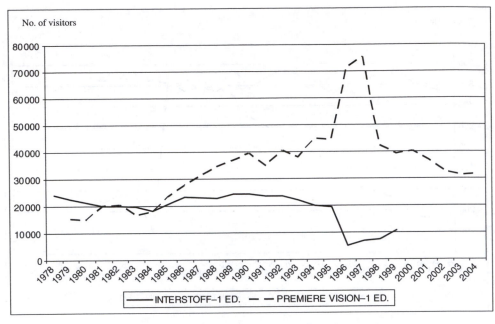

Figure 5.3 *Interstoff* and *Première Vision*: number of visitors (1978–2004) (*Source*: elaborations on FKM and OJS data; data refer to the trade show's spring/summer editions; data for the autumn/winter editions are similar in size and trend)

supply chain, these decisions must be taken around 18–24 months before the fabrics will be incorporated into clothing and be available to consumer markets. New fabric collection development must therefore consider the possible evolution of consumer tastes and preferences in the end-markets many months before they happen. Through the trend concertation process, the Lyonese weavers aimed firstly to identify directions for fabric innovation that would respect trends in consumer tastes, and secondly to share such directions with all the exhibitors before they prepared their own collections. The outcome of trend concertation is a set of relatively simple instructions that reduce variety and improve compatibility among exhibitors' collections. During *Première Vision*, visitors would easily see coherence in supply, as, rather than the result of isolated innovation efforts, fabric collections would reflect a common source of inspiration.

A stylized model of the phases and results of the concertation process is as follows:

- *Trend forecasting*. Trends in consumer society are identified by international panels of "cool hunters", anthropologists and sociologists, fashion experts, designers, textile association executives, and representatives of the most innovative fabric and fibre producers. Consumer trends are then "translated" into directions for new fabric and clothing innovation. The panels are organized twice a year (spring–summer and autumn–winter seasons), 5 or 6 months before the event. It must be emphasized that trend forecasting does not come free of charge: *Première Vision* invests significant financial and organizational resources in this value-creating activity, which is funded through the increased price per square metre paid by exhibitors at the trade show.

- *Consensual agreement upon future styles.* Trends are then validated in the context of concertation meetings. At the "concertation tables", a coalition of exponents of trade associations from upstream and downstream markets in the fabric industry (e.g. fibre and yarn producers, clothing companies) and in complementary products (e.g. accessory producers) meets and decides together which previously identified trends will be collectively pursued. At this level, the decisions are "political" rather than merely technical. Those companies driving the trade associations (mostly French and Italian) are in a significant position to influence the outcome of the concertation process.

- *Communication of validated trends to exhibitors.* Once consensus is reached, the agreed-upon fabric trends are communicated to *Première Vision* exhibitors, the majority of which do not participate in the concertation meetings. The context is that of a workshop on fashion trends, the function of which is to inspire the development of the new collection. To this end, trends are labelled with evocative names (e.g. "quest for equilibrium", "urban soul", "cyber culture"), and documents such as colour palettes and trend books are distributed. In following months, new collections incorporating the trends are developed by the fabric producers that will participate as exhibitors at *Première Vision*. Most of these exhibitors are small-sized companies that lack the end-market knowledge and new product development capabilities to design collections that reflect consumer tastes. The documents distributed by *Première Vision* thus constitute a highly sought-after market research substitute, and are not usually perceived as an imposition from trade associations.

As a consequence of the concertation process, exhibitors launch fabric collections that incorporate the concerted trend during the two seasonal *Première Vision* events. Moreover, visitors are able to browse "trend areas" showing fabric samples combined with artwork, photographs, and other visual materials that have proved extremely popular among visitors. By presenting exhibitors' samples in a visually appealing manner, these artefacts further support clothing manufacturers' information search process and facilitate the sense-making of fashion trends. Media relations ensure that *Première Vision* trends enjoy sustained visibility, even beyond that gained by those who personally attend the trade show. This further reassures the visitors and the exhibitors regarding their choices and contributes to the broader diffusion of the trends. As fabric is a core element for clothing, *Première Vision*'s trends lend themselves to be employed by other producers to reduce variety and improve compatibility in clothing and related products (e.g. knitwear, bags, shoes, accessories). Indeed, other industries interested in the evolution of consumer tastes other than in fashion (i.e. furniture, automotive) incorporate the *Première Vision* trends in their products. *Première Vision* has understood that its business is not just to hire exhibition space to fabric producers (the exhibitors) but also to provide information to clothing manufacturers (the visitors). In so doing, the trade show has also started to guide the innovation trajectories of the fabric and clothing industries. Many fabric producers imitate the trends emanating from *Première Vision* exhibitors, contributing in this way to their diffusion. However, as *Première Vision*'s exhibitors are represented as the innovators in the industry, all other fabric producers are labelled as imitators.

While trend concertation was the backbone of *Première Vision*'s competitive strategy, other factors contribute to explaining its success. The *location*, Paris, was similar to Frankfurt in that it had intercontinental accessibility, but it was superior to the German city in its image as world capital of fashion. Officials at Messe Frankfurt partly attributed *Première Vision*'s success to the fact that, when given the choice, "most of the so-called designer people would much rather be in Paris than Frankfurt" (Spindler, 1990, p. 13). The *timing*, around 3 or 4 weeks earlier than *Interstoff*, was functional to the trade show's positioning of the "first look" for buyers who would place orders later. The *product mix* represented the upper range of the market, as access to *Première Vision* was granted on the basis of product quality, creativity, and financial health.

1999–2006: competition broadens – new challenges

Interstoff reacted in many ways to *Première Vision*'s achievements. The German trade show soon imitated the trend concertation mechanism. According to one of our informants, however, "the Germans lacked the legitimacy to be perceived as style leaders" as a consequence of the exceptional competence of the *Première Vision* organizers and the presence of the main actors from the fashion world among its stakeholders. *Première Vision*'s trends were thus generally considered to be the most influential in the industry. Messe Frankfurt also aggressively marketed *Interstoff* to American and Asian fabric producers as a point of entry to the European Union market, suggesting that other European trade shows could not offer this opportunity. However, in 1999, a new trade fair, *Texworld*, opened in Paris and put an end to *Interstoff*'s monopoly of extra-European exhibitors. Reduced to a fragment of what it once was, *Interstoff* gave up the competition with *Première Vision* and tried to refocus on sportswear fabrics with the launch of a new event, *Techtextil*, dedicated to technical textiles and non-woven fabrics, but this was not enough to stop the exhibitor and visitor drain. The autumn/winter 1999 edition only attracted 2 600 visitors, compelling Messe Frankfurt to terminate one of its historical trade shows.

After 1999, *Première Vision* enjoyed a few years of uncontested trade show leadership in the fabric industry worldwide. However, it was not long before a new menace materialized. Italian companies had long considered *Première Vision* their international showcase, as Paris' intercontinental accessibility and image as fashion capital had provided global visibility to their fine fabrics. The restructuring of the French textile industry, with the closing down of some companies and mergers and acquisitions among others, had left twice as many Italian exhibitors as their French rivals at *Première Vision*. Italian fabric producers had long resented the fact that their most important meeting point was outside Italy. At the end of the 1990s, there were in fact four international fabric industry trade shows in Italy, all held at different times, so creating a disservice to those buyers that would have liked to have a complete view of Italian textile supply. The future seemed full of uncertainty. After years of crises connected with the SARS epidemics in Asia, the 9/11 terrorist attack, and the war in Iraq, the long-feared third phase of liberalization in the textile industry was at the door, and all forecasters agreed that Europe and North America would be flooded by Asian products. Following extensive thinking and long internal discussions, the four Italian textile events decided to join forces and in 2005 launched *Milano Unica*, which aspired to become "the Italian trade fair of the European textile".

The world of Italian trade shows was a complex patchwork that was not easily understood by external observers (see, again, Table 5.1). There were three small events founded in the 1970s (*Ideabiella*, *Ideacomo*, and *Prato Expo*), held in prestigious locations such as Cernobbio's Villa Erba on Lake Como and Fortezza da Basso in Florence. A fourth event of national importance, *Shirt Avenue*, was created in 1999 with a similar concept. The atmosphere of these events was that of a club rather than a crowded trade show in an anonymous fairground. Visitors were personally invited by exhibitors and met them by appointment. Organized by local entrepreneurial associations, these trade shows were generally closed to non-local companies. The panorama of Italian trade shows was completed by *Moda In*, founded in 1984 by two national-level textile industry associations and held in Milan, Italy's most accessible location. While less internationalized than *Première Vision*, *Moda In* used a similar positioning strategy. Exhibitors were selected from western producers only on the basis of quality and creativity and received trend instructions to guide their collection development activities. The same trends were displayed during the trade show in extensive and visually appealing trend areas. While larger than the other Italian trade shows, *Moda In* was nevertheless significantly smaller than *Première Vision*.

In March 2005, when the Italian shows announced to the press the decision to join forces from the following autumn–winter editions, observers started to speculate on the likely effect on the appeal of *Première Vision* if large numbers of its Italian exhibitors supported the Milanese initiative. The all-Italian alliance was not untroubled. According to insiders, organizers from the different trade associations argued over everything, from location and dates to, according to one journalist, the "regional provenance of the food and beverages to be served at the event" (Kaiser, 2005, p. 10B). Moreover, Florence's *Prato Expo* initially declined to participate in *Milano Unica*. Only after long internal discussion and the falling numbers of its September 2005 edition did the Tuscan producers join the other Italian trade shows for the second edition of the event. At stake was the need to preserve the identities of the different shows in *Unica*, which, in spite of the name, remained visibly delineated and kept separate entrances.

Première Vision started its competitive reaction even before the official announcement of *Milano Unica*. In Paris, there were numerous trade shows devoted to related sectors. *Première Vision* acquired two of these, *Expofil* (yarns) and *Indigo* (prototype designs for fabrics), and created partnerships with another two, *Salon de Cuir* (fur and leather) and *Mod'Amont* (trimmings, buttons, zippers). In September 2005, these trade shows were held together with *Première Vision* and proposed fashion and colour trends that were significantly aligned. Moreover, with the aim of saving visitor time, *Première Vision* announced in December 2005 a change in layout from a show organized by product to one subdivided by market destination.

Statistical data for the spring-summer 2006 edition of *Première Vision* and *Milano Unica* suggest that a new war was starting, even if the former remained the most internationalized both from the exhibitors' and visitors' point of view. With its 35 765 visitors, 35% from abroad (February 2006), Milan outnumbers Paris which reported 30 176 visitors, 80% from abroad (March 2005). However, *Unica* attracted only 691 exhibitors, 22% from abroad, compared with *Première Vision*'s 736 (330 from Italy). Only time will tell which of the two trade shows will win the battle for visibility in Europe.

Lessons learned: shaping markets through field-configuring events

In this study, we reported the case of the European clothing fabric industry and of two of its most important trade shows in the period 1986–2006, *Interstoff* and *Première Vision*, the key characteristics of which are reported in Table 5.2. Our findings clearly show that the significance of trade shows goes beyond their use as promotional instruments by individual exhibitors. Similarly to award ceremonies, professional conferences, and spectacular product demonstrations (Anand & Watson, 2004; Garud, 2007; Lampel, 2001), trade shows are important events that contribute to the social construction of the field in which they are embedded.

Competition among field-configuring events

One of the key insights of our study is that more field-configuring events may simultaneously and concurrently exist; a fact that has been neglected by extant literature. In this research, the unit of analysis is a set of interdependent events fighting to obtain critical resources and support from key constituents. The presence of a number of trade shows in an industry, coupled with the fact that most firms have limited resources, means that exhibitors and visitors may not always be able to attend all events. By adopting a longitudinal research design, it has been possible to follow two competitive wars among trade shows: the first ended with the demise of *Interstoff*, the oldest and, for decades, the largest and most important event in the clothing fabric industry; the second started towards the end of our period of observation, and only time will reveal its outcome. In a context of proliferating events catering to the same industry, competitive wars among trade shows are increasingly common and deserve further investigation, as these events may be a representation and, at the same time, an instrument of

Table 5.2 *Interstoff* and *Première Vision*: key differences

	Interstoff	*Première Vision*
Trade show concept	Large number of exhibitors, European and extra-European. Complete range. High, medium, low price/ quality	Selected exhibitors. Innovative firms, mostly European. High-end products. Top quality and fashion content
Organizers' competences and strategic goals	Trade show management competence	End-market orientation and fashion competence. Relational competence (key actors in the fashion supply chain)
	Organizer is the owner of Frankfurt's exhibition centre and has the goal of maximizing rented surfaces and local economic impact	Organizer is controlled by producers' association and has the goal of promoting the local fabric industry
Organizers' role in visitors' interpretation	Emerging sense-making – *"laissez faire"* approach by the organizer; – information about trends emerges spontaneously as visitors compare alternative products and suppliers;	Guided sense-giving – trends are concerted by industry stakeholders; – exhibitors are involved before the trade show; – during the event, fabric collections reflect concerted trends; – exhibitor layout, trend areas, and documentation reinforce visitor interpretations;
	– elaboration is complex and interpretations about trends diverge	– elaboration is easy and interpretations about trends converge

the fight among rival national industries and/or group of producers. In our view, the phenomenon of competitive interdependence among the system of coexisting events can also be generalized to other industries and typologies of FCEs.

Emergent sense-making and guided sense-giving as field-configuring mechanisms

Our findings suggest differences in the field-configuring potential of individual events. *Interstoff* was the first specialized trade show in the clothing fabric industry. Its influence in the field was guaranteed by the enormous number of exhibitors and visitors it attracted. Nowhere else in the world did so many clothing fabric producers and buyers gather together in the same place. What happened at *Interstoff* was, by definition, influential. However, the case of *Première Vision* shows that smaller events may have a greater impact on the field. By restricting access and selecting the "best" producers, its organizers were able to affect the status ordering in the industry. Put differently, exhibitors admitted at *Première Vision* were represented as the innovators in the industry; those excluded from *Première Vision* were the imitators. By restricting its exhibitor base, *Première Vision* acted as a certifier of the product quality and innovativeness of the admitted companies, a function similar to that played by critics and product reviewers in other industries. Our study is thus a first step in understanding the diverse mechanisms through which trade shows and other FCEs may configure their underlying markets.

In this sense, the paper also highlights the fact that the sense-making of FCE participants may be intentionally guided by event organizers. In this respect, we have identified two archetypes of trade show organizers. Some are "neutral" with regard to the dynamics of the underlying markets, adopting a *laissez faire* approach to their evolution and not attempting to guide trends. In these events, the sense-making for event participants is therefore spontaneous. Other trade shows are "non-neutral", selecting and aggregating the most innovating marketers and guiding their innovation efforts. These sense-giving[4] strategies are evident from the vantage point of trade show organizers, but hardly comprehensible to individual exhibitors and visitors. Current research on field-configuring events has so far depicted FCEs as contexts in which sense-making spontaneously emerges as constituents convene together and, through "horizontal" interactions, come to see the world in common framesets. The possible sense-giving activities of FCE organizers – and the interest groups behind them – are thus downplayed. In our opinion, spontaneous and guided sense-making may occur simultaneously and should be jointly investigated to improve understanding of the functioning of field-configuring events.

Collective marketing through standard affirmation strategies

Finally, our study also deals with the role trade shows may have in driving the evolution of the products they display, particularly in industries where there are

---

[4] Sense-giving is "concerned with the process of attempting to influence the sense-making and meaning construction of others toward a preferred redefinition" of reality (Gioia & Cittipeddi, 1991, p. 442).

forces at play that foster the selection of standards or dominant designs (Abernathy & Utterback, 1978; Anderson & Tushman, 1990; Rosenkopf & Tushman, 1998). In these industries, the benefits of compatibility enjoyed by manufacturers, producers, customers, and other relevant actors create inducements for the adoption of designs that thus become dominant (e.g. Anderson & Tushman, 1990; Garud & Kumaraswamy, 1993) even in contexts (such as the present case) where the drivers of innovation are based on style rather than technology (Cappetta, Cillo, & Ponti, 2006). Standards are selected among the many technical-economic options usually available by communities of organizations that have a stake in a particular technology or design. Selection processes of this kind involve compromises and adjustments among all the actors involved, e.g. producers, suppliers, distributors, trade associations, and professional experts (Anderson & Tushman 1990; Tushman & Rosenkopf, 1992). In this chapter, we have shown that, through mechanisms such as the concertation of trends, trade shows may support the encounter of organizational communities involved in the reduction of variety and the selection of designs.

Moreover, our study also demonstrates that trade shows may also affect the process of diffusion of a given design, until a critical mass of supporters is reached and that design becomes dominant. Research has long shown that dominant designs are not necessarily the most technologically advanced or the "best" alternative available (Arthur, 1994; Lee *et al.*, 1995). Schilling (2002) highlighted the fact that trajectories of innovation are highly path dependent. In other words, "random or idiosyncratic events early in the life of the technology can have a profound impact on its final outcome" (Schilling, 2002, p. 387). Trade shows, through mechanisms like trend concertation, may create such path dependence. By supporting the visibility of concerted trends, the stylistic standards proposed by *Première Vision* enjoy an initial advantage over other possible alternatives that is further substantiated through adoption by the trade show's exhibitors. The reputation of these exhibitors as innovators contributes to subsequent adoption by other fabric producers until a critical mass is reached and certain trends that were equally possible at the beginning of the process prevail. Moreover, like concentric circles on the water's surface, the trends selected by *Première Vision* also affect stylistic innovation in clothing, in complementary products (e.g. shoes, bags), and also in more distant industries like automobiles or furniture. In contexts characterized by interconnection among supply chains, the configuring capability of events like trade shows may thus extend beyond the immediate field to which they belong.

There is, however, nothing random in this process. Standard affirmation processes are nowadays seldom the result of spontaneous market forces. Trade show-based trend concertation aims to affirm a group of competitors with respect to others, and is therefore a sophisticated competitive strategy. Significantly, the term concertation comes from the language of politics and refers to processes where "the major interest groups are brought together and encouraged to conclude a series of bargains about their future behaviour, which will have the effect of moving economic events along the desired path" (Shonfield, 1965, p. 231). By convening together at concertation tables, a small coalition of actors can influence the industry's trajectories of innovation by aligning the collective efforts of countless other actors. By leveraging the expertise of trend forecasters and employing a series of artefacts (e.g. trend books, colour palettes, trend areas), *Première Vision* represents the future, and there is nothing neutral in its representation. In a context where alternative innovation trajectories are present, the credible representation of one future before the entire field becomes a self-fulfilling prophecy.

Conclusion

To conclude, the key lesson illuminated by the case of *Première Vision* is that strategic market creation is not a solitary endeavour. In any given moment, there are probably countless individuals – inventors, entrepreneurs, managers – who have great business ideas that have the potential to create new markets or change profoundly existing ones. However, the majority of these ideas fail to get the attention of those actors whose support is so necessary to manifest them in reality. Fifteen weavers from Lyon, a few decades ago, dreamed of a future when their collections would dictate trends in the fashion industry – but they would not be able to manifest that future on their own, without the help of numerous other actors in the field. In this chapter, we suggest that trade shows, and other field-configuring events, may be enabling platforms for collective market creation strategies.

References

Abernathy, W. J. & Utterback, J. M. (1978) "Patterns of industrial innovation". *Technology Review*, vol. 14, no. 1, pp. 40–47.

Anand, N. & Watson, M. R. (2004) "Tournament rituals in the evolution of fields: the case of Grammy Awards". *Academy of Management Journal*, vol. 47, no. 1, pp. 59–80.

Anderson, P. & Tushman, M. L. (1990) "Technological discontinuities and dominant designs: cyclical model of technological change". *Administrative Science Quarterly*, vol. 35, no. 4, pp. 604–633.

Arthur, W. B. (1994) *Increasing Returns and Path Dependency in the Economy*. University of Michigan Press, Ann Arbor, MI.

Banting, P. M. & Blenkhorn, D. L. (1974) "The role of industrial trade shows". *Industrial Marketing Management*, vol. 3, no. 5, pp. 285–295.

Bello, D. C. (1992) "Industrial buyer behavior at trade shows: implications for selling effectiveness". *Journal of Business Research*, vol. 25, no. 1, pp. 59–80.

Bettman, J. (1979) *An Information Processing Theory of Consumer Choice*. Addison Wesley, Reading, MA.

Black, R. (1986) *The Trade Show Industry: Management and Marketing Career Opportunities*. Trade Show Bureau, East Orleans, MA.

Bonoma, T. V. (1983) "Get more out of your trade shows". *Harvard Business Review*, vol. 61, January–February, pp. 75–83.

Borghini, S., Golfetto, F., & Rinallo, D. (2006) "Ongoing search among industrial buyers". *Journal of Business Research*, vol. 59, no. 10/11, pp. 1151–1159.

Cappetta, R., Cillo, P., & Ponti, A. (2006) "Convergent designs in fine fashion: an evolutionary model for stylistic innovation". *Research Policy*, vol. 35, no. 9, pp. 1273–1290.

Carman, J. M. (1968) "Evaluation of trade show exhibitions". *California Management Review*, vol. 11, no. 2, pp. 35–44.

Cavanaugh, S. (1976) "Setting objectives and evaluating the effectiveness of trade show exhibits". *Journal of Marketing*, vol. 40, October, pp. 100–103.

CERMES (2006) *Annual Report on the Trade Fair Sector in Europe*. Bocconi University, Milan, Italy.

Daft, R. L. & Weick, K. E. (1984) "Toward a model of organizations as interpretation systems". *Academy of Management Review*, vol. 9, no. 2, pp. 284–295.

DiMaggio, P. J. & Powell, W. (1983) "The iron cage revisited: institutional isomorphism and collective rationality in organizational fields". *American Sociological Review*, vol. 48, no. 2, pp. 147–160.

European Communities (2001) *The Textile and Clothing Industry in the EU: a Survey*. Office for Official Publications of the European Communities, Luxembourg.

Garud, R. (2007) "Conferences as venues for the configuration of emerging organizational fields: the case of cochlear implants", University of Alberta, Technology, Innovation and Institutions Working Paper Series.

Garud, R. & Kumaraswamy, A. (1993) "Changing competitive dynamics in network industries: an exploration of Sun Microsystems' open systems strategy". *Strategic Management Journal*, vol. 14, no. 5, pp. 351–369.

Gioia, D. A. & Chittipeddi, K. (1991) "Sensemaking and sensegiving in strategic change initiation". *Strategic Management Journal*, vol. 12, no. 6, pp. 433–448.

Golfetto, F. (2004) *Fiere e Comunicazione: Strumenti per le Imprese e il Rerritiorio*. EGEA, Milan, Italy.

Gopalakrishna, S. & Lilien, G. (1995) "A three-stage model of industrial trade show performance". *Marketing Science*, vol. 14, Winter, pp. 22–42.

Hansen, K. (1996) "The dual motives of participants at international trade fairs". *International Marketing Review*, vol. 13, no. 2, pp. 39–53.

Kaiser, A. (2005) "Pulling it together – as several Italian textile shows unite under one name, others go it alone to fill a niche". *Women's Wear Daily*, vol. 10B, May 25.

Lampel, J. (2001) "Show-and-tell: product demonstrations and path creation of techno-logical change", in *Path Dependence and Creation*, edited by Garud, R. & Karnøe P. Lawrence Erlbaum Associates, Mahwah, NJ, pp. 303–328.

Lee, J., O'Neal, D. E., Pruett, M. W., & Thomas, H. (1995) "Planning for dominance: a strategic perspective on the emergence process". *R&D Management*, vol. 25, no. 1, 3–26.

Marzolf, M. (1978) "American studies – ideas for media historians?". *Journalism History*, vol. 5, no. 1, pp. 13–16.

Meyer, A. (2003) How conferences and ceremonies construct technologies and industries. Competitive symposium. *63rd Annual Meeting of Academy of Management*, Seattle, WA, August.

Munuera, J. L. & Ruiz, S. (1999) "Trade fairs as services: a look at visitors' objectives in Spain". *Journal of Business Research*, vol. 44, no. 1, pp. 17–24.

Peñaloza, L. (2000) "The commodification of the American West: marketers' production of cultural meanings at the trade show". *Journal of Marketing*, vol. 64, no. 4, pp. 82–109.

Peñaloza, L. (2001) "Consuming the American West: animating cultural meaning and memory at a stock show and rodeo". *Journal of Consumer Research*, vol. 28, December, pp. 369–398.

Première Vision (2007) *Première Vision*: a permanent evolution. [Online]. Available: http://www.premierevision.fr [8 July 2007].

Rao, H. (1994) "The social construction of reputation: certification contests, legitimation, and the survival of organizations in the American automobile industry: 1895–1912". *Strategic Management Journal*, vol. 15, pp. 29–44.

Rinallo, D. & Golfetto, F. (2006) "Representing markets". *Industrial Marketing Management*, vol. 35, no. 7, pp. 856–869.

Rosenkopf, L. & Tushman, M. L. (1998) "The coevolution of community networks and technology: lessons from the flight simulation industry". *Industrial and Corporate Change*, vol. 7, no. 2, pp. 311–346.

Rosson, P. J. & Seringhaus, F. H. R. (1995) "Visitor and exhibitor interaction at industrial trade fairs". *Journal of Business Research*, vol. 32, no. 1, pp. 81–90.

Schilling, M. A. (2002) "Technology success and failure in winner-take-all markets: the impact of learning orientation, timing, and network externalities". *Academy of Management Journal*, vol. 45, no. 2, pp. 387–398.

Shonfield, A. (1965) *Modern Capitalism: the Changing Balance of Public and Private Power*. Oxford University Press, Oxford, UK.

Smircich, L. & Stubbart, C. (1985) "Strategic management in an enacted world". *Academy of Management Review*, vol. 10, no. 4, pp. 724–736.

Spindler, A. (1990) "Few yanks interested in *Interstoff*". *Daily News Register* vol. 13, 27 April.

Tushman, M. L. & Rosenkopf, L. (1992) "Organizational determinants of technological change: toward a sociology of technological evolution", in *Research in Organizational Behavior*, edited by Staw, B. M. & Cummings, L. L. JAI Press, London, UK, pp. 311–347.

6

Marketing's Role for Firms' Renewal and Innovation Capability

Richard Jones & Karin Tollin

Introduction

Marketing both in the literature and perhaps to a lesser extent in practice has been coming to terms with its role in innovation processes of the firm. As Howard Schultz, CEO of Starbucks recently stated: "To build a great and enduring company, you can't embrace the status quo. You have to keep pushing for reinvention and self renewal" (Schultz, 2007). The onus on innovation stems back to Peter Drucker's (1954) famous observation that only two things in business really count: innovation and marketing. However, to date this link has not been fully exploited.

One key argument in the marketing literature concerns the positive impact of market orientation (MO), as an overall cultural and/or behavioural trait of firms' management and business processes, on new product performance (measured as market share, sales, return on investments, and profitability). A considerable number of empirical studies support this argument (for recent reviews, see Kirca,

Jayachandran, & Bearden, 2005; Baker & Sinkula, 2005; Hauser, Tellis, & Griffin, 2006; Siguaw, Simpson, & Enz, 2006). The conclusion made by Baker and Sinkula (2005, p. 321), after having reviewed studies published in 55 marketing journals between 1990 and 2003, was that "support for a positive market orientation–new product success relationship was nearly unanimous". A second key argument concerns the positive impact of MO on firms' ability to continuously create and implement new ideas, products, and processes. Again, support for this argument can be gleaned from a large number of studies – see Kirca, Jayachandran, and Bearden's (2005) extensive meta-analytical review of studies dealing with effects of MO on innovativeness.

There is also an ongoing debate in the marketing literature about the relationship between MO and the firm's ability to radically innovate. A growing concern in the literature is that MO leads to reactive or responsive product innovation and might actually hinder radical product innovation. In order to put this issue at rest, a number of studies have been conducted over the last few years confirming a strong link between MO and firms' overall innovative behaviour (Atuahene-Gima, Slater, & Olsen, 2005; Baker & Sinkula, 2005, 2007; Narver, Slater, & MacLachlan, 2004; Paladino, 2007; Slater & Mohr, 2006). The overall conclusion appears to be that "Market orientation, properly instilled in the organization, seems to be a business philosophy as important as proffered years ago by Drucker (1954)" (Baker & Sinkula, 2007, p. 538).

Notwithstanding, the arguments for marketing's role and contribution (as a discipline, set of activities, or organizational unit) for firms' renewal and innovation capability still needs further exploration. There is clearly a need in the innovation literature to develop and apply market-oriented resources and capabilities (Hooley *et al.*, 2005); in their recent review of innovation management measurements, Adams, Bessant, and Phelps noted: "The area of commercialization appears to be the least developed of the issues involved in the innovation management" (Adams, Bessant, & Phelps, 2006, p. 38). The contribution from marketing as both a strategic organizational unit and as a set of resources and capabilities needs to be explored, especially given the widespread cynicism towards marketing that apparently exists at the upper level in many companies (Cassidy, Freeling, & Kiewell, 2005; Webster, Malter, & Ganesan, 2005).

This chapter identifies the need for greater empirical insights and the development of managerial frameworks in relation to the following areas: innovation as a key marketing process (in relation to end-user analysis, market planning, and sales), innovation of the overall mindset or paradigm for marketing (such as a shift to a service-dominant logic) (Lusch, Vargo, & O'Brien, 2007; Vargo & Lusch, 2004), innovation of a firm's overall business model or mindset for value creation (such as a shift from a linear to a non-linear mindset for value creation) (Davenport, Leipold, & Voelpel, 2007), and innovation of a firm's corporate brands (such as a shift from a positioning strategy based on purely competitive considerations to a sustainable business brand strategy). Finally, we propose that more attention be given, in the marketing literature, to what sets radical and incremental product innovation apart, their relationship to managerial mindsets, and the consequences for marketing's contribution to the firm's overall innovation ambition.

Central to the arguments presented in this chapter are the results of an explorative analysis of chief marketing executives' (CMEs') mental models, or mindsets. This analysis (undertaken with chief marketing executives in financial services, pharmaceutical, and telecommunications and IT companies) found an almost one-sided engagement with either the company's products or corporate brands (the company brand or key umbrella brands). This was reflected in mindsets oriented towards creating new product values or towards sustaining existing brand values. We also found that within these logics the innovation mindsets are grounded in marketing process, marketing logic, and/or business model innovation and their related capability development.

The overall purpose of the chapter, then, is to encourage theory development about how to strengthen marketing's role, as a discipline, set of activities, or function, for firms' renewal and innovation capability. Our research question is therefore not whether MO leads to improved innovation performance but rather how this is created and maintained. A good starting point for doing this is, in our view, to look into the literature's arguments for taking a marketing perspective on innovation. Thus, the first section contains arguments that we have found by exploring frameworks that deal with strategy implementation in the marketing literature. In addition to this, the first section includes a presentation of key features and principles of some influential frameworks that contain prerequisites for implementing an innovation strategy (as marketing processes, resources, and capabilities). The assumption underlying this chapter, and dealt with in the literature, is that a market-oriented (MO) view on product innovation is desirable.

In the second section it is the mindsets of chief marketing executives that are in focus. This section begins with a discussion of what a mindset is, why mindsets of top managers are important, and for whom, and how to explore managers' mindsets. Thereafter, some key findings from our analysis of chief marketing executives' mindsets are presented. The emphasis here is placed on differences and similarities between mindsets as regards innovation orientation and innovation prerequisites.

Lastly, the chapter focuses on the match and mismatch between marketing management in practice and in the marketing literature. We begin by discussing the match in relation to innovation "space". That is, the apparent preoccupation in marketing with either product or brand innovation, and its consequences on "marketing's role for firms' renewal and innovation capability". This leads to a discussion of the contribution of marketing capabilities to innovation processes.

A marketing perspective on innovation

In the marketing literature, firms' innovativeness and performance with new product development activities are addressed from two perspectives, or overall strategic orientations: "strategy as market orientation" (MO) and "strategy as implementation". As implied by these labels, they represent different views about where the fundamentals to firms' innovativeness and innovation performance are to be found. According to the "strategy as MO" perspective, strategy is about a set of values and/or processes relating to knowledge creation about a firm's customers and competitors with the aim of creating superior customer value. Within the "strategy as implementation" perspective, the focus is on the resources, processes, and capabilities that marketing (as a discipline, set of activities, or function) brings to or has the potential to bring to the innovation process in order to realize new business opportunities and/or to minimize threats of various kinds. Considering the vast amount of studies conducted within the "strategy as MO" perspective and the espoused related arguments for marketing's role, we have chosen to focus on the "strategy as implementation" orientation for marketing. In doing this, we will first consider the processes and resources to which, according to the literature, marketing contributes, followed by a presentation of the capabilities that marketing (as a discipline, set of activities, or function) gives rise to or has the potential to contribute to. To begin with, it will

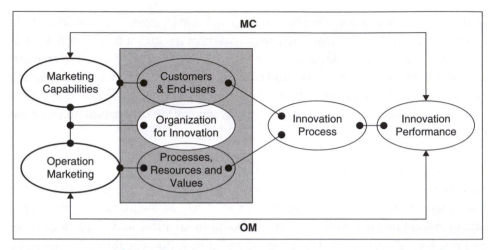

Figure 6.1   A marketing perspective on product and brand innovation

be relevant to present a very general model describing our principal idea of a "strategy as implementation" perspective on innovation.

Figure 6.1 illustrates how we see marketing's role for firms' renewal and innovation capability. According to our analysis of the marketing literature there exist two approaches when addressing a "strategy as implementation" view on innovation. In short, within the first approach the focus is on the role of marketing-related resources, processes, and values, whereas in the second approach it is the capabilities that marketing contributes to innovation processes that are in focus. We have labelled the two approaches "operation marketing" (OM) and "marketing capabilities" (MC). The placement of "OM" and "MC" on the arrows is made to highlight their respective relationship to innovation performance. In this chapter we are interested in exploring the nature of the relationship between each perspective and the innovation processes of the firm. We argue that each perspective offers its own contribution to defining the nature of the innovation space (organization for innovation) within the firm. Furthermore, this innovation space is highly dependent on the mindsets of the organization and not least of CMEs.

The grey box in the model represents the factors influencing the innovation space in the firm. Placed centrally in the model is "organization for innovation". In line with contemporary marketing and strategy literature, the figure expresses a view of the market as representing "a space of potential co-creation experiences in which individual constraints and choices define their willingness to pay for experiences" (Prahalad & Ramaswamy, 2004, p. 122).

At the upper end we have placed customers and end-users where growth is driven by creating value innovations (Kim & Maubourgne, 2005) and co-creating value with customers and strategic partners (Vargo & Lusch, 2004). This requires an understanding of the values, preferences, and behaviour of a firm's customers and end-users, and of their propensities to adopt product and brand innovations. Particularly relevant here are boundary-spanning capabilities that enable the firm to deliver value-creating experiences cost effectively in a dialogue with customers and end-users (Bessant & Tidd, 2007). At the lower end we have placed processes, resources, and values reflecting the resource-based view of the innovation process. This is concerned with managing the processes of innovation from a marketing perspective, where value-based marketing is not couched in terms of the customer but in terms of the organization (Doyle, 2001).

In accordance with the contemporary literature on innovation management and competitive advantage, a multidisciplinary perspective on innovation is emphasized, breaking down the traditional functional silos within the organization (Wind, 2005; Beardsley, Manyika, & Roberts, 2006). Thus, innovation performance is related to both a customer and end-user orientation and is related to the resources and processes of the firm. Within the circle "organization for innovation" are those employees of a firm who are engaged, more or less, with innovation issues and tasks related to a firm's innovation. "Organization for innovation" also encompasses all those cooperating partners of a firm (suppliers, resellers, competitors, and authorities) who interact with the firm's employees, with one another, and with end-users for the sake of not only understanding but also co-creating product and brand expectations and experiences. Some of the tasks that are carried out are closely related to a firm's business process for managing customer relationships (CRM), while others have a basis in a firm's process for managing its supply chain (SCM), its employees (HRM), etc.

Operation marketing: strategy as processes, resources, and values

Srivastava, Shervani, and Fahey (1998, 1999) and Doyle (2000, 2001) present frameworks that approach marketing's role from an integrated and process view of the firm's key business processes (product development, customer relationship management, and supply chain management). Their research is driven by the desire to give marketing a key strategic role in the organization: "If marketing as an intellectual and operating discipline is to be institutionalized in organizations, it must not only pervade the minds of managers within the organization, but also infuse and energize their actions. In short, it must influence the processes by which work gets done" (Srivastava, Shervani, & Fahey, 1999, p. 169).

Srivastava, Shervani, and Fahey (1999, p. 170) suggest two "marketplace shifts": "A product focus is giving way to the need to address customer functionality" and "Product differentiation is evolving into solution customization". They argue that this places marketing processes centrally in the organization's drive to create value. Doyle (2000, p. 21) follows a similar line of argument: "In competitive markets the key to creating shareholder value is possessing a *differential advantage*" which he explains is achieved by "giving customers superior value". He argues that differential advantage is created by focusing on core business processes, namely product development, supply chain management and customer relationship management. Thus, he sees these core business processes as being driven by core capabilities, which in turn derive from the resources of the firm. Among these resources are the firm's intangible assets in the form of the brand. Central here is the focus on processes and tasks. Additionally, it is stressed that the value of cash flow is influenced by how well the company manages to accomplish the following three tasks: "The development of new customer solutions and/or the reinvigoration of existing solutions; continual enhancement of the acquisition of inputs and their transformation into desired customer outputs; and the creation and leveraging of linkages and relationships to external marketplace entities, especially channels and end-users" (Srivastava, Shervani, & Fahey, 1999, p. 169).

While there are broad similarities, Srivastava, Shervani, and Fahey (1999) and Doyle (2000) differ on the extent to which marketing should take the leading role in the implementation of a market perspective. While Doyle (2000, 2001) argues for the importance of placing the development and management of marketing assets (brands, market knowledge, and customer and partner relationships) at the centre in companies' strategy planning process, it is not marketing as an overall discipline, function, or set of activities that should take on the role as the conductor of a market impressed strategy, but general management. This will be made possible, according to Doyle (2000, p. 19), by having marketing professionalism in the boardroom that will provide "expert guidance on how [a company's] customers' and competitors' strategies are changing". Srivastava, Shervani, and Fahey (1999), on the other hand, present marketing as representing the discipline, function, or set of activities that should not only take the initiative to infuse a market perspective into New Product Development (NPD) and SCM but also see to it that the perspective is being implemented. This difference is also apparent in how the issue of assets or resources is dealt with within the frameworks.

Doyle (2001, 2000) discusses assets from a very general, unspecified point of view, whereas Srivastava, Shervani, and Fahey (1998, 1999) take up the issue of "what market-based assets are". According to them, an asset is "any physical, organizational, or human attribute that enables the firm to generate and implement strategies that improve its efficiency and effectiveness in the marketplace" (Srivastava, Shervani, & Fahey, 1998, p. 4). Srivastava, Fahey, and Christensen (2001) present a framework for analysing market-based assets. According to them, market-based assets are of two types: relational and intellectual. Relational assets stem from outcomes of the relationships firms have with external stakeholders that are considered as "key stakeholders" from a marketing point of view. Intellectual assets consist of the knowledge that a firm possesses about market conditions, customers, competitors, suppliers, intermediates, social and political phenomena, and interest groups. This categorization is replicated in other papers. For example, Capron and Hulland (1999) use the term "general marketing expertise" (GME) instead of "intellectual assets". According to them, GME encompasses both individual and group knowledge of the environment and of business practices relating to the creation as well as the implementation of market strategy. Newer work has focused on developing more explicit definitions of marketing resources. Here we have chosen to describe the principal ideas of the frameworks by Hooley *et al.* (2005) and Siguaw, Simpson, and Enz (2006).

Hooley *et al.* (2005, p. 19) define marketing resources as "any attribute, tangible or intangible, physical or human, intellectual or relational, that can be deployed by the firm to achieve competitive advantage". Here, they focus on assets that actively contribute to competitive advantage, which are both requisite and prerequisite for implementing successful marketing activities. In their view, brand reputation, customer relationships, and MO, as an overall cultural and/or behavioural trait of the firm, have these qualities. Their conceptual model of marketing resources encompasses a large amount of different resources that are divided into market-based and market-support resources. They define market-based resources as follows:

- customer-linking capabilities, which are presented as "the first and foremost" of any organization and contain the ability to understand customers' needs and requirements, to provide the right composition and level of customer service and support, and to create and maintain the right kind of relationships with customers;
- the reputation and credibility of the firm within its group of customers, suppliers, and distributors, which, according to Hooley *et al.* (2005), is a potential foundation for sustainable competitive advantage, given that brands, whether product or company brands, take time to develop and require the taking into account of a large and complex bundle of structures and processes;
- the ability successfully to produce innovative market offerings, which concerns the ability to manage the front-end phase of NPD processes in an effective way, and successfully to launch new products and services;
- the human resources of the firm, who "are the conduit through which marketing activities are implemented".

The second category that Hooley *et al.* (2005) identify concerns the value climate within which decision-making is taken. "Marketing support resources" contains the "marketing culture" of the firm and the "managerial capabilities" of the firm's top managers. According to them, MO as a resource is about an overall value orientation (a commitment to serve and to monitor customers closely) and a behavioural trait (a continuous generation and integration of knowledge about customers' needs and experiences). They conclude that "the role of market orientation as a deeply embedded cultural phenomenon affects the whole organization, not just marketing activity" (Hooley *et al.*, 2005, p. 23). The idea of MO as representing a key resource that is capable of creating competitive advantage is a central feature in the hierarchical model of marketing processes and capabilities of Hooley *et al.* (1999). They see a clear relationship between "marketing culture", "marketing strategy" (segmentation, targeting, and positioning) and "marketing operations" (outside-in, spanning, and inside-out processes).

Siguaw, Simpson, and Enz (2006, pp. 560–566) identify the importance of the value climate in achieving positive innovation outcomes (innovation form, type, and rate). They use the term "innovation orientation" (IO), defined as "a set of organization-wide shared beliefs and understanding about learning, the future concept of the firm and its strategies, and the unification of its various functions that shape a firm and lead to competencies supportive of innovation", rather than market orientation. However, they see a clear link between the two, where "innovation orientation is an antecedent of market orientation". Of relevance here is that they see this orientation as a system where the individual elements of learning philosophy, strategic direction, and transfunctional acclimation shift act synergistically. The motivations and meanings given to the three elements by Siguaw, Simpson, and Enz (2006, p. 562) are very much in accordance with frameworks in the marketing literature that deal with antecedents to new product performance and/or to firm innovativeness. Thus, "learning philosophy" is defined as "a pervasive set of organization-wide understandings about learning, thinking, acquiring, transferring, and using knowledge in the firm to innovate". "Strategic direction" contains beliefs and understandings about a firm's identity and what will make innovation happen, expressed as vision and mission statements. Finally, "transfunctional acclimation" concerns the value of different and connected mindsets in a firm, and the mechanisms that capture existing mindsets into a collective body, a system, to facilitate and make innovation happen.

The literature encompassed in the term "operations in marketing" attempts to orient marketing at three levels: processes, resources, and values. It is heavily focused on anchoring the marketing function in the core processes of the firm and on shareholder value creation. This reflects the challenge facing CMEs today to be focused on the bottom line (Ambler, 2003). Following the resource-based view, it argues that innovation processes are linked to key marketing resources that create differential advantage and shareholder value. Evidence shows that innovation performance is strongly linked to the degree to which a market-oriented philosophy is inculcated within the organization. While acknowledging the role of capabilities, these are focused around the key resources of the firm. The next section looks at the literature focusing on marketing capabilities and addresses the issue of how these resources and assets are levered by the organization.

Marketing capabilities

One of the first marketing researchers to create a framework for marketing capabilities was Day, who defines capabilities as "complex bundles of skills and accumulated knowledge, exercised through organizational processes that enable firms to coordinate activities and make use of their assets" (Day, 1994, p. 38). Thus, according to Day, the scope and the antecedents of marketing capabilities are within the firm: its knowledge, skills, and processes. However, as noted by Jarratt (2004, p. 290), the scope of a relationship capability "is likely to extend beyond the functional domain, leveraging assets and skills residing within other functional areas of the organization, as well as from within its network of stakeholders". When addressing marketing's role here, Day's framework (1994, 1999) acts as the overall structure. According to Day (1994), it is possible to classify any firm's capabilities into the following three categories: outside-in, inside-out, and spanning capabilities. In Day's work, as well as in many other studies in the marketing literature, emphasis is put on "outside-in capabilities".

The aim of outside-in capabilities is to reassure that the firm is able to anticipate "market requirements ahead of competitors and create durable relationships with customers, channel members, and suppliers" (Day, 1994, p. 41). Outside-in capabilities are focused around "market sensing" and "customer linking", as these represent the prime means for firms to become more market oriented. Underpinning this argumentation is that "market relationships create sustainable advantages precisely because they are so difficult to manage. Not every firm can or should try to master the market-relating capability" (Day, 2000, p. 24). We begin this section by discussing Day's ideas about market sensing, alongside the contributions from Krepapa and Berthon (2003) and Greenley, Hooley, and Rudd (2005).

Day's (1999, 2002) model for learning about the market contains sensing activities, sense-making activities, and reflection. Sensing activities allow organizations to open up their collective "mind" to new insights about the market. This can be achieved by seeking out latent needs by observing end-users in natural consumption situations, letting prospective or current end-users describe their problems with using a physical product or service, and/or asking end-users to tell their stories about different consumption situations and what experiences they have gained from these. However, when implementing these ways, the following has to be kept in mind: "All this deep digging will be fruitless if the listeners impose their judgements and biases to interpret what they are seeing and hearing" (Day, 2002, p. 245).

All managers can scan the environment. What sets managers in market-driven organizations apart is that they "actively scan the periphery to look for new opportunities" (Day, 2002, p. 245). Here, Day uses the term "scoping" to signify a decision process and a standpoint as regards to "where to look". In defining the scope, Day and Schoemaker (2004) advise top managers to make every effort to expand their scope by having a constant dialogue with employees in other parts of the company, and with customers, retailers, wholesalers, suppliers, venture capitalists, etc. This multisource approach is also recognized as important by Krepapa and Berthon (2003, p. 195). They suggest looking into "the extent to which members of a decision-making team form different interpretations around the content and/or the framing of marketing information". The content of information is about ideas and beliefs as to what the information conveys. The frame concerns beliefs about the credibility and relevance of the information in a particular decision-making situation.

Krepapa and Berthon (2003, p. 199) stress the need for a common framework, or mental model, for classifying and evaluating information, as "excessive source variety is likely to trigger high frame diversity" and thus intensify uncertainty within the organization. They suggest that firms constantly try out new ideas through experiments of various kinds to test the relevance and credibility of information. Over time this will result in a frame, a mental model, against which new sources for information will be evaluated. This is also taken up by Day (2002, p. 247): "These mental models are crucial to making sense of the world and keeping the organization moving in a common direction, but when they are not fully understood they can also blind it to market information and prevent it from developing accurate insights into market realities". Greenley, Hooley, and Rudd (2005) argue that marketing executives should expand their scope to express a multiple stakeholder orientation profile (MSOP). In order to test this proposition, they conducted an analysis of 485 marketing executives' MSOPs. The analysis resulted in a typology of four types of MSOP with the following labels: a shareholder-focus MSOP, a market-focus MSOP, an employee-focus MSOP, and an undeveloped MSOP. As implied by the first three labels, marketing executives have a certain focus in their market sensing activities, although they all have their attention on more than one stakeholder group. The undeveloped MSOP is characterized by a low focus on the above-mentioned stakeholder groups.

The second group of "outside-in capabilities" in Day's (1994) framework is "customer-linking capabilities". According to Day (2000), it is possible to make customer linking become a distinctive marketing capability. However, since it "spans several functions and levels within the organization and incorporates numerous connective links between the buyer and the seller" (Day, 2000, p. 26), it is difficult to identify and manage. As with "market sensing", Day (1999, 2000) presents a framework to make "customer linking" become a distinctive capability. The framework contains the following three dimensions: orientation, knowledge and skills, and integration and alignment of processes; it is very much in accord with other frameworks in the marketing literature. Here we have chosen to let Jarratt's (2004) research findings about the three dimensions supplement Day's framework.

According to Jarratt (2004), Day's three dimensions of market-relating capability coincide considerably with the organizational literature. Jarratt proposes that an organization's (a firm's or the intrafirm marketing function's) relationship management capability is made up of the following three elements: an infrastructure capability, an integrative learning capability, and a behavioural capability. As implied by the name of the first term, it is about the processes, routines, and infrastructure (mindsets and communication technology) that ensure that the firm will be able to successfully manage knowledge-sharing and sociotechnical customer interactions, make potential relationship evaluation, monitor the progress of a relationship, and successfully coordinate the prerequisites and outcomes of customer relationships (Jarratt, 2004, p. 299). When Jarratt discusses the second term, an integrative learning capability, he refers to learning orientation, generative learning, and the dominant logic. He stresses that it is not only about a learning capability oriented towards current customers but also about a capability "that underpins higher-order learning, drawing on relationship memory to proactively advance relationship management practice" (Jarratt, 2004, p. 301). The latter is also expressed in the third dimension, a behavioural capability. This capability should capture, according to Jarratt (2004, p. 302), "the behavioural norms underpinning capability dynamism". Thus, the third dimension emphasizes collaboration that supports joint knowledge creation and dissemination of knowledge between partners, and, furthermore, a willingness and an ability to modify and change the structure and the content of relational exchanges from the outset of being willing to question the existing mindset of relationship management practices (Jarratt, 2004, p. 303).

A number of capabilities are inherent in "a behavioural capability" in relationship management (Jarratt, 2004). One recent comprehensive analysis by van Kleef and Roome (2007) identifies two broad categories of capabilities: capabilities to discover unknown options and capabilities to collaborate in highly diverse teams, including local actors. As regards the latter, the following four capabilities were identified as being essential, i.e. related to a firm's innovativeness and new product development performance: capabilities to create and maintain trust, capabilities to solve problems collectively in diverse teams, networking capabilities, and capabilities to form and maintain strong relationships. From van Kleef and Roome's (2007) overview of capabilities dealt with in the literature it is evident that all four of these capabilities have been dealt with (measured as to their contribution to firm innovation performance and/or being identified as essential from a managerial point of view) from a marketing point of view. That is, the capabilities have been addressed for a firm's customer relationships. However, van Kleef and Roome (2007) note that there exist many other potential partners in firms' innovation processes (suppliers, competitors, authorities, research institutions, etc.), for which capabilities have yet to be explored.

The second category ("inside-out capabilities") in Day's framework (1994) is about capabilities that are the outcome of having acted upon challenges, opportunities, and requirements in the external environment; that is, having worked out a model "that works" for product and/or brand innovation, for instance, a system for cooperating with customers in new product development or a system for recruiting and training employees in customer relationship management. These capabilities provide little value unless they are continuously "activated by market requirements, competitive challenges, and external opportunities" (Day, 1994, p. 41). In a recent analysis by Attia and Hooley (2007), chief marketing executives identified "effective new product development processes" as the most important inside-out capability for successful innovation. The second most important capability mentioned was a so-called spanning capability, namely the "ability to launch new product development which is responsive to customer needs" (Attia and Hooley, 2007, p. 105). In Verona's (1999) resource-based model of new product development there are two categories of inside-out capabilities, namely "technological capabilities" and "marketing capabilities". The first category contains routines in R&D and manufacturing that exert a positive influence on profit generation. Furthermore, technological complementarities are another dimension of functional capabilities related to technology, as stated by Verona (1999, p. 134). And so is knowledge of product architecture, aesthetics, and ergonomics, adds Verona. As regards "marketing capabilities", Verona (1999, p. 136) states that "research techniques employed to capture customer needs, wants, and preferences are a first dimension of marketing capabilities used in product development". In addition to this, Verona proposes that sales, distribution, and service provision may also give rise to profit-generating routines. Although empirical evidence is lacking on the importance of capabilities related to market launch, as claimed by Adams, Bessant, and Phelps (2006), Verona (1999, p. 136) proposes that "the ability to creatively and imaginatively make strategic decisions regarding such issues as market segmentation and product differentiation can positively affect the way customers perceive a new product's ability to fit with their market needs".

The third and the last category in Day's framework, "spanning capabilities", consists of capabilities that will make sure that inside-out capabilities (as the capabilities to manage a new product development process effectively) are successfully integrated with outside-in capabilities (as the capabilities to sense end-user needs and values effectively). Verona (1999, p. 134) clarifies the meaning of this category as follows: "[integrative capabilities] act as an adhesive by absorbing critical knowledge from external sources and by blending the different technical competencies developed in various company departments".

In the marketing literature there is one particular integration issue that has been given considerable attention, namely that between marketing and R&D. An important condition for knowledge creation and innovation is a continuous and frequent communication between actors that differ in training, education, and cultural background. Griffin and Hauser (1996), Leenders and Wierenga (2002), and Maltz, Souder, and Kumar (2001), among others, note that several aspects exist that might have an influence on communication frequency and content, indicating the existence of different integrating mechanisms. Leenders and Wierenga (2002) present a model for analysing the effectiveness of seven groups of integration mechanisms within the pharmaceutical industry worldwide. Their analysis shows that cross-functional boards that review ideas and monitor the NPD process are the ones most strongly associated with integration in the pharmaceutical industry. However, when concluding on this finding, Leenders and Wierenga (2002, p. 314) state that "More research is needed on organizational factors that have an effect on the level of integration in companies such as specific individuals, leadership style, planning procedures, and other factors related to organizational structure in general". In addition to this and the topic dealt with in this chapter, it appears relevant to do more research on the integration of marketing with other fields of competences, for example sales, and its effect on a firm's performance (Guenzi and Troilo, 2007).

In the literature on innovation management it is proposed that a firm's chief executives play a key role in formulating and communicating a visionary strategy for innovation and values for internal integration. In particular, "transactional" versus "transformational" styles of leadership have been identified. Transformational leadership is concerned with generating "a wide strategic vision about the advantages of change and adaptation, significant interest in a communicative culture, attention to the development of people, and acceptance of mistakes" (Aragón-Correa, Garcia-Morales, & Codón-Pozo, 2007, p. 351). The importance of a transformational leadership style is acknowledged in the marketing literature, but only in relation to the CEO. Here, it has been found that transformational leadership is positively related to a firm's inclination to follow the basic ideas of Narver and Slater's (1990) normative market orientation construct. In response to this finding, Menguc, Auh, and Shih (2007, p. 320) conclude that "this result implies that one way to build market orientation is to either nurture or hire a transformational leader".

As implied by the above, spanning capabilities for innovation relate to the integrative management processes with which the transformational leaders are engaged, more or less. Accordingly, one such process deals with establishing or further developing market orientation (MO) as representing an overall integrating resource and/or capability of innovation differentiation driven firms. Thus, the MO concept in the marketing literature is perceived as a key transformational-based competency (encompassing both resources and capabilities of a firm) in that it aims to transform inputs (intelligences about the market) into outputs (values that are appreciated by the market) (Menguc, Auh, and Shih, 2007). In the framework of market-based resources of Hooley *et al.* (2005), two other transformational processes, or spanning capabilities, are taken up, namely innovation management and brand management. However, the findings of their analysis show that marketing alone (as a discipline, set of activities, or function) is not the reason behind the development of companies' market innovation capabilities or brand reputation assets. When commenting on the latter, Hooley *et al.* (2005, p. 26) conclude the following: "This research has demonstrated that capabilities in other functions also impact on reputation. Branding research should usefully be extended to help understand the contributions of these other functions to brand equity and value".

Mindsets in marketing

The ability to implement market orientation in an organization is very much dependent on overcoming the many barriers to organizational learning across the organization (Morgan, Katsikeas, & Appiah-Adu, 1998). Reukert (1992) notes that, while market orientation can have strong benefits for the organiza-tion, it is often difficult to achieve in practice owing to "organizational" factors. As noted above, there is a dearth of research on these "organizational factors", notably the role of specific individuals and leadership styles (Leenders & Wierenga, 2002). Hitherto this paper has focused on marketing capabilities and the role of marketing orientation towards innovation. This approach assumes value-neutral managers to implement and utilize these capabilities. In practice, organizations are characterized by high levels of institutional and functional resistance to interference from competing ideologies, both internally and externally. While there are many sources of resistance, we choose to look at the role of managers' assumptions, values, and predispositions with regard to innovation and strategy. Below, we look in detail at the concept of mental models and present evidence from a survey for how mental models in chief marketing executives vary. We use these results to develop a typology of marketing mindsets for innovation.

The role of managerial assumptions in formulating organizational strategies and in daily practices is widely documented (Bettis & Prahalad, 1995; Prahalad & Bettis, 2004; Senge, 1990; Thomas *et al.*, 1993; Weick, 1979, 1995). Various terms have been used to describe this, including "frames of reference" (Shrivastava & Mitroff, 1983), "management logics" (Bettis & Prahald, 1995), and "sense-giving" (Gioia & Chittipeddi, 1991). What they have in common is their explanatory value in relation to the decision-making processes of managers and their influence on the strategic possibilities for the firm.

Theories of mental models, schema, paradigms, cognitive models, etc., propose that managers carry with them a set of beliefs and assumptions that influence the interpretation of events that they face. Further, these interpretations influence the issues to which managers attribute significance, how they react to them, which solutions they turn to in order to develop a response to them, and how they evaluate the efficacy of their response. For instance, mindsets may consist of "a picture of future customer needs; an understanding of a business model; a set of relationships showing some causality or consequences in the market place; a diagram of critical interdependencies in the value chain; or a mental motion picture of chain of events in a strategic plan" (Karp, 2005, p. 89). They are thus critical to understanding how marketing strategies are developed, implemented, and evaluated.

Understanding managers' mindsets is central to understanding how innovation is approached both by individual managers and by their teams. Individual predispositions as regards the relevance and practicality of radical or incremental innovation respectively, the tasks and information associated with innovation, and the types of relations they define as relevant are all important. Thus, mindsets define the way in which managers sense their environment and how they act upon it: they tell managers how "to categorize an event, assess its consequences, and consider appropriate actions (including doing nothing), and to do so rapidly and efficiently" (Prahalad & Bettis, 2004, p. 76). Importantly, mindsets may act as blinders for the organization in the sense that they direct top managers' attention and attitudes in relation to issues and actions.

Organizational blindness has been treated in the marketing literature under the term myopia. Marketing myopia traditionally describes the short-sightedness of the firm when defining its market and thereby its competition. Myopia is now widely seen as the consequence of holding a particular view, or mindset, about the market and the firm's placement within it that limits managers' ability to assess alternatives. Since Levitt's (1960) first article, myopia has been broadened to encompass specific forms of myopia, including market, competitor, and efficiency myopia (Richard, Womack, & Allaway, 1992). We are interested in innovation mypoia, where managers narrowly define the marketing role in relation to innovation. Francis and Bessant's (2005) four levels of innovation, where they note that managers are often focused on product innovations, are particularly relevant here. This often leaves marketing in the role of "selling" innovations rather than driving them – an innovation mypoia. Alternatively, in the branding literature, innovation is seen as that which is necessary to maintain brand identity – a brand-oriented myopia (Kapferer, 2004). Myopia constrains the innovation space and thereby the processes and knowledge that are sought as inputs to drive the innovation process. Often managers do not consider paradigm or business model innovation, for instance, because of a narrow focus on their own discipline and functional narrowness. It is only when the firm is customer focused and also adopts a multidisciplinary approach that a truly broad view is achievable. The limitation of this view is that it does not address the issue of internal capabilities as a source of innovation, but it does suggest that innovative marketing strategies provide the key to breaking myopic tendencies.

In this way, we see managers' sense-making as central to the successful implementation of innovation strategies. Their ability to define the problem that innovation is set to address is a product of their mindset. In line with the innovation management literature, we regard innovation as an information creation process as managers create meaning in relation to their internal and external environments. This form of directed viewing (Daft & Weick, 1984; Day & Schoemaker, 2004) is important, as it is widely agreed that top management is central in terms of forming and influencing the interpretation framework for the whole organization (Reukert, 1992; Jaworski & Kohli, 1993). Their influence comes from the decisions and other management processes with which they are engaged, but also from the values, knowledge, and fields of interests top managers talk about, more or less explicitly (Leonard-Barton, 1995; Nonaka & Takeuchi, 1995; von Krogh, Nonaka, & Aben, 2001; Armistead & Meakins, 2002). It is at this level that there arises a synergy between the individual managers (their knowledge, experience, and values) and the organizational environment. Success of the innovation process is therefore as much to do with the inculcation of meaning and values at the cultural level of the firm as it is to do with the leadership qualities of a single manager. This we see as an interplay between managers' sense-making and the culture of the organization.

In order to test for the presence of mindsets, we carried out an exploratory study of four financial services, four communications and IT, and nine pharmaceutical companies in Denmark. The study used semi-structured, in-depth interviews with chief marketing executives in each firm. The companies chosen varied considerably in terms of age, size, turnover, and marketing context (see Tollin & Jones, 2009). The purpose of the survey was to uncover the components in the mindsets of chief marketing executives. The context of the study was their decision-making processes, as this provided a concrete framework within which the respondents could reflect over their own decision-making. We asked specifically about the issues, tasks, information, and values that the respondents typically addressed.

The results indicated that the mindsets of CMEs vary considerably. We found that CMEs have varied views and ideas as to what are the key issues, tasks, knowledge areas, and values for corporate-level marketing. However, it was possible to classify four categories: performance-focused management logics, communication-focused management logics, stakeholder-focused management logics, and product-innovation-focused management logics. In accordance with this finding it was found that CMEs differ as to what management capabilities they are creating or nurturing. We found that clear dichotomies emerged around

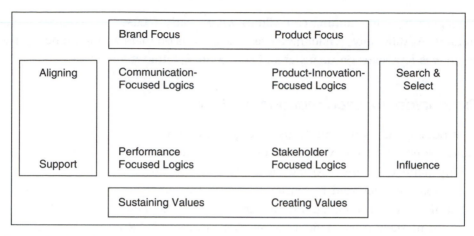

Figure 6.2 Mindsets among chief marketing executives

two dimensions: sustaining values versus creating values, as shown in Figure 6.2. These are described below, but firstly we will summarize the four logics that emerged from the study.

Performance-focused management logics

This logic reflected a strong focus on market sensing capabilities: on gathering and internally disseminating key (brand) performance figures and measurements and documenting the effectiveness of various marketing communication activities. Managers talked about their role in creating shareholder value and as guardians of the key brand, customer relationship, and/or consumer image relationship resources of the firm. They exhibited high levels of spanning activity – both internally and externally, but overall their role was defined (by themselves) as a support function with a focus on advertising, direct marketing, and customer satisfaction/image/loyalty analysis.

Communication-focused management logics

This logic has clear parallels with MO as a strategic approach in its implicit assumptions about marketing's role in the firm. However, it emerged that managers did not have deep insights into corporate strategy but were more concerned with controlling and aligning communication around the brand and new product launches. There was clear evidence of a strong focus on brand management, but spanning capabilities were clearly focused on external stakeholders. Additionally, while there was a clear focus on maintaining brand equity, there was less focus on financial and cost control within many firms.

Stakeholder-focused management logics

A fundamentally different focus emerged through this logic around external stakeholders and the development of network capabilities. Marketing's role was clearly defined around "selling" ideas to many institutional stakeholders. This logic was less interested in sensing the market as an input to product development than in sense-giving around product development. A high degree of political marketing was evident as marketers drew on PR and public affairs to influence key stakeholders and create a positive value climate. Knowledge was disseminated rather than gathered.

Product-innovation-focused management logics

What sets this logic apart from the previous ones is that key issues and tasks dealt with by CMEs concerned transforming their companies' learning orientation from incremental to radical product innovation. Managers were concerned with transformation processes and coordination across the organization. There was a strong presence of integration (as opposed to alignment in communication logics) both internally across the organization (some managers saw themselves as change agents) and externally in terms of developing linking capabilities to customers. However, they also had a strong orientation towards technology and competition.

The emergent dimension of "brand focus versus product focus" and "support versus influence" oriented marketing management can be clearly related to the two marketing approaches to innovation: operations in marketing and marketing capabilities. It was found that CMEs differ as to what management capabilities they are creating or nurturing, based around two clear dichotomies of sustaining values and creating values, as shown in Table 6.1.

Marketing mindset: sustaining values

A central idea of this mindset is that product innovation (of physical goods and services), whether incremental or radical, presupposes a common value platform

Table 6.1 Marketing mindsets for innovation

	Sustaining values	Creating values
Orientation for marketing		
Resources	Brands' identities, market and product knowledge	End-user knowledge and external relationships
Processes	Marketing communication and market performance analysis	Market learning and relationship management
Values	Company performance	End-users' experiences
Marketing capabilities		
Inside-out capabilities	Brand identity formation; sustaining brand equity; brand control; brand communication	Idea generation; end-user integration; technology; business model analysis
Spanning capabilities	Communication; life cycle, and portfolio management	Knowledge management; project management
Outside-in capabilities	Industry, competitor, and brand equity analysis	End-user value analysis, relationship management

throughout the innovation process and implicitly within all processes in a firm's value chain. Ideally, this value platform has its basis in the firm's corporate and/ or key umbrella brands, which was reflected in that group of CMEs with a communication focus. Thus, brands are perceived as representing an important resource, or input, in innovation processes, in the form of their intrinsic or aspired extrinsic values; a brand's identity or visionary image was the key focus for these CMEs. Another resource of importance is made up of quantitative intelligence and data gathering about the company's position and progress in the market in comparison with main competitors, competitors' strengths and weaknesses, developments and trends in the industry, and the image of the company's brand(s) (the corporate and/or an umbrella product brand) among its key and present customers. Accordingly, under this mindset, the marketing process is mostly concerned with the development and safeguarding of strategies for corporate branding and/or umbrella product branding. This is achieved by the design of control systems for continuously monitoring how the brand(s) perform. The values that govern these processes are formulated from an inside-out perspective and express preferable end-states as regards company and brand performance in comparison with main competitors. While marketing executives also argued that they were highly focused on developing outside-in capabilities, it became evident that the "spanning capabilities" they cited in relation to the firm's renewal and innovation capability occurred within a given "branding language", i.e. a common value platform. This impacts both internally and externally: internally, innovation is regarded as that which is necessary to maintain the position of the brand within the tightly defined identity of the brand. The spanning role of, for example, a product manager is defined (and limited) by the notion of what is necessary for the maintenance of the brand. Externally, the spanning role is mostly concerned about effectively communicating the technological, product, and service elements of the brand in relation to its given (presupposed) identity or visionary image. Thus, developing strong communication capabilities becomes highly important in terms of the ability to "translate" product features, attributes, and quality specifications to a brand's identity or visionary image. Other important capabilities were seen in product and brand life cycle management and brand portfolio management and their associated resources and spanning capabilities.

Marketing mindset: creating values

A recurrent theme when the holders of this mindset talked about what resources, processes, and values were important when enacting corporate-level marketing was that they expressed a critical reflective attitude towards their past mindset, and that they regarded themselves as change agents in the process of implementing a shift of mindset within their company or business unit; not just within the marketing department and/or within R&D. Thus, a perception put forward by holders of this mindset is that product innovation presupposes innovation processes throughout the whole value chain of their company. Furthermore, that radical product innovation presupposes abilities "to transform our business models so that we are able to focus on the things that create value" (one of the interviewed managers).

As implied by the name, one central feature of this mindset is a preoccupation with creating end-user values that have not yet been exploited in the particular industry. Additionally, we noted a predisposition towards a qualitative paradigm in relation to market learning processes and detailed microlevel knowledge about end-users' consumption experiences and about processes and process innovations aimed at integrating end-user knowledge into development processes even further. This latter was put forward as follows: "In the future we have to be very much closer to the end-user. We have to work more with details, we have got to fine-tune our offer even more" (one of the interviewed managers). While this mindset appears to be the fulfilment of market orientation, we found that it tended to focus at the tactical and product levels. There was a strong emphasis on specific knowledge about product and process techno-logy, and similarly on being involved with relationship-building processes in the research society, with major client companies, and/or with suppliers of various components or parts of a physical product (packaging technology) or a service (software programs). CMEs were focused on being either agents of innova-tion or supporters of it, in both cases focusing on networking and persuasion. This was reflected in the highly developed external spanning and integrative capabilities.

Marketing's role as creating and/or sustaining values

According to the contemporary management literature, a key task for a firm's top managers is to make sure that processes, resources, and values are "in place" in support for a continuous and successful realization of sustaining values (O'Cass & Ngo, 2007; Beardsley, Manyika, & Roberts, 2006; Homburg, Grozdanovic, & Klarmann, 2007). That is, existing products and brands need to be continuously updated and renewed in response to a "customer-led" or an adaptive market learning model (Berthon, Hulbert, & Pitt, 2004). In addition to this, a firm's top managers must also see to it that a generative learning model is in place and nourished in order to "lead the customer", more or less continuously, with radically new product and brand values (Baker & Sinkula, 2007). However, both in the literature (see, for example, Atuahene-Gima, 2005; Benner & Tushman, 2003; Leonard-Barton, 1995) and in our explorative analysis, the simultaneous existence of the two strategies or mindsets appears to present a paradox. When addressing the problem in the literature, the term "ambidextrous" organization has been introduced, to characterize an organizational form that is composed of subunits: "the tasks, culture, individuals, and organizational arrangements are consistent, but across subunits tasks and cultures are inconsistent and loosely coupled" (Benner & Tushman, 2003, p. 247). However, extant investigations into the ambidextrous organization have focused on the firm level.

In relation to the marketing literature, this is not surprising. As described in the introduction, several studies have provided evidence of the impact of market orientation (MO), as an overall behavioural and/or cultural trait, on companies' innovative behaviour and performance. However, from a functional (the marketing department's) and chief marketing executive's perspective, these studies provide little evidence or guidance on how and why marketing a particular field of resources, processes, values, and capabilities contributes to or is able to strengthen a firm's renewal and innovation capability.

From our literature review on marketing resources, processes, and capabilities and the findings from our explorative analysis of chief marketing executives' mindsets, we perceive that we have the basis for formulating three propositions relating to the "paradox" and to the issue of marketing's present and future role, as a function, for firms' renewal and innovation capability. We propose that marketing's future role, as a function, for firms' renewal and innovation capability is dependent on its commitment to making a contribution to both sustaining and creating values. The first proposition deals with the difference between a sustaining and a value-creating strategy and its effect on the organization of the marketing function. The second proposition concerns the how and why of developing marketing's specific capabilities in relation to creating and sustaining mindsets. Finally, the third proposition concerns the role of the corporate brand in aligning the innovation processes of the organization. Figure 6.3, which is a modification of our original framework as shown in Figure 6.1, aims to clarify the meaning and the relatedness between the three propositions.

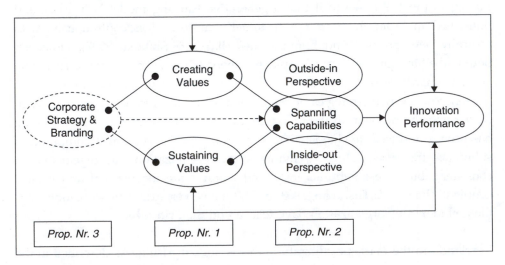

Figure 6.3 An integrated mindset?

> *Proposition No. 1: A continuous and successful realization of creating and sustaining values calls for an ambidextrous corporate-level marketing function.*

The initial motivation for this chapter was to attempt to identify an integrated mindset for centralizing marketing's role in relation to innovation processes. Both our theoretical and empirical work has, however, pointed in the opposite direction. The sustaining and creating mindsets are associated with very different inside-out, spanning, and outside-in capabilities, and to a great extent these approaches are difficult to integrate. We have suggested that the mindsets of CMEs are the source of this difference, but there are compelling reasons for allowing this to persist, because it recognizes quite different commercial contexts and the need for distinctly different resources and capabilities. For example, in markets characterized by strong brand competition and relative stability, where innovation tends to be incremental, organizations need to develop surveillance and metric systems that allow them continually to monitor the health of the brand. Market knowledge is a prerequisite for building and maintaining the brand asset. CMEs develop capabilities around portfolio management, brand identity development, and, not least, strong communicative capabilities, which can legitimize marketing expenditure. Managers adopting a creating mindset, often in rapidly changing markets characterized by high levels of competition, develop a mindset around a deep understanding of end-user requirements and strategic knowledge networks to provide inputs to innovation processes. Key capabilities are focused on bringing people together, either, for example, through idea generation and knowledge networks or through influencing networks of key stakeholders. The greater focus on project management reflects the greater degree of product focus compared with the sustaining mindset.

The consequence of this is that in some organizations the corporate-level marketing department has been split into two sections. One chief business development executive described the organization of marketing within his company by giving the following definition of marketing: "Marketing is on the one hand about communication, traditional marketing communication, and on the other hand about developing new business opportunities, new markets" (one of the interviewed managers). Another similar description was given by a chief marketing executive manager. He stated the following: "The market is so dynamic and we have to separate the strategic part from the operative part of our business. If we had not done that, then we would have lost our orientation – we would have become blind. It's the same with the time perspective, one cannot see both in the short and in the long term. One part of us has responsibility for pushing long-term development, to make sure that we get the right inputs. The other part takes care of implementation and of our short-term strategy. I am engaged in collecting inputs and in formulating the overall strategy: a mantra" (one of the interviewed managers). This appears to be evidence of two trends: firstly, that marketing performs both sustaining and creating roles in the organization that are increasingly being seen as essential for organizational sustainability; secondly, that these roles are not immediately complementary, at least in structural terms, necessitating that they be organizationally separate.

> *Proposition No. 2: Through the market orientation construct, marketing's role for a firm's innovation cannot be questioned (as a philosophy, a business process, or a particular field of knowledge in the literature). However, for marketing's role to develop and become even stronger, more emphasis has to be placed on developing marketing's capabilities for innovation.*

A clear polarization between the two mindsets emerges from the above discussions. This polarization can be said to be a reflection of marketing's own self-understanding. Marketing research and practice have focused on the variables that marketers have in order to reach the market. Central to this is the marketing and communication mix (Kotler & Keller, 2006), increasingly supplemented by brand management strategies focused on building and maintaining brand identity (Aaker, 2001). On the other hand there is an increasing literature on marketing's role in innovation and a paradigmatic move to redefine the nature of the marketing exchange to that of value co-creation (Vargo & Lusch, 2004) and to exploit radically new market opportunities (Kim & Mauborgne, 2005). As argued above, marketing can be seen as a specific set of resources and capabilities that can aid in both a sustaining and a creative mindset. While we have highlighted the way in which these resources and capabilities tend to support the polarization, we believe there is a need to see them as complementary. We have identified a key role for marketing in spanning capabilities. Integrative capabilities are essential for the effective sharing of knowledge within the organization. Coupled to the market sensing capabilities identified by Day (1994), marketing plays an important role in focusing innovation processes on delivering an understanding of customer value creation processes throughout the organization and to its strategic partners. Equally, sustaining mindsets favour the development of resources and capabilities around commercialization of innovations through sensing and reaching capabilities. If these are applied to the innovation process then maybe marketing can contribute to the challenge of commercialization identified by Adams, Bessant, and Phelps (2006).

In a similar vein, the customer-linking capabilities associated with the creative mindset need to be transferred to the sustaining mindset. As traditional mass media communication budgets are being reduced, marketing is being forced to innovate in the area of communication and more widely in terms of business models. The resources, processes, and values attributable to the creative mindset need to be brought into the areas of marketing and brand management in order to reduce the myopic tendencies in marketing. This could thereby reduce the static qualities of the sustaining mindset by allowing brand managers to concentrate brand management more squarely on a customer-focused logic.

> *Proposition No. 3: Corporate branding as a managerial process within the corporate-level marketing function has the potential to act as an important strategic tool in realizing a continuous and ambidextrous innovation strategy in marketing.*

The successful implementation of spanning strategies goes beyond considering resource complementarities in relation to each mindset. There is a need to create an innovation space that breaks down traditional functional boundaries within and external to the firm. In the marketing literature, MO is perceived as a key transformational-based competency (encompassing both the resources and the capabilities of a firm) in that it aims to transform inputs (intelligences about the market) into outputs (values that are appreciated by the market) (Menguc, Auh, & Shih, 2007). However, when we empirically and theoretically examine the ways in which MO is articulated in terms of implementation, the organization-wide, strategic perspective appears to be missing. Both in mindsets and in organizational structures, we found strong tendencies to place marketing in silos and to develop resources and capabilities correspondingly. Significantly, many of the limitations are reflected in the latest definition of marketing to come from the AMA, which narrowly defines marketing as an "organizational function". Recent research suggests that, for marketing to generate successful outcomes, it needs to work across these silos, bringing together product development, customer relationship management, and supply chain management (Doyle, 2001). This proposition suggests that the corporate brand has the potential to perform this role. Increasingly, firms are looking at the symbolic role of branding as a way of integrating the activities across the organization (Knox & Bickerton, 2003). The need to move from a sustaining to a creating role is being realized in the corporate branding literature, where the alignment between purpose, people, and processes is now receiving considerable attention (Schultz, Antorini, & Csaba, 2005). Hooley *et al.* (2005) identify brand management as a key transformational process in innovation management, and importantly as a key spanning function. The key to its success is in aligning its visionary power with practical implementation grounded in individuals in the organization: "A well-conceived brand vision enables employees to appreciate better the journey they are undertaking. Through focusing on . . . the envisioned future, there is an opportunity to consider what environment the firm wants to bring about 10 years ahead" (De Chernatony, 2001). Furthermore, vision can be strategic in nature when it is concerned with organizational sense-making and proaction, i.e. concerned directly with the mindsets of managers. Most importantly, vision provides the umbrella under which organizational strategy develops (Collins & Porras, 1991). Here, the strategic corporate brand can provide the necessary mental framework for managers' sense-making processes and mindsets. Rather than functionally combining the two mindsets, the corporate brand allows the two to exist side by side, enabling each to develop its own resources and capabilities while stimulating complementarities.

Consequences for marketing and future research

We have identified two distinct marketing mindsets which see innovation in quite different lights in terms of the tasks, issues, information, and values that they develop and utilize. Chief marketing executives need to consider the impact of their mindset on their everyday activities, the resources they nurture and utilize, and the capabilities that they develop and apply. We have demonstrated that marketing comes to the innovation process with highly relevant and specialized resources and capabilities that can ensure marketing's strategic role in the organization. However, marketing's most important role is based on its special spanning capabilities, internally and externally. Here we see the corporate brand as playing a central role in creating an integrated mindset across the organization. While working towards an integrated mindset that seeks to develop the strengths of each mindset, we recognize that there are compelling arguments to allow both mindsets to exist within the organization. Anecdotal evidence shows that some organizations are adopting this approach. For it to succeed, we see a vital strategic role for the corporate brand in integrating them at the cultural level. This requires, however, that corporate branding be developed as a strategic function that aligns its visionary power with a process focus that is relevant for employees and stakeholders alike.

We feel that there is a need to better understand the consequences of these mindsets for the organization of innovation in the firm. We have identified a dearth of research looking specifically at the role of CMEs in relation to processes and strategies. Moreover, the dual definition of the role and implementation of branding that overcomes the limitations of each mindset could be an interesting avenue for research. It appears relevant in our view to carry out more research about marketing's integration with other functions and fields of competences. Finally, the need to anchor marketing into the processes of the firm is something that directly concerns the credibility and legitimacy of marketing both in practice and in theory building. The marketing discipline needs to address this issue head on if it is to secure marketing's role in strategic innovation and corporate strategy.

References

Aaker, D. A. (2001) *Managing Brand Equity*. The Free Press, New York, NY.

Adams, R., Bessant, J., & Phelps, R. (2006) "Innovation management measurement: a review". *International Journal of Management Reviews*, vol. 8, no. 1, pp. 21–47.

Ambler, T. (2003) *Marketing and the Bottom Line: the Marketing Metrics to Pump Up Cash Flow*. Pearson, London, UK.

Aragón-Correa, A. J., Garcia-Morales, V. J., & Codón-Pozo, E. (2007) "Leadership and organizational learning's role in innovation and performance: lessons from Spain". *Industrial Marketing Management*, vol. 36, pp. 349–359.

Armistead, C. & Meakins, M. (2002) "A framework for practising knowledge management". *Long Range Planning*, vol. 35, pp. 49–71.

Attia, S. T. & Hooley, G. (2007) "The role of resources in achieving target competitive positions". *Journal of Strategic Marketing*, vol. 15, pp. 91–119.

Atuahene-Gima, K. (2005) "Resolving the capability–rigidity paradox in new product innovation". *Journal of Marketing*, vol. 69, pp. 61–83.

Atuahene-Gima, K., Slater, S. F., & Olson, E. M. (2005) "The contingent value of responsive and proactive market orientations for new product program performance". *Journal of Product Innovation Management*, vol. 22, pp. 464–482.

Baker, W. E. & Sinkula, J. M. (2005) "Market orientation and the new product paradox". *Journal of Product Innovation Management*, vol. 22, pp. 483–502.

Baker, W. E. & Sinkula, J. M. (2007) "Does market orientation facilitate balanced innovation programs? An organizational learning perspective". *Journal of Product Innovation Management*, vol. 24, pp. 316–334.

Beardsley, S. C., Manyika, J. M., & Roberts, R. P. (2006) "Competitive advantage through better interactions". *The McKinsey Quarterly*, The online journal of McKinsey & Co., no. 2.

Benner, M. & Tushman, M. (2003) "Exploitation, exploration and process management: the productivity dilemma revisited". *Academy of Management Review*, 2003, vol. 28, no. 2, April, pp. 238–256.

Berthon, P., Hulbert, J. M., & Pitt, L. (2004) "Innovation or customer orientation? An empirical investigation". *European Journal of Marketing*, vol. 38, no. 9/10, pp. 1065–1090.

Bessant, J. & Tidd, J. (2007) *Innovation and Entrepreneurship*. John Wiley & Sons Ltd, Chichester, UK.

Bettis, R. & Prahalad, C. K. (1995) "The dominant logic: retrospective and xxtension". *Strategic Management Journal*, vol. 16, pp. 5–14.

Capron, L. & Hulland, J. (1999) "Added redeployment of brands, sales forces, and general marketing expertise following horizontal acquisitions: a resource-based view". *Journal of Marketing*, vol. 63, pp. 41–54.

Cassidy, F., Freeling, A., & Kiewell, D. (2005) "A credibility gap for marketers, research brief". *The McKinsey Quarterly*, The online journal of McKinsey & Co., no. 2.

Collins, J. C. & Porras, J. I. (1991) "Organizational vision and visionary organizations". *California Management Review*, vol. 34, no. 1, pp. 30–52.

Daft, R. L. & Weick, K. E. (1984) "Toward a model of organizations as interpretation systems". *Academy of Management Review*, vol. 9, pp. 284–295.

Davenport, T. H., Leipold, M., & Voelpel, S. (2007) *Strategic Management in the Innovation Economy*. Wiley-VCH Verlag, Erlangen, Germany.

Day, G. (1994) "The capabilities of market-driven organizations". *Journal of Marketing*, vol. 58, pp. 37–52.

Day, G. (1999) *The Market-Driven Organization*. The Free Press, New York, UK.

Day, G. (2000) "Managing market relationships". *Journal of the Academy of Marketing Science*, vol. 28, pp. 24–30.

Day, G. (2002) "Managing the market learning process". *Journal of Business and Industrial Marketing*, vol. 17, pp. 240–252.

Day, G. & Schoemaker, S. (2004) "Driving through the fog: managing at the edge". *Long Range Planning*, vol. 37, pp. 127–142.

De Chernatony, L. (2001) *From Brand Vision to Brand Evaluation*. Butterworth Heinemann, Oxford, UK.

Doyle, P. (2000) *Value-Based Marketing*. John Wiley & Sons Ltd, Chichester, UK.

Doyle, P. (2001) "Shareholder-value-based brand strategies". *Brand Management*, vol. 9, pp. 20–30.

Drucker, P. (1954) *The Practice of Management*. HarperCollins, New York, NY.

Francis, D. & Bessant, J. (2005) "Targeting innovation and implications for capability development". *Technovation*, vol. 25, pp. 171–183.

Gioia, D. A. & Chittipeddi, K. (1991) "Sensemaking and sensegiving in strategic change initiation". *Strategic Management Journal*, vol. 12, pp. 433–448.

Greenley, G. E., Hooley, G. J., & Rudd, J. M. (2005) "Market orientation in a multiple stakeholder orientation context: implications for marketing capabilities and assets". *Journal of Business Research*, vol. 58, pp. 1483–1494.

Griffin, A. & Hauser, J. R. (1996) "Integrating R&D and marketing: a review, and analysis of the literature". *Journal of Product Innovation Management*, vol. 13, pp. 191–215.

Guenzi, P. & Troilo, G. (2007) "The joint contribution of marketing and sales to the creation of superior customer value". *Journal of Business Research*, vol. 60, pp. 98–107.

Hauser, J., Tellis, G. J., & Griffin, A. (2006) "Research on innovation: a review and agenda for marketing science". *Marketing Science*, vol. 25, pp. 687–717.

Homburg, C., Grozdanovic, M., & Klarmann, M. (2007) "Responsiveness to customers and competitors: the role of affective and cognitive organizational systems". *Journal of Marketing*, vol. 71, no. 3, pp. 18–38.

Hooley, G., Fahy, J., Beracs, J., *et al.* (1999) "Marketing capabilities and firm performance: a hierarchical model". *Journal of Market Focused Management*, vol. 4, pp. 259–278.

Hooley, G. J., Greenley, G. E., Cadogan, J. W., & Fahy, J. (2005) "The performance impact of marketing resources". *Journal of Business Research*, vol. 58, pp. 18–27.

Jarratt, D. (2004) "Conceptualising a relationship management capability". *Marketing Theory*, vol. 4, pp. 287–309.

Jaworski, B. J. & Kohli, A. K. (1993) "Marketing orientation: antecedents and consequences". *Journal of Marketing*, vol. 57, pp. 53–70.

Kapferer, J. N. (2004) *The New Strategic Brand Management*. Kogan Page, London, UK.

Karp, T. (2005) "Unpacking the mysteries of change: mental modelling". *Journal of Change Management*, vol. 5, pp. 87–96.

Kim, W. C. & Mauborgne, R. (2005) *Blue Ocean Strategy*. Harvard Business School Press, Boston, MA.

Kirca, A. H., Jayachandran, S., & Bearden, W. O. (2005) "Market orientation: a meta-analytic review and assessment of its antecedents and impact on performance". *Journal of Marketing*, vol. 69, pp. 24–41.

Knox, S. & Bickerton, D. (2003) "The six conventions of corporate branding". *European Journal of Marketing*, vol. 37, no. 7/8, pp. 998–1016.

Kotler, P. & Keller, K. (2006) *Marketing Management*. Pearson, Upper Saddle River, NJ.

Krepapa, A. & Berthon, P. (2003) "Making meaning: interpretive diversity and market learning – a model and propositions". *Marketing Theory*, vol. 3, pp. 187–208.

Leenders, M. A. A. & Wierenga, B. (2002) "The effectiveness of different mechanisms for integrating marketing and R&D". *The Journal of Product Innovation Management*, vol. 19, pp. 305–317.

Leonard-Barton, D. (1995) *Wellsprings of Knowledge: Building and Sustaining the Sources of Innovation*. Harvard Business School Press, Cambridge, MA.

Levitt, T. (1960) "Marketing myopia". *Harvard Business Review*, vol 38, no. 4, pp. 45–56.

Lusch, R. F., Vargo, S. L., & O'Brien, M. (2007) "Competing through service: insights from service-dominant logic". *Journal of Retailing*, vol. 83, pp. 5–18.

Maltz, E., Souder, W. E., & Kumar, A. (2001) "Influencing R&D/marketing integration and the use of marketing information by R&D managers, intended and unintended effect of managerial actions". *Journal of Business Research*, vol. 52, pp. 69–82.

Menguc, B., Auh, S., & A Shih, E. (2007) "Transformational leadership and market orientation: implications for the implementation of competitive strategies and business unit performance". *Journal of Business Research*, vol. 60, pp. 314–321.

Morgan, R., Katsikeas, C., & Appiah-Adu, K. (1998) "Market orientation and organizational learning capabilities". *Journal of Marketing Management*, vol. 14, no. 4/5, pp. 353–81.

Narver, J. C. & Slater, S. F. (1990) "The effect of a market orientation on business profitability". *Journal of Marketing*, vol. 4, pp. 20–35.

Narver, J. C., Slater, S. F., & MacLachlan, D. L. (2004) "Responsive and proactive market orientation and new product success". *Journal of Product Innovation Management*, vol. 21, pp. 334–347.

Nonaka, I. & Takeuchi, H. (1995) *The Knowledge Creating Company*. Oxford University Press, New York, NY.

O'Cass, A. & Ngo, L. V. (2007) "Market orientation versus innovative culture: two routes to superior brand performance". *European Journal of Marketing*, vol. 41, no. 7/8, pp. 868–887.

Paladino, A. (2007) "Investigating the drivers of innovation and new product success: a comparison of strategic orientation". *Journal of Product Innovation Management*, vol. 24, pp. 534–553.

Prahalad, C. K. & Bettis, R. A. (2004) "The dominant logic – a new linkage between diversity and performance", in *How Organisations Learn: Managing the Search for Knowledge*, edited by Starkey, K., Tempest, S., & McKinlay, A. Thomson Learning, London, UK, pp. 71–90.

Prahalad, C. K. & Ramaswamy, V. (2004) *The Future of Competition*. Harvard Business School Press, Boston, MA.

Reukert, R. (1992) "Developing a market orientation: an organizational strategy perspective". *International Journal of Research in Marketing*, vol. 9, no. 3, pp. 225–245.

Richard, M. D., Womack, J. A., & Allaway, A. W. (1992) "An integrated view of marketing myopia". *Journal of Consumer Marketing*, vol. 9, pp. 65–71.

Schultz, H. (2007) *Presentation at Apple Special Event, Moscone West, San Francisco, 5 September.* [Online]. Available: http://events.apple.com.edgesuite.net/s83522y/event/index.html?internal=g4h5jl83a [3 December 2007].

Schultz, M., Antorini, Y., & Csaba, F. (2005) *Corporate Branding: Purpose, People, Process*. CBS Press, Copenhagen, Denmark.

Senge, P. (1990) *The Fifth Discipline: The Art and Practice of The Learning Organization*. Currency Doubleday, New York, NY.

Shrivastava, P. & Mitroff, I. (1983) "Frames of reference managers use: a study in applied sociology of knowledge". *Advances in Strategic Management*, vol. 1, pp. 161–182.

Siguaw, J. W., Simpson, P. M., & Enz, C. A. (2006) "Conceptualising innovation orientation: a framework for study and integration of innovation research". *Journal of Product Innovation Management*, vol. 23, pp. 556–574.

Slater, S. F. & Mohr, J. J. (2006) "Successful development and commercialization of technological innovation: insights based on strategy type". *Journal of Product Innovation Management*, vol. 23, pp. 26–33.

Srivastava, R. K., Fahey, L., & Christensen, K. H. (2001) "The resource-based view and marketing: the role of market-based assets in gaining competitive advantage". *Journal of Management*, vol. 27, pp. 777–802.

Srivastava, R. K., Shervani, T. A., & Fahey, L. (1998) "Market-based assets and shareholder value: a framework for analysis". *Journal of Marketing*, vol. 62, pp. 2–18.

Srivastava, R. K., Shervani, T. A., & Fahey, L. (1999) "Marketing, business processes, and shareholder value: an organizational embedded view of marketing activities and the discipline of marketing". *Journal of Marketing*, vol. 63, pp. 168–179.

Thomas, J., Clarke, S., & Gioia, D. A. (1993) "Strategic sensemaking and organizational performance: linkages among scanning, interpretation, action and outcomes". *Academy of Management Journal*, vol. 26, pp. 239–270.

Tollin, K. & Jones, R. (2009) "Marketing logics for competitive advantage?". *European Journal of Marketing*, vol. 43.

van Kleef, J. A. G. & Roome, N. J. (2007). "Developing capabilities and competence for sustainable business management as innovation: a research agenda". *Journal of Cleaner Production*, vol. 15, pp. 38–51.

Vargo, S. L. & Lusch, R. F. (2004) "Evolving to a new dominant logic for marketing". *Journal of Marketing*, vol. 68, no. 1, pp. 1–17.

Verona, G. (1999) "A resource-based view of product development". *Academy of Management Review*, vol. 24, pp. 132–142.

von Krogh, G., Nonaka, I., & Aben, M. (2001) "Making the most of your company's knowledge". *Long Range Planning*, vol. 34, pp. 421–439.

Webster, F. E., Malter, A. J., & Ganesan, S. (2005) "The decline and dispersion of marketing competence". *MIT Sloan Management Review*, Summer, pp. 35–43.

Weick, K. E. (1979) *The Social Psychology of Organizing*. McGraw-Hill, New York, NY.

Weick, K. E. (1995) *Sense-making in Organisations*. Sage Publications, Thousand Oaks, CA.

Wind, Y. (2005) "Marketing as an engine of business growth: a cross-functional perspective". *Journal of Business Research*, vol. 58, pp. 863–873.

7

Linking Technological Innovation Creation to Supply Chain Management

Juliana Hsuan-Mikkola

Introduction

This chapter discusses some fundamental issues related to the management of technological innovation vis-à-vis supply chain management. Technological innovation management topics include the new product development process, portfolio management of innovation, and platform and product architecture modularity. Supply chain management topics include outsourcing, mass customization, and postponement.

We are living in an era that is completely dependent on technology. The faster and more advanced technological development is changing the global economy in the form of outsourcing, the Internet, globalization, and shorter product life cycles, to name a few. These trends pose a tremendous challenge for just about any company that is dependent on technological innovations, be they physical products or services. Having superior technological competence is not sufficient for a firm to compete any more (locally or globally); it also needs to have supply chain management (SCM) competences. In other words, a firm needs to create or sustain competences in order to be able to create markets for its innovations. Dell Computer and Cisco, for instance, have developed product design and restructured their supply chains as a response to achieve mass customization and direct access to customers (Skjøtt-Larsen *et al.*, 2007). Questions faced by companies include: How should firms devise outsourcing strategies related to product innovations? With whom should they partner? To what extent should they share sensitive knowledge, such as the development of sensitive components and related costs? How can firms devise platform strategies in order to create the desired amount of customization while benefiting from savings in production and SCM?

Technological innovation management

New product development (NPD) process

The creation of an innovation rests strongly in a firm's NPD capabilities and the ability to make technical changes, be they incremental or radical. Incremental innovation introduces relatively minor changes to the existing product, often applied to existing markets and customers. Radical innovation establishes new sets of core design concepts, and is driven by technological, market, and regulatory forces (Henderson & Clark, 1990).

A generic NPD process can be analysed in three steps: planning, design, and production (Figure 7.1). In the automotive industry, the planning phase is often referred to as the *functional specification*, whereas the design and production steps are often referred to as the *detailed engineering* (Clark & Fujimoto, 1991; Lamming, 1993; Womack, Jones, & Roos, 1990). The platform/architecture and related outsourcing strategies are often decided during the functional specification phase. Most firms regard their ability to manage platform designs as their core competences.

It is widely known that about 80% of the manufacturing cost of a product is determined at the NPD stage (Clark & Fujimoto, 1991). The longer the errors remain uncorrected after the launch process, the more expensive it becomes to rectify these errors. The creation of an innovation is often realized in conjunction with customers (i.e. a customer need has been identified) and suppliers (i.e. there must be a source for obtaining all the relevant elements necessary for the innovation) (Figure 7.2).

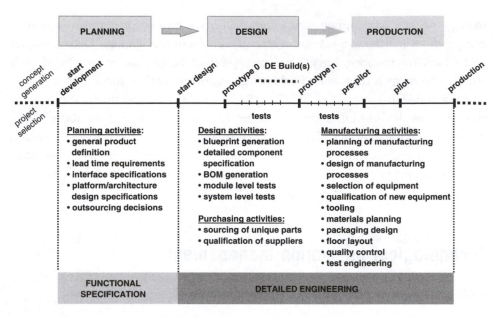

Figure 7.1   A generic NPD process (Mikkola, 2003). Reproduced by permission of Blackwell Publishing

An innovation, in the form of a physical product, for instance, is often created in the NPD function of the focal firm. At this stage, designers and managers are often concerned with how to manage the vast amount of potential projects (i.e. portfolio management of R&D projects) and platform strategies to pursue (i.e. platform and

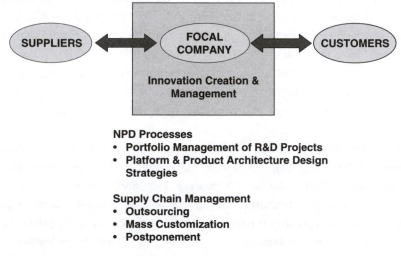

Figure 7.2   Innovation creation and management

product architecture design strategies). Concurrently to NPD, marketing and supply chain managers are concerned with make-or-buy decisions (i.e. outsourcing), the amount of product variety to offer (i.e. mass customization), and efficient distribution strategies (i.e. postponement).

From a focal company's perspective, innovation management has to be linked with SCM. An innovation has commercial value when customers have the possibilities of purchasing it. Without supply chain competences, the firm would lose potential market share against its competitors.

Portfolio management of innovation projects

There is an increasing pressure for firms to introduce innovative products with shortened NPD lead time. The dilemma for these firms is to gain from economies of scale (e.g. from modular components) as well as from economies of scope (e.g. superior technological performance). Another issue related to innovation management is how a firm manages the portfolio of its R&D projects. How does it know what kinds of future innovation should be nurtured? The portfolio approach to innovation management evaluates the innovation in terms of a set of projects, hence such portfolio techniques usually serve to solve a particular set of complex issues faced by innovation management. The R&D project portfolio matrix (Lauro & Vepsäläinen, 1986, Mikkola, 2001), for instance, analyses innovation in terms of the benefits it offers to customers in relation to the competitive advantage of the firm (Figure 7.3).

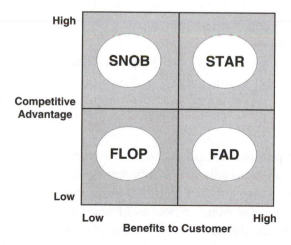

Figure 7.3 The R&D project portfolio matrix (Mikkola, 2001). Reproduced by permission of Elsevier Science

Competitive advantage is the ability of a firm to understand internal as well as external forces that affect the organization: internally a firm must identify its competitive capabilities, and externally it must recognize its relative industry attractiveness (Hax, 1994). In high-tech firms, for instance, the ability to manage the portfolio of products and respective technologies is highly dependent upon the manufacturing processes and technical capabilities in which such products are produced. *Benefits to customers* relate to the perceived value of products provided by a firm. Firms should assess customer needs and translate them into a common language that everyone involved in different departments can understand. For every set of R&D projects there is a different set of competitive advantages and benefits these projects may bring to customers.

The portfolio management approach can provide the following benefits (Mikkola, 2001):

- systematic analysis of projects;
- relative strengths and weaknesses of projects to be revealed;
- consensus among different functions;
- evaluation with respect to business level performances;
- clear gaps and future development opportunities to be highlighted.

However, some pitfalls are as follows:

- orthogonality issues seem to be an inherent challenge;
- technology interdependencies among projects are not so apparent and are difficult to assess;
- a fairly good understanding of each individual R&D project is needed in order to make the proper evaluation, a task difficult for non-technical managers;
- identification of measurement indicators to ensure proper assessment of the projects is difficult.

The existence of portfolios of products (and respective supply chains) raises a challenge for a firm, especially across different product programmes. Reusing a component from another product platform, for instance, might be motivated by the possibilities of gains from economies of scale in production. This is often complicated further by the fact that the reuse might take place within a time span of several years. Most financial systems are not able to capture the benefits from reuse (Mikkola & Hansen, 2007).

Platform and product architecture design strategies

Portfolio management has clear implications for the platform management of products. Good platform communication is a company-specific problem, as the current challenges in the particular industry have to be matched with the organizational structure of the company. This means that the platform communication challenge varies from company to company (Mikkola & Hansen, 2007).

There are several reasons why firms pursue product platform strategies. Some of the benefits of product platforms include reduction of fixed costs of developing individual product variants, greater degree of component and subsystem reuse, increased responsiveness of the firm, higher product variety offered to customers, reduction in development lead time, and improved customer service. However, implementation of the product platform can also be extremely challenging owing to coordination problems that may arise as a result of too much product variety. Customer needs may actually be more difficult to articulate than expected. The firm might exert resistance if the balance between distinctiveness and commonality cannot be leveraged to fit the capabilities of the organization.

An increasing number of firms are applying platform strategies to achieve economies of scale while creating customization of their products. For example, Volkswagen produces the following car models based on a common platform (Muffatto & Roveda, 2000): Skoda Octavia, Seat Leon, VW Golf, Audi A3, and Audi TT. Ford now uses the same "luxury platform" to produce Lincoln, Jaguars, and Volvos (Gartman, 2004).

At the heart of the platform is the organization of components and interfaces making up the product architecture, and the degree of modularity embedded in the product architectures is dependent on the composition of the components, how these components are linked with one another, and substitutability of unique components (Mikkola, 2006; Mikkola & Gassmann, 2003). Product architecture strategy decisions are closely related to the way systems are decomposed, the selection of components to be used, and how these components are linked with one another.

Architectural design decisions consider various trade-offs, and there are no optimal designs. Subsequently, most optimization models offer limited insights. Hence, the focus is not to find the optimal level of modularity in product architectures but to understand the fundamental relationships shared between components and respective interfaces. The goal is also to gain a better understanding about the role of newly developed components and their substitutability in product architectures (needed for long-term survival of firms), which has direct implications for mass customization and subsequently for SCM (Mikkola, 2007).

Product architecture can range from modular to integral. Modular product architectures typically have components with standardized interfaces. This enables mixing-and-matching of components, which increases the degree of customization through combinatorial effects. Such a strategy enables a firm to gain cost savings through economies of scale from component commonality, inventory, and logistics, as well as to introduce technologically improved products more rapidly. Outsourcing decisions are often made concurrently with the design of modular product architectures, and specialization of knowledge is gained through division of labour. Examples of products with modular product architectures include LEGO toys, personal computers, bicycles, elevators, etc.

Integral product architectures, on the other hand, comprise components that are tightly coupled with each other. That is, changes to one component cannot be made without making changes to other components. Integral architectures are designed with maximum performance in mind. Costs of customized components also tend to be higher. This can be prohibitively costly for complex systems. As the interfaces of the customized components become standardized, costs are significantly reduced, as changes to product architecture can be localized and made without incurring costly changes to other components, making outsourcing possible. The Apollo computer in the 1980s, for instance, was a more integral product (compared with IBM PCs and Sun Microsystems). High performance was emphasized and the workstation was designed with a proprietary architecture based on Apollo's own operating and network management systems, and much of the hardware was designed in-house. Apollo's designers believed that it was necessary for various parts of the design to be highly interdependent in order to achieve high levels of performance in the final product (Baldwin & Clark, 1997).

Supply chain management (SCM)

SCM refers to the management and integration of the entire set of business processes providing products, services, and information that add value for customers (Cooper, Lambert, & Pagh, 1997). According to the Council of Supply Chain Management Professionals (CSCMP) (Skjøtt-Larsen *et al.*, 2007, p. 21), SCM "includes coordination and collaboration with channel partners, which can be suppliers, intermediaries, third-party service providers, and customers". It often takes a long time for new products to be developed, evaluated, tested, manufactured, marketed, and subsequently sold in the market. Positive return on investment of a product may not show up in corporate accounting books until many years after its introduction to the marketplace (Aaker & Jacobson, 1994; Hodder & Riggs, 1985). The high degrees of uncertainty and risk inherent in NPD projects pose enormous difficulty for managers to make rational decisions regarding technology selection of product platforms and architecture strategies for the next generation of product families. Furthermore, the complexity of NPD and innovation management policies typically includes other members of the supply chain. These factors make return on investment of NPD projects extremely difficult to assess.

The past decade has seen a strong tendency towards buying more from outside suppliers. In the automotive and electronic industries, typically between 60 and 80% of the product value has been outsourced to suppliers. In the fashion and sportswear industry, outsourcing is even more widespread. Companies such as Nike and Reebok have deliberately planned to retain only design, prototyping, and marketing in-house, outsourcing production and distribution. Increased outsourcing changes the role of procurement from a largely reactive to a proactive activity, searching for and evaluating potential suppliers, establishing contracts, and developing long-term relationships. The recent trend of firms' initiatives to outsource to China and India makes procurement strategies even more crucial in the context of SCM (Skjøtt-Larsen *et al.*, 2007).

Outsourcing

Outsourcing means buying a part from another company rather than making it yourself (Womack, Jones, & Roos, 1990). With outsourcing, a company enters into a contractual agreement with a supplier concerning supply of capacity that has previously been carried out in-house, hence shifting the ownership and decision rights of the outsourced function to the supplier (Momme, Moeller, & Hvolby, 2000). When different components of a technological system require conceptually different kinds of knowledge, it makes sense to partition the system into modules that different members can manufacture in a distributed manner (von Hippel,

1990). Many firms are experiencing financial gains from the outsourcing of non-core activities, as it holds down the unit costs and investment needed to produce products rapidly, and it frees companies to direct scarce capital where they hold a competitive advantage.

Outsourcing decisions are often made concurrently with the design of modular product architectures. Integral architecture designs, on the other hand, inhibit decomposition, as knowledge-sharing and interactive learning take place because team members rely on each other's expertise in designing the architecture (Mikkola, 2003).

Mass customization

Mass customization emphasizes the need to provide outstanding service to customers in providing products that meet customers' needs (through maximizing individual customization) at a low cost (e.g. through modular components) (Feitzinger & Lee, 1997; Pine, 1993). The goal is to produce customized goods (to achieve economies of scope) at low costs (to gain from economies of scale). It allows companies to penetrate new markets and capture customers whose special or personal needs could not be met by standard products (Lee, 1998).

Owing to the evolution of the Internet and advances in IT technology, business-to-business and business-to-consumers information has become almost transparent. When purchasing goods and services, consumers in the western world have become more demanding than before. They want their goods to be customized, with a wide range of selection, they want them cheaper, and they want to get them quickly.

For many firms, the transition from mass production (e.g. make-to-stock products) to mass customization (e.g. build-to-order and engineer-to-order products) has proven to be a challenge. The process of providing individualized solutions forces these firms to change their current operations in order to meet the customers' demands for short times and reduced costs. In spite of considerable investment, many firms nevertheless could not make mass customization a success. For instance, Procter & Gamble, with their experiment to sell personalized beauty products (with $60 million investment), and Levi, with their experiment with customized jeans, have done their best to make mass customization work, but they have failed (Anderson, 2005). What happened? Agrawal,

Kumaresh, and Mercer (2001) mention the following factors: management paradigms, operational changes, supply chain management, dealers' roles, labour and organizational changes, and information technology. Furthermore, in their study of Volvo Cars' activity structure for build-to-order production, Frederiksson and Gadde (2005) found that, in order for customization to be successful, there should be a trade-off between flexibility and rigidity.

Mass customization is enabled through modular product architectures, from which a wide variety of products can be configured and assembled. A firm should have some understanding about the degree of modularity embedded in its product architecture designs before it commits to mass customization.

Postponement

In addition to realizing how to capture customer needs through mass customization, distribution and logistics options should also be considered, such as postponement strategies (Pagh & Cooper, 1998; Mikkola & Skjøtt-Larsen, 2004). In broadest terms, postponement (van Hoek, 2001, p. 161) is "an organizational concept whereby some of the activities in the supply chain are not performed until customer orders are received". According to Lee (1998), postponement delays the timing of crucial processes in which end-products assume their specific functionalities, features, and identities. Customization takes place after obtaining key information about customers' specific needs or requirements at the time of the order. The logic behind postponement is that risk and uncertainty costs are tied to differentiating products by form, place, and time during manufacturing and logistics operations (Skjøtt-Larsen *et al.*, 2007).

One type of postponement closely related to modularization is *form postponement*, which calls for a fundamental change in the product architecture by using designs that standardize some of the components (hence changing the form of the product architecture) or process steps. In order for postponement to be successful, products or processes should be modular in structure (Lee, 1998). In other words, product modularity requires module interfaces to be redesigned so that they can easily be assembled and tested as a total unit. Furthermore, because postponement strategies involve NPD and many members of the value chain, collaboration becomes inevitable between multiple functions (e.g. cross-functional integration) or organizations (e.g. collaborative efforts among multiple firms).

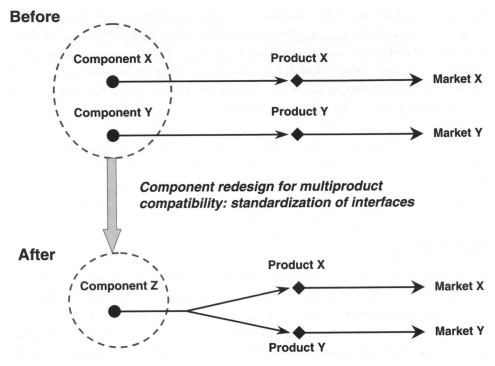

Figure 7.4 Product design for postponement (Mikkola & Skjøtt-Larsen, 2004). Reproduced by permission of Taylor & Francis

The role of product design with respect to form postponement is illustrated in Figure 7.4 (Mikkola & Skjøtt-Larsen, 2004). Under normal circumstances, the same firm produces products X and Y. Component X goes into product X, which is sold to market X. Component Y goes into product Y, which is sold to market Y. With a form postponement strategy, components X and Y are redesigned into a new component Z that can be fed to both products X and Y. The firm needs only to concentrate in producing one component serving multiple markets, hence gaining from economies of scale.

Conclusion

This chapter has briefly discussed some of the fundamental issues of technological innovation creation vis-à-vis SCM. We have only scratched the surface of this complex phenomenon, and one should use these concepts sensibly. For instance,

not all products and related peripherals and services are suitable for postponement and customization. In processing industries it is difficult to decouple
processes into a primary and a secondary phase, and therefore not possible to
obtain both economies of scale and scope.

Furthermore, a modularization strategy is not without drawbacks. According to
Muffatto (1999), the automobile architecture is still relatively integrated (or
closed). Introducing open architecture into cars means that parts must be
designed for an open architecture, which may result in higher costs and heavier
vehicles. Modularization strategies also impact upon a firm's relationship with its
suppliers. A cooperative buyer–supplier relationship in a closed product architecture could be changed to an arm's-length relationship in an open architecture,
where the market mechanism starts to play a more important role. This is due to
the fact that the suppliers are required to develop more standardized components
and subassemblies that fit into an open product architecture (Mikkola & Skjøtt-
Larsen, 2004).

For products that are customized closer to end-customers (downstream activities),
standard components (often owing to economy-of-scale effects) play a more
crucial role than unique components. In this case, the ability to mix and match
components is more relevant than creating specialized customization through
new product development solutions. Firms pursuing this strategy are often more
concerned with short-term survival through cost savings than with long-term
capability development of their product architectures (by introducing innovations
that make imitation difficult).

Not only should the firm understand how to devise technological and supply
chain strategies in order to sustain or to create a new market, its top management
should also be able to translate these strategies into language that everyone in the
firm can understand. This relates to operation management issues, that is, how
capable the top management is of combining qualitative and quantitative tools in
order to plan and control its objectives and goals. Because decisions made by top
managers are related to their knowledge about the innovation and SCM,
integrating these two disciplines into the desired strategy requires managerial
tools for controlling and monitoring such a strategy. Hence, another area that
managers and researchers should consider is the devising of measurement tools to
link innovation management and SCM, so that market creation of innovations can
become a reality with less uncertainty.

References

Aaker, D. A. & Jacobson, R. (1994) "The financial information content of perceived quality". *Journal of Marketing Research*, vol. 31, May, pp. 191–201.

Agrawal, M., Kumaresh, T. V., & Mercer, G. A. (2001) "The false promise of mass customization". *The McKinsey Quarterly*, vol. 3, pp. 62–71.

Anderson, G. T. (2005) "Here's exactly what you wanted". *CNN Money*, 14 June.

Baldwin, C. Y. & Clark, K. B. (1997) "Managing in an age of modularity". *Harvard Business Review*, September–October, pp. 84–93.

Baldwin, C. Y. & Clark, K. B. (2000) *Design Rules: the Power of Modularity Design*. The MIT Press, Cambridge, MA.

Clark, K. B. & Fujimoto, T. (1991) *Product Development Performance*. Harvard Business School Press, Boston, MA.

Cooper, M. C., Lambert, D. M., & Pagh, J. D. (1997) "Supply chain management: more than a new name for logistics". *The International Journal of Logistics Management*, vol. 8, no. 1, p. 10.

Feitzinger, E. & Lee, H. L. (1997) "Mass customization at Hewlett-Packard: the power of postponement". *Harvard Business Review*, January–February, pp. 116–121.

Frederiksson, P. & Gadde, L. E. (2005) "Flexibility and rigidity in customization and build-to-order production". *Industrial Marketing Management*, vol. 34, pp. 695–705.

Gartman, D. (2004) "Three ages of the automobile: the cultural logics of the car". *Theory, Culture and Society*, vol. 21, no. 4/5, pp. 169–195.

Hax, A. (1994) "Defining the concept of strategy", in *Strategy, Process, Content, Context – an International Perspective*, edited by de Wit, B. and Meyer, R. West Publishing Company, St Paul, MN.

Henderson, R. M. & Clark, K. B. (1990) "Architectural innovation: the reconfiguration of existing product technologies and the failure of established firms". *Administrative Science Quarterly*, vol. 35, pp. 9–30.

Hodder, J. E. & Riggs, H. E. (1985) "Pitfalls in evaluating risky projects". *Harvard Business Review*, January–February, pp. 128–136.

Lamming, R. (1993) *Beyond Partnership: Strategies for Innovation and Lean Supply*. Prentice-Hall International (UK) Limited, London, UK.

Lauro, G. L. & Vepsäläinen, A. P. J. (1986) "Assessing technology portfolios for contract competition: an analytic hierarchy process approach". *Socio-Economic Planning Science*, vol. 20, no. 6, pp. 407–415.

Lee, H. (1998) "Postponement for mass customization: satisfying customer demands for tailor-made products", in *Strategic Supply Chain Alignment: Best Practice in Supply Chain Management*, edited by Gattorna, J. Gower Publishing Limited, Aldershot, UK, pp. 77–91.

Mikkola, J. H. (2001) "Portfolio management of R&D projects: implications for innovation management". *Technovation*, vol. 21, pp. 423–435.

Mikkola, J. H. (2003) "Modularity, component outsourcing, and inter-firm learning". *R&D Management*, vol. 33, no. 4, pp. 439–454.

Mikkola, J. H. (2006) "Capturing the degree of modularity embedded in product architectures". *Journal of Product Innovation Management*, vol. 23, pp. 128–146.

Mikkola, J. H. (2007) "Management of product architecture modularity for mass customization: Modeling and theoretical considerations," *IEEE Transactions on Engineering Management*, Special Issue on Mass Customization Manufacturing Systems, vol. 54, no.1, 57–69.

Mikkola, J. H. & Gassmann, O. (2003) "Managing modularity of product architectures: towards an integrated theory". *IEEE Transactions on Engineering Management*, vol. 50, no. 2, pp. 204–218.

Mikkola, J. H. & Hansen, P. K. (2007) "Platform development supported by gaming". *Proceedings of 14th International Product Development Management Conference*, Porto, Portugal, 11–12 June, pp. 933–944.

Mikkola, J. H. & Skjøtt-Larsen, T. (2004) "Supply chain integration: implications for mass customization, modularization, and postponement strategies". *Production Planning and Control*, vol. 15, no. 4, pp. 352–361.

Momme, J., Moeller, M. M., & Hvolby, H. (2000) "Linking modular product architecture to the strategic sourcing process: case studies of two Danish industrial enterprises". *International Journal of Logistics: Research and Applications*, vol. 3, no. 2, pp. 127–146.

Muffatto, M. (1999) "Introducing a platform strategy in product development". *International Journal of Production Economics*, vol. 60–61, pp. 145–153.

Muffatto, M. & Roveda, M. (2000) "Developing product platforms: analysis of the development process". *Technovation*, vol. 20, pp. 617–630.

Pagh, J. D. & Cooper, M. C. (1998) "Supply chain postponement and speculation strategies: how to choose the right strategy". *Journal of Business Logistics*, vol. 19, no. 2, pp. 13–33.

Pine, J. (1993) *Mass Customization – The New Frontier in Business Competition*. Harvard Business School Press, Boston, MA.

Skjøtt-Larsen, T., Schary, P., Mikkola, J. H., & Kotzab, H. (2007) *Managing the Global Supply Chain*, 3rd edition. Copenhagen Business School Press, Copenhagen, Denmark.

van Hoek, R. I. (2001) "The rediscovery of postponement: a literature review and directions for future research". *Journal of Operations Management*, vol. 19, pp. 161–184.

von Hippel, E. (1990) "Task partitioning: an innovation process variable". *Research Policy*, vol. 19, pp. 407–418.

Womack, J. P., Jones, D. T., & Roos, D. (1990) *The Machine that Changed the World*. Harper Perennial, New York, NY.

8

A New Understanding of Market Creation: How CUBEical Thinking Uncovers Competitive Arenas Within Markets

Henrik Andersen & Thomas Ritter

Introduction

Many managers and executives think about market creation as developing a situation where their firm has no competitors but many potential customers. This logic of "outcreating" is compelling: leave the current market with many competitors and find a new market where no competition exists. This strategy has recently received significant attention under the "blue ocean" label (Kim & Mauborgne, 2004). It is the *untouched ground* version of market creation.

Following the "untouched ground" approach, radical innovation efforts often end in new products or product features that serve known customers and solve a known problem but in a very innovative way. Thus, it is not really a new market but rather an *unseen solution* logic of market creation. Every so often, radical innovation results in higher competition, and not "untouched grounds". This is due to competition being quick to adapt or, in some cases, even overtake the original firm with further innovations.

The logic of "untouched ground" and "unseen solution" is based on developing unique solutions and products i.e. goods and services. This indicates that market creation is product and technology driven – even in cases where the original concept is derived from customers' insights. As such, most of the market creation literature deals with temporary monopolies, where competitors will enter the market when they see ample market share opportunities. However, the most common type of market creation follows the logic of "outcompeting" (Hamel, 1991). Outcompeting entails beating competition by employing pre-established success factors, e.g. improving and adding features to existing products, learning quicker, and growing volume faster. This is the *better product* version of market creation. Likewise "unseen solution", this type offers short-term monopolies.

Also, many firms are redefining their market boundaries by changing the span or focus of their operations. For example, more and more airlines are offering hotel and rental car services. Carlsberg, a Danish brewing company, is shifting towards a beverage company (instead of being a brewery), and Sainsbury's offers total household supplies (from groceries to mobile phones, banks, and utilities). Yet while these initiatives have generated new business for these firms, they have not created new markets. In essence, these changes have only managed to make existing markets more competitive as new suppliers enter existing markets – the *new scope* version of market creation.

Of course, market creation depends very much on the definition of markets. Nearly 50 years ago, Levitt (1960) described the difficulties of defining markets from a firm's perspective. Often, firms will narrowly define their markets in a myopic way, thereby losing sight of important competitors: "With enough creativity in delimitating market boundaries, almost any company can claim to be market leader" (Hamel & Prahalad, 1994). This confusion of market definition is not helpful for market creation, as it only concerns the definition of markets and not the actual market exchanges.

Similarly, the academic discussion has also addressed the definition of markets from very different perspectives, e.g. market definition for marketing strategy (Day, 1981; Hamel & Prahalad, 1994; Levitt, 1960), markets as contrasts to alliances and hierarchies (Powell, 1990; Williamson, 1985), and markets as subjects in legal antitrust cases (Horowitz, 1981; Morris & Mostseller, 1991). Given this diversity of opinion, it is therefore necessary to establish a definition of markets before discussing market creation.

This chapter is organized as follows. We will define the term "market" in order to establish a solid conceptual foundation. Based on this discussion, we will explore market creation. We will then focus our attention on "within-market creation", i.e. the (re-)creation of existing markets because our studies revealed that this is the primary mode of real life market creation. The chapter concludes with managerial implications and further research questions.

The definition of markets

In spite of its broad usage, the term "market" is loosely defined in the literature, and market boundaries are "fuzzy" (Day, 1977; Day & Wensley, 1983). Historically, a market is the physical place where buyers and sellers come together to interact. This understanding of "marketplace" has since been enlarged by the emergence of the Internet. E-business solutions enabling suppliers and customers to interact without being in the same place have given rise to the term "market space" (Rayport & Sviokla, 1995). However, mail order businesses exemplified the limitations of a physical market definition long before the Internet was invented. Market participants must also consider both actual and potential actors (Day, Shocker, & Srivastava, 1979). The German retailer Lidl was rumoured to be opening supermarkets in Denmark. This assumption led to price reductions and repositioning of competitors, which became known as the "Lidl effect" – long before the first Lidl shop was opened.

Thus, the physical definition of markets is no longer useful. However, in spite of the limitations of a physical definition of markets, two important points are highlighted:

- A market consists of buyers and sellers.
- Buyers and sellers interact in order to enable exchange of goods, services, financial means, and information.

The first point is actually in contrast to popular usage of terms such as "market research", "market share", and "market segments", which often only take the customer side into account. In this "customers are markets" view, sellers are regarded as an "industry", serving the "market" which is understood to be a collection of buyers (Kotler & Keller, 2006). However, if one element is missing, buyers or sellers, then no transactions can take place and therefore it cannot be considered a market. As the saying goes, "it takes two to tango" – and in market terms it takes *at least* two.

The second point highlights the fact that markets should be seen as exchanges between buyers and sellers (Bagozzi, 1975; Buzzell, 1999). These exchanges require interaction between the two parties in order to determine the details of the exchange. This interaction is typically described as the AIDA model:

- *Awareness.* Customers and buyers must first develop awareness of each other.
- *Interest.* If the initial contact is promising, customers and buyers will invest further time and effort to explore the relationship and its potential value creation.
- *Desire.* Increased familiarity may lead to the development of a special relationship, or preference.
- *Action.* This involves the actual business transaction.

It is important to note that our understanding of the AIDA model is two-sided. Both buyers and sellers move through the stages. Transactions will only take place when both parties arrive at the action stage simultaneously.

The interactions highlight the importance of social elements in economic dealings: It is not firms interacting with firms, but people interacting with people. These social arrangements lead to business relationships that are often long-term in nature (Håkansson, 1982). This also implies that the AIDA model is incomplete. In fact, it should be expanded with an additional retention stage, where buyers and seller interact continuously to enable further exchange (Ford, 1980; Dwyer, Schurr, & Oh, 1987).

Thus, we define a **market** as the social arrangements that allow buyers and sellers to exchange information, goods, services, and financial means.

This definition is based on four elements: buyers, sellers, social arrangement, and exchange. Three conditions, at least one buyer, at least one seller, and the social arrangement, must be fulfilled in order to enable exchange. The absence of any of these elements eliminates the existence of a market. The definition does not imply that all buyers and sellers eventually exchange goods and services. It is possible that buyers and sellers only exchange information. But if no buyer–seller arrangement results in an exchange, we do not consider it to be a market. We deliberately refer to a social arrangement, because it highlights the fact that the particular arrangement may have its own rules and norms.

In the following section, we will apply our definition of a market in order better to understand market creation.

Market creation

Given our definition, markets can change in three ways – change of buyer and seller group (new actors entering, existing actors consolidating or splitting up, or established actors leaving), new social arrangements (different ways of dealing with each other) and new exchange content (new goods and services):

- *Change of buyer and seller group.* In a dynamic world, the group of buyers and the group of sellers undergo constant change. New players enter the market, while existing actors join forces through consolidation. Some of these changes have significant impacts on the market in terms of power. However, these changes are rarely connected with creating markets. Instead, these actions are perceived as changes within existing markets.
- *New social arrangements.* The means of exchange, i.e. the way buyers and sellers meet, interact, and exchange with each other, may change over time. This can be triggered by changes in the legal framework, e.g. new law about customer information. In general terms, the Internet has been a major tool in creating new ways of economic exchange and challenging existing arrangements. While most transactions used to take place in shops, involving sales representatives, the Internet has made it possible to shop from anywhere with access to the Internet. Amazon.com, one of the most famous online retailers, has challenged the market logic that books can only be sold in high street shops. While the final exchange regarding the good is the same (a book), the way the buyer and the seller interact with each other is fundamentally different.
- *New exchange content.* Market creation through new exchange content is driven by product innovation, whereby products are understood to be outputs of a production process and thus include goods, services, logistics,

customization, and advice (Ford *et al.*, 2002). The degree of innovation spans from incremental to radical. Incremental product innovations are normally not referred to as market creation because the implied changes in the market are also incremental. In comparison, radical innovations do have a market creation potential but only when new actors (buyers and sellers) enter the market. Otherwise, also radical innovations will merely support an existing market.

Examples of new exchange content are mobile phones, MP3 players, DVDs, and speciality beer. The products and associated services have not existed before. The infrastructure for using the devices, i.e. mobile networks, MP3 music files on the Internet, and a sufficient number of households with DVDs, had to be established.

However, these examples of market creation can be challenged by defining the boundaries of the market to be sufficiently wide and by looking at the involved actors. Telecommunication firms interacted with their customers around fixed-line solutions long before mobile phones were available. It is rather unlikely that customers without a fixed telephone line were the first ones to adopt the new product. From that perspective, mobile phones made it possible for users to place calls from outside homes and offices but this did not change the social arrangement between buyers and sellers.

MP3 players provide customers with music on the go. This function was earlier provided by Sony's Walkman and Discman and their rival products. As such, the creation of MP3 players is not so much a new market but rather a new product within an existing market. A significant change for using MP3 players is that access to music is gained by downloading files rather than by buying the cassettes and CDs. This potentially changed the social arrangement for the complementary products rather than for the MP3 product itself.

Microbreweries did not invent beer. But their local bars offered a differentiated scene and attracted customers who did appreciate specialized and unique beer instead of mainstream beer – i.e. a different customer type was in target.

The above discussion highlights the dependence of market creation on the perception of the market participants. If an actor, typically a customer, perceives a new form of social arrangement or a new product as a new market, market creation has in reality taken place. With that in mind, it is necessary to see market creation through the eye of the beholder. This interpretative view of market creation is consistent with organizational scientists' interpretation of the "organizational field" (DiMaggio & Powell, 1983). Market creation is a new interpretation of the market – but not necessarily a new market in terms of boundaries. Market creation can be achieved by changing the mindset of the market participants.

In summary, market creation is rarely defined in management and marketing literature. The "total" market creation of radically new products addressing new customers and involving new suppliers is rather seldom to be found. Given that market creation is perceiver specific, there are only a few cases of "total" market creation, i.e. where all involved actors perceive that a new market has been created. Therefore, it is important to turn attention to market creation within existing markets, as this is the most common form of real life market creation. For understanding this type of "micromarket creation", we explore the subdimensions of markets in the following.

Within-market creation: dividing a market into competitive arenas

So far, we have treated a market as one single unit. However, this is an oversimplification of markets because the social arrangements between customers and suppliers vary significantly within a market. Markets are not only created by changing them in their totality but also, and most importantly, by changing the social arrangements within a market, so that market participants will perceive the market as newly created. This reinterpretation of markets focuses, by definition, on existing customers and suppliers and their social arrangements with each other.

Market creation is often, if not always, discussed from the suppliers' perspective. With our understanding of markets, market creation may well be driven by the customer. However, we apply the suppliers' perspective in the remainder of the chapter. Thus, we discuss in the following how a firm can recreate a market by understanding customers in a unique new way.

In almost every market, customers behave differently across the customer base. Given these differences, the social arrangements between suppliers and customers, i.e. the market, can be broken down into social subarrangements tailored to mirror the customer differences. Based on different behaviours, suppliers and customers in a market do not perceive the market in its entirety (all social arrangements) but instead see only that part of the market that is relevant to them. These sets of social subarrangements can be considered submarkets. This understanding, often referred to as customer segmentation, gives a deeper insight into markets. These submarkets offer the opportunity to rethink and differentiate the social arrangements and create a new understanding of submarkets and, thus, of the entire market.

In order to facilitate change within markets, firms conduct satisfaction studies (Fornell *et al.*, 1996; Reichheld, 2003). Such studies provide insights into market potential by looking at areas of dissatisfaction. However, satisfaction studies are only useful in identifying problems (i.e. the area with the lowest satisfaction score) and do not offer specific insights in how to change the situation. The exact issues can only be identified when customer experience is analysed. Increasingly, firms conduct customer experience studies where customers are observed or interviewed about their experience with a product and/or a supplier/customer (Kim & Mauborgne, 2004; Meyer & Schwager, 2007). However, experiences can only be understood when expectations are made explicit. Customer expectations are important because an unsatisfactory experience may have resulted from mistaken expectations and not from goods or service failure. Ulwick's (2002) outcome-driven innovation studies work with this challenge by analyzing expectations and product consequences instead of product features.

In spite of the insights gained from the aforementioned approaches, these studies do not contribute to an understanding of social arrangements, as they address consequences of exchange but not the root causes. Rather, we need to understand variation in social arrangements as behavioural differences. Looking at customers, our study of various markets reveals that differences in social arrangements depend on three dimensions: Customer types, customer roles, and scenes (Figure 8.1). This framework is called CUBEical segmentation due to its three underlying dimensions (Figure 8.1 and the following text are adapted from Andersen & Ritter, 2008).

Customer types. The values and beliefs of an individual person or organization are generally assumed to be mirrored in the behaviours and decisions made by the person or organization in question (Schein, 1992). A personal value is an "enduring belief that a specific type of behaviour (e.g. creativity, caring, honesty)

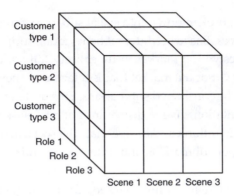

Figure 8.1 CUBEical segmentation of markets

or end-state of existence (e.g. confidence, harmony, status) is personally or socially preferable to the converse" (Rokeach, 1973). Thus, it is widely accepted that people and organizations differ, for example, in terms of their risk orientation (some prefer uncertainty, others prefer predictability), in their orientation towards others (extrovert versus introvert), or in their orientation to nature and sustainability. Firms display their values as statements on websites or badges. For firms, such values are embedded in their organizational culture, also known as firm or corporate culture (Lencioni, 2002). These values affect the employees' behaviours, either consciously or not.

In spite of the existence and impact of values and beliefs, they are hardly usable for market creation purposes as they are often unconscious for the "owner" and unobservable for others. However, as mentioned above, the values and beliefs of an individual person or organization are mirrored in the behaviours and ways decisions are made by the person or organization in question. Therefore, a description of different behaviours and decision patterns captures different customer types and can be used for segmentation (Yankelovich, 1964).

Three important contributions are made with customer type descriptions. Firstly, membership of a customer type is stable over time, and thus firms find their customers in one segment, not different ones. For that reason, the selection of an appropriate differentiation strategy targeted towards each specific customer type is possible. This is the advantage of focusing on values and beliefs instead of experiences and satisfaction. Secondly, customer type descriptions are intuitively understandable for the organization, so that employees are able to segment customers "on the spot". In doing so, they are able to service customers in the appropriate way and execute the chosen differentiation strategy. Thirdly, customer types are directly related to market behaviour because their behaviour is the basis for segmentation. This implies that differentiation strategies have a major market impact and, thus, a high return on investment, because firms offer those products that are appreciated by customers. If segmentation cannot be used for differentiating marketing efforts, customer knowledge is without impact.

Customer roles. Many firms regard a customer or supplier as one actor. In most cases this is a fundamental mistake. Having such a one-size-fits-all attitude mistreats customers and is often a sign of not being customer oriented. All customers are "multividuals", i.e. they perform different roles in their interaction with suppliers. Like an actor on stage, market participants have, or play, different roles. Therefore, we use the role concept to capture these differences. Roles have been discussed in various ways in the marketing literature, but have not been used to differentiate customers:

— roles, and especially role conflict and ambiguity, of salespeople (Ford, Walker, & Churchill, 1975; Singh, 1993);
— roles of firms in networks (Johanson & Mattsson, 1992; Mattsson, 1985);
— roles of members of buying centres (Webster & Wind, 1972).

Roles are defined in relation to other people – or firms in the case of business markets. Typical roles are alone (only thinking of oneself), mother–father–sister–brother (in relation to a family), employee (in relation to a boss), colleague (in relation to coworkers), and functional position (in relation to customers and suppliers). As an example, customers' choices of beverages are quite different across the different roles: a customer may drink tap water alone, sparkling water with the family, tea at work, and coffee in business meetings. Therefore, it is important to understand the role of customers in order to understand their needs and expectations. Customers are very used to shifting roles – they do this various times a day. Sometimes, we are even performing various roles simultaneously when taking a mobile phone call (business) and taking care of the kids (father/mother) at the same time.

Airlines, railway operators, and car rental agencies share a common ignorance of customer roles. These firms have customer loyalty cards and claim to know their customers, but they fail to account for the changing roles of their customers. The busy executive is not interested in a stay-over deal when the plane is overbooked.

But the romantic partner on a weekend-break trip may consider it. A simple question about the purpose of the trip at the desk not only would be friendly but also could make a big difference to their customer relations. Roles are well-suited for market segmentation practice, as they are easily recognizable and their existence over time is stable.

Scenes. Suppliers meet customers in different scenes. Scenes are places, spaces, and physical objects, i.e. the resources that a customer has at hand when meeting a supplier's products and/or personnel. It makes a significant difference if a person travels by car, by train, on a bicycle, or is walking. By varying the resources, i.e. the scene, different needs are important.

Scenes are the places and spaces of interaction, the physical environments. Customers move through different scenes: People drink Coke at home, on the go, in the office, or in a restaurant. Again, different needs are connected with different scenes, e.g. the 2 litre bottle is more suitable for home drinking than on the go. Consider another scene shift, such as a change in resources. The type of beverage desired may change according to the meal, e.g. a hot dog, a salmon sandwich, roast beef, or a cake. Some will suggest other terms like "occasion" and "situation" to capture resource variation, but these terms can be confusing, as they normally combine types, roles, and scenes. Our experience shows that executives can easily understand scenes in parallel to a theatre – and they fully understand the business implications of being able to set the scene. This topic has entered the marketing agenda as occasion and situational marketing.

Strategizing in competitive arenas

Bringing the three elements – customer types, customer roles, and scenes – together, a CUBEical Thinking framework of markets is established (see Figure 8.2). The CUBEical market framework groups customers with similar social arrangements together and defines the competitive arenas of a market vis-à-vis the customers in question. We call a submarket made up of a customer type, a customer role, and a scene a "competitive arena" because it is here where competition unfolds. Customers with similar social arrangements with their suppliers have similar needs, and therefore firms compete to serve these customers with suitable solutions. Suppliers who do not fulfil the needs of a customer within a given competitive arena are not competing because the customer does

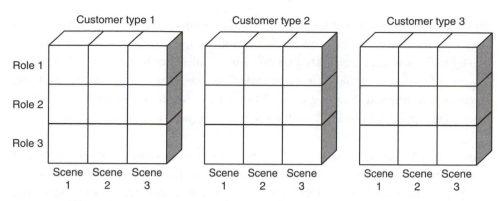

Figure 8.2 Unfolded CUBEical segmentation of markets

not recognize them as interesting. By definition, customers with different needs are in different arenas.

In the CUBEical segmentation model we capture the dynamic of customers' roles and scene changes without having to change the segmentation model of the market. This is a major advantage and differentiates CUBEical Thinking from existing market models, which generally have problems with capturing and explaining customer complexity in recognizable, stable and effective terms. The CUBEical approach offers a stable tool for sales, marketing, and innovation.

Understanding the customer in three dimensions – customer types, customer roles, and scenes – offers unique insight into market creation. Going back to the aforementioned examples, mobile phone firms addressed not customer type and roles but developed a different scene for telecommunication, i.e. the scene when a person is neither at home nor in the office. Similarly, what Amazon.com offered was new scenes, i.e. at home or in the office – as opposed the book shop.

Customers are generally different, and consequently the social arrangement must be designed accordingly. In order to create competitive arenas as a means of within-market creation, competitive arenas must be stable, recognizable, and significant to the market.

Conclusion

In this chapter, we argue that markets are vaguely defined, both in academia and in practice. However, both academics and executives need a working definition to avoid confusion. Similarly to organizational scientists, we define a market as a social arrangement. Within the market creation logic, two different approaches exist. Firstly, markets are created by offering a "killer application" to the market. In spite of the focus of many firms on "total" market creation, our global business environment offers decreasing possibilities for this strategy. Increasingly, market leadership strategies are built on the second logic, within-market creation.

Most firms today operate in existing markets, i.e. in defined spaces of social arrangements with the aim of economic exchange. The true real life potential of market creation lies in the development of a new understanding of markets and, consequently, in a new approach to customers, resulting in a new social arrangement, i.e. a new market interpretation by customers. This new approach is then viewed as a new market by the customer. The most effective market creation is the reinterpretation of the customer universe.

Besides this new interpretation of market creation, we have also described a model for gaining a unique understanding of the customer universe. While most other radical innovation methods focus on customer input, current trends, and dynamic change, our approach is based on stable dimensions: customer type, customer roles, and scenes. With these dimensions, we are able to define competitive arenas – and explore roadmaps for market creation in terms of sales, communication, and new product development.

Technology-driven market creation can be copied by competitors and therefore can only provide a temporary relief from competition. Market creation through the development of new social arrangements cannot be duplicated that easily. Social relationships between customers and suppliers are firm – specific and relatively stable and thus they cannot be easily copied. As such, it is more difficult for a competitor to challenge a firm's market position. With this approach, market creation is established at the micro level – the social arrangement with customers. But it has a far-reaching impact on the market by reshaping the arenas of social arrangements. Or, to use a common saying: "The devil is in the detail".

Acknowledgement

CUBEical and CustomerUniverse are trademarks of Andersen&Partners – Management Consulting, Allerød, Denmark.

References

Andersen, H. & Ritter, T. (2008) Inside the Customer Universe: How Unique Customer Insight Drives Profitable Growth and Creates Market Leaders. Wiley-Blackwell, Chichester, U.K.

Bagozzi, R. P. (1975) "Marketing as exchange". *Journal of Marketing*, vol. 39, no. 4, pp. 32–39.

Buzzell, R. D. (1999) "Market functions and market evolution". *Journal of Marketing*, vol. 63, pp. 61–63.

Day, G. S. (1977) "Diagnosing the product portfolio". *Journal of Marketing*, vol. 41, pp. 29–38.

Day, G. S. (1981) "Strategic market analysis and definition: an integrated approach". *Strategic Management Journal*, vol. 2, pp. 281–299.

Day, G. S., Shocker, A. D., & Srivastava, R. K. (1979) "Customer-oriented approaches to identifying product markets". *Journal of Marketing*, vol. 43, pp. 8–19.

Day, G. S. & Wensley, R. (1983) "Marketing theory with a strategic orientation". *Journal of Marketing*, vol. 47, pp. 79–83.

DiMaggio, P. & Powell, W. W. (1983) "The iron cage revisited: institutional isomorphism and collective rationality in organizational fields". *American Sociological Review*, vol. 48, pp. 147–160.

Dwyer, F. R., Schurr, P. H., & Oh, S. (1987) "Developing buyer–seller relationships". *Journal of Marketing*, vol. 51, no. 2, pp. 11–27.

Ford, D. (1980) "The development of buyer–seller relationships in industrial markets". *European Journal of Marketing*, vol. 14, no. 5/6, pp. 339–354.

Ford, D., Berthon, P., Gadde, L.-E., *et al.* (2002) *The Business Marketing Course: Managing in Complex Networks*. John Wiley & Sons Ltd, Chichester, UK.

Ford, N. M., Walker Jr, O. C., & Churchill Jr, G. A. (1975) "Expectation-specific measures of the intersender conflict and role ambiguity experienced by industrial salesmen". *Journal of Business Research*, vol. 3, no. 2, pp. 95–112.

Fornell, C., Johnson, M. D., Anderson, E. W., *et al.* (1996) "The American customer satisfaction index: nature, purpose, and findings". *Journal of Marketing*, vol. 60, no. 4, pp. 7–18.

Håkansson, H. (1982) "An interaction approach", in *International Marketing and Purchasing of Industrial Goods*, edited by Håkansson, H., John Wiley & Sons Ltd, Chichester, UK, pp. 10–27.

Hamel, G. (1991) "Competition for competence and interpartner learning within international strategic alliances". *Strategic Management Journal*, vol. 12, pp. 83–103.

Hamel, G. & Prahalad, C. K. (1994) "Competing for the future". *Harvard Business Review*, vol. 72, no. 4, pp. 122–128.

Horowitz, I. (1981) "Market definition in antitrust analysis: a regression-based approach". *Southern Economics Journal*, vol. 48, pp. 1–16.

Johanson, J. & Mattsson, L.-G. (1992) "Network positions and strategic actions: an analytical framework", in *Industrial Networks: a New View of Reality*, edited by Axelsson, B. & Easton, G. Routledge, London, UK, pp. 205–217.

Kim, W. C. & Mauborgne, R. (2004) "Blue ocean strategy". *Harvard Business Review*, vol. 82, no. 10, pp. 76–84.

Kotler, P. & Keller, K. L. (2006) *Marketing Management*, 12th edition. Pearson-Prentice Hall, Upper Saddle River, NJ.

Lencioni, P. M. (2002) "Make your values mean something". *Harvard Business Review*, vol. 80, no. 7, pp. 113–117.

Levitt, T. (1960) "Marketing myopia". *Harvard Business Review*, vol. 38, no. 4, pp. 45–56.

Mattsson, L.-G. (1985) "An application of a networks approach to marketing: defending and changing market positions", in *Changing the Course of Marketing: Alternative Paradigms for Widening Marketing Theory*, edited by Dholakia, N. & Arndt, J. JAI Press, Greenwich, CT, pp. 263–288.

Meyer, C. & Schwager, A. (2007) "Understanding customer experience". *Harvard Business Review*, vol. 85, no. 2, pp. 116–126.

Morris, J. R. & Mostseller, G. R. (1991) "Defining markets for mergers analysis". *Antitrust Bulletin*, vol. 36, no. 3, pp. 599–640.

Powell, W. W. (1990) "Neither markets nor hierachy: network forms of organization". *Research in Organizational Behaviour*, vol. 12, pp. 295–336.

Rayport, J. F. & Sviokla, J. J. (1995) "Exploiting the virtual value chain". *Harvard Business Review*, vol. 73, no. 6, pp. 75–85.

Reichheld, F. F. (2003) "The one number you need to grow". *Harvard Business Review*, vol. 81, no. 12, pp. 46–54.

Rokeach, M. (1973) *The Nature of Human Values*. The Free Press, New York, NY.

Schein, E. H. (1992) *Organizational Culture and Leadership*. Jossey-Bass, San Francisco, CA.

Singh, J. (1993) "Boundary role ambiguity: facets, determinants, and impacts". *Journal of Marketing*, vol. 57, no. 2, pp. 11–31.

Ulwick, A. W. (2002) "Turn customer input into innovation". *Harvard Business Review*, vol. 80, no. 1, pp. 91–97.

Webster Jr, F. E. & Wind, Y. (1972) *Organizational Buyer Behaviour*. Prentice Hall, Englewood Cliffs, NJ.

Williamson, O. (1985) *The Economic Institutions of Capitalism*. The Free Press, New York, NY.

Yankelovich, D. (1964) "New criteria for market segmentation". *Harvard Business Review*, vol. 42, no. 2, pp. 83–90.

9

The Role of Unexpected Market Events in Market Creation Strategies

Gabriele Troilo & Salvio Vicari

It all begins with three US sailing enthusiasts, one of whom has bought a pair of foam clogs in Canada, made by a Canadian manufacturer, Finprojects.[1] The clogs are made of a special resin called Croslite which makes the shoe extraordinarily comfortable and odour resistant: perfect for sailing. The three men believe that other sailing lovers may find the clog interesting and decide to build a business around it by distributing Finprojects' product with the brand name Crocs. They set up their base in Florida, to work in the same place where they go sailing. The business starts well, with 1 million US dollars in revenues in 2003. But, completely unexpectedly, Crocs clogs become very popular among doctors, waiters, gardeners, and other people who have jobs that keep them on their feet all day long. Revenues go up at an impressive pace. The new company buys Finprojects and gains full control of the manufacturing process. The product can be slightly changed by adding colour variants and enhancing fashion appeal: that triggers the boom. Crocs spread all over the USA and even become a global phenomenon,

---

[1] For a detailed description of the Crocs case, see *CNN Business 2.0 Magazine*, 3 November 2006.

with celebrities adopting them too. In 2006, revenues reach 322 million US dollars, with 30% coming from foreign markets. At the 2007 Drapers Footwear Awards, which celebrate the best in footwear retailing, Crocs wins the Footwear Brand of the Year, the only award dedicated to manufacturers.

What is interesting about the Crocs story is that it represents the creation of a new market whose success was far beyond the expectations of the company that launched the product. The product was conceived for a single market segment, but the huge market now is made of completely different segments. And this was completely unexpected. The Crocs case is only one of many other stories where no company – neither the innovator nor its competitors – has the capacity to anticipate the birth and fast development of a new market that proliferates beyond all competitors' expectations.

In this chapter we will focus on the concept of unexpected market events as generators of completely new markets. Our point here is that those market events which are inexplicable, surprising, even unbelievable when you try to interpret them with the current conventional wisdom of competitors, have an enormous potential to bring completely new markets to life. Unfortunately, most companies do not give such events the necessary attention just because they do not fit with expectations; businesses find it easier to discard them simply as "chance". In the following sections, we first describe how new market creation, innovation, and unexpected market events are connected. To do that, we elaborate on the concept of market structural holes to identify the discrepancies between the evolution of supply and demand where a new market can nest and take life. Then, we provide a taxonomy of unexpected market events that will help us identify the processes that companies can implement to leverage on such events in order to innovate and create new markets. After describing these processes, exploration, and leveraging, we conclude with the organizational characteristics that make it easier for companies to identify and exploit unexpected market events.

Radical innovation, new market creation, and market structural holes

Innovation has two main driving forces: the market, when demand provides ideas for new product design, and technology, when science is transformed into new technical solutions. These two dimensions can be used to classify product innovation, as Chandy and Tellis suggest (1998). A technology involved in creating a new product may be completely different from, or a derivative of, an existing technology. Or, a new product can better fulfil key customer needs in comparison with existing products, that is, it offers improved or completely new benefits.

As suggested by Chandy and Tellis (1998), incremental innovation is such because it provides relatively low incremental benefits due to slight changes in technology. New products that incorporate existing technology are incremental innovations when customers do not perceive them as really new products. When moderate changes in technology have remarkable effects on customer needs (as perceived by customers themselves), innovations are market breakthroughs. Market breakthrough occurs only when customers perceive a high degree of innovativeness owing to some kind of reconfiguration in, say, product positioning, marketing approach, or distribution channels.

On the other hand, a technology breakthrough occurs when new technical solutions are improved but they have little effect on customer need fulfilment. Radical innovation has a significant impact on customers owing to major technological changes. A radical innovation occurs when new products incorporate a substantially new technology to satisfy existing customers and fulfil their needs better than competing products, that is, with a lower price and/or higher performances.

However, if you consider the degree of newness of customer needs that are satisfied by innovations (compared with needs currently satisfied by existing products), you can reconfigure the previous typology into a different one (Figure 9.1), where new market creation occurs when a new product satisfies completely new customer needs, by incorporating either a totally new technology or an existing one (e.g. Zhou, Yim, & Tse, 2005).

What are the conditions for creating a new market? When does this happen? How can a company identify the opportunity for market creation?

Every day, firms deal with the problem of managing existing products. They regularly face the challenge of incremental innovation, but it is not that common for businesses to focus on new market creation. The fact is that market creation is considered a highly unpredictable issue; it is very rare in the life of a company and extremely difficult to manage.

NEWNESS OF TECHNOLOGY		CUSTOMER NEEDS	
		Existing	New
	Low	Market breakthrough and incremental innovation	New market creation
	High	Technological breakthrough and radical innovation	

Figure 9.1 Innovation and new market creation

Theoretical literature on the creation of new markets is quite scarce, and the few studies on the topic attest to the high risk, uncertainty, and unpredictability in new market creation (e.g. Gort & Klepper, 1982). One explanation is that new markets arise because of technological, political, or regulatory changes (Bala & Goyal, 1994), which create opportunities to be seized by either incumbents or new companies.

According to a different explanation, new market creation can be seen as a social process that involves transforming an environmental opportunity into an innovation and then into a new market operated by a group of interested people. Creating a new market is a highly unpredictable and uncertain process, so people involved are not aware of what information is available, and, of that, what is relevant and worth trying to get (Sarasvathy & Dew, 2005). In this situation, managers and entrepreneurs use a "try and learn" approach. They try to organize some kind of coalition among possible actors (other managers, distributors, venture capitalists, customers) who have a strong enough motivation to work together to choose new possibilities and to bring something new to life. They transform existing solutions and needs into new ones in order to solve the current problems of the actors involved. If this process is successful, it enlarges the initial coalition to include new members, expanding until we have a new market. This usually takes a long time, because the process of creating a social network, which is the basis of the new market, is a time-consuming one.

In order to explain market creation, we consider both these explanations, adding the notion of the *market structural hole*.[2] A market structural hole is a mismatch between the existing offerings and the existing needs of customers (explicitly expressed or latent) in a market.

Every market changes systematically because customer needs, motivations, attitudes, and behaviours are continuously being modified by the thousands of stimuli they receive. Also, competitors regularly change their behaviour, trying to defend themselves from the decisions of their rivals and to outdo them in the struggle for market dominance. Distributors change their approaches as well, taking into account modifications in the supply market and changes in the demand market.

When, for any number of reasons, there is an asynchronous movement in supply and demand, we find a mismatch that can be very large and last for a long time. This mismatch is what we define as a structural hole. The larger and longer-lasting the mismatch, the bigger is the structural hole.

Changes in supply and demand are not synchronized by definition owing to a variety of factors:

- *Different elasticity to modifications in the business environment.* Companies, distributors, and customers have a different capacity to react to environmental modifications because they do not have the same ability to change their decisions and their behaviours. Rigidity can depend on a variety of possible factors, such as scarce cognitive pliability, past investments and exit barriers, path dependency effects, and time and cost of technological improvements. A different readiness to environmental changes brings about a market structural hole.
- *Lack of information about changes made by other actors.* Actors in a market take decisions and behave according to information about market evolution and the moves of other actors. However, when information is lacking, decisions and behaviours are taken on without a thorough representation of the market, and this causes a mismatch between demand and supply, leading to market structural holes.

---

[2] The concept of structural hole is derived from social network theory and was originally proposed by Burt (1992).

- *Cost of change.* Sometimes companies and customers are aware of the mismatch between them, but they think the cost of reducing the distance is too high when weighed up against the potential advantages. This perception can depend on the actual cost structure (for instance, rigidity associated with the fixed cost structure or with non-recoverable past investments) or an under-valuation of possible benefits associated with the change. Again, the existence of this cost leads to a market structural hole.

Whatever the origin, the existence of a market structural hole indicates that there are unmet customer needs that can be potentially satisfied. Therefore, *market creation consists in filling up market structural holes through innovation, by systematically searching, analysing, and replenishing them.* Referring back to Figure 9.1, new market creation occurs when a company is able to leverage on existing or completely new technology to fill a market structural hole and satisfy customer needs that are not satisfied by existing products.

The problem is: how can you identify structural holes? Our answer is: by identifying unexpected market events.

Unexpected market events, market structural holes, and expectations about the future

Unexpected market events (UMEs) are any events that are not in line with managers' expectations. They are not things that happen suddenly, but events that are different from what was expected. Managers usually judge the likelihood of a given event on the basis of how easily they can imagine it happening. They do so because they anticipate future events according to past experience, sometimes based on simple prejudice. When managers have strong expectations about the future, UMEs are more likely to come up. In fact, expectations of market events have to do with customers' behaviours and competitors' moves. These expectations are based on the experience of past behaviours and moves. When there is a mismatch between demand and supply in the market – a market structural hole, in our terms – past expectations cannot make sense of all the changes, and UMEs emerge. Hence, the stronger the expectations, the higher is the probability that UMEs will occur.

Such strong beliefs about the market often depend on a strong market orientation and linkages with customers that are too tight. A strong market orientation has proved to be a key factor in determining successful market behaviour, through better understanding of customer needs and higher customer satisfaction. Loose linkages with customers may have the negative effect of a poor customer orientation but also have positive effects, particularly on the ability of a company to remain flexible in a dynamic environment, and to grab market opportunities when they come up.

Customer tastes can be quite well defined when companies deal with existing products and markets. However, when customers face radically new products and new markets, their needs become evanescent, vague, and ill defined. This means the new market cannot spring up simply from existing or predicted needs. Mowery and Rosenberg (1979) and Dosi (1997) have made strong arguments against demand–pull theories, which add up to the conclusion that abstract demand has little influence on the creation of new markets (Sarasvathy & Dew, 2005). So some literature seems to suggest that firms should forget their customers if they really want to be radically innovative.

Loose ties with customers can allow companies to avoid the trap of a served market, that is, the influence of existing needs and customers on a company's innovative market behaviour (Hamel & Prahalad, 1994). Some empirical research seems to confirm that a strong market orientation leads to less radical innovation (e.g. Gatignon & Xuereb, 1997). Christensen (1997), in his research on innovation in the rigid disk-drive, copier, tyre, and computer industries, found that too strong a tie with customers had a negative impact on the ability of dominant players to maintain their market position through technological innovations. So having loose ties with customers positively affects the ability to innovate (Danneels, 2003), especially in fast-changing markets, where staying flexible and not too closely linked to existing needs can be a good strategy.

Nevertheless, tight linkages with customers produce quite strong expectations on probable future market trends. For instance, having a deep knowledge about customer needs implies that unshakable convictions about what to expect from the market go around the organization. Therefore, expectations about the market and its possible evolution are usually quite strong.

According to our prior definition of unexpected events, that is, something that is not in line with managers' expectations, such strong anticipation of future market events is the condition in which unexpected events are likely to come to light.

When managers are open minded, when they consider as many different out-comes as possible, they may not be surprised when something new happens. But if managers have strong ideas about future market events and something different happens, then they are really amazed. Unexpected market events occur especially when companies have strong market orientation, that is, a tight coupling with their customers.

Consistent with this view, some authors suggest that companies should have a "future-market focus" – that is, they should focus on future customer needs and competitors' moves, instead of and regardless of current ones – because such companies show a terrific ability radically to innovate (Chandly & Tellis, 1998). Firms with a strong orientation towards future markets broaden their horizons and are ready to detect new technologies, new competitors, and new needs (Moorman, 1995). A good example of a company with a future-market focus is Nokia, leader in the cell phone industry. In fact, when Apple announced its intention to launch i-Phone as an evolution of its successful iPod and a potential breakthrough in the telephone market, Nokia immediately began to work on a new product that could outperform the expected features of Apple's new product.

Types of unexpected market event

UMEs emerge when companies face market structural holes with a strong, conventional view of the market. There are three major types of UME: unexpected market re/actions, accidents, and market contradictions.

- *Unexpected market re/actions.* Companies act in a given market according to a view of that market and a planned set of activities. They act expecting a reaction from their customers and competitors. For instance, a company launches a new product after having identified target market segments with certain needs served by specific competitors. This company expects some reactions from both the targeted segments (buying the product, for example) and from identified competitors (launching me-too products). However, what may happen is that customers who were not targeted buy the new product, or competitors from completely different industries launch products to seize the new market opportunity. These events are totally unexpected for the company, and can open the door to new market creation.

Consider the success of SMS (Short Message Service). This means of sending messages of up to 160 characters to and from GSM mobile handsets has progressively become one of the most popular applications in the communication market, for both business and personal use. The first commercial SMS message was sent in the United Kingdom in 1992. Initial growth was slow, among other things because operators did not set up adequate side services for a product they did not see as having a high market potential. Why would the mass market be interested in a way to send simple, short messages instead of speaking directly? Initially, people used SMS to save time and money. No one believed that the service would be used as a means of sending text messages. Unexpectedly, a lot of customers started using SMS as a new and different way of communication. SMS has become one of the most profitable and growing services for mobile operators and is now one of the largest markets in the TLC industry. The number of SMS users in 2006 reached around 1.36 billion.

Unexpected successes and failures are typical examples of unexpected market reactions. According to Peter Drucker (1986), no other area offers a better opportunity for innovation than unexpected success. It occurs when you project positive results in a product launch, but actual revenues or profits are much higher than planned and even hoped. Sometimes this happens because sales also come from customers who were not in the company's target. Other times products are extremely successful because customers use them for a different application that was not projected by the technical or marketing team. In such cases the unexpected success can be an indicator that a completely new category of needs is being satisfied by the new product. Therefore, a market structural hole has been intercepted and a new market can be created.

Managers hardly understand and recognize an unexpected success as an opportunity for a new market creation because this could be a challenge to their ability to judge and to evaluate their own products and markets. And they quite often prefer to consider a success as no more than that, and stop there.

If it is difficult to recognize a success as a source of a big opportunity, it is much harder to evaluate a failure as such. Unexpected failure is quite a common outcome in innovation processes. Most new products fail for technical or marketing reasons, and in many cases such products have to be discontinued; the result is a loss for the company. However, failures are not necessarily bad if they are the take-off point for discovering a new promising market.

When a failure is due to incapacity, ignorance, superficiality, or sluggishness, then it is probably nothing more than a simple mistake; as such there is no opportunity in it, only costs and losses. However, as Drucker (1986) noted, when something is carefully analysed, evaluated, planned, and implemented, the failure is something more. It means that something nobody had understood has happened or is happening: that demand is moving elsewhere, that distribution channels are changing, or that competition is changing in some fundamental way. Understanding what is going on could reveal a very interesting market structural hole.

The story of Jacuzzi is a good example of an initial failure that ended up as a great success. At the beginning of the last century, seven Jacuzzi brothers immigrated to California from Italy. They invented the first enclosed cabin monoplane, an accomplishment that led to the airplane that carried mail for the US Postal Service, and passengers from the San Francisco Bay Area to Yosemite National Park. In 1956, the idea of treating a family member's arthritis symptoms with a hydrotherapy pump came up. The Jacuzzi brothers invented a pump that did not enjoy the hoped-for success, because few arthritis sufferers could afford the expensive bath. A small niche business was developed by providing the J-300, a portable pump, to hospitals and schools. The idea languished until they tried to solve the problem of the high cost of the product, targeting a new market. Roy Jacuzzi, a third-generation family member, sensing the American consumer interest in health, fitness, and leisure activities, marketed the first self-contained, fully integrated whirlpool bath in 1968. While his family members looked on with both surprise and delight, Roy slowly – and nearly single-handedly – created a brand new industry. The Roman whirlpool tub became an icon of free-spirited relaxation in the 1970s. Today, Jacuzzi has become the world's most recognized and largest-selling brand of jetted/whirlpool baths and spas.

- *Accidents.* Accidental market events can be due to a phenomenon called serendipity. According to Wikipedia, serendipity can be defined as "the effect by which one accidentally discovers something fortunate, especially while looking for something else entirely". The word derives from an old Persian tale and was coined by Horace Walpole on 28 January 1754. In a letter he wrote: "I once read a silly fairy tale, called The Three Princes of Serendip: as their highnesses travelled, they were always making discoveries, by accidents and sagacity, of things which they were not in quest of" (Lewis, 1965).

Serendipity is not easy to illustrate, because inventors and managers are reluctant to confess that the merit of their successes is due to an accidental and unexpected discovery. In fact, serendipity is a major component of breakthroughs and scientific discoveries. Aspartame, for example, one of the most popular sugar substitutes, was discovered accidentally.[3] In most food, a sweet taste is frequently associated with calories and carbohydrates, and much effort has long been put into finding alternative solutions. For example, saccharin was discovered in 1879 and used in many different products. In 1965, a researcher at Searle and Co., James Schlatter, was using aspartame in his work on an anti-ulcer drug. Inadvertently, some aspartame spilled on his hand, but he did not wash it off because he knew it was not toxic. Only when he accidentally licked his finger did he discover aspartame's sweet taste. Searle introduced the product into the market in 1983.

Another innovation that is the fruit of serendipity is the Velcro hook and loop fastener.[4] The story begins with George de Mestral, a Swiss engineer, taking a walk through the countryside with his dog one day in 1941. On his return, he noticed that flowers of mountain thistles were tenaciously stuck to his clothes and his dog's fur, and very difficult to detach. He removed them carefully and observed them under a microscope. He discovered that the flowers were covered in hundreds of tiny but strong hooks that allow them to attach themselves to any soft surface. From that day, Velcro – from the French words "velours" (loop) and "crochet" (hook) – became a revolutionary fastening system whose simplicity and strength superseded all previous systems.

One of the innovations reported to be a serendipitous outcome is the discovery of a process that gave life to the inkjet printer at Canon. In 1977, Canon wanted to create a better xerographic technology. Ichiro Endo, one of the company's researchers, accidentally touched the tip of an ink-filled syringe with a hot soldering iron while fabricating a piezoelectric system. The ink inside heated up suddenly, increased in volume, and spurted forth. The squirt of ink changed the course and fortunes of Canon's research and led to the development of a simple inkjet printer that was known as the Bubblejet. Endo became Canon's Director of Product Development.

A more recent example of a successful company created after a serendipitous discovery is Geox, described in Box 9.1.

---

[3] Source: Stacey, L. (ed.) (2002) "Aspartame", in *How Products are Made*. Gale Group, Inc., Blachford. [Online]. eNotes.com (2006). Available: <http://www.enotes.com/how-products-encyclopedia/aspartame> [20 November 2007].
[4] For further information, see www.velcro.com.

Box 9.1 Geox: seek good questions if you look for good answers

In the early 1990s, an Italian wine entrepreneur was in Nevada to present his products at a wine show. At the end of a working day he went for a walk wearing his old sneakers with rubber soles. The hot weather made his feet uncomfortably overheated. To cool them off, he used a knife to make one hole in each sole, and it worked! When he went back to Italy he looked for new shoes with rubber soles that would let his feet breathe, but there were none to be found: the fact was that any hole in the sole would allow water to get into the shoes. Intrigued by this challenging technical problem, he started to work on the idea by looking for technical solutions by scanning specialized technical sources. He discovered that NASA used a special membrane for astronaut spacesuits, with millions of microscopic holes, which permitted body transpiration while being impermeable at the same time. That could be a solution for his problem. He made some sole prototypes with this material – and got a world patent on it – and ended up with a satisfactory product, a good product, he thought, that could be sold to shoemakers both in the casual and in the sport sectors: the breathing shoe. But all the companies he contacted rejected his proposal, as they didn't see any business opportunity in it. In 3 years' time, convinced of the existence of a big market opportunity, the entrepreneur created his own shoe company in 1995 and named it Geox. In 2006, company revenues reached 612 million euros, 50% from 68 foreign markets. Geox is the number-one shoe brand in Italy and the third in the world. It has opened 517 owned shops and sells to 10 000 other shops.

- *Market contradictions.* A market contradiction emerges when two or more market events appear to represent completely inconsistent, paradoxical phenomena. For example, in a market whose customers have a very low income, top-price product sales might reach an all-time record. Or, the technological level of customers in an industry may be very high, but high-tech products sell very few units.

Aristotle's law of contradiction states that "one cannot say of something that it is and that it is not in the same respect and at the same time". This means that what we consider market contradictions are nothing but events we cannot really understand because we use too simple an explanation. When we discover why such events occur, we have probably discovered a market structural hole. An example is the story of Franco Maria Ricci (FMR), an Italian publishing company. In the 1970s and 1980s, book and magazine reading was expected to decline owing to the development of new media and new types of entertainment, like TV, music players, computers, and so on. Many market studies showed that people were less interested in reading than in other pastimes, and there was evidence that consumers were less and less inclined to spend money on magazines and books. Nevertheless, in the same period, a high-quality book publishing company, FMR, enjoyed unexpected success owing to great attention to detail, well-written texts, and cultural and artistic inquisitiveness. It used top-quality paper and printing, perfect graphics, and elegant bindings, as well as texts by famous writers and essayists like Umberto Eco, William Saroyan, Federico Zeri, Octavio Paz, Roy Strong, and Jorge Luis Borges. When everybody expected a decline in turnover for books and magazines and consequently publishers to divest or diversify, why should anyone invest in a publishing company? Nevertheless, this company won success in traditional, high-quality, and expensive books. This was an evident market contradiction. Marilena Ferrari, a sales representative of a publishing company, understood that people wanted to buy high-quality books not to spend time reading but because they wanted something magical, in which beauty, rarity, and exclusivity were the key features: it was a market structural hole. When people buy a volume like an FMR one they are getting an exclusive work of art, and this has nothing to do with reading a book. Ferrari decided to exploit this structural hole, and in 1992 she founded Art'e' ("It's Art"), a company whose business is to promote and sell artwork, fine books, and cultural events. Art'e' started its operations in Italy, and then extended them to Europe; now it is worldwide. The company achieved major success, and, after a sizeable growth in turnover, shares were floated on the stock exchange. In 2003, FMR was acquired, becoming the brand name of the new group.

From UMEs to market creation: exploration and leverage

In order to exploit the potential of UMEs for strategic market creation, a company should implement two processes: stimulate the emersion of UMEs and leverage on them to innovate.

Since UMEs come from market structural holes combined with the existence of strong market conventional wisdom shared among competitors, UME emersion can occur by exploring these holes and by challenging this wisdom. As described above, market structural holes stem from demand and supply evolution that follows different trajectories. So any exploration process of this kind should focus on portions of the market where demand and supply do not match.

Tapping into marginal market segments

Consider [yellow tail] and its huge success in the US wine market.[5] At the beginning of the new century, the US was the third wine market in the world for aggregate consumption, but only the thirty-third for per capita consumption. The market could be considered as split into two main market segments: premium wines and budget wines. Basically, competitors in both segments viewed their customers as informed wine drinkers who considered wine a unique beverage for special occasions. In both segments, strategic efforts of most competitors concentrated on launching more sophisticated wines for the same usage occasions. From the market point of view, the only big difference between the two groups of offerings was price. Given this situation, an Australian company, Casella Wines, focused its attention on the segment of non-wine drinkers, who were 3 times as numerous as wine drinkers. The company came up with the idea that this larger group considered wine as too complex a beverage, and wine appreciation depended on the availability of product knowledge and technical jargon. Thus, Casella Wines decided to launch a new wine brand, [yellow tail], which was targeted at non-wine drinkers as a social, easy drink that every consumer could approach. To build this positioning, Casella Wines eliminated any product feature that could make the product complex: the wine has a soft, fruity taste based on primary flavours that can meet the average consumer's tastes. There is no ageing, no alleged legacy, no technical jargon on the label, which, on the contrary, shows a kangaroo in bright colours, making the bottle very eye-catching and more like other beverage bottles. By August 2003, [yellow tail] was the number-one imported wine in the US, and by 2004 it sold more than 11 million cases. And this result was achieved by broadening the customer base of the whole industry, transforming 6 million non-wine drinkers into actual consumers.

The [yellow tail] case is very informative in showing that, when a market moves towards the maturity stage, customer preferences and competitor actions tend to

---

[5] For a detailed description of this case, see Kim and Mauborgne (2005).

become more stable. On the supply side, competitors tend to pay a lot of attention to each others' moves, and to converge towards similar offerings; by so doing, they also converge towards a shared conventional wisdom about the market. This usually brings about two different market configurations: a concentration of offerings on the largest and most profitable market segments (the so-called "mainstream customers") or market fragmentation, that is, smaller segments each served by more specialized suppliers (the US wine market case). In both circumstances there is a portion of customer preferences that do not match with supplier offerings. In the first case, non-mainstream market segments are forced to adapt their preference curve to that of mainstream customers; in the second case, customers whose preferences are not so well articulated are forced to choose among specialized offerings. Of course, in both cases, customers can decide not to buy products currently available on the market. (Again, this was the case of non-wine drinkers in the US beverage market.) So in both cases there is a mismatch, which gives life to a market structural hole, and a company that focuses its attention on those segments can make a UME emerge. The extraordinary success of Ryanair in the airline industry (see Box 9.2) can give us another important example of market creation following the exploration of new market segments.

Box 9.2   Ryanair: every mainstream market is a niche at the beginning

The growth of the number of Ryanair passengers is astonishing: from 7.2 million in 2000 up to 42.5 million in 2006 (source: www.ryanair.com). How is that possible, especially after 9/11, which proved to be a serious threat to the whole airline industry?

The history of Ryanair began in 1985 when the company was set up by the Ryan family and launched its first route with daily flights from Waterford in the south-east of Ireland to London Gatwick. In 1986, Ryanair obtained permission from the regulatory authorities to operate a Dublin–London route, challenging the British Airways and Aer Lingus high-fare duopoly. The launch fare of £99 return was less than half the price of the BA/Aer Lingus lowest return fare of £209. This strategic price choice would characterize the whole history of the company. Today, Ryanair operates flights all over Europe, and, with a fleet of more than 100 aircraft, it has become the world's largest international airline. However, the peculiar price strategy cannot explain the huge success of the company, which basically created a completely new market in Europe. From the 1970s up to the 1990s in the international airline industry, competitors focused their strategic efforts on the most profitable market segment (at that time): business-class passengers. This strategy was pursued by offering a broad array of on- and off-board services, improving the comfort of the trip, investing in massive loyalty programmes, and developing new international routes to central, attractive locations. A very large part of the potential market was actually kept away from airline services by excessively high fares and, above all, by not having specific reasons to travel. Moreover, small airports are scattered all across Europe, located in cities that are off the main air traffic routes, mostly in economically underdeveloped areas. With its low-fare strategy – combined with intense communication campaigns – Ryanair transformed millions of potential customers into actual customers by giving them a reason to travel. By so doing, the airline has been able to create a connection between a potential demand and a potential supply of tourist attractions. In fact, low fares (that sometimes become no fares at all) make travelling so cheap that many people may find moving around Europe for a few days more convenient than travelling within their own country. This mass of people is also a resource for the underdeveloped areas where small airports are located, which offer Ryanair extremely attractive conditions to fly there. Hence, Ryanair created a completely new business model in the airline industry and a completely new market.

Injecting creativity in gathering and interpreting market information

When most companies share similar conventional wisdom about the market, information regarding market segments and customer preferences and behaviours is usually collected and interpreted in a very similar way. When an undifferentiated view of the market is shared, competitors tend to adopt analogous segmentation strategies and adapt their offerings to the way they represent market segments. Again, a consequence of this behaviour is that offerings tend to be slightly differentiated over time. So a company that uses information in a creative way, and combines data about customers in an unorthodox manner, can build a different view of the market and make underserved segments emerge. The assumption behind this exploration strategy is that every customer can belong to many different segments of preference according to the various segmentation criteria companies use to interpret their markets. By changing interpretation criteria, a company can achieve a completely different view of the market and interpret customer preferences in a novel way. Let's take Linea D'Ombra, the most successful art exhibition organizer in the Italian market.[6] Owing to its immense artistic and cultural heritage, Italy has a long tradition in the organization of art exhibitions. For a long time, large-scale art exhibitions were organized by publically owned museums and institutions that designed temporary shows leveraging on their rich collections. A large number of privately owned organizers operated in the country, but they mostly focused on small-scale exhibitions targeted at local or regional audiences. Based on the conventional wisdom that the main audience of art exhibitions is made up of art-literate citizens – a very small fraction of the population, identified by a high-level education – organizers habitually concentrated their efforts on the quality of the works displayed. What is more, the shared belief was that only large arts cities and historically relevant sites could attract large audiences. Blockbuster exhibitions that were typical of other countries were snobbishly labelled as "pure quality marketing initiatives" for customers with poor cultural capital in search of a way to pass their leisure time. Linea D'Ombra was a small exhibition organizer operating in the north-east of Italy. The experience gained in its small market suggested that the conventional wisdom shared by large-scale organizers could no longer hold true. The belief about large-scale exhibitions corresponded to a shared view of the market that considered only art literates as potential targets for art exhibitions. However, the arts were more and more in the media agenda, and people with a rich cultural background who were not specialized in the arts (a rapidly increasing portion of the Italian population) could also be attracted by arts events. Those people were interested not only in the quality of single artworks but also in a theme that could be represented through the exhibition. Further, visitors were increasingly interested in the full experience of the visit, beyond the exhibition in itself. Thus, the company used this unorthodox view of the market to design an exhibition plan to be deployed in 3–5 years' time, by gathering artworks often never displayed before in Italy, courtesy of individual collectors, and aggregating them around easy-to-grasp themes. Leveraging on the sponsorship of a local bank, they launched a

---

[6] For a detailed description of the evolution of Linea D'Ombra's competitive strategies, see Calcagno, Faccipieri, and Rocco (2005).

programme of temporary exhibitions on the Impressionists in Treviso (a small town in the north-east) in a building that had no historical interest at all. The first four exhibitions (over a 4-years time span) were attended by 600 000 people on average, gaining one of the top spots in the world art exhibition attendance rankings. Now, Linea D'Ombra is considered one of the best art exhibition organizers in Europe.

Setting up market experimentations

Experimenting in a market consists of testing the reactions of customers (and competitors) to an innovative offering that is not developed to its ultimate configuration but is still open to further developments (e.g. Hamel & Prahalad, 1991). The main difference between market experimentation and the traditional innovation process lies in the belief that the innovative offering launched into the market is not the conclusion of the innovation process but the beginning, and that is where UMEs emerge. In fact, the final outcome is the result of many interactions between the actions of the company, the customers, and the competitors which will give the offering its final configuration. Basically, market experimentation is a process of co-creation of the offering with the – often unaware – fundamental contribution of customers and competitors. Consider Italian firm Pastificio Rana, the 200 million euro fresh pasta maker.[7] The company became market leader in Italy, France, Spain, and other smaller European countries by paying extraordinary attention to product quality and the construction of a brand personality based on genuine, traditional values. In 2000, a diversification process was started. The market insight was that an increasing number of people were used to having lunch away from home, and a significant percentage complained about the quality of the food, quite different from what they would eat at home. Since Rana had the product many people consumed at home, managers thought it could be a good opportunity to let customers find the same pasta away from home as well. The company built a partnership with an Italian grocery retailer to open a corner in two of their stores, with the brand "La Trattoria di Giovanni Rana". Basically it was an Italian fast food place that served the company's products. Since this new business required completely new competences for the company, the two corners were used as experiments to learn about the acceptability of the product and the consistency with the company competences. The

---

[7] For a detailed description of the diversification strategy, see the interview with Giovanni Rana, founder and president of the company, in *Micro and Macro Marketing*, December 2005.

experiments were successful, but Rana learned that the investment would have exceeded its possibilities. Rana needed a partner, and it came from France. Casino, the French retailing company, found the idea very attractive, also owing to the large awareness of the Giovanni Rana brand in the country. A partnership was built, and "La Trattoria Giovanni Rana" restaurants were opened in 100 Casino stores, combining the retailing competences of the French partner and the product competences of the Italian partner.

Fostering serendipity

The story of 3M Post-its is one of the most renowned in the history of consumer product innovation.[8] The formula for the sticky back was developed in 1968 – many years before its actual launch – by a 3M scientist, but it was put aside because its technical performance was poor: the sticking capacity of the product lasted for a short time, and was not very strong. Another scientist of the company loved to sing, and he did it regularly in a church choir of the city. He had to deal with a disappointing problem. To find out quickly the songs he had to sing, he used to put bookmarks in the hymnal. Unfortunately, those bookmarks regularly kept falling out, causing him to lose his place. Finding a way to solve the problem, the researcher stepped into the old formula and took it back to improve it and solve his personal problem. This was made possible by the 3M "bootlegging" policy, that is, technical staff members are encouraged to spend up to 15% of their working time on projects they choose. Post-it was market tested starting from 1977, and launched in the whole US market in 1980.

When companies have a consolidated view of the market, they tend to focus only on the part of the market that they can interpret and make sense of from that perspective. This view becomes a sort of a constraint to the import of completely new signals within the organizational knowledge repository, and, in some respects, it raises massive barriers to novelty. For example, for the market segments 3M was serving in the late 1960s, the Post-it formula was uninteresting. The focus on the benefits sought by actual customers narrowed 3M's field of vision, limiting the company's possibility to imagine other applications of the formula. And only a staff member's attempt to find the answer to a personal problem gave life to an unexpected solution. To explore UMEs, a company may encourage its members to seek out completely new information by accessing

---

[8] For a detailed description of the Post-it case, see www.3m.com.

far-from-the-norm environments: different industries, different market segments, geographical markets far afield, and non-business events and situations. The new information collected will offer an enriched view of the actual market or provide the chance to build completely new market opportunities.

Seeking and reconciling market contradictions

As seen above, a market contradiction is hardly an objective characteristic of the market, but it usually depends on the inability of the knowledge structures of current competitors to explain why such contradicting events occur. Reconciling market contradiction basically means building a superordinate cognitive representation of the market that can make those events compatible. It implies the move from an "or...or" view of the market to an "and...and" one, where apparently contradictory events can be tied into a common explanation. To do that, a company should recognize that every representation of the market is based on strong assumptions about customer and competitor attitudes and behaviours. Those assumptions are cognitive simplifications of actors that depend on current limitations of technology, products, customer competences, and more. Building a superordinate cognitive representation implies imagining how market reality could be different if such conditions changed. And so, basically, reconciling market contradictions consists in working out how to remove the constraints that give life to these contradictions.

The huge success of Unilever's brand "Quattro salti in padella" is a perfect example of how to reconcile market contradictions.[9] In the mid-1990s, the Italian frozen food market showed a clear market contradiction. On the one hand, consumer life styles were evolving: the number of women working outside the home had increased dramatically; less time was devoted to cooking; the average cooking competences of young consumers was on the decline; natural, genuine, tasty food was in high demand. The frozen food market was born in the 1970s precisely to serve those life styles, but after 20 years the penetration of frozen food in Italian families was very limited and the size of the market at the time was dropping at a steady pace (from more than 6 000 tons in 1990 to some 5 000 tons in 1995). There was a clear contradiction. However, this contradiction originated in

---

[9] For a detailed description of the development of "Quattro salti in padella", see the interview by Antonella Di Donato, Marketing and Business Director of Unilever's frozen food division, in *Micro and Macro Marketing*, April 2007.

the knowledge shared among competitors regarding the benefits sought by frozen food buyers: time-saving in food preparation and long-term conservation. Thus, most products in the market were precooked pasta dishes and vegetables, the quality of which was very different from home-cooked food. Unilever managers viewed the market differently, by thinking about how to provide customers with a time-saving product that consumers could perceive as being at the same quality level as home-made food. The idea came up to develop traditional Italian dishes, with ingredients that respected the original recipe; customers would prepare this food not just by warming it up in the microwave but by giving it a final touch as well. The quality of the product is ensured because every phase of the production process is carried out internally. The brand name clearly expresses the benefits of the product: in Italian "saltare in padella" is the final activity a cook does to give the perfect taste to a dish, and "quattro salti" is a way of expressing dynamism and movement (like in a disco). "Quattro salti in padella" was launched in 1996 and since then has given a boost to the whole frozen food market: from about 5 000 tons in 1995 to 30 000 in 2006. Its market share today is 60%, with 92% brand awareness.

Conclusion: organizational characteristics supporting exploration and leveraging

Exploring and leveraging on UMEs are highly risky processes. They challenge conventional beliefs, consolidated practices, and efficiently managed activities. This prevents many companies from pursuing an effective exploitation of UMEs and constrains them into the reassuring borders of traditional innovation processes. A company that wants to exploit a UME to foster strategic market creation should be aware of the cognitive, temporal, and financial burden this implies both at an individual and an organizational level.

That is the reason why effective processes of exploration and leverage on UMEs require specific organizational characteristics, in terms of culture, climate, and systems. A *culture* that tends towards conformity hinders the acceptance of the unexpected (cf. Atuahene-Gima, Slater, & Olson, 2005). The ability to build on UMEs depends on the sense of security that organizational members have; they know they are acting in a protected environment where the search for novelty, experimentation, and serendipity are considered fundamental to foster innovation. A culture that is tolerant of errors promotes the willingness to take risks and deal with consequent uncertainty (Smith, Collins, & Clark, 2005).

Beyond organizational culture, openness to the unexpected is favoured by an organizational *climate* that stimulates cooperation and hence interaction. In this regard, an essential element is trust, among members of the organization and in critical actors external to it. In a climate that favours cooperation, employees are more motivated to embark on new paths where the unexpected, and its resulting uncertainty, would find fertile ground. In such a climate, interaction between members of the organization, and between these people and external actors, is based on respect and the conviction that the contribution of the others is indispensable.

Among organizational *systems*, the marketing information system plays a key role in identifying UMEs and amplifying their potential within the company (Vicari & Troilo, 1998; Nonaka, Reinmoeller, & Senoo, 2000). This system must be designed to guarantee that built-in sensors can pick up signals from different parts of the market and various environments. Moreover, this system must be able to disseminate data to all actors who can contribute to challenging traditional views of the market, and must also allow market views to be retained. Only by retaining those views can the company formalize the system of expectations which is then used to compare UMEs and make sense of them.

References

Atuahene-Gima K., Slater, S. F., & Olson, E. M. (2005) "The contingent value of responsive and proactive market orientations for new product program performance". *Journal of Product Innovation Management*, vol. 22, 464–482.

Bala, V. & Goyal, S. (1994) "The birth of a new market". *The Economic Journal*, vol. 104, pp. 282–290.

Burt, R. S. (1992) *Structural Holes: the Social Structure of Competition*. Harvard University Press, Cambridge, MA.

Calcagno, M., Faccipieri, S., & Rocco, E. (2005) "Consumo culturale 'di massa' e nuove forme di offerta: il caso Linea D'Ombra". *Micro and Macro Marketing*, no. 3, pp. 495–514.

Chandy, R. H. & Tellis, G. J. (1998) "Organizing for radical product innovation: the overlooked role of willingness to cannibalize". *Journal of Marketing Research*, November, pp. 474–487.

Christensen, C. (1997) *The Innovator's Dilemma: When New Technologies Cause Great Firms to Fail.* Harvard Business School Press, Boston, MA.

Danneels, E. (2003) "Tight–loose coupling with customers: the enactment of customer orientation". *Strategic Management Journal*, vol. 24, pp. 559–576.

Dosi, G. (1997) "Opportunities, incentives and the collective patterns of technological change". *The Economic Journal*, vol. 109, pp. 1530–1547.

Drucker, P. F. (1986) *Innovation and Entrepreneurship.* Harper & Row Publishers, New York, NY.

Gatignon, H. & Xuereb, J.-M. (1997) "Strategic orientation of the firm and new product performance". *Journal of Marketing Research*, February, pp. 77–90.

Gort, M. & Klepper, S. (1982) "Time paths to diffusion of product innovations". *The Economic Journal*, vol. 92, pp. 630–653.

Hamel, G. & Prahalad, C. K. (1991) "Corporate imagination and expeditionary marketing". *Harvard Business Review*, July–August, pp. 81–92.

Hamel, G. & Prahalad, C. K. (1994) *Competing for the Future.* Harvard Business School, Boston, MA.

Kim, W. C. & Mauborgne, R. (2005) "Blue ocean strategy: from theory to practice". *California Management Review*, vol. 47, no. 3, pp. 105–121.

Lewis, W. S. (ed.) (1965) *Horace Walpole's Correspondence,* Yale edition, in the book, by Remer, T. G., *Serendipity and the Three Princes, from the Peregrinaggio of 1557* (with an Introduction and Notes by Remer, T. G. and a Preface by Lewis, W. S.). University of Oklahoma Press, OK.

Moorman, C. (1995) "Organizational market information processes: cultural antecedents and new product performance". *Journal of Marketing Research*, August, pp. 318–335.

Mowery, D. & Rosenberg, N. (1979) "The influence of market demand upon innovation: a critical review of some recent empirical studies". *Research Policy*, vol. 8, pp. 102–153.

Nonaka, I., Reinmoeller, P., & Senoo, D. (2000) "Integrated IT systems to capitalize on market knowledge", in *Knowledge Creation. A Source of Value*, edited by von Krog, G., Nonaka, I., & Nishiguchi, T. Macmillan, London, UK.

Sarasvathy, S. D. & Dew, N. (2005) "New market creation through transformation". *Journal of Evolutionary Economics*, vol. 15, pp. 533–565.

Smith, K. G., Collins, C. J., & Clark, K. D. (2005) "Existing knowledge, knowledge creation capability, and the rate of new product introduction in high-technology firms". *Academy of Management Journal*, vol. 2, 346–357.

Vicari, S. & Troilo, G. (1998) "Errors and learning in organizations", in *Knowing in Firms. Understanding, Managing and Measuring Knowledge*, edited by von Krogh, G., Roos, J., & Kleine, D. Sage, London, UK.

Zhou, K. Z., Yim, C. K., & Tse, D. (2005) "The effects of strategic orientations on technology- and market-based breakthrough innovations". *Journal of Marketing*, April, pp. 42–60.

10

Beyond Blue Oceans – Implications of Entry Time for Actors in New Markets

Mads Vangkilde

Introduction

In 2005, two extremely well-written and compelling books were published on the subject of competition and timing. Kim and Mauborgne (2005) presented to the world the notion of blue ocean strategies, while Markides and Geroski (2005) described to us the phenomenon of fast seconds. The question that arises after reading these two outstanding books is whether or not firms can or should strive to be fast seconds onto a blue ocean?

This is, of course, a crude way of comparing the two pieces of work, but the basic premise prevails. If we subscribe to the idea of fast seconds as described (and documented) by Markides (2003) and Markides and Geroski (2005), then it becomes apparent that some aspects of blue ocean strategy are uncovered. Reflecting on the literature concerning innovation to understand how a new market is created and the prerequisites on which the firm now competes (Angelmar, 1990; Dollinger, 2002; Garcia & Calantone, 2002; Herbig, 1991; Rogers, 1995; Teece, 1986), we can understand prospective future competition in this new market. Establishing these fundamentals is insufficient, however. While a transition onto a new and less competitive market is desirable, the canon of business strategy remains once competitors follow. Old-fashioned virtues regarding resource imitability still apply, regardless of the market, the order of entry, and the fashion by which early entry into a new market was achieved. Discussing market creation in the context of competition calls for a treatise of sustainability of competitive advantages.

The purpose of this chapter is twofold: I propose a model to analyse the causality of order entry, and the effect on competitive advantages for each actor in a new or establishing market, and I convey the implications of this model for top-level management to secure a long-term (and successful) investment in a blue ocean strategy. The building blocks of this model stem from the areas of pioneering (Lieberman & Montgomery, 1988; Patterson, 1993; Kerin, Varadarajan, & Peterson, 1992; Gilbert & Birnbaum-More, 1996; Vangkilde, 2005) and sustainability of advantages (Barney, 1986, 1991, 1997; Alvarez & Barney, 2002; Dierickx & Cool, 1989; Peteraf, 1993; Wernerfelt, 1984). Work within the area of pioneering provides insights into the mechanisms enhancing or deteriorating advantages of early entry in a market. Looking at the area of strategy, we find insights as to how advantages are built, and how advantages are sustained over time. Combining these two areas provides an understanding and explanation of the causality and implications of entry timing in correlation with the competitive effect. The result is a model that assesses the imitability of the resources applied to produce the specific offerings of each actor in the new market, as well as an analysis of the mutual dependence and relationship between customers and the offering. The first assessment provides a bearing on the resource constellation from a traditional resource-based view of the firm, while the latter indicates the inclination of customers to switch between offerings in the market and the attractiveness of that market.

First-movers and market creators

First-mover advantage is a term that most scholars and businesspeople intuitively find familiar. The term itself is rather self-explanatory at first sight. There is, however, more than meets the eye. When asked more specifically about the nature of pioneering advantages, most people fall short of stating the obvious – that it denotes gains won by acting entrepreneurially. This section seeks to outline the elements of pioneering and to gain an explicit understanding of a first-mover.

Firstly, it is necessary to examine what a first-mover is characterized as, and which functions a pioneer fulfils. The reason why this is necessary links back to a recurring question concerning pioneering advantages – are they a real opportunity? The answer to this very valid question is given via the definition of a first-mover.

There should be no doubt that empirically proving the existence of first-mover advantages is difficult. Lieberman and Montgomery (1988) define a first-mover in the context of earning positive rents as a consequence of early entry. Although simple, this definition is operational and recognizable, leaving discussions on degrees of innovation, processes, and idea creation versus market introduction behind. Two quotes address these more complex elements of pioneering:

- "A firm can achieve first-mover status in numerous ways. For example, the first firm to (1) produce a new product, (2) use a new process, or (3) enter a new market can claim this distinction" (Kerin, Varadarajan, & Peterson, 1992, p. 33).
- "*Inventor* – the firm(s) that develop(s) patents or important technologies in a new product category. *Product pioneer* – the first firm to develop a working model or sample in a new product category. *Market pioneer* – the first firm to sell in a new product category" (Golder & Tellis, 1993, p. 159).

Kerin, Varadarajan, and Peterson (1992) introduce the notion that first-mover advantages can be achieved via new processes and/or new markets. Most often, first-movers are associated with new products. Pioneering advantages can be won through process innovation and new market generation. Golder and Tellis (1993) capture the distinction between idea generation, prototype production, and market penetration. In most instances, market pioneers will be remembered as the "inventor", but this may not be the case.

A crucial factor in discussing first-mover advantages is addressed when looking at the degree of novelty of a new idea. Radical change versus incremental change and disruptive innovation versus dynamically continuous innovation (Cooper, 2000) are terms applied in such a discussion. The disadvantage of engaging in a discussion on first-mover advantages using this terminology is that there is an element of intangibility. It is simply too difficult to make this terminology operational.

Through these statements, the problem of defining a first-mover becomes apparent – who was first, and with what? To sum up, a first-mover is one that earns positive rents from early entry. Early entry can be as an inventor of an idea, the producer of a prototype, or the organization leading the market introduction. Rents can be earned at all three stages, and individual success is not determined by market introduction alone. Lastly, the object of novelty to be introduced may encompass more than a new product. It can be a new process, or the creation of a new market such as that of grocery e-commerce.

The concept of first-mover advantage

The concept of first-mover advantage was broadly recognized with the seminal article by Lieberman and Montgomery in 1988. The developmental stages in the concept of first-mover advantage can broadly be categorized in two phases. The first was one of theoretical pre-understanding. The concept could be logically deduced from a theoretical perspective. In the early 1960s and 1970s, first-mover advantage became an empirically explored concept as well. Studies challenged its existence or explored specific aspects of its nature. The late 1980s marked a concept-based approach to the phenomenon. A brief introduction to the key contribution of all these phases is given here.

Bain (1956) argued that pioneering brands were able to build advantages via consumer awareness. Bain proposed that early entry resulted in early preference and promotional advantages that competitors could not overcome without massive investments in marketing and/or critical cost reductions. Mansfield, Schwartz, and Wagner (1981) examined the cost of imitation and patenting, thus addressing sustainability of advantages implicitly. Mansfield (1985) performed a second study on the phenomenon of technological diffusion. He found that imitation cost on average was 65% of innovation cost, leaving the time lag from pioneer to followers pivotal for success of the first-mover.

Between the two studies led by Mansfield, several other authors contributed to the understanding of first-moving. Lippman and Rumelt (1982) examine pre-emptive innovation, thereby introducing the term "uncertain imitability", addressing the notion that imitation can be more difficult than purely copying a product or process. The term "causal ambiguity" denotes this phenomenon, which is critical in a discussion on sustainability of advantages. Schmalensee (1982) looks at buyer uncertainty and preference asymmetry in the context of product differentiation as a function of entry time. Conrad (1983) focuses on imperfect information as a source for pricing advantages and market shares though pioneering, while Smiley and Ravid (1983) point to cost advantages, pricing, and demand elasticity caused by learning advantages as the key to pioneering advantages.

Robinson and Fornell (1985) and Robinson (1988) investigate the existence of pioneering advantages in the context of consumer and industrial goods respectively, ultimately finding that pioneering advantages are more likely to occur within consumer goods industries. Consumer goods pioneering advantages are influenced by relative consumer information, marketing mix, and relative direct cost, while the industrial goods industry was impacted by switching costs, marketing mix, and direct costs. By looking at 82 brands across 24 product categories, Urban *et al.* (1986) found that pioneering brands held advantages on account of order entry, market position, advertising expenditures, and time lags between competitor entries. Also, Schnaars (1986) found both first-mover advantages and disadvantages by examining entry timing in growth markets. Mechanisms accounting for first-mover advantages were image, experience, brand loyalty, and entry barrier erection, while forces working against first-mover advantages included learning from mistakes, resolving early uncertainty, product enhancements, and lower production costs. This study provided the first explicit account of mechanisms against pioneering advantages. Mary Lambkin (1988) published a study on 129 start-ups and 187 adolescent companies, naming a multitude of mechanisms for first-mover advantage stemming from three sources – relationship to parent organization, entry strategy, and competitive strategy, thereby explicitly acknowledging the overlap with existing business strategies.

In 1988, Lieberman and Montgomery published the first article treating first-mover advantage on a conceptual level, providing a framework for understanding the components and dynamics of first-mover advantage. The origins of first-mover advantages were categorized into three main groups: technological leadership, pre-emption of assets, and buyers' switching costs and uncertainty (Lieberman & Montgomery, 1988). A second important feature of this article was the grouping of second-mover advantages: free-riding, resolution of technological and market uncertainties, shifts in technology and customer needs, and finally inertia by the incumbent. Kerin, Varadarajan, and Peterson (1992) provide a new model for a conceptual understanding of first-mover advantage that encompasses both the strategic choices of first-movers and later entrants and later entrants' advantages as well as identifying four factors of first-mover advantage: economic, pre-emptive, technological, and behavioural. Patterson (1993) addresses the strategic nature of first-mover advantage, building on the preservation of advantages via the creation of strategic barriers. Here, a taxonomy of strategic emulation barriers supporting first-mover strategy is provided. Gilbert and Birnbaum-More (1996) elaborate on the notion of strategic application of timing strategies. This work yields a model to evaluate the advantages of being first or second to enter a new market.

Kardes and Kalyanaram (1992) investigated order entry effects on consumer memory and consumer judgement, stressing the potential for first-mover advantage within consumer goods. As a spin on the consumer aspect, Mahajan, Sharma, and Buzzell (1993) found branding and product life cycles at the heart of their study on instant photography. More recently, López and Roberts (2002) examined entry timing in regimes of weak appropriability; Shamsie, Phelps, and Kuperman (2004) considered market share versus survival rate; and Carow, Heron, and Saxton (2004) examined proprietary technology as a source of pioneering advantages among 1 042 manufacturing companies.

An illustration of these advantages, categorized according to their inherent origin, can be seen in Figure 10.1.

First-mover advantages do exist – there are gains to be won from acting entrepreneurially. However, these advantages do not come automatically. Any advantages that can be identified from acting entrepreneurially, as a first-mover, should be considered on the basis of the premise on which they are achieved and how fast competitors can catch up. Sustainability in the context of first-mover advantage is dealt with – implicitly. The entire concept is built on the balance of exploiting first-mover advantages and avoiding the pitfalls of competitors harvesting second-mover advantages. Essentially, this balance concerns durability of advantages. The problem with this approach in relation to durability is the lack of means of assessing the durability. We are given a frame of reference and a terminology to describe the durability, but no real means of assessing it, and therefore no means of understanding why firms would or would not embark on a new business venture. This applies to both the conceptual work of Lieberman and Montgomery (1988) and the application-oriented (decision support) work of Gilbert and Birnbaum-More (1996). To extract any real value from the concept of first-mover advantage, we need to develop a model to assess the durability of first-mover advantages.

Economic mechanisms: economies of scope, economies of scale, learning curve economics (lower unit costs) and use of excess production to build barriers	Pre-emptive measures: input factors, location, product characteristics, investments in plant and equipment, distribution channel, pre-empting scarce resources, pre-emptive innovation (developing product or product range).
Business strategy mechanisms: advertising intensity, managerial competences (decisions, risk taking and reward systems), firm policy, exit strategy, clarity & consistency of strategies, efficient scale to market size, research & development, marketing efforts (pricing, promotion and distribution),	Collaboration and strategic partnering: connection to technological infrastructure, decision to integrate and collaborate and minimising strategic dependence
Firm resource mechanisms: patens & trade secrets, organisational learning (from early start or multi-market participation), causal understanding, team proficiency, organisational values, broader product range, proprietary technology	
Mechanisms associated to innovation: degree of novelty of product, uniqueness, uncertain imitability, difficulty of production, complexity, compatibility, product form, product function, product intangibles, radical or incremental innovation.	
Firm capabilities	**Securing external capabilities**
Customer related mechanisms	**Industry related mechanisms**
Uncertainty mechanisms: demand uncertainty, buyers choice under uncertainty, price advantage (when purchase frequency is low and high costs are associated with product failure), more frequent trials and repeat purchases of pioneer product, uncertainty toward new products, pioneer status enhances purchase intention & credibility of firm, incomplete information/cognitive limitations/knowledge asymmetry.	Market related mechanisms: market type, market evolution, velocity of industry, fragmentation/concentration of industry, rate of innovation diffusion, technological change or discontinuity, entry scale, creation of new market, redefined markets or new technologies, advantages strongest in BtC over BtB
Switching costs: contractual, supplier specific learning, buyer adaptation, investments in co-specialised assets	Competitors: followers face vast investments in marketing, response time, degree of existing and future competition, average industry market shares
Brand building mechanisms: awareness from being first, brand building, sequential entry strongest, new products stronger than extensions, brand extensions stronger than new brands, new products in a brand extension strongest, information search costs, higher involvement (recall, retrieval in pioneer product) and occupying product characteristics shapes consumers perception of the entire product category.	Barriers by pioneer: deterrence (investments by pioneer – signalling resolve), competitive reputation, position of pioneer (brand, cost leader, niche) and better exploitation of Product Life Cycle by pioneer.

Figure 10.1 Mechanisms enhancing advantages of early entry

Assessing first-mover advantages

In order to understand the influence of durability of advantages on the first-mover advantage concept, the dynamics or causalities in offering a new product or service must be explained. To be successful in servicing a new market, two aspects need to be fulfilled: customers in sufficient numbers must value the new offering and temporal barriers must exist to prevent potential competitors from duplicating the offering. An illustration of this can be seen in Figure 10.2.

Causal ambiguity and durability

A critical element contained in the above model is causal ambiguity (in this context, causal ambiguity explains the potential gap between what firms produce

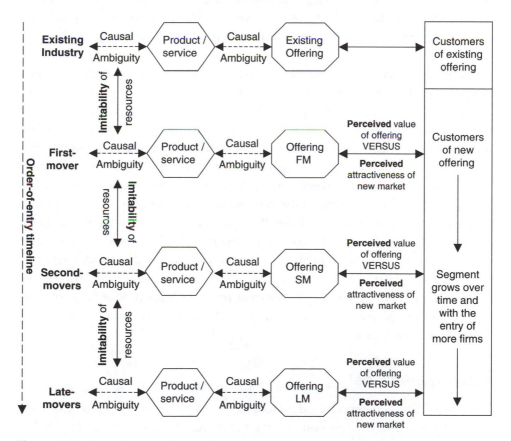

Figure 10.2 Causality of early entry

and what customers buy) between a product or service and the offering that consumers ultimately judge. This distinction is crucial because of the two prerequisites mentioned for successful pioneering of a new market: consumers valuing the offering and temporal barriers. When investigating durability of advantages, both need to be accounted for, as the new offering needs to be perceived as valuable in order to generate rents. An early problem encountered by e-grocers (in the case of San Francisco-based Webvan, even fatal) was the number of customers. As the market has developed, critical mass has been reached and rents can be earned. Now, the perceived value of the offering by the single e-grocer needs to be distinct from others to attract or retain consumers. Multiple, seemingly similar, offerings that consumers cannot differentiate will decrease the durability of (first-mover) advantages. Likewise, if a new market has proven to be profitable, temporal barriers need to be in place to prevent the erosion of resources applied in producing the product/service. Durability is therefore a function both of the imitability of resource constellations applied to produce a product or service and of the perceived value of a specific offering.

Arguing that durability of advantages (effectively addressing competitive advantages) stems both from the relative number of alternative choices (externally derived) and from resources applied in the production (internally derived) is rare – not because of the individual external and internal view, but because of the combination of them. When discussing competitive advantages, research often subscribes to one particular line of reasoning for the existence of such advantages. Very often this choice is between a model based on the resources found within a firm and a model that builds on the external environment of a firm. Adopting a view solely concentrated on either the internal or external view would be inappropriately limiting in the context of first-mover advantages. A first-mover is dependent on the procurement of an innovative idea and on the acceptance by the market of this idea, thus implying that the external environment (consumers' perception of alternatives) and the internal functionalities (resources applied in the production) play an equally significant role in the analysis of durability of first-mover advantages.

Applying the model

From an analytical perspective, the model indicates that the process of dissecting durability lies in analysing consumer perceptions and then proceeding to the resource constellations underlying the production of these value propositions. It is necessary to have an indication of which elements in an organization to analyse in order to keep the internal analysis on a manageable level. This means asking consumers about the perceived value of the offerings in the market. When dealing with a consumer–market problem, a single consumer may not be significant. Exposing the potential in different segments and quantities is, however. It is therefore necessary to identify relevant segments and to place each customer in these segments.

With these insights, the dependence analysis can then be performed on both the focal firm and the market to construct the indicated value, and also on the competitive environment to determine the imitability of those resources producing different offerings for the market. This implies an investigation of the value proposition as indicated by the consumers as well as the underlying resource constellations. Both the value proposition and the resources for this should, in order to yield a representative picture, be reflected upon by both the focal firm as well as the later-movers and potential competitors with substitute product offerings. Performing these two analyses will yield an answer about the durability of advantages gained by the first-mover.

The resource-based view (RBV) of the firm and resource dependence theory (RDT) will provide the models for analysing the perceived value of offerings by consumers and imitability of resource constellation by competitors. Barney (1997) provides a framework for the internal resource constellation and its imitability by competitors via the VRIO model. Pfeffer and Salancik (1978), on the other hand, support a model of relative dependence to understand the possible durability of advantages in a relationship. Treating the relationship between the first-mover and the consumers on a dyadic level provides an effective tool to understand how this can result in durable competitive advantages.

The VRIO model examines the competitive implications of resources by analysing each resource, capability, or core competence on four variables: value, rareness, imitability, and organization (to be exploited).

Tied into a relationship

A precondition of gaining competitive advantages from any kind of network or relationship is power. Mutual dependence and power in a cooperative relationship are determined via the control over resources (Weber, 2002; Gelderman &

Importance of resources	Scarcity of resources	Discretion over resource allocation and use
Measured on:	**Measured on:**	**Measured on:**
Relative magnitude of resource	Concentration of resources	Ownership
	Relative number of alternatives	Access
Criticality of the resource		External use

Source: Own illustration after Pfeffer & Salancik (1978).

Figure 10.3   Assessing perceived value of resources

van Weele, 1999). Applying this approach to the subject of evaluating the durability of advantages in a firm external perspective provides the tool necessary to supplement the VRIO analysis for the firm internal perspective. Gelderman and van Weele (1999) present a model on the situation of dependence. The relative dependence between two actors determines the relative power. As both parties in a relationship must be assumed to draw a benefit, a mutual dependence must exist. This dependence is described as the net dependence of each actor. Pfeffer and Salancik (1978) and Emerson (1962) propose that the relative power position between two actors be determined via three variables: importance of resources, scarcity of resources, and discretion over resource allocation and use.

As explained, the intent of this framework is to perform the analysis on consumer perception firstly. The implication is that, by looking at perceived output through offerings, the factors that go into the creation of advantages are already explored. Implicitly, these need to be organized by the firm to be exploited – otherwise there would be no effect to observe. I will be applying a modified model – value, rareness, and imitability – for the sake of my study on the imitability of resource constellations causing advantages. Modifications are also applied to the RDT analysis. The perceived value is analysed on the importance, scarcity, and discretion over resource allocation and use. While importance (relative magnitude and criticality) and scarcity (concentration of resources and relative number of alternatives) impact upon the dependence between the firm and the customers, discretion (ownership, access, and external use) does not influence this relationship. The reason is found in the buyer/seller relationship of the context. Ownership is changing for the purpose of *access*. Discretion in this study is not a relevant factor, and I will be applying a modified model consisting of importance and scarcity.

Is there a difference?

Semantically, the elements found within RDT are closely linked to those applied within the RBV theory. The all-important distinction lies in the context in which it is applied – in firm internal resources versus the perceived value of an offering in the external environment. I argue that the VRI(O) model is crucial in identifying how fast competitors can copy the elements of a given offering. It cannot, however, evaluate the *perceived* value of a firm's offering in the market. Causal ambiguity or the chance of it occurring denies the theoretical possibility of using just one of the two approaches. Under the assumption of causal ambiguity, the VRI(O) analysis does not allow for the estimation of the end-effect (offering) of resources that create value in the market. Also, RDT does not necessarily reflect the ease with which competitors could imitate a given valuable offering.

Looking beyond semantics, it is relevant to examine how the two approaches differ and are comparable. To do so, it is necessary to revisit the variables.

Barney (1997) links the question of *value* to the capability of resources with regard to their impact on strengths and weaknesses in the internal analysis and opportunities and threats in the external analysis. Resources are valuable if they harness strengths, eliminate weaknesses, support opportunities, and prevent threats. More specifically, resources need either to reduce a firm's costs or increase its revenue compared with a situation where the firm does not possess these resources. Rareness is dealt with in terms of its relative existence measured by the potential to generate competitive advantages. If a valuable resource is not rare, then this can never be more than a competitive parity. Valuable and rare resources, however, can result in a temporary competitive advantage.

Imitability of resources	Perceived value of offering		
Valuable	Important	Attractiveness	
Rare	Scarce		Durability
Imitable			

Source: Own illustration.

Figure 10.4 Modified variables for analysis

Imitability is dealt with in an economic sense, i.e. what would the cost of acquiring the resources be, if not possessed already? This notion is built on the concept of strategic factor markets where resources can be acquired, and of relevance is the relationship between the cost of the resources and the returns to a strategy once implemented (Barney, 1991). If the cost of acquiring these resources is low, then the imitability is easy and these resources may become no more than a source of competitive parity. However, cost of duplication can vary, and sustained competitive advantages can stem from such resources given four special conditions. Unique historical conditions are the first of these conditions. First-mover advantages and path dependence are the sources of unique historical conditions. Secondly, causal ambiguity explains the lack of understanding between resources and competitive advantages. Social complexity, including relations between managers, the firm's culture, and the firm's reputation among suppliers and consumers, is the third condition for costly imitability. Lastly, patents are mentioned as a condition. Patents are only a source of sustained competitive advantage in some industries, and may even ease imitation in other industries (Barney, 1997).

The concept of strategic factor markets and the costliness in acquisition of resources has been contested by Dierickx and Cool (1989), who argue for the existence of non-tradable assets. Non-tradable assets are accumulated over time in asset stocks that cannot "simply" be acquired in a market. The argument is that factor markets are not imperfect but rather incomplete, thus implying that certain asset stocks cannot be bought freely but must be built over time. The point here is both to demonstrate the elements contained in imitability and to show the difficulty in determining the exact nature of imitability. With the insights from Barney (1997) and Dierickx and Cool (1989), this element and especially its complexity are analysed.

The relative magnitude and criticality of a resource determine its importance, according to Pfeffer and Salancik (1978). These two variables are not completely inseparable. The relative magnitude of an exchange is assessed via the proportion of total inputs, or the proportion of total outputs, entailed in the exchange. Dependence, in other words, increases towards consumers, as the number of output(s) is low or one primary input to operations is critical. Criticality is more intangible by nature and describes the degree to which an organization can continue functioning in the absence of an input resource or in the absence of an output market. Scarcity is related to concentration. In other words, it is important whether many or few actors possess the resources that are perceived as being valuable. It becomes pivotal whether the focal firm has access to this resource. Sanctions become an issue here, as the relative number of alternative firms, their size, and their importance in the industry influence the scarcity of resources. Freely opting to source a resource from an alternative firm can be restricted because of these factors. Fear of retaliation by a powerful actor can lock other firms into a relationship.

In applying the knowledge of a firm's internal resource constellations and the impact on imitability of resources by competitors from RBV with the relational focused knowledge of RDT, we find a tool to dissect the complexity of sustainability of first-mover advantages. The fundamental premise here is that the dependence between the perceived values of respective offerings will determine the worth of a new market, as well as the worth of a single offering by a firm. If a relative and mutual attraction should exist, the value, rareness, and imitability of the resources acquired to produce a given offering will determine the overall sustainability of this offering in the market.

Conclusion

I believe that the concept of first-mover advantage in combination with insights from resource theory can contribute greatly to the unveiling of how marketers can assess the benefits of new ventures, thereby elaborating on the notion of blue oceans, and explicitly take into account the fact that even the most shark-infested red oceans were once blue, that firms succeeding in creating a new market (that is profitable) will soon find themselves surrounded by sharks, and that, while firms can establish new boundaries for themselves, this does not automatically guarantee profits.

Moreover, considering the perspective presented by D'Aveni and Gunther (1994) and the notion of "hypercompetition", firms would have constantly to swim towards new blue oceans. Here, the constant movement would be the source of survival – not the achievement of reaching a new pool of water once. While these contributions are valuable in their own right, it is through a concept like first-mover advantage that a holistic understanding is achieved. Both the concept offered by Kim and Mauborgne (2005) and that offered by D'Aveni and Gunther (1994) depart from a basic premise of innovation as a necessity. Fundamentally, both contributions suggest redefining firm boundaries (innovation of products, processes, markets, etc.) as a means of competing successfully.

What will happen once a firm has redefined the boundaries of its competitive landscape? In order to make an assessment, we need to revisit some of the discussions conducted earlier, especially those leading to the creation of Figure 10.1 from the literature review. Here we can characterize the sources upon which a firm would be dependent in its future endeavour. A five-step assessment plan could help a firm understand the premise of its future competitive position:

- **Step 1.** *Wherein lies the novelty of your offering?* Is the novelty associated with a product, a process, a market, or a combination of these? If it is associated with a product, then an incremental change to an existing product will most likely not change the competitive landscape. If it is a radical change from the existing products, then two questions need to be considered: What barriers are in place to hinder competitors from imitation? How much will customers need to adopt new routines in order to use the product? Imitation by competitors relates to the aspect resource heterogeneity (see step 3) – if the product is produced by a new process, then imitation is more complex. Creating infra-structure for a radical new product is cumbersome and expensive (sales channels need to be created and educated, marketing efforts must establish a need for customers to demand the product, and customers also need to be trained in the use of the product). Therefore, the degree to which customers need to adjust their habits can be decisive for the ease (and thereby time) of adoption – the more difficult it is to use the product, the more expensive the education.
- **Step 2.** *What advantage(s) are associated with being first to your offering?* Securing external capabilities involves the pre-emption of input factors, location, or other investments. These activities can extend to collaboration with vital actors in this new competitive arena (sales and distribution channel controllers, skilled personnel or associated products, i.e. hardware producers for software, and vice versa).

  Advantages include firm capabilities (assessment via resource-based analy-sis) such as the exploitation of economic mechanisms (Can I create economies of scope or scale? Will I benefit from a learning curve advantage? Can I use excess capacity to build barriers?) or business mechanisms (Can advertising intensity build barriers? Do I possess managerial or organizational advan-tages? Is my R&D unit equipped to compete?).

Do customer-related mechanisms pertaining to uncertainty (buyer's choice, pricing, trials, or incomplete information), switching costs (contractual, supplier learning, buyer adaptation, or investments in cospecialized assets), or branding (awareness from media or marketing spending, line extensions, lower search costs for customers, higher involvement by customers, or the possibility of creating a dominant design) support this strategy?

- *Step 3. Can the resources applied to produce the offering withstand imitation?* Are these resources valuable? (Are the firm's resources heterogeneous (markedly different from those of competitors) and able to generate rents (environmental opportunities)? and/or Can resources build barriers to entry and sustain value (environmental threat)?)

  Are these valuable resources rare? (Do competing firms possess similar resources (resources with the ability to deliver the same value as competitors' resources)?)

  Can these resources be imitated easily or at a low cost? (Can competing firms acquire the same resources? Are the resources tradable or mobile? At what cost could competitors acquire the resources? What conditions have shaped the resources as known today?)

- *Step 4. Will I be able to tie in customers to my new offering?* Is my offering important enough for customers to retain them (measured on the degree of use of a resource in relation to the total amount required)?

  Is this perceived importance sufficiently scarce? (How many other sources of a given resource exist and, among the given sources of alternatives, how many are accessible?)

- *Step 5. What would I do if my competitors made this move first, and how do I respond to their pursuit of me?* In relation to the first part, this will help you understand if there are any advantages associated with being first – Is everything lost if I am not first? Could I easily catch up? Where are the (dis)advantages rooted?

  The second part should help you understand that, if this new venture is worth spending time and resources on, the chances are that others will feel the same. How long do I need to be in the market alone to generate a profit? Are my investments lost? Can I build other barriers once I get started?

  It should be stressed that the success or failure of a new idea cannot be foreseen. We can, however, apply models to approximate an understanding – and also apply it retrospectively to understand the evolution of a new market. When the movie "Blade Runner" was released in 1982, the producers chose 10 multinational corporations (Pan Am and Atari, among others) to be featured in the movie to create a realistic picture of society in 2019. The companies were chosen because they most realistically would still exist nearly 40 years later. Of the 10 companies expected to survive into the twenty-first century, only Coca-Cola has existed continuously until today. Regardless of the nature of a business idea, nothing is everlasting, and advantages gained by pioneering need to be supplemented to secure longevity.

References

Alvarez, S. A. & Barney, J. B. (2002) "Resource-based theory and the entrepreneurial firm", in *Strategic Entrepreneurship – Creating a New Mindset*, edited by Hitt, M. A., Ireland, R. D., Camp, S. M., & Sexton, D. L. Blackwell Publishing, Oxford, UK, pp. 89–105.

Angelmar, R. (1990) "Product innovation: a tool for competitive advantage". *European Journal of Operational Research*, vol. 47, no. 2, pp. 182–189.

Bain, J. S. (1956) *Barriers to New Competition*. Harvard University Press, Cambridge, MA.

Barney, J. B. (1986) "Strategic factor markets: expectations, luck, and business strategy". *Management Science*, vol. 32, no. 10, pp. 1231–1241.

Barney, J. B. (1991) "Firm resources and sustained competitive advantage". *Journal of Management*, vol. 17, no. 1, pp. 99–120.

Barney, J. B. (1997) *Gaining and Sustaining Competitive Advantage*. Addison-Wesley Publishing, Ontario, Canada.

Carow, K., Heron, R., & Saxton, T. (2004) "Do early birds get the returns? An empirical investigation of early-mover advantages in acquisitions". *Strategic Management Journal*, vol. 25, no. 6, pp. 563–585.

Conrad, C. A. (1983) "The advantage of being first and competition between firms". *International Journal of Industrial Organization*, vol. 1, no. 4, pp. 353–364.

Cooper, L. G. (2000) "Strategic marketing planning for radical new products". *Journal of Marketing*, vol. 64, no. 1, pp. 1–16.

D'Aveni, R. A. & Gunther, R. E. (1994) *Hypercompetition: Managing the Dynamics of Strategic Maneuvering*. The Free Press, New York, NY.

Dierickx, I. & Cool, K. (1989) "Asset stock accumulation and sustainability of competitive advantage". *Management Science*, vol. 35, no. 12, pp. 1504–1511.

Dollinger, M. J. (2002) *Entrepreneurship: Strategies and Resources*, 3rd edition. Prentice Hall, Upper Saddle River, NJ.

Emerson, R. M. (1962) "Power-dependence relations". *American Sociological Review*, vol. 27, no. 1, pp. 31–41.

Garcia, R. & Calantone, R. (2002) "A critical look at technological innovation typology and innovativeness terminology: a literature review". *Journal of Product Innovation Management*, vol. 19, no. 2, pp. 110–132.

Gelderman, K. & van Weele, A. (1999) "New perspectives on Kraljic's purchasing portfolio approach". Paper presented at the 9th International Annual IPSERA Conference, London, Ontario, Canada.

Gilbert, J. & Birnbaum-More, P. H. (1996) "Innovation timing advantages: from economic theory to strategic application". *Journal of Engineering and Technology Management*, vol. 12, no. 4, pp. 245–266.

Golder, P. N. & Tellis, G. J. (1993) "Pioneering advantage: marketing logic or marketing legend?". *Journal of Marketing Research*, vol. 30, no. 2, pp. 158–170.

Herbig, P. A. (1991) "A cusp catastrophe model of the adoption of an industrial innovation". *Journal of Product Innovation Management*, vol. 8, no. 2, pp. 127–137.

Kardes, F. R. & Kalyanaram, G. (1992) "Order-of-entry effects on consumer memory and judgment: an information integration perspective". *Journal of Marketing Research*, vol. 29, no. 3, pp. 343–357.

Kerin, R. A., Varadarajan, P. R., & Peterson, R. A. (1992) "First-mover advantage: a synthesis, conceptual framework, and research proposition". *Journal of Marketing*, vol. 56, no. 4, pp. 33–52.

Kim, W. C. & Mauborgne, R. (2005) *Blue Ocean Strategy – How to Create Uncontested Market Space and Make the Competition Irrelevant*. Harvard Business School Publishing, Boston, MA.

Lambkin, M. (1988) "Order entry and performance in new markets". *Strategic Management Journal*, vol. 9, Special Issue: Strategy Content Research, pp. 127–140.

Lieberman, M. B. & Montgomery, D. B. (1988) "First-mover advantages". *Strategic Management Journal*, vol. 9, Special Issue: Strategy Content Research, pp. 41–58.

Lippman, S. A. & Rumelt, R. P. (1982) "Uncertain imitability: an analysis of interfirm differences in efficiency under competition". *Bell Journal of Economics*, vol. 13, no. 2, pp. 111–118.

López, L. E. & Roberts, E. B. (2002) "First-mover advantages in regimes of weak appropriability: the case of financial services innovations". *Journal of Business Research*, vol. 55, no. 12, pp. 997–1005.

Mahajan, V., Sharma, S., & Buzzell, R. D. (1993) "Assessing the impact of competitive entry on market expansion and incumbent sales". *Journal of Marketing*, vol. 57, no. 3, pp. 39–52.

Mansfield, E. (1985) "How rapidly does new industrial technology leak out?". *Journal of Industrial Economics*, vol 34, no. 2, pp. 217–223.

Mansfield, E., Schwartz, M., & Wagner, S. (1981) "Imitation costs and patents: an empirical study". *Economic Journal*, vol. 91, no. 364, pp. 907–918.

Markides, C. C. (2003) "Racing to be second: innovation through imitation", in *The Future of the Multinational Company*, edited by Birkinshaw, J., Ghoshal, S., Markides, C. C., *et al.* John Wiley & Sons Ltd, Chichester, UK, pp. 211–221.

Markides, C. C. & Geroski, P. A. (2005) *Fast Second: How Smart Companies Bypass Radical Innovation to Enter and Dominate New Markets*. Jossey-Bass, San Francisco, CA.

Patterson, W. C. (1993) "First-mover advantage: the opportunity curve". *Journal of Management Studies*, vol. 30, no. 5, pp. 759–777.

Peteraf, M. A. (1993) "The cornerstones of competitive advantage: a resource-based view". *Strategic Management Journal*, vol. 14, no. 3, pp. 179–191.

Pfeffer, J. & Salancik, G. R. (1978) *External Control of Organizations. A Resource Dependence Perspective*. Harper & Row, London, UK.

Robinson, W. T. (1988) "Sources of market pioneer advantages: the case of industrial goods industries". *Journal of Marketing Research*, vol. 25, no. 1, pp. 87–94.

Robinson, W. T. & Fornell, C. (1985) "Sources of market pioneer advantages in consumer goods industries". *Journal of Marketing Research*, vol. 22, no. 3, pp. 305–317.

Rogers, E. M. (1995) *Diffusion of Innovations*, 5th edition. The Free Press, New York, NY.

Schmalensee, R. (1982) "Product differentiation advantages of pioneering brands". *American Economic Review*, vol. 72, no. 3, pp. 349–365.

Schnaars, S. P. (1986) "When entering growth markets, are pioneers better than poachers?". *Business Horizons*, vol. 29, no. 2, pp. 27–36.

Shamsie, J., Phelps, C., & Kuperman, J. (2004) "Better late than never: a study of late entrants in household electrical equipment". *Strategic Management Journal*, vol. 25, no. 1, pp. 69–84.

Smiley, R. H. & Ravid, S. A. (1983) "The importance of being first: learning price and strategy". *The Quarterly Journal of Economics*, vol. 98, no. 2, pp. 353–362.

Teece, D. J. (1986) "Profiting from technological innovation: implications for integration, collaboration, licensing and public policy". *Research Policy*, vol. 15, no. 6, pp. 285–305.

Urban, G. L., Carter, T., Gaskin, S., & Mucha, Z. (1986) "Market share rewards to pioneering brands: an empirical analysis and strategic implications". *Management Science*, vol. 32, no. 6, pp. 645–659.

Vangkilde, M. (2005) "First-movers in the e-grocery sector: a framework for analysis", in *Grocery E-Commerce*, edited by Kornum, N. & Bjerre, M. Edward Elgar Publishing Ltd, Cheltenham, UK, pp. 241–275.

Weber, O. J. (2002) "Resource dependency as barrier or driving force for grocery BtC e-commerce and subsequent changes in the supply chain". Paper presented at the 14th NOFOMA Conference, Trondheim, Norway, June 4–6, 2002.

Wernerfelt, B. (1984) "A resource-based view of the firm". *Strategic Management Journal*, vol. 5, no. 2, pp. 171–180.

11

Supplying Value to Customers through Innovation in B2B Services

Fabrizio Zerbini

Introduction

Distinctive value propositions are fundamental for business marketers, lying at the heart of their ability to gain and defend a strategic status, and to sustain performance over time (Anderson, Narus, & van Rossum, 2006).

Innovation is key in this respect, because it drives the effectiveness function of a supplier's value for its customer, and thus sustains the relationship on a long-term basis (Möller & Törrönen, 2003). Indeed, innovation facilitates the reframing of value creation strategies, changing the rules of the game and shifting the battle-field where competition is less relevant and the firm's ability to distinguish itself is greater (Kim and Mauborgne, 1999, 2005).

In this chapter, we are interested in one specific innovation modality – service innovation – as a key component of suppliers' strategies in business markets.

More specifically, we are interested in exploring the role that radical innovations in the service concept have within the value-supplying process, and definitely in the supplier's differentiation capability within value creation and delivery phases (Anderson & Narus, 1990).

There are at least three reasons why focusing on service innovation is a promising research avenue to understand value creation and delivery in B2B settings. Firstly, services are increasingly included by companies as components of the augmented product within a baseline-value proposition, and are therefore the key elements on which the value proposition can be insulated from competition and become distinctive. Secondly, being services intrinsically featured as activities where production happens jointly with usage (e.g. Zeithaml, Parasuraman, & Berry, 1985), they are a peculiar context to understand how value creation – which is focused on production – is intertwined with value delivery – which is focused on the utilization of the product by the customer. Thirdly, although innovation is considered central in value creation (e.g. Möller & Törrönen, 2003), little is said about the service component of innovative supplies.

To contribute to the understanding of the role of service innovation within the value-supplying process, this chapter will be developed as follows. Firstly, we review prior research on value-for-customer and its relationship with innovation, focusing on service innovation as a key medium for creating and delivering value within the market. Then, we describe the research methodology and present evidence from two case studies on innovation-based service value. Finally, we discuss our results with reference to service and innovation management research, deriving key managerial implications and highlighting the limitations of our study.

Theoretical background of the study

Services have been claimed to play a pivotal role in innovation processes that deliver value to the customer (Hertog, 2000). Such a claim especially holds in business markets, where the relational nature of exchanges demands the supply of value-added services in order to pursue and maintain a strategic status (e.g. Ulaga & Eggert, 2006; Tuli, Kohli, & Bharadwaj, 2007). Industrial buyers are particularly keen on service innovations, and display peculiar procurement strategies for those suppliers supporting innovation and collaboration (Kadefors, Björlingson, & Karlsson, 2007).

Surprisingly, however, little systematic assessment of service innovation value-for-customer emerges in current research (Hipp & Grupp, 2005). Hints have to be derived from related bodies of study, including those on the degree of service innovativeness and the relationship with innovation performance (e.g. Avlonitis, Papastathopoulou, & Gounaris, 2001; Cooper *et al.*, 1994), as well as those on the domains (Hertog, 2000) and typologies (Berry *et al.*, 2006; Hipp & Grupp, 2005) of service innovation.

More specifically, value creation is indirectly considered in those studies focusing on the performance of service innovations. Broadly taken, these studies have shown that service industries are equally effective as goods industries in succeeding through innovation, thus providing value to customers. Indeed, small but non-significant differences exist between goods and service industries, and mostly at the level of process innovation. However, these studies have mostly referred to the performance at the level of innovators' outcomes, not of innovations' users (e.g. Cooper *et al.*, 1994; Leiponen, 2006).

Advancements towards an understanding of value-for-customer have been further provided by those focusing on the degree of innovativeness rather than the type and level of innovation as a discriminator, but findings are mixed on this subject across industries. Indeed, there are studies reporting that discontinuous innovations breed competitive advantage (e.g. De Brentani, 2001), and studies finding positive impact on performance of both incremental and radical innovations (Oke, 2007). Others, however, suggest that radical innovations are not always optimal from a market perspective (e.g. Atuahene-Gima, 1996). Key findings on this aspect are reported within the financial services industry, where Avlonitis and colleagues have measured innovativeness along the operating/delivering process newness, the modification of extant components, and the newness for the market and for the company, and have found that an inverted U-shaped relationship exists between innovativeness and performance in the marketplace (Avlonitis, Papastathopoulou, & Gounaris, 2001). Albeit lacking an explicit focus on value creation, findings of this study constitute a first building block towards an understanding of value of innovation, calling for intermediate solutions between incremental and radically new services.

Interestingly, the issue of tying service innovation with value-for-customer has emerged indirectly in those studies categorizing service innovation types as well. On this subject, prominent work has been developed by Hertog (2000), who distinguished across four domains of service innovation. The first domain is service *concept innovation*, which is developed throughout a variation of service components and usually targets mostly the immaterial dimension of service. Examples are conceptual elements that define concept stores and flagship stores such as in the fashion distribution industry (Hertog, 2000). The second domain is innovation at the *client interface* level, which captures the ability to re-invent the processes tying buyer and sellers. Examples are data and knowledge exchanges, which have been fostered by EDI (electronic data interchange) innovation. The third domain lies at the *service delivery* level, and refers more specifically to organizational arrangements among the parties. A case in point is the emerging outsourcing modalities, which are developed on demand in the enterprise software business (e.g. Gibbert *et al.*, 2006). Finally, the fourth domain lies at the level of *technological support*, which includes innovations such as tracking systems in logistics.

Others have focused on typologies of innovations adopted by service industries (Hipp & Grupp, 2005). Accordingly, knowledge intensity innovations are mostly diffused within technical and R&D services, software, and business services. They are typically aimed at bridging the gap between knowledge producers and knowledge users. Network-based innovations are spread over business services, financial services, and technical and R&D services. They typically deal with data processing (e.g. financial services) and communication networks (e.g. telecom services). Additionally, scale intensity innovation becomes relevant whenever standardized services are offered, such as in the case of financial and retail trade services. Supplier dominance innovation occurs whenever third parties are key in allowing the service firm to conceive and implement the innovation.

Finally, recent studies have probed further into the nexus between service innovations and value-for-customer, by categorizing new services not only on the basis of their type (separable versus inseparable consumption and production) but also according to the key benefit they deliver (core product or delivery facilities) (Berry *et al.*, 2006). Specifically, there are four types of service innovation: (1) flexible solutions; (2) controllable convenience; (3) comfortable gains; (4) respectful access. Flexible solutions include best practices such as FedEx delivery services or eBay never-closed garage sale; their offerings point to the ability to innovate in core service by separating production and consumption. Controllable convenience embodies excellence cases such as Google or Skype, which have used technologies to identify innovative modalities of delivering value to the customer in terms of efficiency increases, still with separable services. Comfortable gain examples are offered by companies like Starbucks, which offers non-separable services that innovate in the core offering by means of experiential consumption at the point of sale. Finally, a respectful access case may be represented by South-west Airlines, which innovated in its service formula by creating a new market for affordable and reliable passenger transportation, based upon innovative delivery of an inseparable service, thus creating a discontinuity in the airline transportation market.

Taken together, these studies suggest that services are a key medium for delivering value through innovation: (1) by assessing their impact on innovators' performance and their equal contribution as compared with goods, and (2) by suggesting that value to customers can be delivered in different modalities, both through joint production and consumption and through separation of the two, and both in the core service and in the delivery modalities. However, they do not provide conclusive evidence on the impact of different degree of innovativeness; moreover, they consider services mostly as stand alone, and do not take into account value delivery strategies where services are a component of broader value propositions.

Directions covered in this study

Services have been considered increasingly relevant in marketing research, as they have grown to become the largest part of today's economy. As scholars noted, services represent 70% of the OECD aggregate production and employment, and 75% of US GDP (Berry et al., 2006).

Accordingly, beginning from the 1990s, researchers have paid greater attention to innovation not only in goods but also in services, by adapting theoretical models well established in manufacturing industries (e.g. Lievens & Moenaert, 2001).

The relevance of services for innovation being undisputed (e.g. Hertog, 2000; Hipp & Grupp, 2005), the question has been progressively shifted towards what types of innovation better suit value creation and delivery. With few notable exceptions (e.g. Berry et al., 2006), such an issue is not directly covered in current research, which has mostly dealt with service innovation implications for the innovator's, not the innovation user's, processes (e.g. Avlonitis, Papastathopoulou, &

Gounaris, 2001; Cooper *et al.*, 1994). Only recently, scholars have begun to consider that service innovations add value at different levels, including both a core concept and a client interface/service delivery level (Berry *et al.*, 2006; Hertog, 2000).

Such a view seems particularly relevant to exploring further the role of service innovation in business markets. Indeed, prior research on supplier's value posits that such value is delivered both through the core product and to the relationship, and is displayed throughout increases in efficiency, effectiveness, and networking, which are increasingly tied over time to the innovation function (e.g. Möller & Törrönen, 2003; Walter, Ritter, & Gemünden, 2001). Moreover, recent research probes further into this direction, by showing that value has a core dimension and a sourcing one (Ulaga & Eggert, 2006), and that it is rooted into solution offerings, where the interaction process is central (Tuli, Kohli, & Bharadwaj, 2007).

In keeping with these insights, this study aims to disentangle the nexus between service innovation and value-for-customer at the level of (1) the content dimension of service innovation, which collapses into the core offering, and (2) the process dimension of service innovation, which lies in the supplier–customer interaction. In doing so, we aim to show evidence of value creation and delivery modalities that go beyond such a repartition of innovation domains, and to explore the value of novel approaches that explicitly point to the integration of core and sourcing innovation modalities, consistent with the emerging view of business supplies as bundling processes (Tuli, Kohli, & Bharadwaj, 2007).

Methods

In consideration of the lack of research on the nexus between service innovation and value creation in business markets, this study adopts a qualitative case study method. This approach is consistent with the purpose of combining exploratory with explanatory purposes, and allows an in-depth understanding of research issues to be gained (Yin, 1984). More specifically, a multiple case study approach is followed in order to allow service innovation to be considered in different market settings. Given the relational nature of value creation in business markets (e.g. Lindgreen & Wynstra, 2005; Möller & Törrönen, 2003), we focused on cases where service innovations occur within a relational context. Moreover, as service innovations have been mostly studied within the context of knowledge-intensive business services (KIBS) (e.g. Hipp & Grupp, 2005), we managed to obtain variance on the type of service, including both cases of innovation throughout KIBS and cases of innovation not only based on KIBS. Controlling for such conditions and for our ability to access key company managers to get endorsement for our analysis, four lead suppliers in their industry were selected. For each supplier, we performed data collection beginning with a preliminary analysis, based on dialogues with managers and/or document analysis, to identify key traits of service innovation. Of the four cases, two were discarded because of the lack of apparent and significant service innovation content in their value creation strategies.

Two cases were thus retained, and constituted the object of this study. The first was IBM, belonging to the knowledge-intensive business of information technologies and services. The second was Arvato Services, part of the Bertelsmann group, and operating both in the labour-intensive business of customer care and in the knowledge-intensive business of CRM.

Data acquisition was then performed between June and October 2007, referring to the firms' administrative records and documents and, when possible, combining document analysis with in-depth interviews with the marketing managers, the pros/cons of which have been discussed by Bailey (1978). In-depth interviews were used to capture information on the strategic content of service innovation, engaging managers in ongoing dialogues, as recommended by the grounded theory approach (Glaser & Strauss, 1967). Based on this analysis, we managed to identify a recurring structure in service-based value innovation, which is presented in the results section of this chapter.

Case presentation

IBM: supplying "business on demand"

IBM is one of the largest companies worldwide, operating in the information technology (IT) business, with 356 000 employees, a revenue of $91.4 billion from 164 countries and net profits of $9.4 billion in 2006. Over the years its reputation has spread as the leader in IT products owing to its ability to develop and affirm radical innovations, which established new standards within the market and allowed IBM to gain leadership positions in different segments (e.g. mainframes, servers). Relatively less well known, on the other hand, is IBM's orientation towards services and service innovation, which has become increasingly relevant since the start of the new millennium.

At the beginning of the decade, the IT market was facing a transition: on the one hand, the *dot com* bubble was affecting financial markets; on the other hand, the market was slowing down, because IT buyers had concentrated their expenditure prior to the year 2000 on dealing with the risks of the *millennium bug*. Such market conditions were, however, expected to vary: on the one hand, the *Internet* market was expected to shift from 800 million users in 2001 to 2 billion in 2007; on the other hand, IT suppliers were increasingly moving from a closed standard to an open-ness policy in order to favour the diffusion of new technologies having intrinsically short life cycles. Both trends, according to IBM, were opening up the opportunities for IT users to boost their operations owing to easier interconnectivity and communication between IT products (e.g. industrial servers, transaction manage-ment tools, interconnectivity tools such as personal digital assistants, portable hard disks).

From a supplier perspective, such trends could have impacted on the demand for IT services, aimed at leveraging information technologies within their users' operations. It was estimated that business customers were spending about $23 600 billion per year in operations, including sales, purchasing, and admin-istrative and R&D functions. Of these, $1 400 billion was outsourced to service providers, and, more specifically, $500 million was expected to come from supply chain management, human resource management, engineering, customer care, and after-sales services, all of which were heavily dependent on information technologies. IT suppliers thus had the opportunity to expand from tangible technologies to immaterial services, integrating IT into the customers' business processes.

IBM was in a convenient condition to exploit such an opportunity. During the 1990s, the company had moved from proprietary architectures to open standard, and from hardware to communication technologies. Additionally, it had invested in a direct channel of distribution, to ensure maintenance of the direct relationship with its customers, besides increasing market coverage. In doing so, IBM accumulated over the years a valuable and specific expertise throughout its business specialists. As customers began to demand not single components or bundles but effective solutions and continuous assistance, the ability to merge know-how on IT with specific expertise on the customer's business emerged as a key success factor to anticipating market evolutions and capturing innovation opportunities.

In 2001, IBM reconfigured its business model according to a "service-led" approach, and acquired PricewaterhouseCoopers, one of the largest companies in management consulting, to complete its endowment of business experts devoted to offering business solutions to the market. At the same time, it invested over $700 million in career development, becoming the world's heaviest spender, according to Training Research results, in 2004. Of this, $400 million was focused on "market value skills", which included: (1) professional competencies, such as business process transformation and consultative selling; (2) industry trend and marketplace dynamics competencies, focused on the primary target of banking, public administrations, retailing, life sciences, and small–medium enterprises; (3) on-demand strategy competencies, including operating environment analytics, service-oriented architectures, and business componentization; (4) IT competencies, including web servicing, wireless systems, security, Linux, data management, and system architecture and design. As such, a company traditionally based on technological intensity began its shift towards a labour-intensive configuration, called by IBM managers the "service science".[1]

Service innovation

A new value proposition directly followed IBM's organizational restructuring process. In 2005, IBM explicitly formalized the new course with the "business on demand" formula, which made explicit the shift from offering products and services such as hardware and software to offering a continuous availability of computing and professional services, accessible via network resources, on a pay-for-use basis. Business on demand was defined as "an enterprise whose business processes are responsive to any demand, opportunity, or threat; integrated end-to-end across the company; and capable of integrating fluidly across extended business ecosystems of partners, suppliers, and clients".[2]

---

[1] From records of P. Maglio's talk at Bocconi School of Management, 23 May 2006.
[2] IBM annual report, 2004, p. 13.

The concept targeted customers with a strong orientation to the value of innovations and was developed on the basis of continuous relationships with business partners, rather than on a transactional basis. Such an approach aimed at offering greater flexibility in customer procurement policies, as well as facilities and know-how to develop process innovations based on IT. It was based upon flexible IT infrastructures, known within the industry as service orientation architectures (SOAs), which were expected to become the standard for over 80% of new product development processes by 2008, according to Gartner projections. SOAs included business applications, portals, and workflow tools, using open standards and integrating people's work with information services and business processes, to allow improvement in front-end applications, as well as real-time access to and use of business information.

Interestingly, such infrastructural elements were but one of the components of the business on demand concept, which was grounded mostly on the "market value skills" component. The expertise of IBM's professionals was significantly reorganized to suit an "on demand" approach, targeting four main areas: (1) professional competencies, including skills on cross-brand selling, business process transformation, deal pricing, and consultative selling; (2) industry trend and marketplace dynamics, including skills mostly focused on key industries such as banking, public administration, retail, life sciences, and small–medium businesses; (3) on-demand strategies, including skills on operating environment analysis, SOA projecting, and the redefinition of business activities and support tools; (4) IT competencies, including skills on web services, wireless systems, security systems, Linux, total system management, system design, and architecture.

Added value of service innovation

Value-for-customer in the IBM case is provided both at the level of the efficiency and at the level of the effectiveness dimension.

At the efficiency level, IT buyers are allowed to gain access to remote services, leaving the ownership of IT systems and infrastructures to the supplier, and gaining additional flexibility in scaling the cost component. For instance, IBM has innovated in the data management processes of travel agencies, establishing new mechanisms for strategic outsourcing. Leveraging upon open-source software (Linux), it allowed customers to access web and database management tools operated at IBM, letting them pay directly for the data elaboration, storage, and networking activities. In doing so, it enabled travel agencies to deal with demand fluctuations, minimizing their installed production capacity.

At the effectiveness level, the approach made it possible to integrate domains of knowledge usually lying separately at the supplier and customer level, thus fostering innovation. For instance, in the healthcare services, the availability of IBM experts in customer teams facilitated the combination of data analysis techniques with the doctors' knowledge, and led to integration of archival data on patients with genetic information, resulting in the development of new and customized diagnosis methods and treatment definition procedures.

Value creation through business on demand is therefore based upon two main components. The tangible component includes IT products, such as servers and data warehousing, and IT infrastructures, such as middleware and data management applications. Such elements are based upon open-source platforms and thus add value by facilitating the interoperability across systems. The intangible component includes the expertise accessed via business relationships, which embodies personalized services aimed at providing customers with IBM's expertise in their own markets, and applying it throughout the endowment of IT components and infrastructures. Such skills include advanced data analysis techniques and business optimization modelling; engineering skills, targeting R&D on components, and developed throughout computer-aided design; innovation skills, developed through scientists along with industry experts, for idea generation.

Value delivery is performed mostly throughout ongoing relationships. These relationships were the basis allowing the customer access to IBM's know-how, and allowing IBM to enter within the customer's process, to foster innovation via the exploitation of its own IT products, infrastructure, and management expertise. In doing so, IBM innovated by breaking with the tradition of IT implementation processes, which often failed because of their project-based focus. Discrepancies between the technical knowledge of suppliers, who had only partial knowledge of their customers' business requirements and functioning, and the business process expertise of buyers, who had little know-how on the adaptation and customizing of IT systems to the business requirements, had been a key issue in the IT business. The business on demand approach inverted the emphasis between the IT system implementation and its day-to-day operability, implying a key role of the IT supplier in the latter phase. Thus, the business on demand approach innovated mostly in the value delivery process, allowing IT buyers to access their supplier's know-how and effectively outsource part of their knowledge management processes.

Arvato Services: CRM as "one-stop shopping concept"

Arvato Services is a division of the Bertelsmann group, accounting for 27 000 employees and revenues of €1.8 billion from 65 countries in 2006. It offers services in B2B markets, focusing on those components that integrate customer relationship management (CRM) practices. These services include activities of geomarketing, data mining, and direct marketing, as well as customer care and contact services, loyalty management, logistics, information technologies, and e-commerce.

Arvato Services has reached a leading position in Europe where it offers CRM services to large and leading companies and has spread out in a large number of countries, becoming, over the years, the strategic supplier for CRM in a variety of industries, including financial services, entertainment, oil stations, telecommunication, and utilities, besides automotive and air transportation.

Its success is interesting particularly when considering that Arvato Services has constantly grown within a business area that has suffered massive downsizing in the 2000s. CRM services were expected to grow from $35 billion in 1999 to $135 billion in 2004 worldwide, but mostly failed to attain such a projected growth owing to heavy failure rates over the years. According to some (e.g. Rigby, Reichheld, & Schefter, 2002), over 55% of CRM projects fail to attain the planned outcomes, while in some cases companies have invested significant resources only to find their customer relationships damaged rather than reinforced. Additionally, practices such as loyalty programmes have been largely criticized for their inability to produce significant outcomes (e.g. Sharp & Sharp, 1997).

In such a scenario, Arvato Services managed to succeed by entering into a relationship with its customers progressively, with small but highly focused projects, and then extending the scope of interaction to the wide set of CRM services available in its offering. The ability to integrate different CRM service components was central in this respect. Indeed, while competitors were mostly focused on specific services, Arvato Services was recognizable for its wide-spectrum approach and its attention to a continuity of interaction, what it called "full service reward programme management" or "one-stop shopping".

Service innovation

Arvato Services' success in gaining a primary supplier positioning was not tied to key innovations in the service content. Indeed, Arvato Services' strategy was mainly grounded upon well-established business practices in the domain of customer care, loyalty management, and e-commerce services.

These service components were defined in order to target specific customer benefits. More specifically, customer care and contact centre services were designed to pay particular attention to peak and seasonality issues, developing inbound and outbound advanced techniques and integration tools with database management, as well as multichannel services, making it possible to answer customers' calls for "one-call solutions" throughout integrated services with high quality standards, such as 90% of calls answered within 30 seconds and 90% of emails answered within 2 hours. Loyalty programme management services were conceived to answer customers' calls for a programme configuration able to discriminate between high-value and low-value customers, developing integrated solutions with IT solutions making it possible to assess the effects of marketing actions at the level of single customers, and to measure their value. Marketing techniques for customized targeting were integrated within the knowledge management system in order to allow improvement of CRM tactics. Accordingly, data mining techniques and logistic services were integrated, to ensure on-time delivery of rewards to customers, addressing one of the most common issues of loyalty management practices. Additionally, tools for managing programme subscriptions and communicating with subscribers according to a one-to-one approach were developed, in response to customers' calls for reliability of customer databases and their exploitation for purposes of personalized communication. Finally, Arvato Services' value proposition was completed with e-commerce services, which integrated commercial activities, such as the display of catalogues, with CRM activities, such as customer data management, and with logistics, such as order management, goods issue, and warehouse management.

In fact, the novelty of Arvato Services' approach was very strongly tied to the servicing process. The value proposition was indeed conceived according to an integrated solution approach: Arvato Services was the primary supplier for "integrated loyalty management" services, being able to merge in an overall process a variety of service components, including customer care along with loyalty management and e-commerce services. However, Arvato Services did not engineer a solution-selling strategy but worked to develop a process approach to customer relationships. Indeed, the company leveraged on a modular tactic to acquire a strategic status for its customers by progressively extending the scope of its supply on the strength of its ability to exploit synergies between service activities, and shifting from a project-based contractual relationship to one of continuity servicing.

Added value of service innovation

Arvato Services' focus on delivering integrated CRM services on a continuity basis has implications for value-for-customer both at the effectiveness and efficiency levels.

On the effectiveness side, integrated CRM solutions offered to customers improvements in the reliability of customer data, by means of data collection techniques reducing data entry errors on customer records, and also increases in quality of information flows, by means of analytics at the single customer level, as well as reporting facilities allowing continuous updates and therefore higher responsiveness to market signals.

On the efficiency side, integrated CRM solutions allow customers to leverage upon CRM data to improve the logistic function by minimizing slack of resources on the stocks of rewards, and by reducing time-to-delivery of rewards at the point of sale or customer site. Additionally, reliability of customer databases enabled failure rates on communication activities such as direct mailing to be reduced.

Value creation was performed mostly by splitting the hard component of material and human resources requested to perform the service activities, which were owned and operated by Arvato Services, and the soft component of knowledge resources and customer management skills, which were accessible to the customer on a continuity basis.

On the first side, value creation was performed while paying attention to a continuous optimization of information and goods flows, as well as the integration of separate knowledge domains (logistics, customer databases, contact centre data). Such integration lay at the heart of Arvato Services' success, because it made it possible to capture the synergies embedded in market-oriented processes, the identification and exploitation of which is often hampered by the separate carrying out of the customer centre, marketing and loyalty, and logistics activities.

On the second side, value creation was performed by means of key account managers fully dedicated to one customer, and charged with the responsibility of the customer team. Additionally, formalized reporting systems were defined, warranting customers a continuous accessibility and flexibility in inquiry modalities. Finally, consulting meetings were organized for customers in order to allow sharing of tacit knowledge on customer management. Such interorganizational interfaces were, moreover, central to facilitating value delivery by means of direct access to Arvato Services' business expertise.

Findings

Evidence from the IBM and Arvato Services cases provides key insights into service innovations that foster value creation in business markets and help suppliers in attaining a strategic status in front of their customers. Findings from our analysis will be set out with reference to three key peculiarities of such service innovation: (1) the emerging shift from an approach oriented towards solution selling to one oriented towards continuous servicing for problem-solving; (2) the evolution of bundling from a customization logic to a synergy-seeking one; (3) the implications of problem-solving servicing for key supplier status.

Process innovation: from solution selling to problem-solving servicing

The quest for supplies conceived in terms of specific solutions – rather than mere goods or services with a variety of functionalities – has been apparent since the mid-1990s (e.g. Bosworth, 1995). However, looking at the growing diffusion of solution sellers, scholars have started to observe that suppliers' response to the market needs for problem solvers has often been inappropriate. In most cases, and consistent with traditional prescriptions from theory (e.g. Galbraith, 2002), suppliers conceive solutions as packages of products and services that have to be bundled in a customized manner and sold to the customers who will gain added value in dealing with their business issues. However, buyers have a different view of what a solution should consist of: they pay limited attention to the bundle per se, and are rather interested in a relational process, where the supplier is able to carry over the customer's problem from its emergence until post-deployment support (Tuli, Kohli, & Bharadwaj, 2007).

Our analysis probes further into this direction, by offering novel empirical evidence about innovation-based value creation based on a process view of solutions. IBM's shift from supplying IT products to delivering on-demand business solutions is key in this respect. Please note the following:

> *The company helps its clients transform their businesses and gain competitive advantage by applying its skills and experience to business performance challenges specific to the client's industry or across industries and processes. The company enters into long-term relationships and creates solutions for clients, driving on-demand business innovation. (IBM annual report 2004, p. 14)*

Similarly, the case of Arvato Services reports on the company's willingness to engage in ongoing relationships to foster continuous innovation in its customers' processes: while competitors may be stronger in supplying specific services, Arvato Services grows and gains a key supplier status because of its distinctiveness in offering the ability to deal with the CRM issues of its customers on a 360° basis. Please note what has come to light during the interviews:

> *The problem is that every competitor operates only some parts of the service, they do, for instance, CRM and rewards but not sourcing of rewards, or they do not operate in logistics or financial services. Sometimes we can lose on this, but in tenders we normally face groups of suppliers, not integrated ones. One-stop shopping, that's the concept.*

> *It's a process, it needs changes, and we follow the customer as much as possible . . . our solutions are renewed year after year according to emerging needs . . . our account stimulates the customer. It's a knowledge management process. They go to the customer and propose variations continually . . . when they perceive they have only one key account rather than a few suppliers offering services and systems that do not communicate among themselves, the time to react is much shorter. It's much better to call myself and have everything under control than to call a dozen different suppliers and understand what is happening. (Interview with Arvato Services Italia marketing manager)*

Such a novel focus more on the interaction process than on the bundling of service components was key in allowing both companies to distinguish themselves from competing suppliers and to gain a leadership position within their own business. IBM and Arvato Services people were able to shift the focus from the technological content of their supply to the added value of maintaining tight interaction, and exploiting it throughout forward-looking approaches to issues emerging in current operations.

It turns out that solution selling is reconceptualized as a servicing process oriented towards problem-solving, breaking out of the dichotomy of service innovations, which interprets flexible solutions as alternatives to accessibility-oriented services (Berry *et al.*, 2006). Indeed, the cases of IBM and Arvato Services show how the adoption of a process focus shifts the interaction modality from a spot basis to a relational one, thus (1) allowing customers an easier and continuous access to the supplier's know-how and skills and (2) giving to both parties a greater ability to react flexibly to emerging issues in the customer business. Such an approach was distinctive with respect to industry models in both cases, and made it possible to add value for the customer with respect to prepackaged solutions, the problem-solving effectiveness of which was confined to the ability to anticipate business issues prior to their concrete emergence, and the flexibility of which in dealing with them was mostly confined to what was forecast *ex ante*, by means of contractual agreements.

Content innovation: bundles as ongoing synergy seekers, not prepacked tools

Bundling techniques have spread in recent years as suitable means to integrate immaterial and material components within the same supply. This tendency seems consistent with the transition towards the service economy that is now emerging, pushing towards a convergence of goods and service offerings (e.g. Oke, 2007). Criticisms of bundling have, however, emerged over time, because bundling has been associated with a predefined supply, customized a priori, and thus allowing little flexibility in the face of unexpected market variations (Tuli, Kohli, & Bharadwaj, 2007).

Our cases provide evidence that bundling could be valuably reinterpreted as a flexible approach to identifying synergies and innovation opportunities throughout the integration of service components, consistent with a focus on an ongoing relationship. Bundles are therefore not stable and predefined but varying and rearranged depending upon emerging needs.

For instance, the "on demand" approach of IBM is based upon the ability to bundle tangible IT components with the intangible component of IBM people's expertise accessed via the consultancy services. In our analysis we found the following:

> Competitive advantage today comes from expertise and expertise is not static. IBM has the world's deepest, most diverse collection of business and technology innovators, supported by advanced collaboration systems and a culture that enables continuous learning. (IBM, Understanding Our Company, March 2005)

> Services is rapidly expanding and evolving in some surprising ways. It now encompasses not just labour-intensive consulting, but also the utility-like delivery of computing . . . we see the beginning of this trend . . . in our own "e-business on demand" offerings, where customers don't buy computers, but acquire computing services over the Net, on a pay-for-use basis. (Chairman's letter, IBM 2001 annual report)

Interestingly, IT infrastructures and software remain a property of IBM, as it is their use that is sold to the customer. Access to IT allows scalability of business processes and flexibility, thus constituting a value-added immaterial component of the supply. However, value-for-customer is grown not only by means of innovative modalities to exploit IT but also by integrating the access to IT capacity with the ability to exploit IT for business purposes, which is ensured by bundling within the "on demand" supply the continuous availability of IBM experts, systematically trained in specific skills, and dedicated to the customer. Hence, IBM's emphasis in bundling IT with consultancy services probes much more in the direction of finding synergies to be exploited within the customer's business processes, rather than in defining specific supply configurations to be crafted *ex ante* and sold to the customer within a predefined package.

Similarly, in the Arvato Services case our interviewee observed the following:

> If the service is, for instance, a mere call centre, or a telemarketing, then the customer looks at the reporting outcomes and things end there. But when then

you have a structure of team working besides the mere call centre or rewards component, this is always ready to react to the customer feedback, it's a partnership, it won't be possible otherwise in companies so relevant and on services so much integrated. (Interview with Arvato Services Italia marketing manager)

Accordingly, the attention is not focused on how different CRM components and consultancy services are mixed, but on the ability to offer accessibility to an integrated system where the supplier is in charge of managing service components on the spot in order to find out the most suitable configuration of CRM solutions to be adopted by the customer in the face of the emergence of a specific business issue.

It follows, therefore, that bundling is reinterpreted here as a continuous recombination of service components upon request. Within the framework of a strategic orientation towards servicing for problem-solving, the suppliers' offering results in bundles of material components, such as IT infrastructures and software, and immaterial components, such as the suppliers' expertise in exploiting technologies, which makes it possible to tackle strategic and operational issues specifically emerging within the customer's business environment.

Servicing for problem-solving and key supplier status

The shift from prepackaged bundles to a continuity servicing approach, where the supply is continuously adaptable on demand, was key in allowing these two suppliers to attain and retain a leading position in the market. Please note the following:

It's not only efficiency, the company is made of people. When you have standards of interaction and relationships, it's also easier to approach and solve problems. That's the idea of Arvato Services, multiyear contracts for long-standing relationships, it matters in the long term. (Interview with Arvato Services Italia marketing manager)

At the end, business on demand makes it possible to look at and manage the company as an integrated entity. Such an approach is relevant when parts of the structure are controlled by others. This is much more than mere production efficiency: it's the ability to generate additional value. (IBM, Living in an on demand world, Report, October 2002)

There are three main reasons why IBM and Arvato Services were allowed to gain a strategic status in front of their customers (Table 11.1).

Firstly, because of the effect that servicing for problem-solving had on value-for-customer. In both cases, increases in efficiency were allowed by delivering scalability of business processes, while effectiveness was fostered by adding specific know-how on IT (IBM) and CRM (Arvato Services) practices to the baseline offering, to guide customers in exploiting the installed IT and CRM

Table 11.1 Comparison of findings

Key features of servicing innovation	IBM	Arvato Services – Bertelsmann
Process innovation	On-demand approach: shift of emphasis from IT implementation to IT exploitation in day-to-day operations. Supply of continuous access to IBM's experts for leveraging upon technologies for scalability and innovation	Ongoing interaction with Arvato Services' project leaders and team. CRM facilities support internal communication and the management of the relationship with the end-customer, but emphasis is on the accessibility, scalability, and re-engineering of the integrated system of CRM services
Content innovation	Bundling of IT components and professional services is not predefined in detail. Supply of full and flexible access to IBM's IT and business skills, applied to IT components. Focus on recombination, not pre-packaging	One-stop shopping approach: orientation towards continuous servicing, allowing customers fully to outsource CRM practices, and using knowledge management facilities to allow customers to maintain full control of the supplier's activity, and the possibility of intervening promptly and redirecting decisions
Key supplier status	Efficiency (installed capacity reduction) and effectiveness (flexibility) facilitating scalability Continuous interaction in problem-solving, driving trust and reconfirmation Leverage on tacit knowledge inhibits imitation by competitors and customers' switch propensity	

components. Interestingly, such know-how was fundamental to gaining effectiveness in current customers' processes, but, at least in the case of IBM, constituted also a basis for opening the customers' processes towards new avenues of development, thus exerting also an innovation function (e.g. Möller & Törrönen, 2003; Walter, Ritter, & Gemünden, 2001).

Secondly, because a continuity focus made it possible to reinforce extant relationships, which were guided by the supplier's ability to solve problems as they emerged in the customer's business. This approach was consistent with the processual focus sought by the customers (Tuli, Kohli, & Bharadwaji, 2007), thus allowing these suppliers to emerge from critical accidents with stronger reliability as trustworthy partners.

Thirdly, because these content and process innovations were based upon a competence-based strategy (Zerbini, Golfetto, & Gibbert, 2007) and were therefore difficult to reproduce for extant competitors in the market. Indeed, both Arvato Services and IBM added value to their customers' processes by merging traditional CRM and IT services with distinctive skills, in the service practice (Arvato Services) or in the service practice and in the customers' businesses (IBM). In both cases, the ability to engineer organizational and technological facilities to interact with customers continuously was central in warranting these customers access to know-how and skills mostly tacit, and therefore accessible mostly by context-sharing approaches (Nonaka, 1994).

Therefore, in our cases, servicing for problem-solving constituted a valuable means to grow in the customer relationship towards a strategic status, but also an innovation-based strategy suitable for gaining sustainability of competitive advantage through being deeply intertwined with the exploitation of supplier's strategic assets within the customer relationship.

Conclusion

There are a few implications for theory and practice that derive from this analysis.

With respect to prior research, this study contributes firstly to the emerging view of solution selling as a process-centric rather than a product-centric approach

(Tuli, Kohli, & Bharadwaji, 2007). More specifically, both the "on demand" and "one-stop shopping" concepts offer evidence about the modalities through which firms in service industries can cope with the growing demand for continuity of interaction, by innovating not only in the content but mostly in the process dimensions of their offering.

Secondly, the analysis offers novel evidence that breaks the service innovation recipe (Berry *et al.*, 2006) by showing that innovations aimed at supplying flexible solutions can converge in new access modalities. Indeed, when services are interpreted as ongoing processes and supplied on a continuity basis, relationships can serve both as a means to allow direct access to suppliers' know-how and skills and as a means to facilitate interaction, thus enabling a continuous re-engineering of the offering content that serves a solution, depending upon the concrete emergence of problems in the customers' operations.

Thirdly, the analysis offers insights into the nexus between value creation in business markets (Walter, Ritter, & Gemünden, 2001), supplier functions (Möller & Törrönen, 2003), and service innovation (e.g. Hertog, 2000). More specifically, evidence from the IBM and Arvato Services cases suggests that some concept innovation, such as reinterpretation of bundling modalities, and service delivery innovations, such as continuous access modalities, can be profitably integrated in a value-for-customer logic to allow the supplier to cover not only its customers' needs for efficiency but also its attention to effectiveness and innovation. Indeed, it is the joint ability to adapt the content of the supply and to perform ongoing interactions that increases the responsiveness of the supplier to the emergence of the customers' problems, suggesting that in some cases such innovation modalities are interdependent for value creation purposes. Moreover, this study offers a follow-up to the growing evidence on value-for-customer strategies grounded on suppliers' competencies (Golfetto & Gibbert, 2006) by deepening value creation and value delivery modalities that occur after the marketing phase (Zerbini, Golfetto, & Gibbert, 2007) when the relationship is in place.

With respect to practice, this study shows firstly how suppliers could valuably shift from an *ex ante* customization to an ongoing adaptation approach towards the service concept definition. Indeed, value is delivered to customers mostly through responsiveness to emerging needs during the servicing process, rather than by fixing *ex ante* the conditions of the supply.

Additionally, the analysis suggests that suppliers should not underestimate the relevance of material components of service bundles, such as IT systems or CRM infrastructures, both because of their direct contribution to the efficiency and effectiveness function of the supplier and because they act as a context that gives evidence of the value of the supplier's distinctive skills in exploiting those components. However, increasing attention must be paid to the modalities through which such skills are not only nurtured within the organization but also targeted by specific interfaces, making it possible to foster access by the customer, and therefore value delivery.

In conclusion, it must be noted that the findings of this study should be carefully considered in light of the limitations of the research design and implementation. Two limitations warrant specific consideration in this respect. Firstly, this analysis was based upon qualitative research methods, and thus lacks external validity. Further research based on quantitative approaches should be conducted in order to assess the extent to which servicing for problem-solving constitutes a structured path of innovation within other business markets for the systematic creation and delivery of value to customers. Secondly, data were collected at the supplier level. Although these data included insights from company representatives and from internal archives, documenting case histories at the customer level, which included not only subjective but also objective data about outcomes and the structure of servicing for problem-solving, we didn't have the opportunity to look at the customer perspective. Therefore, further analyses are needed in order to verify and close any emerging gap of perspectives within the dyadic relationship inherent in this type of value creation approach.

References

Anderson, J. C. & Narus, J. A. (1990) "A model of distributor firm and manufacturer firm working partnerships". *Journal of Marketing*, vol. 54, no. 1, pp. 42–58.

Anderson, J. C., Narus, J. A., & van Rossum, W. (2006) "Customer value propositions in business markets". *Harvard Business Review*, vol. 84, pp. 91–99.

Atuahene-Gima, K. (1996) "Differential potency of factors affecting innovation performance in manufacturing and services firms in Australia". *Journal of Product Innovation Management*, vol. 13, no. 1, pp. 35–52.

Avlonitis, G. J., Papastathopoulou, P. G., and Gounaris, S. P. (2001) "An empirically-based typology of product innovativeness for new financial services: success and failure scenarios". *Journal of Product Innovation Management*, vol. 18, no. 5, pp. 324–342.

Bailey, K. D. (1978) *Methods of Social Research*. The Free Press, New York, NY.

Berry, L. L., Shankar, V., Parish, J. T., *et al.* (2006) "Creating new markets through service innovation". *MIT Sloan Management Review*, vol. 47, no. 2, pp. 56–63.

Bosworth, M. T. (1995) *Solution Selling, Creating Buyers in Difficult Selling Markets*. McGraw-Hill, New York, NY.

Cooper, R. G., Easingwood, C. J., Edgett, S., *et al.* (1994) "What distinguishes the top performing new products in financial services". *Journal of Product Innovation Management*, vol. 11, no. 4, pp. 281–299.

De Brentani, U. (2001) "Innovative versus incremental new business services: different keys for achieving success". *The Journal of Product Innovation Management*, vol. 18, pp. 169–187.

Galbraith, J. R. (2002) "Organizing to deliver solutions". *Organizational Dynamics*, vol. 31, Autumn, pp. 194–207.

Gibbert, M., Golfetto, F., & Zerbini, F. (2006) "What do we mean by 'marketing' resources and competencies? A comment on Hooley, Greenley, Cadogan, and Fahey (JBR 2005)". *Journal of Business Research*, vol. 59, pp. 148–151.

Glaser, B. G. & Strauss, A. L. (1967) *The Discovery of Grounded Theory: Strategies, for Qualitative Research*. Aldine, Chicago, IL.

Golfetto, F. & Gibbert, M. (2006) "Marketing competencies and the sources of customer value in business markets". *Industrial Marketing Management*, vol. 35, pp. 904–912.

Hertog, P. D. (2000) "Knowledge-intensive business services as co-producers of innovation". *International Journal of Innovation Management*, vol. 4, no. 4, pp. 491–528.

Hipp, C. & Grupp, H. (2005) "Innovation in the service sector: the demand for service-specific innovation measurement concepts and typologies". *Research Policy*, vol. 34, no. 4, pp. 517–535.

Kadefors, A., Björlingson, E., & Karlsson, A. (2007) "Procuring service innovations: contractor selection for partnering projects". *International Journal of Project Management*, vol. 25, no. 4, pp. 375–385.

Kim, W. C. & Mauborgne, R. (1999) "Strategy, value innovation, and the knowledge economy". *Sloan Management Review*, vol. 40, no. 3, pp. 41–53.

Kim, W. C. & Mauborgne, R. (2005) *Blue Ocean Strategy: How to Create Uncontested Market Space and Make the Competition Irrelevant*. Harvard Business School Press, Boston, MA.

Leiponen, A. (2006) "Managing knowledge for innovation: the case of business-to-business services". *Journal of Product Innovation Management*, vol. 23, no. 3, pp. 238–258.

Lievens, A. & Moenaert, R. K. (2001) "Communication flows during financial service innovation". *Journal of Bank Marketing*, vol. 19, no. 2, pp. 68–88.

Lindgreen, A. & Wynstra, F. (2005) "Value in business markets: What do we know? Where are we going?". *Industrial Marketing Management*, vol. 34, pp. 732–748.

Möller, K. K. E. & Törrönen, P. (2003) "Business suppliers' value creation potential. A capability-based analysis". *Industrial Marketing Management*, vol. 32, pp. 109–118.

Nonaka, I. (1994) "A dynamic theory of organizational knowledge creation". *Organization Science*, vol. 5, no. 1, pp. 14–37.

Oke, A. (2007) "Innovation types and innovation management practices in service companies". *International Journal of Operations and Production Management*, vol. 27, no. 6, pp. 564–587.

Rigby, D. K., Reichheld, F. F., & Schefter, P. (2002) "Avoid the four perils of CRM". *Harvard Business Review*, vol. 80, no. 2, pp. 101–108.

Sharp, B. & Sharp, A. (1997) "Loyalty programs and their impact on repeated-purchase loyalty patterns". *International Journal of Research in Marketing*, vol. 14, pp. 473–486.

Tuli, K. R., Kohli, A. K., & Bharadwaj, S. G. (2007) "Rethinking customer solutions: from product bundles to relational processes". *Journal of Marketing*, vol. 71, no. 3, pp. 1–17.

Ulaga, W. & Eggert, A. (2006) "Value-based differentiation in business relationships: gaining and sustaining key supplier status". *Journal of Marketing*, vol. 70, no. 1, pp. 119–136.

Walter, A., Ritter, T., & Gemünden, H. G. (2001) "Value creation in buyer–seller relationships – theoretical considerations and empirical results from a supplier's perspective". *Industrial Marketing Management*, vol. 30, pp. 365–377.

Yin, R. K. (1984) *Case Study Research: Design and Methods*. Sage Publications, Beverly Hills, CA.

Zeithaml, V. A., Parasuraman, A., & Berry, L. L. (1985) "Problems and strategies in services marketing". *Journal of Marketing*, vol. 49, no. 2, pp. 33–46.

Zerbini, F., Golfetto, F., & Gibbert, M. (2007) "Marketing of competence: exploring the resource-based content of value-for-customers through a case study analysis". *Industrial Marketing Management*, vol. 36, no. 6, pp. 784–798.

PART II

Co-creation of Meaningful Experiences with Customers

12

Co-creating Consumption Experiences: an Endless Innovation

Stefania Borghini & Antonella Carù

Introduction

The role of the customer in the co-creation of product and service offers is very relevant in recent discussions on the relationship between companies and the market, especially when we adopt the vision according to which the customer is an active player in the creation of value (e.g. Vargo & Lusch, 2004; Lusch & Vargo, 2006).

It is true that consumers have always used all the material resources offered by the market to construct their experiences in a personal and individual way by creatively and proactively manipulating these objects as cultural resources. Without the awareness of marketers and beyond their control, brands, products, objects, and servicescapes are continually appropriated and modified by consumers. Consumer value is created through experiences and solutions that allow the co-creation and sharing of resources, including skills and knowledge, involving both the company and the customer.

Co-creation has been extensively debated in work on product innovation (e.g. Griffin & Hauser, 1993; Leonard-Barton, 1995; Thomke & von Hippel, 2002; Prahalad & Ramaswamy, 2004). In this new light, the boundaries of innovation are extended beyond the company to include the customers and their cultural resources and skills as an active part of the creative process.

The aim of the present chapter is to contribute to theory development on the ways this co-creation may occur, from the consumer agency in the construction of solutions and experiences to the production of meanings through material resources provided by the market (e.g. Arnould & Thompson, 2005).

More specifically, the work will focus on the identification of the multiple domains of co-creation in order to provide new insights and managerial implications. We suggest it is necessary: (i) to understand the way consumers identify possible meanings ascribed to specific solutions and experiences; (ii) to include the "philosophy of multiple meanings"; (iii) to adopt the vision of "infinite possibilities"; and (iv) to manage different levels of consumer participation and involvement during the experience and/or solution creation process. In so doing, we will argue that there are multiple means to support managers in mobilizing consumers' competence and resources in the areas described above.

The co-creation of value in the managerial perspective

Recent literature on the creation of unique value for customers has extensively shown that one of the new key principles for managerial practice is co-creation of value which sees customers as an active part of this process (e.g. Prahalad & Ramaswamy, 2004; Gilmore & Pine, 2002; Kozinets et al., 2004). Indeed, consumers are increasingly aware of what they buy and what they consume, they are more informed and competent, and they pay greater attention to consumption actions and the implications of the products and services they acquire. In the search for information, they are less isolated and more interconnected, willing to share the experiences and skills with others. The same argument stands for industrial customers who always play an active role in defining and influencing their suppliers' offer.

The history of many successes (or failures) of new products and/or services launched on the market shows without doubt that any action by a company cannot simply be taken from a unilateral point of view. Ultimately, it is always the customers who determine the success of an innovation by adopting it and including it in their consumption choices. Even more importantly, value is not created within the firm and then exchanged with the customer. Through continual interaction based on dialogue, transparency, risk assessment, and customer access to direct experience of the product, rather than just the product features (Prahalad & Ramaswamy, 2004), managers and customers divide the work of creation and innovation between themselves. Value is thereby co-created via the continual interaction between companies and consumers, in what has been termed the *new value creation space* (Prahalad & Ramaswamy, 2004, p. 10), i.e. the competitive space where interactions between the consumer and a network of companies and consumer communities occur.

As various authors have demonstrated (e.g. Prahalad & Ramaswamy, 2004; Gustafsson & Johnson, 2003), the new best practices highlight not only a trend towards the joint creation of products but also a shift towards an experience-centric view of the co-creation of value. In this view, ongoing interactions that enable consumers to co-create unique experiences with the company and its products and services are proposed to be the key to unlocking new sources of competitive advantage. Products and services are but means around which experiences are created.

Innovating experience environments create strong linkages with customers and allow experience personalization based on individual involvement and the derivation of personal meaning (Prahalad & Ramaswamy, 2004).

By focusing on two core drivers (the locus of competences and the locus of innovation), Prahalad and Ramaswamy (2004) propose a new conceptualization of the competitive space in which companies act to achieve competitive advantage (Figure 12.1). The authors consider three different loci of innovation: product space, solution space, and experience space. The implicit hierarchy identifies experience space as the final and highest opportunity for innovation.

Moving from left to right along the bottom of the figure, the *product space* is based only on product innovation and derives from a product-oriented approach. Firms operating within this space are continually involved in new technology development and product performance improvement. The focus of innovation is devoted

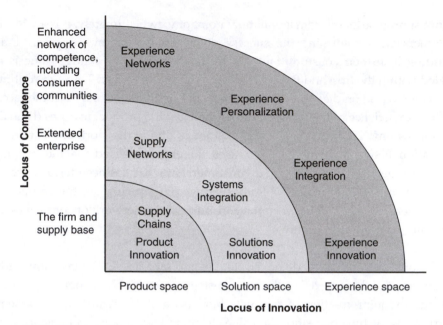

Figure 12.1 Towards an experience-centric view of competitive space. Reprinted by permission of Harvard Business School Press. Exhibit from Prahalad, C. K. and Ramaswamy, V. (2004) *The Future of Competition: Co-creating Unique Value with Customers.* Harvard Business School Press, Boston, MA, p. 147. © 2004 Harvard Business School Publishing Corporation, all rights reserved

to improving the components and functions of the supply chain in order to manage product innovation at an appropriate cost. Competitive advantage is achieved with a better combination of cost, efficiency, quality, and variety.

The *solution space* is considered as a step forward in the new logic of achieving a competitive advantage, especially when considering business markets. Here, the idea is to sell complete solutions and systems to customers. This approach requires significant skills in integrating components from several suppliers that can have different levels of participation in the creation process. Suppliers that are able to offer solutions provide a combination of hard components – embodied in physical products – and competence (Zerbini, Golfetto, & Gibbert, 2007). This soft component based on the supplier's competencies and capabilities is the main source of competitive advantage and a barrier to imitation.

The *experience space* is considered by Prahalad and Ramaswamy as the most challenging and promising strategy to provide superior value for customers. In an experience-centric view of innovation, the opportunities for change derive from the capability to manage heterogeneous consumer experiences, interact directly with their communities (especially the more proactive and engaged ones), and consider the evolvability of the experiences for each customer, etc.

In a similar perspective, Gustafsson and Johnson (2003) consider the shift towards the experience economy as a natural evolution of contemporary management thought within the service industries. IKEA, for example, clearly shows a strategic focus based on the creation of a whole experience for the customer within the stores and through the product design and usage. The experience in the IKEA shops is designed around the customer's experience in the sense that customers can find not only a pleasant exhibition of the products but also a system of supplementary services – e.g. restaurant, areas for children, delivery services, office and kitchen planning tools, return policies, etc. Product design that makes all pieces easy to transport, easy to build up, provides a rich offer of integrated products that can be combined together and adapted to different types of home space.

Different levels of and opportunities for experience innovation can be achieved, depending on the competencies and capabilities available in the organization (Prahalad & Ramaswamy, 2004). Companies can compete at the level of experience integration and experience personalization, or even cooperate in a system of experience networks extending the locus of competence and integrating external actors in the innovation processes. The maximum level of innovation is achieved when the company can rely on an enhanced network of competence that includes consumer communities as well as suppliers. Prahalad and Ramaswamy highlight how this strategy requires specific infrastructures for experiences and a proper methodology. These two elements are in fact crucial in order to engage customers and consumers actively in the co-creation process. Briefly, the managerial environment that can support these approaches is based on various tenets: (i) flexibility in knowledge creation and integration of multiple forms of information; (ii) development of new capabilities and managerial mindsets based on discovery strategy, collaboration, and ability to cope with instability and disequilibrium; and (iii) ongoing dialogue with customers.

Overall, this literature has made a significant contribution to managerial practice, highlighting the role of customers in the co-creating process and going beyond the traditional view of firm-centric value creation.

Moving our attention to the active role played by customers, these contributions open the way to a more complex view of everyday managerial practice. Nevertheless, in-depth investigation of consumer practices and related opportunities for innovation is still lacking.

In the following sections of this chapter, our aim is to reveal this side of co-creation by focusing more on consumer behaviour. A general understanding of recent trends among consumers can provide insights and implications for the management of co-creation and, at the very least, identify potential areas for investment when innovating products or services.

We would also suggest adopting a more flexible view when considering the potential space available for innovation. According to the studies discussed above, the key concept is based on the hierarchy of steps through which experience creation (or better, co-creation) can provide greater value for customers. Many authors consider experience creation a better strategy than solution selling, especially when considering individual consumers or families. Examples of solution selling are typically related to business markets rather than consumer markets. In contrast, we argue that individual consumers, and not only industrial customers, also look for integrated solutions that can improve their everyday life.

In this study, we propose to consider the possibility of innovation based on co-creation in both the experience and solution spaces, including the construction of meanings that consumers ascribe to these spaces. We will discuss these issues below.

Consumers and the markets: the cultural perspective

In order to identify opportunities for innovation in the spaces based on co-creation and consumer participation, it is useful to explore the various planes on which consumption activities develop. To this end, some recent contributions from psychological, sociological, and cultural perspectives can be considered particularly illuminating.

In this section we will focus on three fields that in similar ways have explored and unpacked the active roles played by consumers while consuming products and services provided by the market: psychology, sociology, and consumer research.

The common matrix in these fields, which would not appear to be that closely related, is the central position assigned to consumption activities in the process of *identity construction*, be it single or collective. In this view, products, services, brands, and commercial spaces are material resources used by consumers to build and communicate their self in all its dimensions.

In psychology, for instance, Breakwell (1986) suggests that the end-states that are desirable for identity are defined by a sequence of phases of assimilation, accommodation, and evaluation of materials and consumption experiences. Her model of identity process is based on the argument that identity is a dynamic product of the interaction between two dimensions: on the one hand there are the capacities for memory, consciousness, and organized construal, on the other there are societal structures and influence processes that derive from the social context within which such activities are developed.

According to a cognition-centred view, the phases of assimilation and accommodation are linked to the memory system. Memory absorbs elements such as values, attitudes, style, group memberships, and interpersonal networks and adjusts the existing structure to locate them. In the evaluation phase, these elements are allocated to identity elements.

Four major principles typically guide this process: (i) self-esteem, (ii) continuity, (iii) positive distinctiveness, and (iv) self-efficacy.

The desire for *self-esteem* is a basic tenet of any theory of identity. It influences many cognitive processes and the attribution of meanings. Every consumer evaluates and selects products and services that will allow a certain level of self-esteem. When we need to decide among alternative purchases, we tend to choose the one that gives us the perception that we are achieving the goals and objectives at the basis of our life, in terms of beliefs, values, and attitudes. If we are adhering to environmentally friendly consumption ideologies, for instance, we will be happy to choose goods and services considered to inflict minimal harm on the environment. These purchasing decisions help us to keep our level of esteem high.

Consuming products according to the *continuity* principle means choosing goods that help us to maintain a connection between past and present conceptions of the self. Overwhelmed by the marketplace offer, one typical decision criterion is based on the need to keep an ongoing sense of self over time. Loyalty to brands or places can be led by this principle.

A third typical force that drives the choices of contemporary consumers is the *distinctiveness* principle. In both modern and postmodern economies and ways of life, any consumer strives to achieve distinctiveness from other people; there is no need to push towards total distinctiveness. Distinctiveness among subcultures can be an acceptable compromise for many people. Being the first to buy all new products launched on the market and behaving like typical pioneers in the adoption of innovation can be explained by the desire to achieve a certain level of distinctiveness. Consumers can choose to pay for these products not because of their performance per se, but because of the symbolic benefits attached to the fact that they are new.

Finally, a desirable end-state is represented by *efficacy* (or *self-efficacy*). Individuals always try to maintain an identity that is characterized by competence and control over actions and decisions. Consumption activities that give the perception that the individual is able to solve any consumption-related problem effectively allow positive feelings to emerge. On the other hand, a lack of efficacy can be associated with feelings of alienation and helplessness. Even though the market provides alternative solutions to problems offering different levels of technical quality and performance, consumers tend to choose those solutions that give them the feeling that they are good problem-solvers and able to obtain what they need. It does not matter if they are choosing the best solution overall, it is rather the feeling that they relate to their choice, how satisfied they feel about the level of competence and control experienced during the decision process.

How many times are we unaware of the technology behind a product or a service innovation and we make decisions based only on the sensation that we will feel comfortable with a particular product or service? It is difficult to define when and how these principles operate. Probably, it will depend on specific consumption situations, which may even be culturally specific. Very often they interact, influencing the processes of decision-making or meaning attribution.

From a complementary perspective, it is widely recognized in sociology, too, that consumption practices have increasingly become the domain within which people explore and build their own identities. In simpler words, our identities are enhanced by what we consume. Consumers have definite strategies for engaging in consumption, as they tend to apply the same rhetorical components when they verbalize their hopes, fears, aims, and aspects of self through discussing their way of shopping (Gottdiener, 2000).

Self-identity formation through consumption is based on a complex set of social interactions that happen in multiple cultural domains where the marketplace culture plays a greater role compared to the past (e.g. Baudrillard, 1998). People are engaged in multiple lifestyles as they belong to different subcultures: they work and have families, friends, leisure activities, and many cultural interests. Their consumption ideologies are complex and intertwined. Products and services provided by the markets are means for identity construction and social discourses. Consumer goods do not have only a functional or economic value, they make a statement about the self of the users/owners. They are used to communicate lifestyles, manifest resistance to the market, build social identity related to ethnicity or subcultures, and so on. In this way, consumption becomes a form of identity.

Fashion, furniture, cars, and many other products have always been used to build identity and communicate lifestyles, values, and beliefs to others. Attachment to brands like Harley-Davidson or resistance to the cultural and ideological power of major companies such as Nike or Coca-Cola represent these ways of communicating personal values and identities dramatically.

Using these premises, *consumer culture theory*, the label that refers to the complex set of theoretical contributions catalogued by Arnould and Thompson in 2005, emphasizes and investigates the productive and constructive aspect of consumer practices. Consumers do not only use products to build an identity often deployed as a fragmented self (Belk, 1988), they actively rework and transform symbolic meanings encoded in advertisements, brands, retail settings, or material goods to manifest their particular personal and social circumstances and further their identity and lifestyle goals. Products and services are seen as a heterogeneous palette of resources from which to construct individual and collective identities (e.g. Thompson & Hirschman, 1995; Murray, 2002; Schau & Gilly, 2003).

In this way, the market provides models and references that consumers can choose to inhabit or not. The market as a cultural forum defines symbolic boundaries among mainstream norms and opposing lifestyles. The coexistence of different ideologies allows consumers to choose and display multiple opportunities for identity. They even combine, rework, and innovate the proposals offered by the market by interpreting its signs and codes creatively.

We use very different brands, combining luxury goods with unbranded or self-made products, and feel comfortable with the potential fragmentation and confusion that this choice may convey. Different consumers will ascribe different meanings to the same value proposition provided by companies and feel free to adapt their products to their personal purposes. The manipulation of advertising and the recombination of its messages fuelled by the social discourses pervading the web give consumers the power to modify brand image and manifest their agency as consumers (e.g. Kozinets *et al.*, 2004). The creative use of products and services for purposes that are different to those that motivated their launch on the market are common every day.

The "real world" can no longer be considered monolithic or rational, as consumers tend to experience realities that are different from everyday life. Through consumption practices and the experience of fantasies, aesthetics, desires, and identity, they construct multiple realities linked to the same goods or commercial places (for a detailed review, see Arnould and Thompson, 2005). The consumption of physical or virtual spaces shapes our practices, but, at the same time, provides a setting where we can take on multiple identities. We can build an ideal self while living on Second Life, present a temporary actual self during leisure activities or single experiences, or maintain a sense of belonging with a mythical past by consuming brands based on retromarketing strategies. We can buy the bedroom for our kids at IKEA because we want to save money, because we like Scandinavian design, or for completely different reasons. Some can satisfy the desire to feel good fathers or good mothers who can take care of their children. Using their hands to build their beds or bedside tables enhances the feeling that they are building a family legacy. In this way, consumers are not consuming a product; they are building their own identity as parents.

The brief picture of these three perspectives on consumption and their role in identity projects opens the way to an exploration of broader potential areas for experience and solution creation. It suggests wide areas for innovation and supports the experimentation of challenging managerial approaches, revealing promising opportunities that are less tied to company limitations and more open to unexpected alternatives.

The innovation space in the identity construction perspective

Taking together the various prospective theories based on the idea of consumption as a tool to construct identity, it is interesting to note how the space for innovation enlarges to include not only functional and symbolic improvements but also changes due to the various interpretations and appropriations undertaken by consumers (Figure 12.2). There is no need to keep a strict hierarchical structure of innovation options that sees experiences as a more developed frontier with respect to solutions in consumer markets (Carù, 2007).

In the next paragraphs, we will describe a broader area for innovation, considering both the area of solutions and the area of experiences. Moreover, we will identify the specific role ascribed to competencies in designing the context for experiences and solutions.

In a broad view, we can agree that a solution is more like a functional fact integrating company and customer resources which allow the customer to respond to a complex system of sought benefits, while an experience is a subjective fact, marked by emotion and linked to elements within the individual. On the other hand, experiences may vary considerably and even include the

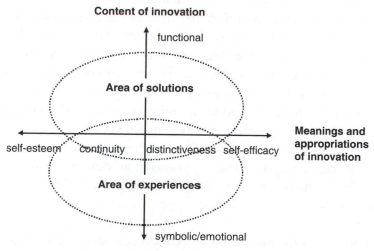

Figure 12.2 The multiple innovation spaces

aspect of problem-solving, which is at times central in the relationship between companies and consumers and the condition that allows an experience to develop.

The same package of products or services may in fact constitute a solution for one consumer and experiential context for others. In terms of the process of identity building, the same products/services may represent different principles at different occasions of consumption: offering a sense of continuity (functional, symbolic, or both together), increasing the perception of self-effectiveness in resolving problems and thus satisfying that part of identity linked to that need (gender, family role, social or professional position, etc.), providing an opportunity for escapism and multireality, reducing the tension of living a fragmented self (e.g. being a serious and scrupulous professional, but also feeling like a bold and reckless sportsperson), etc.

This new perspective widens the boundaries of potential innovation, both in terms of symbolic/emotional and of technical/functional content. With regard to the former, for example, innovation may not be so much a question of new symbolic positioning that gives a new image to a specific product, service, or brand. It could involve the creation of cultural meanings, of symbolic resources that are not totally defined, but leave consumers the liberty to realize a freer and more subjective appropriation, or, at least, to take on those proposed to resolve different problems linked to the building of identity. For example, a cosmetic product for women may for teenagers represent a means to construct their gender identity, while offering a guarantee of continuity and self-esteem for older women aware of their own selves. Even if at first sight this suggestion might appear to disagree with the principles of positioning and communication (which recommend to propose clear and unambiguous meanings), there are company cases demonstrating that a certain complexity in the meanings carried by brands is able to satisfy consumers with differing symbolic/cultural needs. This is so in the case of the well-known American brand for young girls, *American Girl*, which, through products and services carrying multiple meanings tied to motherhood, femininity, the sense of friendship, and multicultural society, actually offers a cultural platform that can be appropriated, obviously in different ways, by young children, their mothers, grandmothers, or entire families (Kozinets, Sherry, *et al.*, 2005).

In the second case of the innovation of technological and functional content, the innovation may be realized around a different use or combination of products, which again offers a response to the principles of identity-building. Incorporation of a new technology in a product may prove successful with consumers if the benefits offered are tied to their needs to maintain their sense of self. A new electronic tool could simplify consumers' lives and heighten the perception of self-efficacy and self-esteem. Feeling competent in the processes of consumption and the choices of the underlying products, services, and brands is one of the fundamental aspects in the process of identity-building, reducing the sense of alienation or futility. Many marketing myopias derive precisely from difficulties companies have in realizing how simple consumers' requests can be. Acquiring a high-quality, home audio-video system that everyone can understand and that works immediately even with old products that the consumer already possesses will always make the latter happy with his/her choice.

Designing the context for experiences and solutions: the role of competencies

Companies do not create experiences or solutions but may help customers to experience them (Carù & Cova, 2007). On the basis of this consideration, it is therefore important to address the topic in a different way, more in terms of supporting the customer in the processes of experience creation than in producing marketing stimuli.

Interesting and successful examples of such cases can be found in those companies that have developed significant relations with customers precisely owing to their ability to create a unique and inimitable set of activities that provide a solution to complex needs. IKEA, for example, manages to generate a unique shopping experience by offering integrated products and services that constitute solutions for customers and allow them to construct their experiences. The fundamental elements on which IKEA's strategy is based are, on the one hand, customer participation in all phases of the interaction process with the company, from the choice of product (the customer is completely autonomous, as the entire range is on show at the points of sale) to the assembly of the furniture, and, on the other, a low-cost production system based on modular components (Gustafsson & Johnson, 2003).

Many companies are moving in this direction by expanding their concept from a company-based production perception towards a concentration on the resources and competencies that the customer needs. At an operational level, providing such resources to consumers represents an effective way to support their life projects and identity construction.

To pursue their life projects, consumers use various material and immaterial resources. Taking the classification proposed by Vargo and Lusch (2004) for company resources, Arnould, Price, and Malshe (2006) propose the distinction between *operand resources* and *operant resources* also for consumers. The *operand resources* are the set of tangible possibilities available to consumers; typically these are economic and social (e.g. income, health, social relations, personal credit) or goods (raw materials and goods available to consumers). Some of these goods are acquired by exchanges with operators in the market, others can come from varying sources (gifts, inheritances, etc.). In contrast, the *operant resources* are the set of immaterial assets that consumers use in exchanges and that influence their purchasing and consumption decisions:

- physical and mental resources;
- social resources;
- cultural resources.

Each of these resources is tied to cultural schemes including conventions, traditions, and inherited gestural and verbal habits that are part of the consumers' world. Physical and mental resources embrace health, energy, strength, and emotional and sensorial perceptions. Social resources are relations or networks with other people, including the traditional demographic reference categories (e.g. the family, ethnic groups, social classes) as well as other emerging groupings (groups of friends, brand communities, subculture, and consumer tribes) on which consumers can exercise differing levels of command and control (Arnould, Price, & Malshe, 2006). Taken together, these cultural assets comprise the set of resources for various types of knowledge and cultural scheme, including cultural capital, and personal aims and abilities.

The important aspect is that the individual's resources vary not only in quantity but also in quality, and have an impact on the single life projects and on consumption practice. A number of studies have revealed that people with ample cultural resources tend to be oriented towards abstraction, affirmation of their own subjectivity, and the expression of self. In contrast, those with fewer resources appear directed more towards managing material limitations related to aspirations, functionality, and tradition (Holt, 1995).

Customer competences can be developed in various ways:

(a) creating innovations that bridge gaps in customer resources (resources that customers do not have or that they can use, for example, to create meanings);
(b) creating innovative experiential solutions or platforms that facilitate customer participation (simplicity, immediateness) and that offer the possibility to discover the experience progressively, enriching it with individual significance;
(c) providing the customer with the necessary functional skills and creating platforms that aid the construction of meaning.

With regard to the first alternative (creating innovations that bridge customer gaps), Philips Medical Systems offers a range of products to support its customers in the creation of value for the consumer (Box 12.1). In this case, the supplier acts as a partner with its own direct customer (typically from a hospital or diagnostic centre), supporting staff in the process of creating experience for the consumer, i.e. the patient. The idea is to extend the company's activities to include support for its customers, starting with the experience of the end-users and seeking to understand this experience and, consequently, help health sector organizations to create environments that reflect a particular positioning within the community. In practice, Philips bridges a gap among its customers, relieving them of the task of developing skills and resources that go beyond the principal supply environment.

Box 12.1   Philips Medical Systems

The strategy of Philips in recent years is synthesized in the brand promises "sense and simplicity" which make evident the mission and the values of the firm. Strongly committed in this perspective, the Medical Systems Division includes hi-tech medical products for various specializations, e.g. image diagnostics and cardiology. Its strategy is focused on technology and process innovation: the idea is to develop solutions in the forefront, simple to use for the people working – the doctors and the technical employees in the hospital – and carefully designed in order to enhance a pleasant experience for the patients. These ideas are well described on the website of the company:

We at Philips Medical Systems are driven by the passion and commitment to save human lives. With the help of doctors and experts, we develop technologies and processes for the health sector that render the diagnosis, treatment, and prevention of illness, as well as the management of health services, simple, accessible, and effective.

In the section *Products and Solutions* on the website, the company writes:

> *... Sure we develop breakthrough technology with sleek designs and meaningful ergonomics. But we're more about helping people save lives. Go through our product portfolio. Peruse our online literature. Learn more about the tools that can change outcomes for patients and professionals alike.*

The company's attention is focused on products and technologies, but above all on the awareness of the support that hospital staff need to use these instruments. They support their customers in choosing the instruments, considering their present and future goals, and in using them.

This attention goes as far as the consumer, the patient, or, better, starts from there. It is no surprise that in the *Products and Solutions* section on the website there is a part dedicated to the *ambient experience*, the context in which the customer experience occurs, which is centred on the patient's physical and emotional comfort, and especially on children's experience. When patients enter the room, they find the images of a selected theme projected on the wall, and they are immersed in some very relaxing light effects (Figure 12.3). The problem is one not only of product design but also of the environment in which the products are used. It is interesting to note that, in the search for solutions for their customers, the idea is that the starting point should not be the design of a system of products and services but rather the experience for the customer (from *system design* to *experience design*). This idea evokes the concept of the servicescape not only in its functional version but also in an emotional form with explicit reference to imagining something that goes beyond what we are used to and, maybe wrongly, consider obvious, but that may constitute a significant source of differentiation for a hospital:

> *Imagination takes flight*
> *Imagine if you could break down the barriers that can make a visit to the hospital an intimidating experience for patients, harnessing technology to*

enhance patient comfort and understanding, while providing each patient with a personalized experience that eases anxiety.

Imagine if you could create a world so inviting that your hospital becomes the premier choice for patients.

This is the world of Philips Experience Design. Experience Design refocuses space, lighting, and technology to create a positive experience for patients as well as hospital staff.

The areas of attention are physical and emotional comfort, the contact personnel, the customization of the experience, and the flow of hospital activities. With reference to the first aspect, the idea of an environment offering patients physical and emotional comfort is expressed as follows:

Destination: Happy place

When your patients enter your doors, they enter a foreign land. The language is strange. The customs are alien. The landscape is unfamiliar. While they are certain of the quality of care and comforted by the professionalism and kindness of staff, many patients experience feelings of helplessness and unease. We can help you change that.

Our vision focuses on using technology as a nearly invisible enabler, rather than an intrusive intimidator.

We have long been experts in designing patient-friendly medical products. Now we are focusing that expertise on the entire patient experience. We will help you evaluate your hospital – by meeting with patients and staff, conducting focus groups, and facilitating workshops – to create an environment that reflects your unique vision and place in the community.

This attention to the patients' experience has some positive effects because it allows a non-traumatic approach to the clinical test: it help patients, especially children, to relax and to experience the waiting time and the exam time without the anxiety often connected with these kinds of clinical test in the hospital. As a consequence it can reduce the use of drugs often required in order to relax patients.

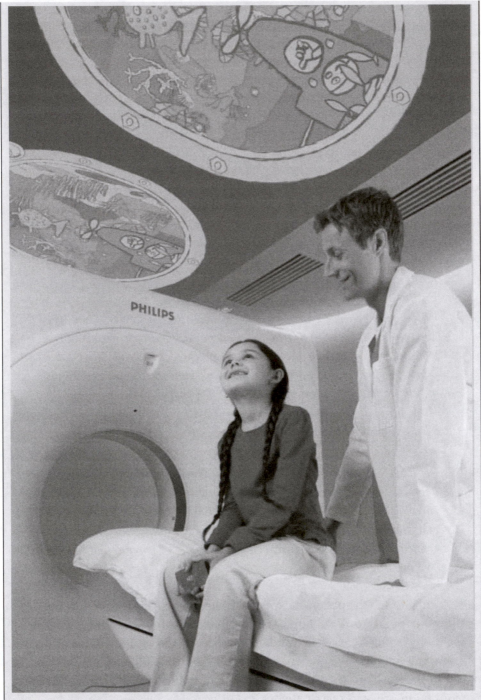

Figure 12.3 Philips ambient experience design in hospitals. Reprinted by permission of Philips Medical Systems, Italy. © 2007 Philips Medical Systems, Italy

Source: Carlo Camnasio, General Manager of Philips Medical Systems, personal interview, November 2007; *http://www.medical.philips.com* [July 2007]. Reproduced by permission of Dr C. G. Camnasio, Philips Medical Systems.

For the second alternative (creating innovative experiential solutions or platforms that facilitate customer participation and offer the possibility to discover the experience progressively, enriching it with individual significance), an interesting example is the Jyske Bank in Denmark which has tested a servicescape aimed at attracting customers to the bank by progressively reducing the gap in skills relating to the banking service that the average consumer might perceive (Box 12.2).

Box 12.2 Jyske Bank: a destructured context for an experiential bank

Jyske is the second largest private bank in Denmark, with 4 000 employees and 119 branches, and operates in both the retail and corporate sectors. The bank's founding value is the principle of balance: it places the shareholders, customers, and staff on the same level. Its vision includes being different from other banks and adopting an unpretentious style. Since September 2006, this approach has taken form in an original servicescape for the banking sector. The environment presented to Jyske Bank customers is unusual. Even from the outside, the institution offers a different welcome: through a window you can see the café where customers can take a cup of coffee (the bank wants to be remembered for its generosity).

At the *askbar*, customers can enquire about the bank's services. Flat plasma screens show news, weather forecasts, and other information. One branch has, on average, 10 screens. Operations are conducted at the *moneybar*. This area differs from the classical counter separated by glass and is furnished more like a trendy bar. Behind the teller, a screen presents financial and banking offers as packaged products. The space between the different bars forms the *market square*. Here customers find the *theme island*: areas offering the financial products packaged like software or CDs. Customers can take one and look at it as they would in a supermarket. There are about 40 products on offer, and each is presented in its own 2 minute video.

At the centre of the area, there is the *trybar*. The barcode on the package of the product that the customer wishes to check is read by an optical reader, and the screen shows the details of the "product".

The *oasis* is a corner of the branch where customers can sit down, relax, and read brochures or even books and magazines; it breaks the continuity with the banking theme.

In adjacent areas there are meeting rooms and "amusement arcades" where simulations can be carried out with the help of a financial consultant. The arcades have touch-screens that make presentations simple and interactive.

Jyske Bank's eye-catching packaging makes banking and financial services tangible in a literal sense. This is intended to intrigue customers and make them more prepared to seek information on alternatives, so reducing the distance that would be created by a simple, anonymous brochure. Customers can collect the information needed to choose a financial service in successive steps of increasing complexity according to individual needs for detail: from the packaging, to the video, to the financial consultant in the meeting rooms; from curiosity to an informed professionally explained choice.

In the branch environment, the bank wishes to mix the rational and the experiential dimensions. It is not a place for relaxation and leisure (in spite of the oases), but a bank with typical functions. However, customers face the experience of going to the bank in a freer and less structured way, similar to how they would act in a bar or place of entertainment. Technology plays a fundamental role not as the cold interface of the self-service but rather as an easily accessible and interactive means to understand and inspire customers' investments.

The bank's initiative is still too recent to forecast future development. Nevertheless, the first empirical evidence shows that it has almost doubled the net influx of customers over the last year compared with the comparable period the year before. This undoubtedly signals from the outset a trend towards an experiential approach even in a context such as a bank that is dominated by rationality and functionality.

Source: Frank Pedersen, Director Communication and Marketing, Jyske Bank, personal interview, November 2007; *http://www.jyskebank.dk* [August 2007]. Reproduced by permission of Frank Pedersen.

Finally, regarding the third possibility (providing the customer with the necessary functional skills and creating platforms that aid the construction of meaning), an interesting case is that of Andria, a residents' cooperative in Correggio (Reggio Emilia), Italy, which started its activities building houses (Box 12.3).

Box 12.3   Andria: integration of solutions and experiences

Andria is a residents' building cooperative founded in 1975 in Correggio (Reggio Emilia), Italy. The name is inspired by that of the ideal city imagined by the famous author Italo Calvino in one of his stories. The cooperative has built over 2000 houses, 70 rented apartments for immigrants, and eight nursery centres for infants. There are approximately 5000 members of the cooperative, who are also residents in the houses that have been built.

Every project is designed according to the specific needs of target customers. For example, Andria designed the "Case per GioCo" (i.e. houses for play), a type of house for young couples that can be progressively modified in relation to their financial budget, the birth of children, and any other family change. Another project has been dedicated to children. Based on research that has originated a "Manifest of the housing needs of children", Andria has designed Coriandoline (Figure 12.4), a boys-and-girls-friendly neighbourhood, which recalls a sense of magic, shaped around children's needs and desires, rich in space for play, with walls representing images from fairy tales.

Figure 12.4   Andria – Coriandoline. Reprinted by permission of Andria, Italy. © 2007 Andria, Italy

Andria uses an approach that expressly integrates solutions and experiences. Every housing initiative takes account of the fact that a house purchase is not only a rational decision but also an extremely emotional choice for a family. It is a question not merely of square metres and solicitors' contracts but also of dreams and unique personal and family investments in the life of an individual. Andria's approach is at both levels.

In technical terms, Andria assists the customer from their first meeting in the cooperative's offices up to the handing over of the keys. Over the years, Andria has recorded its technical skills in its "Building-site Guide", a short vade mecum describing the various phases of the house-building process. For example, it indicates what is customizable and to what extent and when the customer can request any customizations; it explains that site visits are only possible together with a representative of the cooperative; it indicates who will have technical responsibility and act as the essential reference point for the customer throughout the project.

The second level is imaginative and experiential. Over the years, Andria has developed know-how regarding the emotions involved when families buy houses, known in the vernacular as "mal della pietra" (stone-ache). Building a house is a dream that, in the face of the difficulties involved in such a complex project, is also accompanied with a streak of real suffering for the customer. The cooperative has developed a model that divides the process into four phases: customer interest in buying a house; signing of initial contract; building; completion and life in the new house. Each phase is marked by an emotional state ranging from the euphoria that the project is starting to the distress caused by the complexity of the work. In each of these phases, Andria intervenes with services and communication to smooth these fluctuations.

For example, the family entering the new house at the end of the process experiences a sense of abandonment. Small imperfections are exaggerated, while some delusions are the result of unrealistic expectations. To help the family at this difficult moment, a member of Andria's staff is on hand when they move in to expel any feelings of misery that may have accumulated during the long building period.

Solutions and experiences refer not only to single houses but also to the entire estates in which Andria operates. They pay attention to the communal areas to make them welcoming; and they are introducing nursery schools in the estates with a conception of housing that is being extended in the light of the complexity of people's living conditions. Andria works in close contact with local authorities to help resolve urban problems, such as the recovery of degraded areas, or the demand for low–medium-cost houses for immigrant families. The cooperative's initiatives aim to celebrate the local area, starting with its historical and cultural features. In this way, Andria becomes a reference partner for the community of Correggio.

From the experiential point of view, Andria seeks to create in the estates a harmonious community life. To this end, it creates "really false" legends to root the origins of its activities in an imaginary world. The Lemizzone site has a brochure illustrating the legend of the mythical King Lamizzo, a character created by a local author. Tired of fighting, King Lamizzo settled down happily in the area where the estate that now bears his name has been built and where the medieval king's "really false" tomb can also be found. A relaxed sense of community has been created around the story of King Lamizzo, such that the residents, taking up and taking over the stimulus from Andria, organize carnival festivals in historical costume. The experience of the house is thereby extended to an experience of a village community.

Source: Luciano Pantaleoni, General Manager, Andria Cooperativa di abitanti, personal interviews; *www.andria.it*, June 2007 (Carù *et al.*, 2004). Reproduced by permission of Luciano Pantaleoni.

From a position of strength founded on continual dialogue with its customers/associates, the cooperative analysed individuals' needs in depth. Initially, housing for particular market segments with specific requirements was designed (e.g. "Case per Gio.Co" – houses for young couples that could be progressively developed internally by the residents themselves on the basis of their family needs and economic resources – or for families with elderly parents). Next, they moved on to the creation of entire estates with particular attention to the communal areas that are an important part of people's living experience. They are currently designing nursery schools on the estates. The question of housing has broadened to that of living, and it has become more complicated, just as the lives of many people are becoming more complicated. By analysing their experience in housing, Andria is developing projects able to provide solutions to a broad and complex system of required benefits. In so doing, the cooperative has also assumed the role of resource and competence integrator. The engineering skills linked to construction have been joined by expertise regarding the local territory and the pedagogic skills to design the schools and give them their specific imprinting (Carù *et al.*, 2004). The case demonstrates an approach that offers customers the information necessary to interact with a building site during the construction process while also developing an experiential platform in which customers can freely use their imagination to build meanings that enrich their experience.

All of these examples help to identify some necessary basic principles required to set up co-creation strategies. In particular, it is important to underline the need to make every form of innovation understandable and accessible to customers, bearing in mind the operand and, above all, operant resources that the latter possess and generally use in exchanges.

Conclusion

Taking account of the principles aimed at maintaining intact the sense of identity desired, together with the co-existence of very different pressures even within a single individual, we suggest some summary guidelines that may be useful in designing and defining the spaces for innovation. These indications can serve to innovate both content and processes and, as stated above, concern the functional and symbolic aspects of an innovative offer:

- identify possible meanings that consumers can ascribe to specific product/ service concepts;
- include in the strategy the "philosophy of multiple meanings";
- adopt the vision of "infinite possibilities";
- take into account different levels of consumer participation and involvement during the experience and/or solution creation process.

1. *Identify possible meanings that consumers can ascribe to specific product/service concepts.* The first important aspect obviously concerns the awareness of the existence of multiple significances that consumers may attribute to product/ service concepts. In practical terms, this means trying to identify the range of possible meanings, understanding how a specific product, service, or brand fits into consumers' lives and life projects. What aspects of consumers' identities can a specific product/service satisfy? How big is this class? How much space does a company have to intervene in these aspects? How valid is the principle of continuity with respect to others? How do the products and services fit into consumers' current system of objects, solutions, and experiences?

2. *Include in the strategy the "philosophy of multiple meanings".* The second aspect, linked to the philosophy of multiple meanings, specifically emphasizes the need to resort always to the logic that suppliers themselves will inevitably produce a multiplicity of meanings that can be attributed by consumers, even for the same single consumer. If well managed, this philosophy allows the space for innovation to be expanded considerably and the competitive advantage horizon to be raised.

3. *Adopt the vision of "infinite possibilities".* Obviously tied to this basic principle, the idea of adopting a vision of infinite possibilities also marks the need to take account of the directions that the multiple meanings produce in terms of perceptions of innovation. Multiple meanings can be attributed not only to the

innovative products themselves; rather they are multiplied for each different dimension of identity that they can fill with content. The same innovation can be a playful experience, a functional solution, a tool to increase consumption competence, and a means of enhancing self-esteem in the professional dimension of individual identity. Who says that people choose iPods just for the beautiful design, the ease-of-use, and the myth of an anti-mainstream brand? The iPod is also an instrument to satisfy identity ideals tied to the need to feel able to play a professional or social role, etc.

4. *Take into account different levels of consumer participation and involvement during the experience and/or solution creation process.* The co-creation of value by companies and consumers requires an understanding of the roles that the two players assume and the marketing tools that companies can use in these processes. However, this is not everything. Another fundamental aspect is the need to identify the different levels of involvement that consumers them-selves wish to establish with companies and the bundle of resources (operand and operant) that are at their disposal.

Companies do not create consumer experiences, but can contribute to their creation by offering their resources to consumers. The latter will decide whether and how to use these resources, assuming then the main role in modelling their experiences. Not all customers and consumers are prepared to play an active part in this process of involvement.

Each innovation based on this logic must be flexible and consider contexts that allow various levels of appropriation and participation.

Figure 12.5 summarizes the considerations in this chapter, highlighting the role of companies and customers in the co-creation of value generated from the combi-nation of competences and responsibilities and activities that both players must present.

Returning to Vargo and Lusch (2004), a company's products and services can be seen as the expression of its competences and resources, which customers exploit to their own advantage, using, in turn, their own tangible and intangible resources (Arnould, 2007) (see Chapter 6 of Carù, 2007).

Companies and consumers act with their own resources, and the processes of value generation lead to the joint use of these resources. In this framework,

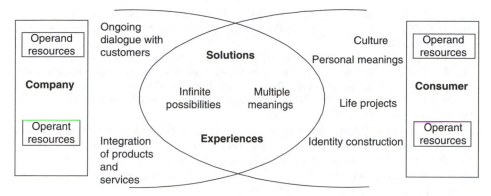

Figure 12.5   The co-creation of solutions and experiences

companies cannot govern all the processes, but must consider the active role of the consumer. Consumers contribute to the process, guided by their own life projects and the construction of their own identities. Many significances full of different meanings are generated, so designing potentially new combinations of experience and solutions.

The natural corollary of these considerations is the importance of defining, and the necessity to define, the system of integrated resources required to offer a solution to consumer needs. If contexts are generally created by companies, they must, nevertheless, leave some freedom to consumers, whose participation has to be facilitated by appropriate means, and take account of their resources and competences.

References

Arnould, E. J. (2007) "Consuming experience, retrospects and prospects", in *Consuming Experience*, edited by Carù, A. & Cova, B. Routledge, Oxford, UK, pp. 185–194.

Arnould, E. J. & Thompson, C. J. (2005) "Consumer culture theory (CCT): twenty years of research". *Journal of Consumer Research*, vol. 31, March, pp. 868–882.

Arnould, E. J., Price L., & Malshe A. (2006) "Toward a cultural resource-based theory of the customer", in *The Service-dominant Logic of Marketing: Dialog, Debate, and Directions*, edited by Lusch, R. F. & Vargo, S. L. ME Sharpe, Armonk, NY, pp. 91–104.

Baudrillard, J. (1998) *The Consumer Society. Myths and Structures*. Sage Publications, London, UK.

Belk, R. W. (1988) "Possessions and extended self". *Journal of Consumer Research*, vol. 15, September, pp. 139–168.

Breakwell, G. M. (1986) *Coping with Threatened Identity*. Methuen, London, UK.

Carù, A. (2007) *Consumo e Marketing dei Servizi. L'Evoluzione verso Esperienze e Soluzioni*. EGEA, Milan, Italy.

Carù, A. & Cova, B. (eds) (2007) *Consuming Experiences*. Routledge, Abingdon, UK.

Carù, A., Cova, B., & Pace, S. (2004) "Project success: lessons from the Andria case". *European Management Journal*, vol. 22, no. 5, October, pp. 532–545.

Gilmore, J. H. & Pine, B. J. (2002) "The experience IS the marketing". *Strategic Horizons*, vol. 26, August, pp. 1–14.

Gottdiener, M. (2000) "Approaches to consumption: classical and contemporary perspectives", in *New Forms of Consumption. Consumers, Culture, and Commodification*, edited by Gottdiener, M. Rowman & Littlefield Publishers, Inc., Lanham, MD, pp. 3–31.

Griffin, A. & Hauser, J. (1993) "The voice of the customer". *Marketing Science*, vol. 12, no. 1, Winter, pp. 1–27.

Gustafsson, A. & Johnson, M. D. (2003) *Competing in a Service Economy*. Jossey-Bass, San Francisco, CA.

Holt, D. B. (1995) "How consumers consume: a typology of consumption practices". *Journal of Consumer Research*, vol. 22, June, pp. 1–16.

Kozinets, R. V., Sherry Jr, J. F., Borghini, S. *et al.* (2005) "American Girl: the family brand", in *Advances in Consumer Research*, edited by Menon, G. & Rao, A. R. Association for Consumer Research, Provo, UT, vol. 32, pp. 10–11.

Kozinets, R. V., Sherry Jr, J., Storm, D., *et al.* (2004) "Ludic agency and retail spectacle". *Journal of Consumer Research*, vol. 31, December, pp. 658–672.

Leonard-Barton, D. (1995) *Wellsprings of Knowledge. Building and Sustaining the Sources of Innovation*. Harvard Business School Press, Boston, MA.

Lusch, R. F. & Vargo, S. L. (2006) "Service-dominant logic: reactions, reflections and refinements". *Marketing Theory*, vol. 6, no. 3, pp. 281–288.

Murray, J. B. (2002) "The politics of consumption: a re-inquiry on Thompson and Haytko's (1997) 'Speaking of Fashion'". *Journal of Consumer Research*, vol. 29, December, pp. 427–440.

Prahalad, C. K. & Ramaswamy, V. (2004) *The Future of Competition: Co-creating Unique Value with Customers*. Harvard Business School Press, Boston, MA.

Schau, H. J. & Gilly, M. C. (2003) "We are what we post? Self-presentation in personal web space". *Journal of Consumer Research*, vol. 30, December, pp. 385–404.

Thomke, S. H. & von Hippel, E. (2002) "Customers as innovators: a new way to create value". *Harvard Business Review*, vol. 80, no. 4, pp. 74–81.

Thompson, C. J. & Hirschman, E. C. (1995) "Understanding the socialized body: a poststructuralist analysis of consumers' self-conceptions, body images, and self-care practices". *Journal of Consumer Research*, vol. 22, September, pp. 139–153.

Vargo, S. L. & Lusch, R. F. (2004) "Evolving to a new dominant logic for marketing". *Journal of Marketing*, vol. 68, no. 1, pp. 1–14.

Zerbini, F., Golfetto, F., & Gibbert, M. (2007) "Marketing of competence: exploring the resource-based content of value for customer through a case-study analysis". *Industrial Marketing Management*, vol. 36, no. 6, pp. 784–798.

13

How Market Perceptions Influence Knowledge Strategies on User Involvement

John K. Christiansen, Anne Sofie Lefèvre,
Claus J. Varnes, & Astrid S. Wolf

Introduction

Researchers have used different arguments to explain how user involvement can develop knowledge in innovation processes and why it is important. To many, user involvement is a prerequisite for successful innovation that leads to successful product launches in the market. User involvement is presented variously as a matter of strategic concern (Prahalad & Ramaswamy, 2000, 2004a), as a strategy to reduce risk (Ogawa & Piller, 2006), as a source of obtaining novel ideas and solutions from lead users (von Hippel, 1986, 1998; Jeppesen, 2005), or as a way to create user communities around firms and/or products (Franke & Shah, 2003). Other researchers regard user interaction as a way to uncover functional requirements of a product and ensure these are incorporated into new product specifications (Griffin & Hauser, 1993), or as a matter of getting users involved in the right phases and in the right way (Gruner & Homburg, 2000). Studies have found that, while competitor orientation increases the introduction of me-too products and reduces the launching of line extensions and new-to-the-world products, customer orientation increases the introduction of new-to-the-world products and reduces the launching of me-too products (Lukas & Ferrell, 2000). Critical voices have been raised as "firms lose their position of industry leadership...because they listen too carefully to their customers" (Christensen & Bower, 1996, p. 198).

Others have presented radically different approaches and views on the role and perspective of the relationship between users and companies. The design-driven approach (Verganti, 2003) and the constructivist perspective on the relationship in innovation (Latour, 1991; Kreiner & Tryggestad, 2002) are two such approaches. The design-driven approach claims that companies should propose and design new futures, while the constructivists maintain that markets, technologies, and products are co-produced in an ongoing interaction between companies, users, and technology.

Thus, companies can choose between different approaches with reference to user interaction with varying objectives. The choice of strategies for user interaction might be influenced by different factors. However, we claim that the company's perception of the market and the relationship between the market and the firm must be a major – if not the most important – factor when companies design and choose their interaction strategy and the manner in which they utilize the results of this interaction. The perception of the market and how it relates to the company not only influences the methods and approaches chosen for user interaction but also influences the company's understanding of the relationship between itself, the product innovation process, and users and how the knowledge can and will be utilized (Berthon, Hulbert, & Pitt, 1999; Verganti, 2003).

The differences between market perceptions and user involvement rely on different epistemological assumptions on knowledge and markets and their relationship to firms. The issue of different market perceptions and the relationship to the choice of strategies for user interaction has not been addressed in previous research. Some have addressed the need to distinguish between customer orientation and market orientation (Slater & Narver, 1998, 1999). We follow this line of thought to claim that different perceptions of markets have implications for the meaning of market creation and its execution, and thus on how the user-related knowledge is utilized in the innovation processes.

The chapter starts with an overview of four different definitions of markets and their implications: structuralism, reconstructivism, interactional, and constructivism. Subsequently, methods for user involvement are discussed and divided into two groups: "traditional" marketing methods and "context-oriented" approaches. Thirdly, we discuss the relationship between perceptions of markets and the use of different knowledge strategies on user involvement from a theoretical point of view. The observations from an empirical study of four companies and their use of various approaches – and how these relate to different perceptions of markets – are then discussed. Finally, we discuss the observations and the implications of the study for theory and managers.

Four market perspectives

A market is often defined as a place where exchanges between the products/ services and customers occur. In this view, the concept of the market represents the sum of potential customers (Porter, 1980). However, various definitions of markets, market orientations, and customer orientation have been offered and discussed in many publications (Berthon, Hulbert, & Pitt, 1999; Shapiro, 1988; Narver & Slater, 1990; Slater & Narver, 1999). Yet, for the present purpose, four perspectives on markets have been identified, as we are interested in how companies relate to their market, which, in this context, includes customers and customer orientation.

The structuralist perception of the market

The structuralist market perception assumes that the market has a stable structure and a boundary, which can be identified beforehand (Kim & Mauborgne, 2005) and which cannot be influenced by a single company assuming perfect competition (Kim & Mauborgne, 1999a, 1999b; Porter, 1980). The company's strategic goal is to position itself inside the industry where it can best defend itself against competing forces. Positioning often results in a competition-based approach to strategy (Kim & Mauborgne, 2005; Porter, 1980). Within this logic, companies ideally select among cost, differentiation, and niche strategies to optimize the position in the market (Porter, 1980). The market and the sum of customers are therefore perceived as relatively fixed entities with a certain market potential (e.g. target customers in segments). While competing for the same customers, the pivotal point for companies is to retain and increase the customer base. The tools used are segmentation and customization (Lampel & Mintzberg, 1996), where focus is directed to differences in customer preferences (Kim & Mauborgne, 2005).

This perception departs from an assumption that companies act autonomously in relation to the development of products, production processes, marketing messages, and managing sales channels without any – or only a very weak – degree of user involvement. Thus, users are primarily involved in the exchange of offerings (Prahalad & Ramaswamy, 2004a, 2004b), and the company and users have different roles – one as the producer and the other as the consumer (Prahalad & Ramaswamy, 2004a; Prahalad, 2004). The company is the value creator, because value creation exclusively takes place inside the company through exchange activities (Prahalad & Ramaswamy, 2004a, 2004b; Prahalad, 2004), and the product or service is perceived as the *carrier* of this value.

The reconstructivist perception of the market

As an alternative to the structural understanding of the market, Kim and Mauborgne (2005) advance a *dynamic* perception of the market – what they label as a reconstructivist point of view. The argument is that market structures are constantly reconstructed and reconfigured owing to the higher intensity of competition faced by companies, which in turn makes profitable growth hard to accomplish through a structuralist-oriented approach to strategy (Kim & Mauborgne, 1997).

This view states that market creation should be based on the notion of designing products possessing a superior value for the customer, thereby making the competition irrelevant. This requires transcendence from existing market structures (Kim & Mauborgne, 1999b), a strategic logic that denotes value innovations (Kim & Mauborgne, 2005, 1999a, 1997). Similarly to the structuralist market perspective, products are perceived as carriers of values, and equally it is a company-centred value creation process, where the company is the creator of this value. The customer is again the passive recipient of a given service; however, during the innovation process the user can have a more active role in the creation of a given service or product (Prahalad & Ramaswamy, 2003).

Exploration beyond the needs of existing customers in the market is pivotal while making value innovations. This assumption is based on untouched and/or not yet identified demands that enable the creation of new markets (Kim & Mauborgne, 2005, 1999a). To generate new markets, and not only capture market shares in the existing market, companies must develop an understanding of how to attract consumers from other markets into new needs. Companies pursuing this reconstructivist logic should therefore not be restricted by conditions defined by the conventional perceptions of the industry, competitors, or market segments. On the contrary, they must seek to expand their creative scope by breaking these external conditions and assumptions about markets and needs, as this will make it possible to identify more opportunities (Kim & Mauborgne, 1999b).

The interactional perception of the market

Prahalad and Ramaswamy (2000, 2003, 2004a, 2004b) challenge the view that the market represents the place where economic extraction is allocated, that the company creates value through its output, and also dispute that products themselves are carriers of value. Instead, this view claims that value creation takes place in the interaction processes between the company, customer, and communities (Prahalad & Ramaswamy, 2003), and it becomes important to create an environment where users can obtain a personalized experience.

This perspective builds on the claim that the asymmetry that previously existed between companies and customers' access to information has been equalized because of the arrival of connected, informed, powerful, and active customers (Prahalad & Ramaswamy, 2000). This view challenges the conventional perception of the customer as passive in the value creation process. Another challenge is the prevailing overlap between industries and convergence of technologies, and accepted distinctions of products and service channels (Prahalad & Ramaswamy, 2004a, 2004b, 2003).

By acknowledging that value is created *with* the customer and not for the customer, the market is no longer perceived as a given sum of potential customers. In this view, interactions with the customers and with the diverse customer communities are important for companies. The process is one of concurrent value creation and consumption. This interaction requires that the company continuously gets ideas for new interactions, for example, by linking to different and new communities and companies that the consumers can interact with, thereby creating an experience environment, which enhances the possibility of creating personalized experiences for the customers.

Thus, the meaning of market changes, as the market is now perceived as a forum in which conversation and interaction between customers, communities, and companies takes place. The market becomes inseparable from the value creation process (Prahalad & Ramaswamy, 2004b) and the focus is on the exchange and interaction processes. The customers' co-creation of the product's value fundamentally changes the traditional division between supply and demand, as demand in this perspective is contextual. Value creation is defined by the experience of the respective customer in a given time and place, and in the context of a specific event.

The constructivist perception of the market

The constructivist perspective is based on recent works in sociology and organizational theory, which address the continuous creation and re-creation of entities and relationships by focusing on relationships and networks in processes. Therefore, it is impossible – in this perspective – to identify something or a group of customers as a market or a segment of a market "out there". What are relevant here are the more or less stable networks between entities (Latour, 2005). Lately, the importance and impact of the constructivist perspective have been recognized in marketing, as it has a profound impact on providing new insights into what constitutes markets, consumers, companies, and their relationships (Araujo, 2007).

The constructivist market perspective represents the most dynamic and fragile perception of what constitutes a market, because it is constructed through a process of framing that allows many possible associations and relations to be sorted and classified. A frame establishes a boundary around which interactions take place independently of their context (Callon, 1998b). For example, companies are developing segmentation models that can help to sort different types of customers, and are calculating market size by estimating how big a market share they possess. In this way, companies construct models of what is "out there". However, the constructed models are not "true" reflections but images or representations (re)produced through investigations, experiences, education, and negotiations.

As the constructivists perceive the market as a temporary construction, what constitutes a market at a given point of time has dynamic characteristics, as it is continually constructed. Furthermore, in the constructivist perspective, elements such as customers or a product are the outcome of a stabilization of certain characteristics for a longer or shorter period (Callon, Méadel, & Rabeharisoa, 2002). The stabilization or creation of what is represented as a product can be seen in the relationships between the manufacturer, the designers, customers, and the available technologies and tools (Kreiner & Tryggestad, 2002). This perspective changes the meaning of the concept of goods:

> *A product is an economic good that can be seen from a variety of perspectives: production, circulation, and use. Thus a product corresponds to a process, a trajectory in time, whereas a good corresponds to a state at a point in time. Services can be turned into goods too by defining and objectifying their properties making them tradable – e.g. a rented car available for a limited period of time and for pre-specified users. (Araujo, 2007, p. 213)*

The distinction between being a customer and being a company is pointless within this perspective (Kreiner & Tryggestad, 2002). However, it is not only in relation to the development of products that the constructivists claim that a distinction between company and customer becomes obsolete. Pushed to extremes, these authors will claim that the distinction between company and customer will have little significance, because the roles can change from one day to the next (Kreiner & Tryggestad, 2002). It is the use of something that turns it into a credible product. Thus, the customer shows trust and confidence in what then becomes a product (Callon, Méadel, & Rabeharisoa, 2002). The relation to the customer creates the product as something. Otherwise it would be nothing.

This blurring of roles of the company and the customer shows that it is not the product itself that carries value, but value is attributed only through relationships. How the establishment of networks and relationships creates a "product" is illustrated with an example of a process ending with a new camera (Box 13.1), which represents the outcome of a long co-creation process between multiple actors.

Box 13.1   The creation of a product through relationships

In 1887, Kodak introduced the Eastman's camera, which was the first amateur camera on the market. An examination of the sequence illustrates how the product development process and the development of the mass market for amateur photographs are created simultaneously in an inter-woven process. During the process, the technical, the economical, and the social structures are changing. Different players, both human and non-human, are replaced by other players. We are thereby not following the development of a camera through a given context, but on the contrary the simultaneous production of "text" and "context" (Latour, 1991).

Throughout the development process, until the Kodak camera is a reality, every new initiative is dependent on how the players are receiving it. Hence, the process cannot be seen as a linear process that is building on a technological development, as every step can change both the camera and the players in a dialectic process. The point is that we are always integrated in a chain of human and non-human players; hence, the social is not only a chain of humans and the technical not only a chain of non-humans, as "... nothing becomes real to a point of not needing a network in which to upkeep its existence" (Latour, 1991, p. 118).

Pushed to extremes, it could be proposed that the idea of uncovering customer needs conflicts with the constructivist logic, as it is not obvious who the customer is, as the customer is defined through the process and multiple heterogeneous possible relationships exist that are performative, i.e. of a temporary nature (Callon, 1998a). Also, customers in this perspective are seen as performative constructs that are only stable owing to a temporary strong network around some actors.

Approaches to user involvement

User involvement in innovation and market creation is done through multiple methods. Inspired by Slater and Narver (1998), we will distinguish between traditional methods and context-oriented methods. Traditional customer-oriented marketing methods focus on understanding the expressed desires of the customers in the served markets of companies (Slater & Narver, 1998, p. 1002). One common denominator characterizes traditional marketing methods: whether using focus groups, the voice of the customer (Griffin & Hauser, 1993), in-depth interviews, or questionnaires, the approach is to ask the users/consumers in different ways about a given product or situation to map needs and desires. It is assumed that it is possible to explicate and articulate desires and needs, which subsequently delivers input to new concepts and products (Kumar & Whitney, 2003).

Differing from the market-driven approaches, the practice of other methods such as empathic design, lead user approach (with user communities), and the design-driven approach represents context-oriented approaches. These approaches, in different ways, take into account that users are not always capable of articulating their needs, that companies need to understand the context, scan the market more broadly, and have a long-term focus, and that companies need to go beyond immediate articulated needs (Slater & Narver, 1998, p. 1004) or even design the future for customers (Verganti, 2003) to come up with unique selling propositions through new products and services. A number of context-oriented methods can be found, but four have been of special interest to many companies in recent years.

Empathic design

In 1997, Dorothy Leonard introduced empathic design based on an increased understanding of the functioning of the human mind (Leonard, 2000). According to Leonard, traditional marketing methods are insufficient to uncover user needs, as each individual possesses tacit knowledge about his/her work routines, surroundings, and experiences. Some people automatically innovate if a product does not seem to make sense in the context in which it is being used. Maybe the product is being used differently than imagined by the designer, or the user changes the usability and hence unconsciously changes the design or use of the product. These types of modification innovation are often unconscious and unarticulated – they happen through the practice of using products – and users/consumers are often unaware of their needs or have experienced problems that led to the changes. Empathic design thus focuses on the latent needs of users (Leonard & Rayport, 1997; Leonard, 2000) which cannot be directly expressed or formulated and are therefore not exposed by using traditional marketing methods.

Empathic design provides techniques that enable companies to reach users' tacit knowledge or latent needs (Leonard & Rayport, 1997). Instead of asking the users about their needs, managers should gather a cross-functional team and employ anthropology and ethnographic methods to observe users in their own settings and environment, e.g. equipped with videos and cameras. The essence of this approach is listening and empathizing with consumers or users being observed rather than interrupting and asking questions (Leonard, 2000). Through their observations, the team get visual feedback on how users approach different products and services and their latent needs are revealed. These needs will provide input and ideas to innovative products that could lead the company to establish new markets (Leonard & Rayport, 1997; Leonard, 2000).

The lead user approach

Eric von Hippel introduced the lead user approach in 1986. Similarly to the assumptions underlying empathic design, the lead user approach considers user insight in new product and service needs and in potential solutions, limited by users' "real-world experiences" (von Hippel, 1986). Thus, "ordinary" users will almost certainly not be able to generate new product concepts, whereas some user practices could point to future conditions. Also, traditional marketing approaches have been found to produce too many incremental product modifications and me-too products (Christensen & Bower, 1996) and even lead to complete misunderstandings of what customers and markets might want. It has been suggested that approaches such as the lead user approach can be relevant when companies have high innovation orientation and want to interact with or shape the market (Berthon, Hulbert, & Pitt, 1999).

Von Hippel aims to address a special type of user, namely the lead users. They are able to provide companies with knowledge about future needs and solutions. The lead users are ahead of trends and might address needs that are still latent in the general market and that will become noticeable months or years later. A further characteristic of lead users is that they benefit from innovating. Therefore, the task is to incorporate lead users and extract their knowledge, seize the latent needs of the market, and get ideas for new products or knowledge of potential solutions. It is important to note that lead users are not necessarily found within a company's own industry (von Hippel, 1986) but might be users in related or distant areas that can provide solutions, ideas, or knowledge as input to the innovation processes. The inputs provided from the lead users thus represent a rather broad spectrum, from specific ideas for new surgical instruments, to new ways of treating skin problems, to more general inputs about methods or approaches (von Hippel, 1986) that can be transferred from one domain to another. The first two examples need little translation, while the latter requires long and many translations to be applied. Recently, the lead user concept has been especially popular within software development, as user communities have been seen as an example of lead users (Shah & Franke, 2003).

Communities approach

The communities approach is complementary to the lead user approach in the sense that users in the user communities are often – but not always – themselves lead users who, as opposed to "ordinary" users, will be able to articulate their latent needs and in addition will benefit from innovating (von Hippel & Katz, 2002; Jeppesen, 2005). An example of a community could be a surf club, in either a virtual/online or physical form, which means that it is a gathering of people who share similar interests, explore possibilities, and look for solutions. For example, in a user community, if a member has a suggestion for improving the design of a surf board, not only does the member share this idea with other members of the community but other members also contribute with ideas and suggestions for further developments. Members who reveal interesting ideas or valuable contributions obtain recognition from other members (von Hippel, 2005; Shah & Franke, 2003). In some user communities on the Internet there is a "grading" system based on the number and/or quality of helpful solutions submitted to the forum.

Companies can search for communities or try to create and support them. By listening to, or participating in, communities, companies not only obtain ideas for new products but might also find that members already have developed new ideas, concepts, or solutions (Jeppesen & Molin, 2003). Furthermore, companies can offer communities a free toolkit enabling users to complete the product development or to pursue their own ideas (Jeppesen & Molin, 2003; von Hippel, 1998; Franke & Piller, 2004). In this way, companies can tap into the sources of creativity and solutions.

Design-driven innovation

Design-driven innovation is based on the idea that every product has its own language and meaning (Verganti, 2003) and that companies might "make proposals to customers about the future" and use the design of products and services actively. The products' meaning "... proposes to the user a system of values, a personality and identity that may easily go beyond style" (Verganti, 2003, p. 36). In design-driven innovation the message and the design language of a product are in focus, not the functional or technological characteristics (see Box 13.2).

Box 13.2   Design-driven innovation in action

The designers play a crucial role within a design-driven approach, and the selection of designers and the design language are of strategic importance. The computer company Apple noticed that many people bought computers to have at home in living areas and not in designated office spaces. Therefore, Apple wished to design a computer that could be perceived as any other piece of design furniture. In other words, the company wanted to design a computer with a "homelike" language, as it was observed that computers were often hidden in the living rooms. Apple looked for a designer who could interpret and understand the users' homelike sphere to develop a computer with a new design language. They identified a designer who had designed bathrooms and other home equipment. The result of that collaboration was the organic shaped and coloured computer, with integrated screen and computer drives, which turned out to be a great success. This design was originally launched in 1998 and later introduced as the "all-in-one" computer, with several major modifications and new releases since then (adapted from Verganti, 2003).

By designing and offering integrated computers to be displayed in the homes of customers, Apple probably also addressed some needs of the users, e.g. not having a clutter of wires lying around, but this might have been a side effect of the product language.

Design-driven innovation does not include a direct involvement of the users and could be regarded as more closely related to technology-driven approaches than to customer- or market-driven approaches. The basic idea rests on the construction of a specific and unique product language that is created through a network of different interpreters, e.g. designers, architects, design schools, cultural events, and studies of sociocultural trends. These interpreters are able to understand sociocultural phenomena that are not visible in the present but will be trends of the future and transform these into proposals that are included into the design of products. By understanding the sociocultural phenomena or models, which consist of infinite interactions between users, companies, designers, products, schools, etc., interpreters identify new product languages. The interpreters read the users' current world and envisioned future, and the users in that sense merely provide the background and only indirectly take part in the innovation process.

Through these interpretations, companies obtain knowledge about future trends and insights into the subtle dynamics of values and meanings of society (Verganti, 2003) that deliver the input to the design and development processes in companies. Design-driven innovation does not focus on the development of products that fulfil the functional and operational needs of users. Instead, it focuses on producing new meanings or product languages that speak to the emotional needs of the users, and in that way creating unique offerings to customers.

Relating market perception and strategies for user involvement

How strategies for user involvement relate to market perceptions will be discussed in the following. These relationships are presented in a framework (Table 13.1) and empirically explored in the next section.

The structuralist market perception and the user involvement strategies

If a company undertakes a structuralist market perception, the choice of a user involvement strategy would be traditional marketing methods. This view focuses on how to deliver goods and services to identified segments of customers, and the

Table 13.1 The relations between the four market perceptions and user involvement approaches

	Structuralism	Reconstructivism	Interactional	Constructivism
Traditional marketing methods	A	A	C	C
The lead user approach	B-C	A	B	B
Empathic design	B-C	A	B	B
Communities	B-C	A	A	B
Design-driven approach	C	C	C	A

A – the market perception and the practice suit each other well.
B – the market perception and the practice suit each other partly.
C – the market perception is in conflict with an employment of the practice.

main challenge is to extract knowledge about their needs as input for product and service innovation. The company produces the value and the market is created through segmentation, as market boundaries are regarded as stable, and the company has to compete within these limitations to seize market share. Gaining market share calls for application of the traditional marketing methods, since it is possible to either segment through objective factors, which could be geographic and demographic, or segment through psychographic factors such as lifestyle or different social classes because segments must be measurable (Pelsmacker, Geneuens, & den Bergh, 2004) and data are mostly collected using questionnaires and other methods. Segmentation through life style, for instance, requires the use of focus and/or in-depth interviews. Using marketing methods for segmentation reflects the (implicit) understanding that the needs of users can be articulated, extracted, and analysed and used to produce an image of the optional market and its segments.

All the more, the inherent non-dynamic view in this structuralist market percep-tion suggests that, if methods like empathic design, the lead user approach, or communities were employed, their potential could not be explored fully. For instance, a structuralist market perception might not be sufficiently open actually to exploit information on the user's context when observing and analysing through empathic design. In the structuralist market view, the notion of what is interesting in the user's context is a priori framed by the perception of relevance within the industry in which the company competes. This line of argument applies to the use of the lead user and communities approaches as well. Companies with a structuralist market perception are supposed to work only within the identified market boundaries when (un)covering existing or potential customers' needs which exclude the use of design-driven innovations as this practice focuses on broad sociocultural phenomena where the customers or users only play a minor part. Conceptually, design-driven innovations do not include the notion of a specific user base.

The reconstructivist market perception and the user involvement strategies

Companies with a reconstructivist market perception can make use of traditional marketing methods and several of the context-oriented approaches: empathic design, lead user, and the use of communities. These practices can facilitate the redefinition of markets and segments by providing new and interesting observations on identified user needs that can help a company to redefine or identify new products and services and/or new ways to segment customers.

In contrast to the structuralist market perception, the dynamic character of the reconstructivist market perception fits in with empathic design, lead user approaches, and the use of communities because a company with a reconstructivist market perception looks beyond the borders of its own industry to identify users' needs. The design-driven approach does not focus on uncovering needs and is outside the scope of this perspective.

The interactional market perception and the user involvement strategies

Within this perception of the market, market creation refers to the creation of an experience environment. By this we mean that value is not inherent in the product itself but instead exists in the creation and exploitation of interactions between companies, customers, and communities.

By regarding users and customers as co-creators of the value production, the involvement becomes critical, and traditional marketing methods, as well as empathic design and lead users, can provide additional information. A community-oriented approach is the strategy for user involvement that matches the inherent reasoning of the interactional market perspective. As illustrated in the Apple case (see Box 13.2), design-driven innovation does not focus on the development of products that fulfil users' needs for interaction or experience. Instead, the strategy is concerned with producing new meanings (or product languages) that speak to the emotional needs of users.

Stimulation, creating and supporting communities around the offerings of the company, can be regarded as a way of crafting interactions between companies, customers, and communities themselves, but the uses of this approach need to be carefully managed if the company is not to take control and be "... still in charge of the overall orchestration of the experience" (Prahalad & Ramaswamy, 2004b, p. 8). According to this view, too much interference from companies in the users' experiences and communities will actually decrease the user experience, as the objective is to enable customers to perceive themselves as co-creators. A modification of this view is the more modest, but widely used, approach to present many opportunities through offerings to customers, which enhances the users' own abilities to create their own solutions and to personalize products and services (Berger & Piller, 2003). The lead-user approach and empathic design can provide input to the interactional perspective, but are not in themselves "interactional".

The constructivist market perception and the user involvement strategies

The constructivist market perspective claims that products are not themselves carriers of value. Value is created through the relations that the product or service might facilitate and make possible. These relations can be more or less stable, and one relation can be abandoned for another. Changes in relations are frequent, which means that neither the company nor the customers are seen as having a static position – they are in a constant flux as the "market itself" is a construct of shifting relations. Uncovering user needs would be a Sisyphean task, impossible or of less relevance here. Traditional marketing methods, as well as empathic design, lead user approaches, and the use of communities, do not a priori support this perception of a "market".

The logic in the design-driven approach is not concerned with specific customer types or groups, with no attempts to uncover specific user needs. This approach actively uses the constructive features of the market, not to adapt but to propose and influence new designs and solutions. The focus on relations and creating new ones is central to creating new product meanings and therefore makes a design-driven innovation strategy compatible with the constructivist perspective. In addition, the product meanings offer users a system of values that may well exceed style and aesthetics (Verganti, 2003). Again, this is compatible with the constructivist market perception, which places value in relations. In constructivist terms, the integrated coloured and organic shaped Apple computer became a success, partly because it was not another anonymous grey box but was actively given meaning, making it possible for the customers to establish another relation to the computer. Apple presented a language and interpretation that enabled a new product meaning – a relation representing a lifestyle or a dream of a possible future. Additionally, there are very explorative elements in the original lead user approach (von Hippel, 1986) and in the co-construction that can happen with user groups and user communities. Both the lead user and communities approach thus can be relevant in this market view, and there is much potential in both approaches, but often these are not fully exploited by companies.

Illustrations from practice: perceptions of market and user involvement strategies

The ways in which perceptions of markets are related to user involvement strategies in practice will be analysed and discussed in respect to four different case companies below. Data for the cases have been collected through various sources including five interviews in each company, surveys, and annual reports, but the companies have asked to remain anonymous. The explorative analysis and the sample of companies have been made to investigate how differences in market perception influence the creation of user interaction strategies. We do not claim the findings to be statistically significant, but they are of great relevance for a better and deeper understanding of company behaviour with respect to their knowledge strategies.

- The Snack Company is in the "snack" industry and manufactures, markets, and sells a large variety of crisps and fruit snacks internationally. The company employs approximately 200 people. Headquarters, R&D, and production are located in Denmark.
- The Kitchen Company is one of the dominant market players in the Northern Europe kitchen industry. The company develops and distributes kitchens to more than 11 countries in Europe. The kitchens are distributed through more than 100 independent franchise stores. The company employs approximately 800 people.
- The Sports Company is an SME that develops sports clothing, mainly for the running and bicycling sports and for the European markets geographically. The Sports Company has approximately 30 employees. Development activities are based in Denmark, while production is outsourced to the Far East.
- The Phone Company is a major player in the European telecom industry. The company is organized into four business units and employs more than 1 000 people located mainly in Denmark.

Observations on the market perceptions of the four companies

The market perceptions of the respective case companies are summarized in Table 13.2. Nine different parameters are used to present the dominant market logic identified and followed by the four case companies. The marking along the dotted line in the table presents the dominant market perception of each company. The

Table 13.2 The market perception in the case companies

	Market as an entity	Market as dynamic		
	Structuralist	*Reconstructivist*	*Interactional*	*Constructivist*
Market boundaries	◆ ■ ●	▲		
What is the market?	◆ ■ ● △	▲ ○ ◇		
Where is the market?	◆ ■ ●	▲		
Knowledge of user needs	◆ ■ ● △	▲		
Relation between the producer and the consumer	◆ ■ ○ ▲	●	○	
Location of value creation	◆ ■	▲ ●	○	
Who creates value?	◆ ■ ○ ▲	△ ●	○	
How is value created?	◆ ■ ● △	▲	○	
Strategic focus	◆ ■	▲ ●		

◆ — the Snack Company; ■ — the Kitchen Company; ● — the Sports Company; ▲ — the Phone Company.

markings outside the dominant logic line indicate fragments of a given market perception outside the dominant perception for a given company.

Three companies – the Snack Company, the Kitchen Company, and the Sports Company – possess a dominant structuralist understanding of the *market boundaries*. This suggests that they all have a non-dynamic market perception. The companies do not look to expand or to break out of the industry to which they belong, but are instead searching, in different ways, to satisfy the different user needs in their industries and thereby gain competitive advantage. The Snack

Company and the Kitchen Company, especially, employ this narrow perception of the market, as they define competitors as being similar companies. The Phone Company, on the other hand, has a reconstructivist understanding of the market boundaries, implying that they are not limited by a narrow industry view. Instead, this company continually tries to expand the market and create new markets. For example, the Phone Company is systematically searching for new segments of users to target in developing countries. Among other things, the company developed a technology that made it easier for multiple users to share one cell phone, recognizing the economic situation in these countries.

The case companies perceive *what the market is* in different ways. The Snack Company, the Kitchen Company, and the Sports Company compare the *market* with the general segments they are supplying. This indicates that the market for these companies is the sum of the different segment sizes. They are constantly hunting for market share from competitors. The Phone Company, alternatively, represents a more dynamic understanding of what its market is and not only focuses on capturing market share from competitors but is also allocating resources to create and expand its market.

Where the market is for the Snack Company, the Kitchen Company, and the Sports Company is equivalent to a measurable geographic area; in other words, it exists "out there". The Snack Company and the Kitchen Company are actively working with relative measurements of market shares. Also, the market represents something that exists out there for the Phone Company. However, in contrast to the other three companies, this company does not perceive the market size as a given constant, as it regards market boundaries as something that can and should be expanded and changed.

The *grasp of user needs* of the Snack Company, the Kitchen Company, and the Sports Company shows that they are focusing on mapping existing user needs. The companies highlight the identification of differences in user preferences, which they are investigating through more or less advanced segmentation of the market. In contrast, the Phone Company analyses similarities in user needs across groups of present and future potential users.

In practice, *value* in the Snack Company, the Kitchen Company, and the Sports Company is created through a higher effectiveness in the value chain and also through segmentation of the market, whereas the Phone Company continually seeks to create superior value for the users by targeted product modifications and innovations. For instance, it was among the first to find that users in general spend a lot of time on transportation and therefore integrated FM radios in many of their cell phones. The product complied with different user needs across user groups, because the company succeeded in creating a new market where users did not have to choose either a phone or a radio but could have both. The Phone Company managed to attract prior non-users into their market and redefined or expanded the meaning of a cell phone.

In terms of *location of value*, the Snack Company and the Kitchen Company represent a structuralist perception. These companies assume that the physical products are the carriers of value. Thus, they solely work on improving their physical products. The product focus is also explicit on the companies' home-pages, the primary function of which is to inform the users about their products. The Sports Company and the Phone Company, besides some attention to physical products, also focus on the user context and how their products add value for the customers. Hence, the latter companies are developing not only products but also whole product solutions. The Sports Company has, for example, developed a running jacket that is very simple to fold while running, to adapt to the need to change outfits while running. For this product solution, they received a European innovation award. The Phone Company's attention to complete product solutions can be illustrated by the above-mentioned example of their integration of FM radio with cell phones, or the multi-user solution in developing countries.

The Snack Company, the Kitchen Company, and the Phone Company all reflect a structuralist logic in terms of *who creates the value*. These companies assume that they as a company can arbitrarily decide what has value to the user, because the value is embedded in the products or product solutions they market. The Sports Company also tends to think that it creates the value, but at the same time users have a more active role in the product development process in this company, reflecting a reconstructivist perception.

That the Snack Company, the Kitchen Company, and the Phone Company represent a structuralist view on *the relation between producer and consumer* implies they operate under an (implicit) assumption that they alone create value for the user, where users provide input to the innovation processes – not participate in a dialogue. Thus, their users do not have an active role in the product development processes, and the roles, as producer and consumer respectively, are distinct. As mentioned earlier, the Sports Company places users in a more active role. They therefore attain characteristics of a co-producer in the product development process.

The focus on competitors in the Snack Company and the Kitchen Company also reflects that the primary *strategy* is inward looking, i.e. into the perceived industrial segment and their competitors there. These companies often use benchmarking against competitors when they make decisions; likewise, the competitor's initiatives are closely monitored and analysed. The Sports Company and the Phone Company follow a different strategy that has qualities from the reconstructivist perspective; its concern is to create superior value for the users, and the competitors are perceived as of less relevance. Among other things, these companies accomplish this strategy by thinking in terms of complete product solutions for users' "all round needs".

The companies' user involvement strategies

The user involvement strategies identified in the respective companies were mostly the traditional marketing methods. The use of traditional methods was more formalized than the context-oriented approaches, which were only rarely and used ad-hoc.

In the idea generation and concept development phases of the product development process, the Snack Company applies focus groups and different types of hall tests as the primary method for user involvement. Hall tests can be in different types, as interviews, phone interviews, questionnaires. We found fragments of the lead user approach in the idea generation phase where the company interacts with its different suppliers to obtain inputs on new trends in snack products.

The Kitchen Company has no user involvement strategy. Inspiration is gathered from the different kitchen franchise stores where the customers occasionally make requests to the sales staff. These requests are reported from stores to the company. When a large number of similar requests from customers or users are collected, the company then considers how to respond and eventually uses the requests as inputs for new products or modifications. The supplier of drawers to the Kitchen Company uses empathic design as a standard practice, and the Kitchen Company subsequently makes use of this knowledge in its own product development.

The Sports Company occasionally uses some practices for user involvement in the idea generation phase. The company runs an online club where members occasionally write to the company if they are satisfied or dissatisfied with something, and this produces inspiration for product modifications or new products. Furthermore, the Sports Company gets ideas from the sales staff who represent the company's brand at different running marathons around the world. The sales staff from time to time make interesting observations about marathon participants, which provide useful information to the innovation processes of the company. The role of the sales staff can be characterized as an informal and limited use of empathic design. However, the lead user approach is used in a structured manner in the Sports Company. Formal agreements about sponsorships to professional sportsmen include the obliga-tion of these sportsmen to provide feedback and ideas and participate in innovation projects in the company. This lead user approach ensures that the company collects ideas to implement modifications and new solutions. The Sports Company also uses so-called concept groups where they invite profes-sional sportsmen from a specific sport discipline together with designers and instructors to a joint workshop for idea generation. In the later concept development stage, focus groups consisting of professional sportsmen provide feedback.

The Phone Company deploys qualitative interviews and focus groups in the idea generation phase as well as in the concept development phase. Further-more, empathic design is used, and is widely accepted in the firm. For their "entry market business unit", in which the Phone Company is concentrating its efforts on the developing countries in Asia and Africa, the company uses empathic design as standard practice following its own guidelines. Never-theless, the objectives are not to understand users' unexpressed (latent) needs which are normally considered the main driver of empathic design. Instead, the use of empathic design in the emerging market business unit started as the company identified a need to understand the cultural differences of the markets and behaviours of customers, and difficulties encountered while obtaining relevant and valid information on the developing countries. The Phone Company was the only company where use of the design-driven approach was identified. The company works actively with designers to construct different meanings in cell phones, exceeding the functional proper-ties of the phone.

Table 13.3   Market perceptions in relation to user involvement strategies in companies

	Dominant market perception	Dominant user involvement strategy	Supplementary – but infrequently used – user involvement strategy
Snack	Structuralist, with a few features from the reconstructivist perspective	Traditional marketing methods	Lead user
Kitchen	Structuralist	Traditional marketing methods (informal use)	Empathic design (used suppliers employ it and firm benefit)
Sports	Structuralist, with features from both the reconstructivist and the interactional market perspective	Traditional methods (informal use). Lead user approach to some extent	Empathic design
Phone	Reconstructivist, with a few features of the structuralist logic	Traditional methods and design-driven approach. Empathic design in entry market business unit	Empathic design (ad-hoc use in western markets)

Discussion of the observations

Table 13.3 illustrates the observations regarding the different market perceptions and the companies' user involvement strategies. The table is simplified, but shows how the three companies dominated by a structuralist market perception are also nearly exclusively using more traditional approaches to interact with the market and customers. This fact supports our initial assumption that structural market perceptions will lead to a view on the customers and users as sources of knowledge on expressed and latent needs, but not as actively engaged in the market creation of these firms.

One observation is that in the Snack Company and the Kitchen Company, where the structuralist market perception is most noticeable, the traditional methods are very dominant. The logic of the structuralist market perspective is to segment the market to identify and fulfil different user preferences. This explains why the traditional methods are preferred to the context-oriented approaches in both the Snack Company and the Kitchen Company, given that the context-oriented approaches do not produce measurable segmentation data compared with the traditional methods. In both companies, context-oriented approaches or techniques are rather meagre.

The Snack Company used the lead user approach for idea generation with their suppliers only to a limited degree. That "lead users" were the suppliers and not identified on the basis of a strategic search limits this special application of the lead user approach.

In the Kitchen Company, no structured application of the traditional methods was perceived, and the innovation was mostly based on the collection of user and customer requests from staff in stores. Having a structuralist mindset in both the Snack Company and the Kitchen Company implies that the company is considered to be the one that designs and delivers value to the customers. Customers are subsequently assigned a rather limited role as merely "consumers" – not as sources or, even more radical, co-creators.

The Sports Company also employs several of the traditional methods in a non-structured manner, but applies the lead user approach in several sophisticated ways. This can be explained by several perceptions stemming from the reconstructivist market perception where the users have a more active role in the innovation process. As the Sports Company actively involves customers and (lead) users in both the initiation and design of new products, it has a static market perception with respect to what the market is, but a dynamic view of the relationship to customers.

The Phone Company is the only company out of the four case companies where the dominant logic is not mainly structuralist. It is also the only company that uses the context-oriented approaches actively, among these empathic design and the design-driven approach. However, empathic design is still a smaller part of the knowledge generation techniques and mainly used in emerging markets. In traditional markets, on the other hand, qualitative interviews and focus groups are widely used. The Phone Company at the same time has some traces of structuralist market perceptions – predominantly expressed by those employees involved in established markets, and this could explain why the company does not interact with users outside the industry in western countries. That the Phone

Company, in spite of its dynamic market understanding, also makes use of the traditional methods in the western markets could indicate that, the more defined a given market is, the greater is the tendency to apply the traditional methods – even though the company represents a dynamic market understanding. It is not possible from our case study to conclude whether this is a general observation. But the observations indicates that this might be the case.

Conclusion

Based on previous research, four perspectives on markets have been identified, and we have suggested that each perspective has implications for how companies interact with their customers and users in innovation processes, and how they exploit knowledge from users. The following two main approaches on user involvement in product development have been identified: the traditional marketing approaches, which regard the user as a more or less passive source of information on behaviours and needs, and the context-oriented approaches, which foster, and fit nicely into, an interactive view of the customer/user/ consumer relationship. These interactive methods include the lead user approach, empathic design, communities, and the design-driven approach, but they are not restricted to those described here. However, identifying the two groups and the four dynamic approaches makes it possible to analyse how market perceptions and user involvement approaches correspond in practice.

The preliminary assumption on the relationship between market perceptions and user involvement approaches was confirmed by a small explorative study. The overall picture from the explorative study confirmed that companies with a structuralist view of the market tend to focus on traditional marketing methods, while those (only one case) that have more dynamic perspectives frequently employ context-oriented user involvement strategies.

The analyses suggest that a relationship exists between market perception and user involvement approaches. Although a distinction was not made between radical and incremental innovation, it could be suggested that the context-oriented approaches support radical innovation, but these measures would require a different market conception. On a socioeconomic meta level it can be argued that the meaning of a kitchen, for instance, changed before industry combatants realized it. They would have benefited from a design-driven approach to "a kitchen" in an interactional or even constructivist market perspective.

Viewing the market as dynamic or even co-constructed will pose a significant challenge to many companies. A change in organizational identity and culture might be needed and make it a strategic issue and a concern for top management. Innovation management and the issue of market perceptions and user involvement are thus strategic and not operational issues. Abandoning the omnipresent notion that value is not only intrinsic to the product, and acknowledging that it is a relational concern, opens many strategic possibilities, as it confronts the mindset of a company and industry logic. A change would require courage and leadership.

User involvement can produce different effects and increase the level of knowledge, but the utilization of the knowledge – or, rather, the outcome of the interaction between users and firms – is influenced by the market perceptions of those involved. Not only do the different approaches to user involvement address the "users" differently and uncover various aspects of users but also the information provides different types of input to the innovation processes. The input can be utilized to create distinctly different types of knowledge depending on the market perception of a company and its employees. For example, user communities can be regarded as an add-on to other marketing information if the market view is a structuralist one. The company will therefore not engage actively in the user community or be able to benefit from or exploit its full potential. For some companies this might be a relevant position to take, while others might want to explore the opportunities presented using the more dynamic market perspectives.

References

Araujo, L. (2007) "Markets, market-making and marketing". *Marketing Theory*, vol. 7, no. 3, pp. 211–226.

Berger, C. & Piller, F. (2003) "Customers as co-designers". *IEE Manufacturing Engineer*, August/September, pp. 42–45.

Berthon, P., Hulbert, J. M., & Pitt, L. F. (1999) "To serve or create. Strategic orientations toward customers and innovation". *California Management Review*, vol. 42, no. 1, pp. 37–58.

Callon, M. (1998a) "Introduction: the embeddedness of economic markets in economics", in *The Laws of the Market*, edited by Callon, M. Basil Blackwell, Oxford, UK, pp. 1–57.

Callon, M. (1998b) "An essay on framing and overflowing: economic externalities revisited by sociology", in *The Laws of the Market*, edited by Callon, M. Basil Blackwell, Oxford, UK, pp. 244–269.

Callon, M., Méadel, C., & Rabeharisoa, V. (2002) "The economy of qualities". *Economy and Society*, vol. 31, no. 2., pp. 194–217.

Christensen, C. & Bower, J. (1996) "Customer power, strategic investment, and the failure of leading firms". *Strategic Management Journal*, vol. 17, no. 3, pp. 197–218.

Franke, N. & Piller, F. T. (2004) "Value creation by toolkits for user innovation and design: the case of the watch market". *Journal of Product Innovation Management*, vol. 21, no. 6, pp. 401–415.

Franke, N. & Shah, S. (2003) "How communities support innovative activities: an exploration of assistance and sharing among end-users". *Research Policy*, vol. 32, no. 1, January, pp. 157–178.

Griffin, A. & Hauser, J. R. (1993) "The voice of the customer". *Marketing Science*, vol. 12, no. 1, pp. 1–27.

Gruner, K. E. & Homburg, C. (2000) "Does customer interaction enhance new product success?". *Journal of Business Research*, vol. 49, pp. 1–14.

Jeppesen, L. B. (2005) "User toolkits for innovation: consumers support each other". *Journal of Product Innovation Management*, vol. 22, no. 4, pp. 347–363.

Jeppesen, L. B. & Molin, M. J. (2003) "Consumers as co-developers: learning and innovation outside the firm". *Technology Analysis and Strategic Management*, vol. 15, no. 3, pp. 363–384.

Kim, W. C. & Mauborgne, R. (1997) "Value innovation: the strategic logic of high growth". *Harvard Business Review*, January–February, pp. 103–112.

Kim, W. C. & Mauborgne, R. (1999a) "Creating new market space: a systematic approach to value innovation can help companies break free from the competitive pack". *Harvard Business Review*, January–February, pp. 83–93.

Kim, W. C. & Mauborgne, R. (1999b) "Strategy, value innovation, and the knowledge economy". *Sloan Management Review*, vol. 40, no. 3, pp. 41–54.

Kim, W. C. & Mauborgne, R. (2005) *Blue Ocean Strategy*. Harvard Business School Press, Boston, MA.

Kreiner, K. & Tryggestad, K. (2002) "The co-production of chip and society: unpacking packaged knowledge". *Scandinavian Journal of Management*, vol. 18, pp. 421–449.

Kumar, V. & Whitney, P. (2003) "Faster, cheaper, deeper user research". *Design Management Journal*, vol. 14, no. 2, pp. 50–57.

Lampel, J. & Mintzberg, H. (1996) "Customizing customization". *Sloan Management Review*, vol. 37, pp. 21–30.

Latour, B. (1991) "Technology is society made durable", in *A Sociology of Monsters: Essays on Power, Technology and Domination*, edited by Law, J. Routledge, London, UK, pp. 103–131.

Latour, B. (2005) *Reassembling the Social*. Oxford University Press, Oxford, UK.

Leonard, D. A. (2000) "Tacit knowledge, unarticulated needs, and empathic design in new product development", in *Knowledge Management Classic and Contemporary Works*, edited by Morey, D., Maybury, M., & Thuraisingham, B. The MIT Press, Boston, MA, ch. 9, pp. 223–237.

Leonard, D. A. & Rayport, J. (1997) "Spark innovation through empathic design". *Harvard Business Review*, vol. 75, no. 6, November–December, pp. 102–113.

Lukas, B. A. & Ferrell, O. C. (2000) "The effect of market orientation on product innovation". *Journal of the Academy of Marketing Science*, vol. 28, no. 2, pp. 239–247.

Narver, J. C. & Slater, S. F. (1990) "The effect of a market orientation on business profitability". *Journal of Marketing*, vol. 5, pp. 20–35.

Ogawa, S. & Piller, S. T. (2006) "Collective customer commitment: reducing the risks of new product development". *MIT Sloan Management Review*, vol. 47, no. 2, Winter, pp. 65–72.

Pelsmacker, P., Geneuens, M., & den Bergh, J. (2004) *Marketing Communications – a European Perspective*. Pearson Higher Education, London, UK.

Porter, E. M. (1980) *Competitive Strategy: Techniques for Analyzing Industries and Competitors*. The Free Press, New York, NY.

Prahalad, C. K. (2004) "The blinders of dominant logic". *Long Range Planning*, vol. 37, no. 2, pp. 171–179.

Prahalad, C. K. & Ramaswamy, V. (2000) "Co-opting customer competence". *Harvard Business Review*, vol. 78, no. 1, pp. 79–87.

Prahalad, C. K. & Ramaswamy V. (2003) "The new frontier of experience innovation". *Sloan Management Review*, vol. 44, no. 4, pp. 12–18.

Prahalad, C. K. & Ramaswamy, V. (2004a) *The Future of Competition: Co-creating Unique Value with Customers*. Harvard Business School Press, Boston, MA.

Prahalad, C. K. & Ramaswamy, V. (2004b) "Co-creation experience: the next practice in value creation". *Journal of Interactive Marketing*, vol. 18, no. 3, pp. 5–14.

Shah, S. K. & Franke, N. (2003) "How communities support innovative activities: an exploration of assistance and sharing among end-users". *Research Policy*, vol. 32, no. 1, January, pp. 157–178.

Shapiro, B. P. (1988) "What the hell is 'market oriented'?". *Harvard Business Review*, vol. 66, November/December, pp. 119–125.

Slater, S. F. & Narver, J. C. (1998) "Customer-led and market-oriented: let's not confuse the two". *Strategic Management Journal*, vol. 19, no. 10, pp. 1001–1006.

Slater, S. F. & Narver, J. C. (1999) "Market oriented is more than being customer-led". *Strategic Management Journal*, vol. 20, no. 12, pp. 1165–1168.

Verganti, R. (2003) "Design as brokering of languages: innovation strategies in Italian firms". *Design Management Journal*, vol. 14, no. 3, pp. 34–42.

von Hippel, E. (1986) "Lead users: a source of novel product concepts". *Management Science*, vol. 32, no. 7, pp. 791–805.

von Hippel, E. (1998) "Economics of product development by users: the impact of 'sticky' local information". *Management Science*, vol. 44, no. 5, pp. 629–644.

von Hippel, E. (2005) *Democratizing Innovation*. The MIT Press, Cambridge, MA.

von Hippel, E. & Katz, R. (2002) "Shifting innovation to users via toolkits". *Management Science*, vol. 48, no. 7, pp. 821–834.

14

Tribal Entrepreneurship: "Consumer Made" and Creative Communities as Market Makers

Bernard Cova & Stefano Pace

Introduction

Marketing expertise is no longer a tool exclusively in the hands of companies. Today, consumers create services, goods, and experiences, and they participate in the design of many of them, update them, and reconfigure them. Consumers are not mere receivers of companies' offerings but active participants in the creation, if not hijacking, of companies' strategies. "Consumer made" is the concept that can synthesize the emerging features of current marketing practices by consumers. This process has emerged strongly during the last few years owing to the development of the Web 2.0 capabilities. Today, the Internet is characterized by its power to aggregate communities and tribes. Communities are the new actors of the "consumer made" phenomenon. They represent a new form of collective participation by consumers. In this contribution, we would like to analyse the roots of this participation by consumers, the growing role of communities as entrepreneurs, and how companies can deal with this phenomenon.

At the roots of "consumer made": consumer resistance, technology, and community

The roots of the "consumer made" phenomenon can be traced in three interconnected aspects: consumer resistance to traditional marketing, enabling technologies, and communities.

Consumer resistance

Postmodern consumers nurture an antimarketing stance: "Today's consumers are wise to the wiles of marketers. They possess a 'marketing reflex', an inbuilt early warning system that detects incoming commercial messages, no matter how subtle, and automatically neutralizes them" (Brown, 2003, p. 37). This marketing reflex arose against the backdrop of consumers' renewed resistance to marketing: "the new antimarketers are not against the free market as such ... But, the antimarketers today argue that the process has gone too far, the system is out of whack, and our consumer paradise has turned into a quagmire of commercialism, consumption, and materialism. Marketing, they say, is a major culprit" (Johansson, 2004, p. 41). According to a recent survey by the consultancy firm Yankelovich Partners, 60% of consumers have a much more negative opinion of marketing and advertising now than a few years ago, 61% feel that the amount of marketing and advertising is out of control, and 65% feel constantly bombarded with too much marketing and advertising. As the authors of the research state:

> Marketing resistance is not a desire to stop shopping altogether. Consumers just want a better way to interact with marketers. Smarter, technologically empowered, time-starved consumers want marketing that shows more respect for their time and attention. Until we get better at engaging consumers, they're going to continue to push back and resist what advertisers are trying to deliver to them. (www.yankelovich.com)

However, marketing per se is not in danger. What is in peril is an old concept of marketing that would put the consumer at the centre of the stage to delight him or her in any need or caprice; a consumer considered as passive receiver of marketing decisions taken outside his or her control. Postmodern antimarketing consumers do not show a *pars destruens*, but a *pars construens*: they are not willing to remove marketing from their daily life. They would like to save marketing by renovating its nature through an active participation in the creation and exchange of goods and services. That creation would integrate – or even substitute, in extreme cases – the firm's activity. Yet all this is really nothing new! If we look more closely, we find that the consumer has always had a creative role to some extent, silently rebelling against the product/service use specifications prescribed by firms, and inventing his or her own everyday uses and meanings owing to ingenuity, clever insights, and the subversive tactics he or she employs to rearrange objects and instructions imposed on the consumer in order to reappropriate the marketing system (de Certeau, 1980). However, there is now something else in the air (Denegri-Knott, 2006): consumers are said to "behave badly" online and to defy the conventionally accepted norms of consumer/producer interaction in offline environments.

Enabling technology

The resistance to the old marketing practices explains the consumer's willingness to participate. However, this willingness would be empty without the abilities to create. These abilities have increased, on the one hand, owing to the growing "professionalism" of consumers. On the other hand, the threshold to enter the field of creation has lowered. This happened through the spread of technologies that can be used by ordinary people. Building a car is still a complex bundle of competencies that only an organization can have. Other products or services, on the other hand, can easily be manipulated by the consumer owing to technology. Finance, for instance, is no more an esoteric discipline reserved for bankers. The private investor can try to do it personally by using the flow of information of financial media and through e-trading systems. The Internet is an ideal platform to solicit users' participation in product innovation on account of its peculiar features, namely "extended reach, enhanced interactivity, greater persistence, increased speed, and higher flexibility" (Sawhney, Verona, & Prandelli, 2006, p. 6). The exchange between firm and users is rich and intense, and it overcomes the limitations of offline forms of collaboration. In the real world, consumers can be engaged in poor forms of collaboration, such as surveys, where the information exchange is large in number but not very deep. A real dialogue cannot occur but in limited numbers, as in focus groups. The Internet extends and enriches the interaction between company and users, giving a boost to the users' participation (Sawhney, Verona, & Prandelli, 2006). In summary, a second leg of the "consumer made" phenomenon is the availability of technologies that enable people really to produce things. The Internet is certainly one of the best cases. Internet services are inherently open to consumers' participation. The open-source operating systems represent the best example of how consumers (with enough capabilities and motivations) literally collaborate together to create or update a new product, in this case, software.

Community

Communities foster the strength of the previous two factors. The resistance of consumers to marketing reaches its extreme when consumers aggregate together. If resistance to marketing is a root of the "consumer made" trend, the community would exalt this root. By the mere fact that people gather and associate together, the group that is formed shows a tendency to express some form of hostility towards the rest of the world, towards the outsiders. This phenomenon is well known in the social psychology field. By simply assigning subjects to one or another group totally at random, the two groups can develop quite hostile feelings towards each other when competition over resources is at stake. In the case of brand communities, the scarce resources involved are the brand meanings, the product, and the decisions to take about it. Some communities identify themselves as oppositional in nature against other brands (Muñiz & O'Guinn, 2001). The stigma that is sometimes involved in some practices pushes individuals to seek the protection and comfort of like-minded people in a community, and then the community will assume a defensive posture against the mainstream society. The examples are various: *Star Trek*'s true believers stigmatized by some for their passion (Kozinets, 2001), *Warhammer* enthusiasts criticized for the aggressive content of their preferred game (Cova, Pace, & Park, 2007), and Apple Newton lovers who would be considered oddly out of date with their attempt to revive an old portable computer (Muñiz & Schau, 2005, 2007). The same enhancing effect played by communities for the antimarketing approach can be observed for the technologies. The new technologies are often socially oriented. New technologies exalt the opportunity to aggregate to form a social group. Second Life, for example, is a society based on the essential technological nature of the Internet: bits. Anyone who knows how to manipulate bits can create a rich existence in Second Life and interact with other people.

Communities today are both an environment where business can be created and creators of businesses by themselves. The first case still represents the traditional approach towards communities. The first management authors to study the collective aggregation over the web would suggest how to create business opportunities by leveraging on existing communities or promoting new ones. In some way, this top-down approach is still present when offline companies try to figure out which type of business would better fit an environment like Second Life. The questions are whether a carmaker should open a showroom in Second Life to advertise its new product. That question is still about Web 1.0. Seen in the entrepreneurial community approach, the real question the carmaker should ask is: How to let people in Second Life build my new car? The second case – community as creator of business – is the core of a communitarian "consumer made" phenomenon. Bookcrossing (Dalli & Corciolani, 2007), for instance, is a grass-roots type of initiative that creates and exchanges value without any help by publishers, which are kept outside the project. The very nature of bookcrossing lies in the fact that a multitude of subjects are part of the project. The network is necessary to initiate a sustainable and sufficiently varied exchange of books. Publishers usually frown on this activity, arguing that it would divert books from the bookshops, subtracting value from the industry and the economy in general. Bookcrossing supporters, on the contrary, would emphasize the fact that the practice could act as word-of-mouth advertising for less known authors or minor publishers. They also add that, on strict economic terms, often one buys two books instead of one: one for one's own library and the other to be delivered in the circuit. Significantly, in coherence with the antimarketing stance that communities some-times show and that is at the root of "consumer made", those who practise bookcrossing call themselves ironically "pirates". They do not commit any misdemeanour; however, they play with the stigma of being pirates to signal their peculiar position at the periphery of the marketplace.

Communities as competitors

Tribes can be entrepreneurial (Cova, Kozinets, & Shankar, 2007), showing their new nature that is both different from individual passion and from the previous form of social aggregations. Entrepreneurs are creators of new products and new markets as well. A market is intended as a platform (not necessarily physical) of exchange (not necessarily involving money). Communities create a market alternative to the official one by hijacking the brand (Wipperfürth, 2005). The market created by the community can have three different positions with respect to the "official" market of the company:

- *Conflicting* position against the official market. In this case it is an overt expression of a negative antimarketing position.

- *Integration* of what normal markets could not provide to the true believers. A fan searching for a rare vintage version of a song of his or her preferred band should refer to the community to satisfy this particular need, both in real terms (having the vinyl) and symbolically (enjoying the song with other connoisseurs).
- *Extension* of the official market. In this case, any consumer of the brand – regardless of whether or not that consumer belongs to a community – can find objects or activities linked to that brand both in the official market and in the community creations. The community creates a market that integrates the company's offer for the common user. A fans website that eagerly provides gossip news around a celebrity can be a source of information for normal users too.

The three situations can coexist. Videos made by fans of a TV series as a form of gift for the fellow members of the community can be posted on open websites and enjoyed also by an audience that does not belong to the community. The markets created by the entrepreneurial communities have a role to complete some gap that is left open by the normal economy. Like flea markets, the markets created by the communities can be seen as strange by the mainstream, but they represent a source of creativity that completes the offer of the company.

This integrative action is particularly relevant for brands. A brand can be considered a polysemous system: many meanings combine together to form a constellation. For the most complex brands, this system is rich and incomplete. Nutella (the famous hazelnut spread) has several meanings. A community can help by adding new ones that are coherent with what already exists. For instance, the hedonism of Nutella is one of its meanings. The dialogue that can develop in a community of Nutella lovers could integrate that meaning with a mild sense of guilt or with a dichotomy between the good of Nutella and self-discipline. All these variations of meanings cannot be conveyed by a single source, that is, the company. A community can help in this operation. The world of a brand is applied in many instances and translated in different forms by the community, since the company could not do it alone.

One could observe that this operation of integration really would not need a community. An individual could do the same alone. Actually, the concept of community is necessary. Like languages, the creation of a meaning occurs through a dialogue, that is, within a community, a group with a shared language that has spent time interacting. The word "home" gets its sense through daily use among people. Similarly, the Nike logo acquires a sense through a dialogue among consumers. The preferred source of this dialogue is the community of those passionate about that brand. At the other extreme, one can argue that the entire market formed by all the consumers does the same: it redefines the meaning of a brand the same way as a community. The difference with the community is still present. The community is organized to create and take action very quickly, more critically, and with more competencies, compared with the slow formation of a public opinion or a fad.

Communities as creators of collective outcomes and market makers differ from individual consumers and the market as a whole. Communities develop "we-intentions" that are of a higher order with respect to the individual or the anomic masses. We-intentions are: "(1) mutual responsiveness among participants to the intentions and actions of others, (2) collective commitment to the joint activity, and (3) commitment to support others involved in the activity" (Bagozzi & Dholakia, 2006, p. 1101). We-intention is the willingness of the community as a whole. The community can be considered as a single head with many neurons represented by its members. People in communities wish to contribute owing to their social identity, their identification with the group. The utilitarian consideration of giving something to the community in order to receive something else is of secondary importance. The identification with the community positively impacts on we-intentions (Bagozzi & Dholakia, 2002, 2006). Collective endeavours like the operating system Linux (Bagozzi & Dholakia, 2006) are explained by we-intentions, that is, by the community as a subject in itself. These features of the community would explain the different nature of communities' creations compared with individual creations. When individuals create something and share it with others, what is created is a repository of different contributions (see Box 14.1). When the community is at stake, the outcome is collective, with all authors at the same level and none superior. The result is unique and is expressed by a single collective mind that cannot be referred to any individual. This would explain also why communities remain the same even when members leave.

Box 14.1   Wikipedia

At its origin, the Internet was considered a library with no boundaries at all, as in the Jorge Luis Borges tale ("La Biblioteca de Babel"). Anyone could take a huge amount of information about his or her preferred content, regardless of the topic. Then the web showed its social nature, consisting in people contacting and socializing with other people in chats, communities, e-mails. In a way, these social connections are a form of social creation by themselves, since the members of the community create the posts and messages that substantiate the relations. As a third wave, today the Internet presents the opportunity to create things, both in individual forms (for instance, in blogs) and in collective forms. That third dimension shows the very nature of the Internet. The Internet is a platform made of texts and multimedia content that can be reduced to bits that can be elaborated by computers. Hence, it is the best space for people to create things or modify what has been created by others: a simple connection, a keyboard, and then the user can enter and manipulate that space. Second Life is among the most-known examples of such manipulation of online reality. However, another project shows the real sociality of creation: Wikipedia. In Second Life, anyone can build his or her own avatar, accessories, and space. In Wikipedia, any contribution is based on the contribution of someone else. An article is written by previous users and then it can be modified. The final result is not personal objects that populate the space, as in Second Life. The result is the article around a topic, behind which the personal effort is hidden. The article in Wikipedia is a true collective creation, developed through ideation and successive refinements.

There is a difference from open-source software too. The competences to write a software code to share with fellow programmers, as in an open-source project, are quite rare and at a high level. In Wikipedia, instead, anyone can participate for two reasons. Firstly, on the technical side, Wikipedia is user friendly, and anyone who is able to use the Internet or common software applications (for instance, Microsoft Word for Windows) would be able to use the Wikipedia interface too. The Linux users and other open-source users were once the bulk of the Wikipedia community. Today, their relative presence is smaller, but they still represent the main resource when it comes to the more complex programming tasks. Secondly, since any topic can be dealt with in Wikipedia, virtually anyone can make a contribution to something about which he or she is an expert or knowledgeable.

Wikipedia today is among the most visited Internet domains, with an annual positive trend of 30% in visits (source: compete.com). Wikipedia has a certain turnover rate, with new members entering and others ending their activity. Anyway, the rules of the system are respected, which shows the robustness of the community. Drawing on data from the French version of Wikipedia, around 100 primary members produce more than 1 000 contributions per month, and around 1 000 secondary members produce 100 contributions. As in many collective endeavours or communities, a few subjects would produce the major part of the content.

Companies are sometimes at odds with this new space. For certain topics (among them, the description of the companies themselves) a firm may have something to say. Usually, companies use their press statements to post a contribution. These statements are easily spotted by Wikipedia members and changed to attain a tone that is less institutional and more Wikipedia style. When the company inserts its copyrighted content, the community often would prefer to erase it rather than change it. Aware of the dynamics in Wikipedia, companies that notice mistakes in content referring to them would prefer to single out the errors to the community, rather than correct them directly.

The challenge posed by Wikipedia to traditional encyclopaedias is noteworthy. Some competitors (such as *Universalis* and *Larousse*) emphasize their being certified encyclopaedias, leveraging on the credibility of the source. Others, like *Encarta*, try to adopt a Wikipedia-like method, accepting modifications suggested by readers, but under the final responsibility of the editorial panel. Hachette left the industry. Generally, the encyclopaedias are repositioning themselves as service providers, rather than content providers. This witnesses the power of the Wikipedia approach.

Source: interview with Pierre Beaudouin, President, Wikimédia France, September 2007. Reproduced by permission of Pierre Beaudouin.

In this framework, the resources of the company seem quite poor compared with the resources of a community. The firm is an activator of a process that is then partially in the hands of forces outside it. What is the role that a company can have? It depends on its cultural approach to the new phenomenon of tribal entrepreneurship and the strategies adopted.

Company partnering strategies

Company's approach

The typical reaction of companies can be exemplified by the case of Diet Coke and Mentos (see Box 14.2).

Box 14.2   Diet Coke–Mentos: consumers' experiments

A flood of home-made videos recently invaded the Internet, on websites like YouTube. In these videos, the authors conduct a funny and bizarre experiment, dropping Mentos candies into a bottle of Coke and producing a rich explosion of the beverage. In one of the most famous of these, two persons organize a quite complex game of Diet Coke fountains resembling the patterns of fountains in the gardens of noble palaces. Other individuals try it and post online variations of the experiment, soon creating a wave of videos. Different versions of the experiments feature rockets propelled by the newly discovered fuel at college science festivals. The avalanche of videos is so massive that even mainstream media have to acknowledge it. David Letterman makes his own experiment in his talk show on CBS. These experiments have the three facets illustrated above:

- *Resistance to marketing practices.* In this case there is no open and hard conflict against the two brands. The intent is ironic and funny. The consumer makes fun of the brands: a light form of non-acceptance of boring and renowned marketing tricks.
- *Enabling technology.* Internet and amateur video equipment. Anyone could upload a video made with a mobile phone camera.
- *Community.* Videos are made to be shared, although not in specialized brand communities. One of the main venues of the videos is YouTube, which is a main social gathering over the web.

The reaction of the two companies involved shows the difficulty that a firm faces when the phenomenon of consumer empowerment emerges. As a first reaction, the Coca-Cola Company distanced itself from the videos,

---

> pinpointing that they did not fit with the brand personality of Diet Coke. But later on, both Coca-Cola and Mentos tried to leverage on the viral phenomenon by collaborating with the video makers.

The initial protective reaction by Coca-Cola is typical of companies that are accustomed to design and control all facets of their brand. Managerial practice and academic literature have traditionally emphasized the building of the brand equity through heavy marketing investment by the company. The consumer is considered a subject who can adhere or not to this effort, but without changing it. Viral marketing is based on the grass-roots word-of-mouth by consumers; thus, it would be a form of outsourcing marketing by companies. But, even in this case, traditional marketing rules apply, since the viral idea is instilled by the company and possibly controlled by it. Facts like the Coke–Mentos experiment have a new nature. The company does not promote or assist initiatives like the Coke–Mentos videos. The firm assists passively in the spontaneous growth of semi-professional endeavours referred to its brand. Given the stance of traditional brand management of controlling anything that is related to the brand, companies are at odds with this passive position.

A firm facing any act of consumer empowerment should assume a sort of antimarketing stance. A brand manager should not try directly to control or direct the expression of consumer empowerment, but rather promote and leverage the positive features of it. The first requirement to face the "consumer made" phenomenon is cultural: to avoid the traditional marketing reaction of considering the consumer as the receiver of the marketing decisions and actions. The most interesting case under the "consumer made" view occurs when the company actively enables its consumers to develop new solutions, create products, and engage in other activities linked to the company's business. The British Broadcasting Corporation (BBC) provides its viewers with software that enables them to edit the original content of BBC television (Berthon *et al.*, 2007). A resistant stance, on the contrary, would have considered any use of such content as a copyright infringement to prosecute. One of the risks of the enabling approach is that even a positive stance of the company towards the community could spark a negative reaction. In fact, the enabling strategy could possibly be interpreted by the community as an attempt to control its activity. The tribal approach to marketing should be attentive to the invisible fences often raised by communities, even when the intent is definitely positive. As a blogger said, refusing the hypothesis of being paid by sponsors, "the fun is the freedom" (Cova, Kozinets, & Shankar, 2007, p. 17).

Which culture would characterize a given company? Naturally it depends on the history of the company, on the role of marketing, and the experiences with consumers.

Company strategies

Depending on its culture, the company can adopt different strategies to leverage fruitfully on "consumer made". In Prahalad and Ramaswamy's important book, *The Future of Competition: Co-creating Unique Value with Customers* (2004), firms are encouraged to consider consumer empowerment as a managerial opportunity, not as a threat. That opportunity is divided into contribution and cooperation. The first of these refers to co-creation by co-opting the consumer's competencies in the company's process. The latter refers to the co-creation of the consumer's experience through personalization. Companies can involve consumers both as small groups of creative consumers or as average ones (Berthon *et al.*, 2007). Building on that, one can divide the "consumer made" concept into two dimensions. The first dimension refers to the competencies of consumers, whether experts or laymen for the brand. The second dimension refers to the object of the co-creation, whether the product or the experience. In the first case, the consumer participates in the definition of the offer. In the second case, the consumer freely defines his or her experience with the product.

The quadrants in Figure 14.1 are as follows:

- *Co-innovation*. The company involves communities of creative consumers in the new product or service design process. Examples of this strategy are IdeaStorm from Dell (see Box 14.3) and its invitation to propose and vote for new products or services to be developed by Dell, and the "Share your Ideas" programme by Nokia. The web browser Firefox Mozilla was created by a thousand software developers. At a smaller level, we can cite the experience of Andria, an Italian construction firm. In its residential project "Case per Gio.Co" (short for "Giovane Coppie", and meaning "houses for young couples"), the young couples themselves build part of their new house.

Figure 14.1   "Consumer made" typologies

Box 14.3   Co-innovation – Dell's IdeaStorm "Where your ideas reign"

Everyone knows about Dell's troubles of late, especially after the counter-communication made by Jeff Jarvis with his posts entitled "Dell Hell", detailing his day-to-day problems with Dell computers and Dell services. The hardware maker's once industry-leading build-to-order supply chain systems are now the norm, and it has fallen behind in design – areas where competitors such as Apple and Sony excel. Consumer service has deteriorated since it was outsourced to India, so that consumers can no longer rely on a timely and informative service. At the beginning of 2007, Michael Dell prepared an answer to all these troubles: "We are at our best when we are hearing directly from our customers", said Mr Dell. "We listen, learn, and then improve and innovate based on what our customers want. It's one of the real advantages of being a direct company".

Launched on 16 February 2007, Dell's IdeaStorm (www.dellideastorm.com) represents a new way to listen to customers' views on how to build the best products and services. It is an online community where customers can post their ideas on technology and Dell products, services, and operations. The community will vote for the best ideas and discuss the ideas with other users. Dell will share the ideas throughout its organization to trigger new thoughts and evolve everything that is done at the company. It looks and feels a lot like Digg.com, the popular tech news aggregator: users post suggestions and the community votes, so that the most popular ideas rise to the top. Just 5 days after launch, the Dell site boasted 1 384 ideas that had been voted on 122 388 times and generated 2 189 comments. Admittedly, not every idea is great. And some communities speak louder than others – a large open-source contingent, for example, is demanding preinstalled Linux and Open Office, among other things. As of 21 February, this was the most popular suggestion, with some 67 000 votes. Above all, the comments on the site reflect some real passion.

On 13 March 2007, Dell noted that the IdeaStorm community's interest in open-source solutions like Linux on Dell platforms had come through loud and clear. Many people had suggested a survey to help Dell determine which distribution is most popular. Based on this idea, Dell launched a short survey (10 days) where everyone could tell Dell more about their favourite distribution of Linux, their preferred method of support, and more. More than 100 000 people took part in the survey. Here are some of the highlights from the survey:

- More than 70% of survey respondents said they would use a Dell system with a Linux operating system for both home and office use.
- Survey respondents indicated they want a selection of notebook and desktop offerings.
- The majority of survey respondents said that existing community-based support forums would meet their technical support needs for a tested and validated Linux operating system on a Dell system.

Survey respondents indicated that improved hardware support for Linux is as important as the distribution(s) offered. Dell has heard these voices and decided to expand its Linux support beyond the existing servers and Precision workstation line. The first step in this effort for Dell would be offering Linux preinstalled on select desktop and notebook systems.

Finally, on 1 May 2007, Dell announced officially that it would begin offering Canonicals' latest version, Ubuntu 7.04, as an option on selected

Dell consumer models in the USA in the coming weeks. And, on 24 May 2007, Dell unveiled its three consumer systems – the XPS 410n and Dimension E520n desktops and the Inspiron E1505n notebook – with the Ubuntu 7.04 Linux distribution factory installed. These systems target the Linux enthusiast community and are a direct result of consumers' ideas and feedback on IdeaStorm.

(Data gathered from the Dell website, from Business Week, *and from www.Buzzmachine.com)*

- *Co-promotion.* A large group of consumers is involved in producing visuals or films for upcoming advertising campaigns of the company. The promoter usually uses a contest. The competition in itself is already a form of communication. Ferrero organized something similar in its photographic contest among the fans of Nutella, the renowned hazelnut spread. Each image should support the brand slogan, "What would the world be without Nutella?". The experience of General Motors, with its "Chevy Apprentice Challenge", was not successful, however. The initiative created an opportunity to express opposition to SUVs (see Box 14.4). That case shows the risks inherent in "consumer made" initiatives promoted by companies.

Box 14.4   Co-promotion – Chevy Apprentice Challenge

In early 2006, General Motors launched an online contest named the "Chevy Apprentice Challenge", where people were invited to submit their own commercials for the Chevy Tahoe online. Via an online form, anyone was able to select different audios and images provided by GM and combine them with their own screen captions and texts to create "unique" commercials. It was all part of a creative new advertising campaign for the Chevy Tahoe, and those who submitted commercials were eligible for great prizes. But did GM's creative efforts backfire? Many marketing experts called the outcome a failure. At the same time, GM claimed victory, while anti-SUV pundits claimed they were the victors.

GM's plan was to generate some serious word-of-mouth with their effort. They thought they would get their audience participating and bloggers spreading the buzz. But GM confused participation with an uncontrolled free-for-all: GM's approach to this attempted word-of-mouth campaign allowed many of the commercials to be created by environmentalists whose interest was nothing more than to damage the brand. Actually, those commercials were attacks against large four-wheel-drive vehicles (SUVs) like the Chevy Tahoe. GM did not pull the ads while the contest was running, and left the ads posted on the Internet for all to see.

According to marketing experts, the mistake made by GM was to open the door to the general public. A much better approach would have been for GM to approach all current owners of Tahoes. They could have asked those loyal fans to create commercials using the same material, plus their own videos, images, and music, to create truly personalized commercials.

Source: AdvancedBusinessBlogging.com and RPM Success Group Inc.

- *Co-production*. In this case the consumer directly participates in his or her own consumption experience. The firm enables the consumer to customize the product which is offered through self-service platforms. A good example is provided by the US winemaker Crushpad which advertises on its website:

  Now you can make unique, ultra premium wines no matter where you live. Crushpad provides grapes from California's top vineyards, industry-acclaimed winemakers, and a state of the art winery 100% focused on small lots. You choose your level of involvement and we do the rest. The Custom Wine service is designed for non-traditional winemakers who work hand-in-hand with Crushpad staff and consulting winemakers to define and create their wine. You can choose from among our excellent grape sources or identify your own, and are encouraged to participate in the roughly 30 decisions necessary during the process. The end result is the finished product – a world-class wine with your brand. (www.crush padwine.com)

On a symbolic level, the meaning given to the brand is not unique, but it is free to be redefined by consumers. Red Bull is an example (see Box 14.5). Nutella is again another case. The company Ferrero establishes the boundaries of the acceptable meanings for its brand Nutella through traditional advertising campaigns in mass media. The meanings are family, flavour, and social gatherings. Then the company opens an Internet platform where consumers can freely play with these meanings and redefine them: regression towards infancy, comfort and friendship in hard times, and mild sense of guilt over hedonistic consumption.

Box 14.5   Co-production of meaning – "Red Bull gives you wiiiings"

Since the early 1990s, Red Bull has carefully and intentionally cultivated the mystery surrounding its product. This myth-building strategy and the latent uncertainty about Red Bull's ingredients (taurine!) and effects still work today. The public has filled in the blanks with speculation and innuendo. Meanwhile, headquarters clearly don't mind. "I always have to fly to Pamplona to source bull's testicles," jokes CEO Mateschitz. "Those rumours have never hurt," he adds joyfully.

Indeed, Red Bull means different things to different people, and caters for different occasions. Furthermore, Red Bull ensures that consumers do not feel pressured to drink Red Bull in a certain way. During their sampling, they always provide a full and closed can, so that consumers can decide when and how much to try. "We don't try to control how people use Red Bull," explains North American spokeswoman Emma Cortes. There is not a right way to use Red Bull, no code of conduct (for consumers). It effortlessly crosses socio/economic boundaries. Consumers are asked to use their imagination in fitting Red Bull into their lives. It helps get them deeper into the Red Bull experience and truly understand its role.

Ask someone to define his or her Red Bull experience and the answers will vary. For instance (Wipperfürth, 2005), the *Fire Island (NY) News* has dubbed it "The new sex drink", while a 13-year-old boy in a local deli said, "Me inspira a bailar" ("It makes me dance"). And, according to a waitress in a New York City wine bar, "If you mix it with cough syrup, it makes your cold go away."

- *Co-imagination*. Here, the company encourages anything that might foster interactions within the fan communities of a brand, product, or activity. The major part of this practice involves stories. Fans and consumers are producers of stories centred on their favourite brand. These stories can take the form of legends around the brand or personal accounts of brand use. Stories are a main feature of communities (Muñiz & Schau, 2005; Muñiz & O'Guinn, 2001). Community members establish and reaffirm their mutual connections and their commitment to the brand through a storytelling ritual that nurtures the myth of a brand. Consumer behaviour as a whole can be seen under a narrative paradigm (Shankar, Elliott, & Goulding, 2001). Consumers "write" their consumption: brands are systems of meanings that are socially determined through a process that is linguistic in nature. In fact, language and narrative are the ways to provide a meaning to objects and facts. This dialogue is inherently a social process, where each individual contributes to a final collective result. For some communities, the language is not a metaphor or a hidden structure, but the overt form of collective result (see Box 14.6).

Box 14.6   Co-imagination – TV series communities and writing stories

TV series fans are so committed to their beloved programme that their discussion can take the form of real suggestions about the scripts of the episodes. Through discussion, the most involved viewers develop the standards regarding aesthetic and taste with which each episode should comply, otherwise an episode, a character, or even a detail would not be considered really coherent with the spirit of the series (Kozinets, 1997). These standards would be a dictionary, a set of interpretive conventions necessary to read or appreciate an episode. In fact, a story cannot be read unless points of reference are provided. The hidden and deep meanings of a TV series and its nuances can be defined by a community. In summary, the community defines a canon. The producers of the series can draw suggestions from the discussion of characters and stories.

Within the established canon, the fans can imagine variations of the stories and alternative scripts. *Lost* is a famous TV series broadcast in the USA by ABC and well known in other countries as well. Part of the mystery of the show is in the gradual discovery of ties among the main characters well before the actions that occur in the episode. In "Lostpedia", a community of fans of the series, there is a rich matrix where previous connections between the characters are imagined by the fans.

Communities can try to impose alternative stories on the producer of a show. Fans of *Star Wars* complained against Jar Jar Binks, a character introduced in the prequel of the George Lucas saga, soliciting its deletion from the films. Webpages such as "Death to Jar Jar Binks" were posted. Around 700 die-hard *Star Wars* fans formed the "International Society for the Extermination of Jar Jar Binks". The complaint was also active: some fans suggested alternative scenes to delete the character without affecting the plot. One of the "hated" features of Jar Jar was its strange accent. Hence, on the web one could find videos depicting the character using impeccable British language. Self-made episodes were common as well. Among them, the most famous were "Die, Jar Jar, Die" and "Attack of the Flaming Ewoks" (www.salon.com).

The previous examples show the brand literacy (Bengtsson & Firat, 2006) necessary to develop stories that nurture the imaginative field surrounding TV series and brands in general. Brand literacy means the consumer's ability to understand the meanings of brands and consumption and to play with them in a way that is understandable by fellow consumers. That is, rhetoric. Communities create the rhetoric and the code of understanding of brands, hence co-imagining them together with the company.

Limitations to the companies' strategies

The exploitation of the "consumer made" phenomenon by companies has some limits. We can identify some of them.

Consumer fatigue

Permission marketing emphasizes the frustration that consumers may feel being bombarded by a plethora of marketing initiatives. We could extend this frustration possibly to include even the marketing actions freely chosen by the consumer:

a quite active consumer can reach a threshold of "consumer fatigue" that prevents any further participation. The participation in a community, for instance, can be so deep and time consuming that the subject can reach a noticeable stress level. Hence, willingness to participate and the ability to do so are not sufficient to grant the consumer's involvement.

Double exploitation

Consumers' participation is depicted in the "consumer made" approach as a bottom-up impulse coming from the consumers themselves. However, the process can be the other way too: companies can be the initiator and promoter of consumer participation. This is common in the service marketing field, where the concept of "prosumer" has been adopted for some time. For efficiency purposes and on account of the goal of personalizing the offer, consumers are involved in the definition and the delivery of services. ATM is the classical example of self-delivered service. One of the recommendations of service marketing is to check the actual willingness of the consumer to participate. Not all the consumers wish to participate and not in any circumstances. This lack of willingness might be due to simple time constraints. But in some cases (and at a cultural level) consumers may consider their active participation as another form of a predatory marketing approach that would exploit consumers by giving them a false freedom. The final economic value of "consumer made" is still in the hands of the companies, and this can be interpreted as double exploitation: the firm would exploit the consumer's activity, creativity, and energy and draw all the benefits of the new or modified product (Cova & Dalli, 2007).

New technology adoption limits

Service marketing and management seems particularly fruitful in identifying the drivers of the adoptions of new technologies (Bitner, Ostrom, & Meuter, 2002) that play a major role in "consumer made". Models on adoption of new technologies by consumers show that they are willing to adopt a new technology when they feel able to use it, and also if they can figure out their role in the process of service delivery. Hence, the discussion about the culture of consumers should be integrated with a more operational consideration of how the consumer adopts the technology. Technological advances make available two types of technology. One is user friendly and easily accessed by individuals; Wikipedia is an example, and this would explain part of its success. On the other hand, complex platforms like Second

Life are also available. The forces of competition compel firms to launch these sophisticated technologies before the market is totally ready for them. In this case the new technology adoption models derived from service marketing can be helpful. In summary, new technologies cannot be considered just as an enabler of participation, but should be seen in terms of their adoptability.

Positive drivers of participation

The willingness to act as marketers is rooted in the resistance posture towards marketing. In this view, the consumer acts for negative purposes: preventing the company from making something or correcting its actions. But that framework would not take into full consideration the behaviour of those who may wish to participate for a positive motivation: doing something for the sake of it, for the pleasure and personal gratification. This behaviour is particularly frequent for communities. A member of a group is often led to a deep participation by the social enhancement, self-discovery, and entertainment value (Dholakia, Bagozzi, & Pearo, 2004). No direct oppositional stance is involved, even in communities born to express an opposition.

Conclusion

The "consumer made" phenomenon and the creative communities' trend can be included in a broader framework based on the service-dominant (S-D) logic (Vargo & Lusch, 2004; Lusch & Vargo, 2006a). According to the S-D logic, any offer to the market is a bundle of potential competencies that are finally extracted by the consumer and used for his or her own benefit. This is typical in the service field, where "prosumption" and co-creation necessarily occur to generate value. Also, physical goods derive their market value from the actual action executed by the consumer over them. Goods and services are *operand resources*, defined as those "resources on which an operation or act is performed to produce an effect" (Vargo & Lusch, 2004, p. 2). *Operant resources* are those employed on the operand ones. In this view, the consumers are the main operant resources: they use their own ability and creativity to extract benefits from the offer. Thus, the "consumer made" perspective can add some specifications to the S-D logic. In the S-D logic, the operand resources are produced by the company and then put on the market. In "consumer made", the operand resources are not made available just by the company. Consumers create resources that are almost independent of those of the firm. A video posted in an online community showing a new or funny use of a product is an operand resource that can be used by other subjects, both as a suggestion of the alternative use or as an inspiration for a new video contribution. In all this, the company remains in the background. In the S-D logic, knowledge is the main operant resource. The "consumer made" also emphasizes the emotional side. Nothing can be truly extracted from a TV series for which no passion is involved. Emotion is the activator of the process. The S-D logic advocates the evolution from a "market to" to a "market with" approach. The final offer is the result of a collective and networked effort among the company, its suppliers, and the consumer. The consumer is still seen as an individual acting alone on the offer, as a "consultant". The "consumer made" shows that consumers can form a network by themselves; a network that can assume the form of close-knit communities too. While S-D logic argues for integration between the networks, the consumer warns that the consumer's network could be an outsider and oppositional, and not a bundle of nodes in a constellation of coordinated actors. All in all, the "consumer made" approach does not negate the S-D logic, rather it defines some facets of it and adds other aspects (see Table 14.1).

Table 14.1 S-D logic and its "consumer made" specifications

Goods-dominant logic concepts	Service-dominant logic concepts	"Consumer made" specifications on S-D logic
Goods	Services	Competencies, abilities
Products	Experiences	Ties
Feature/attribute	Solution	Consumer's competencies and emotions
Value-added	Co-creation of value	Self-determined value
Profit maximization	Financial feedback/learning	Co-optation of consumers' competencies
Price	Value proposition	Value formed within consumer-created market
Equilibrium system	Complex adaptive systems	Firm system and consumer system: collaboration or opposition
Supply chain	Value-creation network/ constellation	Constellation of networks
Promotion	Dialogue	Negotiation
Market to	Market with	Markets
Product orientation	Service orientation	Creativity orientation

Source: adapted from Lusch & Vargo, 2006b, p. 286.

References

Bagozzi, R. P. & Dholakia, U. M. (2002) "Intentional social action in virtual communities". *Journal of Interactive Marketing*, vol. 16, no. 2, Spring, pp. 2–21.

Bagozzi, R. P. & Dholakia, U. M. (2006) "Open source software user communities: a study of participation in Linux user groups". *Management Science*, vol. 52, no. 7, July, pp. 1099–1115.

Bengtsson, A. & Firat, A. F. (2006) "Brand literacy: consumer's sense-making of brand management". *Advances in Consumer Research*, vol. 33, no. 1, pp. 375–380.

Berthon, P. R., Pitt, L. F., McCarthy, I., & Kates, S. M. (2007) "When customers get clever: managerial approaches to dealing with creative consumers". *Business Horizons*, vol. 50, pp. 39–47.

Bitner, M. J., Ostrom, A. L., & Meuter, M. L. (2002) "Implementing successful self-service technologies". *Academy of Management Executive*, vol. 16, no. 4, pp. 96–108.

Brown, S. (2003) *Free Gift Inside: Forget the Customer, Develop Marketease*. Capstone, Chichester, UK.

Cova, B. & Dalli, D (2007) "Community made: from consumer resistance to tribal entrepreneurship". *EACR Conference* (European Association for Consumer Research), Università Bocconi, Milan, Italy, 11–14 July.

Cova, B., Kozinets, R., & Shankar, A. (2007) *Consumer Tribes*. Elsevier-Butterworth-Heinemann, Oxford, UK.

Cova, B., Pace, S., & Park, D. J. (2007) "Global brand communities across borders: the Warhammer case". *International Marketing Review*, vol. 24, no. 3, pp. 313–329.

Dalli, D. & Corciolani, M. (2007) "Consumption between market and community: evidence from the bookcrossing case", in *4th Workshop in Interpretive Consumer Research*, 26–27 April 2007, Marseille, France, edited by Cova, B. & Elliott, R.

de Certeau, M. (1980) *L'Invention du Quotidien. Arts de Faire*. Gallimard, Paris, France.

Denegri-Knott, J. (2006) "Consumers behaving badly: deviation or innovation? Power struggles on the web". *Journal of Consumer Behaviour*, vol. 5, no. 1, January–February, pp. 82–94.

Dholakia, U. M., Bagozzi, R. P., & Pearo, L. K. (2004) "A social influence model of consumer participation in network- and small-based virtual communities". *International Journal of Research in Marketing*, vol. 21, no. 3, September, pp. 241–263.

Johansson, J. K. (2004) *In Your Face, How American Marketing Excess Fuels Anti-Americanism*. Pearson, Upper Saddle River, NJ.

Kozinets, R. V. (1997) "'I want to believe': a netnography of the X-Philes' subculture of consumption". *Advances in Consumer Research*, vol. 24, no. 1, pp. 470–475.

Kozinets, R. V. (2001) "Utopian enterprise: articulating the meanings of Star Trek's culture of consumption". *Journal of Consumer Research*, vol. 28, no. 1, pp. 67–88.

Lusch, R. F. & Vargo, S. L. (eds) (2006a) *The Service-dominant Logic of Marketing: Dialog, Debate, and Directions*. ME Sharpe, Armonk, NY.

Lusch, R. F. & Vargo, S. L. (2006b) "Service-dominant logic: reactions, reflections and refinements". *Marketing Theory*, vol. 6, no. 3, pp. 281–288.

Muñiz Jr, A. M. & O'Guinn, T. C. (2001) "Brand community". *Journal of Consumer Research*, vol. 27, no. 4, pp. 412–432.

Muñiz Jr, A. M. & Schau, H. J. (2005) "Religiosity in the abandoned Apple Newton brand community". *Journal of Consumer Research*, vol. 31, March, pp. 737–747.

Muñiz Jr, A. M. & Schau, H. J. (2007) "Vigilante marketing and consumer-created communications". *Journal of Advertising*, vol. 36, no. 3, pp. 35–50.

Prahalad, C. K. & Ramaswamy, V. (2004) *The Future of Competition: Co-creating Unique Value with Customers*. Harvard Business School Press, Boston, MA.

Sawhney, M., Verona, G., & Prandelli, E. (2006) "Collaborating to create: the Internet as a platform for consumer engagement". *Journal of Interactive Marketing*, vol. 19, no. 4, Autumn, pp. 4–17.

Shankar, A., Elliott, R., & Goulding, C (2001) "Understanding consumption: contributions from a narrative perspective". *Journal of Marketing Management*, vol. 17, no. 3–4, pp. 429–453.

Vargo, S. L. & Lusch, R. F. (2004) "Evolving to a new dominant logic for marketing". *Journal of Marketing*, vol. 68, pp. 1–18.

Wipperfürth, A. (2005) *Brand Hijack: Marketing Without Marketing*, Portfolio, New York, NY.

15

Three Types of Firm-related Online Communities

Niels Kornum

Introduction

People and citizens have always gathered to share common interests, but consumers also have a long record of collaboration focused on some topic of shared interest, e.g. the cooperative movement. The Internet has not changed this fundamental human curiosity and urge for sharing and, indeed, has reduced the exchange-related transaction costs dramatically and enabled a global reach where people with very specialized interests can quickly identify who shares their enthusiasm and afterwards connect quickly and make exchanges in cost-efficient ways.

By 2001, 100 million Internet users said they belonged to an online community: 50% of these users attended groups with shared interests and hobbies, 31% were fans of a particular team, 28% shared the same lifestyle, and 28% were part of a support group for a medical condition or personal problem (Thorson, Duffy, & Schumann, 2007). Clearly, the numbers, multitude, and complexity of the online community phenomenon have increased since then. The social networking phenomenon is a recent example of these complexities. Here, firms like MySpace and Facebook are providing the infrastructure for social interaction, and the number of registered users is large.[1]

But why is it interesting for firms to initiate or engage with online communities in the first place? Some of the possible reasons why working with online communities might be attractive are: (a) overcrowded markets; (b) decreased effect of promotion efforts on traditional media such as TV; (c) consumers are increasingly ignoring or being irritated by being exposed to more and more extensive promotion effort, and therefore want to control the promotion inflow to a higher degree. Thus, increased support of and interaction with online communities may open a new channel between the firm and lead users, new users may learn from lead users, and information or promotion may be available in the right amount seen from the perspective of the community member. This may in addition strengthen and stabilize the relationship between the firm and the community members and promote loyalty and emotional attachment (Keller, 2001). Concerning the firm's motivation for engaging with online communities, this chapter reveals one general trait across community types, that is, the search for ways to enhance the long-term relationship with core customers or lead users and thereby potentially increasing value creation for both the customer and the firm. Other types of motivation actually vary between different community types, e.g. to strengthen brand relationships or collect customers' use experience knowledge, which furthermore may strengthen innovation. This will be discussed in more detail later in this chapter.

Against this background, the rest of the chapter focuses on firm-initiated or firm-related online communities, which demands some amendments to existing studies, because they have primarily been based on studies of user-initiated communities. Examining the firm–community link means that community concepts must reflect to a greater degree the relationship between these parties and the processes around which the relationship evolves. To characterize this phenomenon distinctly, three types of firm-initiated online community are proposed: "brand community", "CSR community", and "innovation community". These three types are analysed in detail after the next section. Whereas the brand community and the innovation community have been examined previously, the CSR community type is new. It is precisely this "missing link" that solves important conceptual problems that arise, for example, when using brand community concepts to understand the community–firm relationship in a healthcare setting. These conceptual problems are dicussed in more detail in the "Outlining and defining the topic of the chapter" section below. The findings of the chapter as a whole are summarized in Table 15.1 and in the "Three community types revisited and conclusion" section. These findings indicate that the proposed typology can incorporate in a precise manner what is found empirically, but also pinpoint that much work remains to be done, both theoretically and empirically.

Outlining and defining the topic of the chapter

Initially, it is important to define what the basic characteristics of an online community are in general. Inspired by Kozinets (1999, p. 253), an *online community* in this chapter is understood as: *social interaction in an online setting between people who share some communal objects or elements and where the setting and at least some activities are initiated by a given firm.* The communal elements that participants share will differ on a number of dimensions, and these will be revealed when the three types of online community are compared and discussed in detail later.

But, before the three types are developed, there is a need to clarify how online communities in general have been typified. Thus, online communities have been characterized in a number of ways (Armstrong & Hagel III, 1995; Kozinets, 1999; McWilliam, 2000; Wenger, 2000; Wenger & Snyder, 2000; Williams & Cothrel, 2000; Cova & Cova, 2002), for example whether they are communities of interest, relationships, fantasy, or transactions (Armstrong & Hagel III, 1995). The latter authors admit that the four types are "not mutually exclusive", but, in addition, there seems to be a significant overlap between some of the types which in addition may not apply to a community definition with social interaction as the primary denomination.[2] In addition, these typologies have focused on a very broad spectrum of online phenomena, and mostly on *member*[3] or *user-initiated* communities. However, as briefly discussed above, this chapter will specialize and draw the attention to *firm-initiated* and *firm-related* communities and how they can be characterized.

In this quest to examine firm-initiated online communities, it might be fruitful to begin to examine the concept of brand community. With reference to Muñiz and O'Guinn (2001), Andersen (2005) defines a brand community as a "group of actors who are fans of a particular brand" or the potential to become ones. The community is being organized and managed by the brand supplier to further marketing aims. Andersen uses this brand community focus to analyse two communities initiated by Coloplast, a Danish corporation that has three main business areas: ostomy-related activities, incontinence, and wound-care products. One of the communities is called SpinalNet, established for patients, nurses, and relatives with the purpose of helping persons who have suffered a spinal injury.

On the one hand, in the entire analytical set-up of the paper, Andersen focuses on branding, and he also mentions that the online-community-mediated dialogue between the firm and the customers can enhance "brand involvement and loyalty". On the other hand, the empirical evidence presented seems to question the proposition that these communities should be characterized as brand communities. Thus, Andersen reports that, in Coloplast's view, healthcare personnel are "extremely sensitive towards suppliers' possible attempts to market their products through the 'back door'", and "too much focus on product branding aspects is believed to be counterproductive". Consequently, "too much product pushing would immediately raise suspicions and we would lose whatever backup and goodwill we had", as the community manager notes (Andersen, 2005, p. 47).

Now, there is a clear contradiction between the ideas of the brand community as brand involvement and the empirical evidence that only allows a very, very indirect connection between the online community activities and the relevant products and corporate brand. This very indirect connection more resembles how stakeholders are seen in a corporate social responsibility and stakeholder theory perspective, where stakeholders are not just instrumental to marketing and branding but viewed "in their own right", e.g. as "real people with names, faces, and children" and "with the aspiration of fulfilling our dreams and theirs" (Freeman & Velamury, 2006, pp. 17–20). It is therefore suggested that, besides the brand community type, it is important to develop a new community type where ethical considerations are crucial and a direct connection to brand and product pushing will be at least counterproductive and at worst devastating for the trust between the community members and the hosting firm. This type is called a corporate social responsibility, or CSR, community, and it will be defined and discussed at length below.

A third distinct type of company-initiated community proposed here is the product development or innovation community (von Hippel, 2005). This type differs from the two already mentioned in that the interaction of the community focuses explicitly on product development and innovation, whereas the brand community revolves around the brand and the CSR community focuses on solving a personal problem of common interest to the members. It is well documented that lead users in different sectors contribute significantly to the product innovation of the firms, and that they are willing freely to share this knowledge; each (lead) user may only have one or a few innovations to offer, but these innovations may be widely distributed, for example, within an innovation community (von Hippel, 2005).

The discussion of the three community types focuses on a firm perspective. Online communities could be studied solely from a community perspective without reflecting that some of the activities relate to a brand or a product of a firm. However, this chapter emphasizes the *relationship* between the firm and certain types of community by recognizing that firms must have some kind of motivation for initiating or relating to a certain community, but also that firms must consider that communities have their own dynamics, even those that are initiated or hosted by a specific firm, and therefore the firms need to know why users and subgroups of these participate and share experiences, etc., with other users. The managerial aspect of this is that, in order to design marketing communication efforts to communities, managers should be able to distinguish between three major types of online community that are likely to respond quite differently to marketing efforts because the reasons why users engage in the communities differ markedly. As already indicated (e.g. Armstrong & Hagel III, 1995), online communities can be typified on the basis of a number of different dimensions, but in this chapter the typology will underline to what extent and how community activities *relate* to the brand, product, innovation, or, in the case of the CSR community, only indirectly to the firm, although it is still relevant to the firm to consider how to link to this type of community, because the long-term results may be encouraging, e.g. increased value for all stakeholders. Thus, the first of the six elements that contribute to distinguishing between the three types is the *focal point of interaction in the community* (element 1). It signifies the object or the topic around which the interaction evolves, e.g. the "brand" in the brand community? This element is easy to identify empirically and needs no further elaboration here. The next three elements relate to why community users or members participate in activities and are willing to share knowledge and experiences. Element 2 is *experienced members' motivation for contributing*. Element 3 is *novice members' motivation for contributing*. From the firm's perspective it is important to know why unpaid experienced members engage because experienced members will often represent the community and channel important decisions, and furthermore they play a significant role by setting the norms and controlling certain aspects of the community's development. The novice members' motivation for contributing is included in this chapter because it signifies what would motivate outsiders/consumers to join the community and is therefore important for the further recruitment of users or when a firm wishes to initiate a community from scratch. In addition, it is important for a firm to distinguish between certain subgroups of a community when considering how to interact with a community. There might be a number of subgroups, but in this chapter the opposition between experienced and new members is chosen in order to maintain clarity and overview when comparing between the three types. Whereas elements 2 and 3 focus on members' *community*-oriented motivations for participating, i.e. the "we-ness" aspect (e.g. Muñiz & O'Guinn, 2001), the reason to join may also originate from element 4 – *members' personal needs or benefits from participating*. Such knowledge is of immediate interest to a company when preparing interaction with and marketing communication to a given community, because such expressions may represent values to which the firm can link its communication efforts. This chapter will show significant differences between members' motivation in the three communities – differences that a firm should take into account. The last two elements include why and how *firms* choose to initiate online communities. As regards element 5 – *firm's motivation for initiating and relating to a community* – it seems rather obvious that condensing the experience of why firms engage with communities would be interesting to other firms. This is also valid for element 6 – *firm's intervention method* – and this includes how directly and intensely, e.g. in terms of marketing push, the firm tends to intervene. These six elements will form subsections of the three main sections examining the three types of community.

Against this background, this chapter will review research that studies online communities in order to address two questions: Can firm-initiated or firm-related online communities, specifically the proposed new CSR community type, be distinguished and characterized consistently when compared with the branding and innovation community types? In the process of developing the CSR type through discussion of the six elements, what are the differences and similarities between the three types?

Brand community

Focal point of interaction

That the focal point for interaction in a brand community is the "brand" is rather obvious, yet addressing this topic in detail is somewhat more complex. Typically, branding research has focused on the *brand* and the customers' identification with the brand (e.g. Aaker, 2002). Still, Keller widens this notion by proposing that the strength of the relationship can be evaluated on the basis of the extent to which the customers (a) are loyal in their behaviour in terms of, for example, repeat purchases, (b) exhibit strong personal attachment, (c) feel a sense of community, e.g. kinship or affiliation with other people associated with the brand, and (d) exhibit active engagement (Keller, 2001, p. 15). Thus, Keller includes both the traditional perception of brand relationship in (a) and (b) and points forward to the meaning and importance of brand communities in (c) and (d). In line with this, Muñiz and O'Guinn (2001) and Antorini and Andersen (2005) focus on the interaction *between* community *members* evolving around a brand.

Experienced user's motivation for contributing

How do the *experienced* members *contribute* to the community interaction? The largest contribution is directed to the novice member, and here the process unfolds as a kind of initiation ritual where the experienced member in an exemplary manner shows how the brand and community cultural codes are lived and the novice can copy this or the experienced member can help via more explicit "teaching" (Schouten & McAlexander, 1995; Muñiz & O'Guinn, 2001; Kozinets, 2002). Such processes are sometimes perceived as negative by other members (Algesheimer, Dholakia, & Herrmann, 2005). Lead users also provide knowledge to the rest of the community (McAlexander & Schouten, 1998; Muñiz & O'Guinn 2001; Kozinets 2002; Bagozzi & Dholakia, 2006).

Why do experienced members contribute? The background is that the experienced members have co-created the community together with other members of the same credence and thus want to ensure that the "right" brand perception and subculture are maintained, and therefore their contribution by being a role model or "teacher" is perceived as "natural" (Schouten & McAlexander 1995; Muñiz & O'Guinn, 2001). Yet, the help is limited, specialized, and embedded in the community, and not some universal principle like altruism (Muñiz & O'Guinn 2001; Wang & Fesenmaier, 2003, 2004). As a spin-off, the contributor may gain recognition from peers and even admiration from newcomers (Schouten & McAlexander, 1995).

Novice user's motivation for contributing

How do the *novice* members of a brand community *contribute*? This is done by giving recognition to the experienced user (Schouten & McAlexander, 1995; McAlexander & Schouten, 1998; Kozinets, 2002). Living the brand and the culture may gradually raise their status in the community (hierarchy), and thereby as a whole they contribute to the sustainability of the brand community. This act is motivated by their wish to learn and live the brand fully, and via this process their status in the community is gradually raised (Schouten & McAlexander, 1995; McAlexander & Schouten, 1998).

Members' personal needs or benefits from participating

Besides social aspects of community interaction, what have the members reported about their perceived *personal sociopsychological gains* from participating? Initially, it is important to note that the sentiments around brand communities represent only a part of the members' life expressions. Hard-core Harley bikers see their life style as an all-consuming totality, but, to most of the other subgroup members, this life style is primarily a leisure activity (Schouten & McAlexander, 1995). And in the case of the Mac, Bronco jeep, and Saab car communities, "Members know it isn't the most important thing in their lives – not even close – but neither is it trivial" (Muñiz & O'Guinn, 2001, p. 418).

Although brandfests primarily satisfy "basic hedonic needs" (McAlexander & Schouten, 1998, p. 381), they may also provide extraordinary experiences that touch deeper layers, such as "flow", self-affirmation, or self-discovery. But such deep experiences are not reported for *online* brand communities. Therefore, members' primary psychological gain from participating is to fulfil basic *hedonic needs*, and this is valid for online (Muñiz & O'Guinn, 2001; Kozinets, 2002) as well as for some offline brand communities (Schouten & McAlexander, 1995; McAlexander & Schouten, 1998). Linked to hedonic needs are potential psychological gains stemming from *public self-expression and self-exposition* when living the brand (Schouten & McAlexander, 1995; McAlexander & Schouten, 1998; Muñiz & O'Guinn, 2001; Kozinets, 2002; McAlexander, Schouten, & Koenig, 2002). This is especially pronounced in brandfests and even more in a public and audiovisually "noisy" formation of, for example, Harley bikes (Fournier *et al.*, 2000; Fournier & Maas, 2001). But web-based communication in online brand communities can, given the potentially wide publicity on the Internet, also satisfy such needs, albeit in a less intense manner (Muñiz & O'Guinn, 2001; Kozinets, 2002; Bagozzi & Dholakia, 2006).

Firm's motivation

Interaction and socialization in cases like Linux user groups, car clubs, and coffee communities (Bagozzi & Dholakia 2006; Algesheimer, Dholakia, & Herrmann, 2005; Kozinets, 2002) influence behavioural intentions. This is directly or indirectly pronounced in potentially increased sales. However, this does not mean that a brand community should be a battlefield for hard or soft sales, as mentioned above. Instead, the firm might focus on potential long-term value gains.

Brandfests (McAlexander & Schouten, 1998 [motorcycle rallies and jeep brandfests]; Fournier *et al.*, 2000 [motorcycle rally: the posse ride]; McAlexander, Schouten, & Koenig, 2002 [jeep brandfests]) seemingly provide both stronger product–customer, brand–customer, and firm–customer relationships. Furthermore, these brandfest studies all indicate that these stronger relationships generate a number of pecuniary spin-offs, such as merchandise on the brandfest and intentions of buying (new versions of) the product/brand after the brandfest.

Firm's intervention method

The firm's intervention methods are found to be twofold. Firstly, the intervention may vary in intensity depending on the degree to which the community is self-sustained. Yet, the above-described online communities are user initiated. Or, if they are firm initiated, the firm's intervention intensity and methods are not reported. Still, for the German-speaking car club community, there are indications that certain firm influences may increase normative pressure, and for new members this may lead to a negative outcome. However, the authors characterize this finding as preliminary. For the brandfests where the intervention method is well reported, the question addressed is to what extent the firm should create and actively manage the community processes, or whether it should just support and facilitate. A detailed account of different intervention methods and their strengths and weaknesses is given by Fournier and Maas (2001).

Another issue is the extent to which brand communities are or should be the "space" or "place" for intensive, involuntary, and explicit direct branding and merchandise exposition. The case of the Mac, Bronco, and Saab online communities (Muñiz & O'Guinn, 2001) indicates that the members actively search for information about the brand and products, but, as they are user-initiated communities, the firms' potential direct promotion efforts are not reported. The general impression from the brand communities under discussion is that the members are very open to information about the brand or products, but they prefer to be able on their own account to choose when and how. This is most explicit in relation to brandfests, where the opportunities and temptation to initiate a promotion push would be greatest. Some brandfests entirely abandon hard and soft sell, and the participants seem to notice this as positive input to their goodwill "account" (McAlexander, Schouten, & Koenig, 2002), whereas others allow some sales and promotion, although as a minor and indirect part of the whole brandfest activities (Fournier *et al.*, 2000). Again, refer to Fournier and Maas (2001) for a detailed account on specific intervention methods (i.e. the posse ride).

CSR community

Focal point of interaction

This type of community does not take a brand perspective as the focal point of interaction; rather, it is the members' personal and social problems and their need for safety, related to physiological, psychological, and social issues, that drive the community interaction and purpose. An example of such a community, besides the already mentioned SpinalNet, is DepNet.com, which is sponsored by the Danish pharmaceutical firm Lundbeck and designed for members who suffer from depression.

The examples of CSR communities used in this chapter are all from the healthcare sector, so why not call this community type the "patients" or "healthcare" community? The reason for choosing the CSR name is, firstly, that "healthcare" is a sector or industry term and therefore does not fit with a brand term referring to a firm feature. Secondly, the CSR name gives the most precise distinction between a brand community and CSR community, because it refers to the much more indirect and ethically demanding role that the *firm* plays in the CSR community and thus signifies that the focus of the typology in this chapter is the firm–community relationship.

The number of studies related to this type of community is sparse. Andersen's (2005) SpinalNet study is the only scientific account of *firm-initiated* CSR communities found. Still, three other communities are *user initiated*, and one is co-founded by 14 hospitals in the Stuttgart area of Germany.

Experienced user's motivation for contributing

According to a study of 15 communities related to different diseases (Josefsson, 2005), *experienced users* contribute primarily because they have had their own harsh experiences with the illness, and this gives them a strong emotional drive to share this experience with others in order to make the process less painful: "I want to help others so they don't have to go through the same thing I have" (p. 146). In addition, an investigation of cancer-related *user-initiated online* forums (Turner, Grube, & Meyers, 2001) indicates that the online exchange was evaluated to be as supportive as face-to-face help from family and friends. Users seem to help each other primarily concerning topics that supplement the expert-provided information, for example, topics of sociopsychological importance and exchange of additional information. And the users act in line with this: "experience reports from other users were important reasons for visiting the community" (Leimeister, Ebner, & Krcmar, 2005, p. 120), and they trust the other users, in spite of the very intimate and private topics that are interchanged. Coloplast, a *firm* already introduced above, has *initiated* an *online community* called SpinalNet. Andersen (2005) has analysed this community, but the data are based on interviews with the firm, not with the users. Persons with spinal cord injuries are not able, or are very restricted in their ability, to move around. Therefore, usage of an online community gives them the safety from being better informed by professionals or the opportunity to chat with other members who perhaps have greater experience in potential problems and know how and where to obtain help to solve these problems. In most of the support event cases mentioned above, the experienced users are probably the main contributors of the support.

Thus, *experienced* users' motivation for participating and contributing, based on their own bitter experience, is to prevent others from encountering the same problems. The thanks and recognition they receive from user feedback is perceived to be rewarding.

Novice user's motivation for contributing

The *new user* is normally in the first phases of the disease or problem, and may not, as described above, receive sufficient face-to-face support, or the explanations from healthcare professionals may have been hard to understand, even in situations where face-to-face consultations have been obtained. Consequently, the new user may be confused about the facts, in addition to potentially being distressed and suffering from other sociopsychological symptoms (Turner, Grube, & Meyers, 2001; Leimeister, Ebner, & Krcmar, 2005; Josefsson, 2005). The situation, which is often delicate for the user, asking questions and the bitter experiences of those who answer, induces a communication form of "empathy and human understanding" (Josefsson, 2005, p. 150). Furthermore, humour is an important element, and jokes about seemingly incompetent professionals are common. Consequently, the *new* user gets help to understand the illness or problem and, in a broader context, to go on with his or her life in spite of the problems.

Members' personal needs or benefits from participating

According to the preceding sections, we now know that users of this type participate actively and think that the support and information they get is important. The type of help that is transferred can be called *empathic* and *specialized* to the problem and its context. Seen in general, this type of community fulfils the basic need for *safety* in a physiological and sociopsychological sense.

Firm's motivation

As the only firm-initiated community is Coloplast's SpinalNet, the study of this firm is the only one to represent the firms' perspective. One of Coloplast's motivations to participate is that product use forums give access to valuable market information. The discussion in these forums also includes competitors' products, and this reduces the problem of user-perceived product push. In addition, these forums and the entire community represent a resource from where to spot a lead user with innovative ideas. More about this in the "Innovation community" section below. Concerning the broader motivation, the project manager for SpinalNet notes that ". . . we are not doing this to promote short-time sales" (Andersen, 2005, p. 47). Moreover, concerning the long-term perspective, the firm, in its 2003/2004 Stakeholder report, mentions that "Our stakeholders' interests converge across the board. To generate good financial results, a company needs satisfied customers and successful employees. Improved processes and new technology can reduce the environmental impact and ensure even more effective utilization of materials, all for the benefit of society and Coloplast's performance". Thus, besides improved market intelligence and innovation capability, not short-term but rather long-term financial results from the synergistic effect are also a motivation.

It can be difficult in an absolute sense to establish if the imperative to include the community as an important stakeholder is morally founded or founded on the prospect of long-term value creation/profit, or both (Kornum, 2007). According to Jones, Felps, and Bigley (2007), broadly moralist stakeholder cultures do exist, where "humanistic values for their own sake" are organizationally rooted. However, with the rudimentary empirical base on the topic in this section, the question remains open.

Firm's intervention method

The case of Coloplast and SpinalNet (and StomaNet) has already shown that ethical concerns from professionals and other users are important factors in the relationship between the firm and these stakeholders. The firm therefore avoids product push and states that the relation to "particular product brands is of relatively little importance and downplaying these activities" is part of Coloplast's community strategy (Andersen, 2005, p. 47). The only direct product intervention that is allowed for in both communities is discussion forums centred around product use and assessments thereof, but this includes both Coloplast's own and the competitors' products and is not used for brand or product promotion purposes. As mentioned above, Coloplast is very much aware of the ethical background for avoiding a direct marketing push, and instead uses indirect methods of funding and provides organizational processes, infrastructure, and expert knowledge.

Innovation community

Focal point of interaction

Now, as has been mentioned above, both brand and CSR communities may form the basis for finding lead users with innovation potential, and the individual community member may be a member in more than one type of community. Consequently, the difference between a brand community and an innovation community is that, whereas members of the former will focus on (hedonic) aspects of product usage and living the brand culture, a member of the latter will be involved in a systematic quest to translate brand living into *new* products and services, which may be seen as more demanding than just usage, and this normally involves lead users. For the CSR community, only a minor part of their interaction may relate to forums that discuss products in use, whereas the major part of their interaction relates to solving problems in a broader socio-psychological context. Yet, it may be useful to understand both the use-experience feedback and its context in order to grasp the full implications for users/patients of a product innovation. The difference here will also be a more *systematic and intense focus on developing new features*. For example, Coloplast in 2001 had more than 25 customer groups involved in product development, and the SpinalNet community has made it much easier for the firm to recruit users to innovation focus groups (Andersen, 2005, p. 48).

Experienced user's motivation for contributing

Franke and Shah (2003) find that user motives for participating are more oriented towards sharing and assisting others (community factors) than towards individual-focused benefits such as money or recognition (personal benefit factor). Specifically, in relation to lead users, Füller, Jawecki, and Mühlbacher (2007) have developed a netnographic study of participation and innovation in five *user-initiated* basketball communities. It shows that participation in each community is structured with a small group of "highly active, broadly respected, well-known, long-standing, and knowledgeable insiders" (Füller, Jawecki, & Mühlbacher, 2007, p. 64). For example, in one of the communities, 3.4% of the members make 80% of the postings. Extensive use experience is shared, not only to support purchasing decisions or to modify existing designs but also to propose entirely new designs. The motives for sharing innovative ideas are reported to be: a desire to give back, recognition, hope of useful feedback, inner satisfaction from revealing an idea, and community norm (Füller, Jawecki, & Mühlbacher, 2007, p. 65).

The study by Jeppesen and Molin (2003) is the first in this section to be based on a *firm-initiated* innovation community. The firm is part of the game industry, and the results from the study indicate that peer recognition induces knowledge-sharing. In work by Jeppesen and Frederiksen (2006), results from another *firm-initiated* community are presented. This firm develops and sells computer-controlled musical instrument software. The lead users or innovators in this community are mostly IT-skilled persons who are involved in the community as hobbyists, and nearly all these innovative users share their innovations with the rest of the community, which has a positive knowledge diffusion effect on the other users. Because the innovators are hobbyists, they do not have so much to lose from sharing. But another reason for sharing is, contrary to what has been reported for *user-initiated* communities, not peer recognition, but instead firm recognition. This may be due to the characteristics of these innovative users, in that they are interested primarily in "technical aspects of product development and [they] therefore identify less with 'non-technical' peers, but more with firm-based developers" (Jeppesen & Frederiksen, 2006, p. 56). With these they seem to have, if not a personal, then a kind of close relationship where they can identify individual employees. The innovative users even to some extent honour the firm and its developers, and some lead users may even see them as idols.

Thus, across the studies reviewed above, lead users or innovators can be identified as the main contributors in a broad array of dimensions. Being part of a community enhances their contribution. As only one of the studies focuses directly on *firm-initiated* innovation communities, it is worth noting that here the primary reason for lead users to participate is *firm* recognition, as opposed to peer recognition. Yet, because rather unique circumstances have influenced the characteristics of this community and because many of the other innovation communities as well might be firm initiated, the motivation for participating in user-initiated communities should also be considered. In user-initiated communities, lead users also possess a prominent position, because they drive innovation.

As elaborated above, there seems to be agreement that both community and personal sociopsychological benefit oriented factors *motivate lead users to share and participate*. Concerning the latter factor, this will be discussed below. As for the former, across the studies presented, lead users are found to participate because they (a) share community norms or value systems, (b) feel obligations to assist, and (c) hope for useful feedback in the long term (reciprocity).

Novice user's motivation for contributing

As for less frequent participants and less innovative members, based on the sections above, they generally participate because they want to (a) learn about innovation and (b) share use experience and their own modifications.

Members' personal needs or benefits from participating

The motivational base of lead users is more other-regarding than the rest of the contributors. Other-regarding in this context because members participate for the reason that they support the basic value system (ethos) of the community, may feel moral obligations to the group, and finally are "highly motivated by social relationships and emotional bonds they value" (Hemetsberger, 2006, p. 29). Füller, Jawecki, and Mühlbacher (2007, p. 65) separate innovators' possible gains into "excitement driven" (80% of all ideas posted in the community) and "need driven" (20%). The former members are driven by enjoyment and fun attached to the process in itself, whereas the latter are driven by "so far unsatisfied needs when using equipment" (Füller, Jawecki, & Mühlbacher, 2007, p. 65). Füller (2007) surveyed 727 members' reasons for participating in 10 communities innovating in widely different product categories. It is not specified to what extent activities are *firm or user-initiated*. This investigation seems to support the contention that excitement/enjoyment on the one hand and dissatisfaction with existing products on the other are important personal drivers for participating in innovation activities. The former is also confirmed by Jeppesen and Molin (2003). As just mentioned, Hemetsberger (2006) reports that the main contributors in an open-source software community were found to be more other-regarding than the rest of the members. However, they were also found to be "significantly more intrinsically motivated" (Hemetsberger, 2006, p. 30) than the rest; that is, enjoyment or passion drives members to do their programming task, but pursuing the task is also motivated by self-regard as being competent and a sense of self-efficacy.

Thus, *personal sociopsychological gains* in the form of excitement, enjoyment, or passion are often mentioned as drivers, but also innovation-specific issues may drive the member, e.g. until now unsatisfied product-related needs.

Firm's motivation

According to Jeppesen and Frederiksen (2006), sharing innovation in a community means that new products can become available to all users at low costs, and that the firm can pick the best and most innovative ideas for free and integrate them in future innovations.

Firm's intervention method

In the case of computer-controlled musical instrument software, the firm intervenes by hosting the community, i.e. infrastructure, by letting the individual firm developers participate in community exchange and by giving members with promising innovations recognition by exposing their accomplishment to the community (Jeppesen & Frederiksen, 2006).

Three community types revisited and conclusion

The findings in the "Brand community", "CSR community", and "Innovation community" sections are summarized in Table 15.1, where the characteristics of the three community types are presented. The content of this table will form the basis for the following revisit to, and comparison of, the three types. The distinguishing features of the "focal point for interaction" dimension are rather straightforward and have been indicated above. Before we proceed, and in order not to make repetitions in every subtheme below, it is important to mention that, because no empirical study that compares across the three types is available, the findings below concerning cross-type links will be indicative. But they will hopefully function as an inspiration for future empirical scrutiny.

What is the *experienced member's motivation for contributing*? There seems to be a similarity between the brand and innovation community types in that mainte-nance of the community norm is found to be important across the two types. There is no direct indication pointing to any reason for this, but a possible explanation could be that both community types evolve around a product/brand, whereas CSR communities evolve around a problem. Thus, the two former communities should protect the product/brand spirit, but the latter has a more indirect relation to products. In CSR communities, indeed, it is reported that founders of a community influence the norm setting, but it has not broadly been reported as a significant motivator for participation. Instead, the lead users' primary motivation is to share their former harsh experiences in order to prevent other members from facing the same problems or at least to some extent to help relieve their suffering. There might be some similarity to the innovation commu-nity type element "obligation to assist", yet the motive of sharing harsh experi-ences has not been labelled in (moral) obligation terms, although it can be interpreted in this direction. As regards the "feedback in the future" dimension, i.e. contributing because of expected reciprocity, this is somewhat more instru-mental than obligation and is often contained in the definition of fairness (e.g. Ring & Van de Ven, 1994). However, slightly different uses of constructs may prompt me to avoid any concluding explanation and leave it to further research.

Peer recognition is probably not the reason why users start participating in a community, rather it is an element that maintains or even reinforces existing members' motivation. On the face of it, there seems to be a significant difference

Table 15.1 A typology of firm-related online communities

	Brand community	CSR community	Innovation community
Focal point for interaction	Brand	Members' personal and social problems	Innovating the product or service
Experienced members' motivation for contributing	- Maintain brand and community culture - Status/peer recognition	- Share harsh experience - Avoid other same experience - Peer recognition	- Firm recognition - Support community norm - Obligation to assist - Feedback in the future
Novice members' motivation for contributing	- Learn and live brand and culture - Raise status	- Learn about problem/illness - Learn to live with it	- Learn about innovation - Share use–experience and own modifications
Members' personal needs or benefits from participating	- Hedonic - Self-expression - Public self-exposition	- Physiological, psychological, and social safety	- Enjoyment or passion - Unsatisfied product-related need
Firm's motivation	- Brand relationships - Long-term brand value (equity) enhancement - Brand intelligence?	- Use-experience intelligence - Long-term value enhancement - Moral obligation?	- Innovation intelligence - Innovation relationships - Long-term value enhancement through innovation
Firm's intervention method	- Direct (providing, for example, brand icons, stories, fun, sentiments, etc.) - Indirect	- Indirect (providing, for example, funding, infrastructure, expert knowledge, etc.)	- Direct (providing, for example, innovation recognition, innovation cooperation) - Indirect

between the innovation community type and the other two, because the former has firm recognition as an important motivating factor, whereas this is not the case for the other two. The general explanation here might be that, in order for firm-initiated user innovation to be successful, it will be a narrower circle of lead users in the community that will drive the community part of innovation. This indicates that these users are advanced in a number of aspects and can match firm-employed developers and therefore will have an inclination to be oriented towards these developers. However, the number of firm-initiated communities reviewed is small, and this also calls for further research. In addition, during brandfests it is reported that technical seminars are very popular, and some firm employees may reach a "star status", where some participants even ask for an autograph. This is indeed firm recognition, but is this their primary reason for participating? Maybe for some of them, but not for the majority. But what are the differences and the similarities here, and to what extent could brandfests be used for recruiting lead users of innovation communities?

For natural reasons, *novice members* have a slightly different motivation for participating in online communities than experienced members. But, across the three types, the motivation of the newcomer seems to be more alike, as compared with the experienced user. The object around which their motivation evolves is of course different (brand, personal problems, innovation), but the processes seem to exhibit some similarities. A common motivation found is to learn about the object of the community and to live within the processes that surround it. Yet, how this can be obtained differs widely between the types. In the case of brand communities, the learning is a cultural adaptation process and, because of a more pronounced status hierarchy, the so-called neophytes here are, for good reasons, eager to raise their status. An innovation community learning process is more closely related to knowledge and use experience and much more cognitively driven, as opposed to brand communities which are more affectively driven. CSR communities have both cognitive (know the problem/illness) and affective elements (coping sociopsychologically).

Concerning members' *personal needs or benefits* when participating, brand and innovation communities have a common trait, because concepts such as excitement and enjoyment are frequently mentioned. The open question here is whether or to what extent we talk about the same phenomenon in the two types. It is hard to know from the data. But one explanation could be that the members in the two types can be located at different ends of a continuum but overlap in the middle. Fun and enjoyment could be situated on the left side, excitement in the middle, and passion on the right side, and from left to the right there would be a gradual change in motivations from hedonic via excitement to motivations of a more spiritual stance,[4] or from experiential and immediate (left) to something private and enduring (right) (Keller, 2001, p. 14). From this it is possible to suggest that *online* and some *offline* brand communities are primarily situated from left to middle, whereas participators of *brandfests* and some *offline* brand communities may cover the entire spectrum. For lead users in innovation communities it can be proposed that they are situated primarily in the middle, yet with different reach to right or left, depending on, for example, product or member characteristics. Following the ideas of the suggested continuum, the "self-expression" and "self-exposition" proposed in Table 15.1 fit well with the most hedonic (right) part of the continuum.

In the case of the *firms' motivation* for engaging in work with online communities, an important synergistic interaction is found between relationship building on the one hand and brand/use experience/innovation intelligence on the other. From these intelligence initiatives, companies can gain access to an invaluable pool of sentiments and knowledge in relation to members' needs, wishes, use experience, innovative ideas, etc., and the synergetic effects from this may generate resources that can enhance new initiatives that again can strengthen the firm–community relationship and ultimately support in the long term the value creation of the firm and its stakeholders. Owing to the sparse numbers of cases where the firm–community link is part of the study, it is not possible here to indicate which of these are the primary motivators or propose some causal chain. This will demand a cross-type examination. Furthermore, it seems interesting to study the member feedback originating from brand or CSR communites and how it can be transferred to innovation communities (Andersen, 2005). In addition, which role can CSR communities play when a company deals with corporate social responsibility or stakeholder responsibility issues. (Freeman & Velamury, 2006; Morsing & Oswald, 2006)? This directly furthers discussion on the firm's *intervention methods*. CSR communities work with members' problems that are personal, private, sometimes intimate, traumatic, or otherwise sociopsychologically demanding. Because these members and professionals normally have very mixed feelings towards the product and brand push, the firm must be sensitive and consider all related ethical aspects. Although it is often mentioned in relation to brand communities or brandfests that the firm should be cautious with product push, most brandfests include some elements of marketing and sales. As mentioned above, in CSR communities the brand or product is much less visible, e.g. direct product marketing is replaced by giving the users an opportunity to share their use experience in relation to both the focal firm's products and competing products. In the link between the firm and related innovation communities there seems to be few restrictions, because both parties are committed to the product and the furthering of promising innovations.

To *conclude* and answer the research question, the content of this chapter indicates that three distinct online community types have indeed been identified. Although there are a number of similarities between the three types, the typology described above includes a number of dimensions that make the individual type distinct, and it has been indicated that the above cross-type comparisons can lead to fruitful discussions and new research questions. Concerning the distinction between the three types, the major contribution from this chapter is to indicate that the brand and CSR community differ on most dimensions and that marketing efforts should accordingly differ. In both instances the communities have their own dynamics independent of the related firm, but brand communities are much more open to promotion and marketing push, and often the community is the active party to search for information, merchandise, and ads. At certain brandfests some participants have stated that they recognize that the event is not being used for a direct sales effort, and online communities may follow a general tendency where consumers indicate that it is fine that product information and sales opportunities are easily available, but, for example, they would like actively to find the information they need themselves instead of too much marketing push. For instance, in the case of a brandfest it is possible to hear (technically) detailed information or news about the products and possible selling spots for accessories, collectibles, etc., but all this should be in the form of activities that run parallel to the main event and do not disturb the main event, and the participant should have the opportunity actively to choose these product/marketing-oriented activities in pauses in the main event. CSR communities, on the other hand, are *very* sensitive to marketing push, and, from the perspective of members, including professionals, marketing push will be considered unethical and intrusive, as seen against a background where these communities are trying to help other members in difficult personal circumstances. As the examples from the Coloplast case show, the influence is much more indirect, as the firm finances the online infrastructure, compensates experts' time usage when answering questions, and collects use experiences from both its own and competitors' products. Thus, it creates a forum from where it can get useful input about all aspects of product use and the firm's products as compared with those of its competitors, and such inputs are, as discussed in the "Innovation community" section, potentially very valuable for innovation. Hereby it is also indicated how the three types can support each other, because both brand and CSR communities can provide input to innovation. Developers and other employees at the related firm can scan the online activities to see if some use-experience problems need to be solved in further innovation and whether entirely new ideas prevail. A brand community and an innovation community may share the same online community infrastructure and even the same name, where the "community" would signify different activities under the same umbrella. As regards the CSR community–innovation community relationship, they are more separate in nature, because a strong and direct product focus is considered inappropriate in a CSR community. Besides scanning the CSR community for relevant use experience, the CSR community could serve as a recruitment base for selecting lead users for innovation activities. If the brand community and the innovation community are separate, the brand community could have a similar function.

Endnotes

1. Refer to the link: http://en.wikipedia.org/wiki/List_of_social_networking_websites
2. The discussion relates to Armstrong and Hagel III (1996) "Real value from online communities". *Harvard Business Review*, May–June, p. 136. The authors suggest three criteria or dimensions on which the typology should be based. The first dimension is the amount of desired interaction by community members, the second is the breadth of subjects that form the basis and content for members' interaction, and the third is the depth of desire to escape reality. The intention of the authors seems to be to capture the broad spectrum of member-initiated online communities. However, seeking to achieve this objective, a number of open questions seem to materialize. Two examples:

   (a) The chosen criteria/dimensions are not applied systematically in the four types. For example, the initially suggested dimensions do not characterize communities of transactions.
   (b) Although the authors mention that the types are not mutually exclusive, they do not discuss in detail what the consequences of this will be.

   For example, if an online community in general were defined by the property of "interaction" between members, then the type "Community of relationships" would become redundant, or alternatively type one, two and four could be called "Communities of relationships", and the typology would collapse.
3. The terms "member", "user", and "participant" will be used synonymously throughout this chapter. It would be interesting to study the extent to which there is a significant difference between members on the one hand and users/

participants on the other when it comes to, for example, participation intensity and type of motivation for joining. But this is not the focus of this chapter.

4. There are some similarities here to three (four) of Schwartz' eleven motivational domains: hedonic (left), stimulation (middle) and self-direction or spirituality (right). However, these and a number of the other dimensions require a closer examination to become comparable between different studies (see, for example, Schwartz & Bilsky, 1987, "Towards a psychological structure of human values". *Journal of Personality and Social Psychology*, vol. 53, pp. 550–562).

References

Aaker, D. A. (2002) *Building Strong Brands*. The Free Press Business, Simon & Schuster, New York, NY.

Algesheimer, R., Dholakia, U. M., & Herrmann, A. (2005) "The social influence of brand community: evidence from European car clubs". *Journal of Marketing*, vol. 69, no. 3, pp. 19–34.

Andersen, P. H. (2005) "Relationship marketing and brand involvement of professionals through web-enhanced brand communities: the case of Coloplast", *Industrial Marketing Management*, vol. 34, pp. 39–59.

Antorini, Y. M. & Andersen, K. S. (2005) "A communal approach to corporate branding", in *Corporate Branding*, edited by Schultz, M., Antorini, Y. M., & Csaba, F. F. Copenhagen Business School Press, Copenhagen, Denmark.

Armstrong, A. & Hagel III, J. (1995) "Real profits from virtual communities". *The McKinsey Quarterly*, no. 3, pp. 127–141.

Bagozzi, R. P. & Dholakia, U. M. (2006) "Open source software user communities: a study of participation in Linux user groups". *Management Science*, vol. 52, no. 7, pp. 1099–1115.

Cova, B. & Cova, V. C. (2002) "Tribal marketing: the tribalisation of society and its impact on the conduct of marketing". *European Journal of Marketing*, vol. 36, no. 5/6, pp. 595–620.

Fournier, S. & Maas, J. (2001) *Building Brand Community on the Harley-Davidson Posse Ride*. Teaching note, Harvard Business School Cases, Boston, MA.

Fournier, S., Sensiper, S., McAlexander, J. H., & Schouten, J. W. (2000) *Building Brand Community on the Harley-Davidson Posse Ride*. Harvard Business School Cases, Boston, MA.

Franke, N. & Shah, S. (2003) "How communities support innovative activities: an exploration of assistance and sharing among end-users". *Research Policy*, vol. 32, no. 1, pp. 157–179.

Freeman, R. E. & Velamuri, S. R. (2006) "A new approach to CSR: company stakeholder responsibility", in *Corporate Social Responsibility: Reconciling Managerial Strategies Towards the 21st Century*, edited by Kakabadse, A. & Morsing, M. Palgrave MacMillan, New York, NY.

Füller, J. (2007) *What Motivates Creative Consumers to Participate in Virtual New Product Development?* American Marketing Association, Summer.

Füller, J., Jawecki, G., & Mühlbacher, H. (2007) "Innovation creation by online basketball communities". *Journal of Business Research*, vol. 60, no. 1, pp. 60–71.

Hemetsberger, A. (2006) *Understanding Consumers' Collective Action on the Internet: a Conceptualization and Empirical Investigation of the Free- and Open-Source Movement.* Research synopsis, April, Department of Strategic Management, Marketing and Tourism, University of Innsbruck, Innsbruck, Austria.

Jeppesen, L. B. & Frederiksen, L. (2006) "Why firm-established user communities work for innovation: the personal attributes of innovative users in the case of computer-controlled music instruments". *Organization Science,* vol. 17, no. 1, pp. 45–63.

Jeppesen, L. B. & Molin, M. J. (2003) "Consumers as co-developers: learning and innovation outside the firm". *Technology Analysis and Strategic Management,* vol. 15, no. 3, pp. 363–383.

Jones, T. M., Felps, W., & Bigley, G. A. (2007) "Ethical theory and stakeholder-related decisions: the role of stakeholder culture". *Academy of Management Review,* vol. 32, no. 1, pp. 137–155.

Josefsson, U. (2005) "Coping with illness online: the case of patients' online communities". *Information Society,* vol. 21, no. 2, pp. 133–153.

Keller, K. L. (2001) *Building Customer-Based Brand Equity: a Blueprint for Creating Strong Brands.* Working paper, Report no. 01-107, Marketing Science Institute, Cambridge, UK.

Kornum, N. (2007) *Company Stakeholder Responsibility – a Resource Based Perspective.* Working paper no. 1, Department of Marketing, Copenhagen Business School, Copenhagen, Denmark.

Kozinets, R. V. (1999) "E-tribalized marketing?: the strategic implications of virtual communities of consumption". *European Management Journal,* vol. 17, no. 3, pp. 252–264.

Kozinets, R. V. (2002) "The field behind the screen: using netnography for marketing research in online communities". *Journal of Marketing Research,* vol. 39, no. 1, pp. 61–72.

Leimeister, J. M., Ebner, W., & Krcmar, H. (2005) "Design, implementation, and evaluation of trust-supporting components in virtual communities for patients". *Journal of Management Information Systems,* vol. 21, no. 4, pp. 101–135.

McAlexander, J. H. & Schouten, J. W. (1998) "Brandfests servicescapes for the cultivation of brand equity", in *Servicescapes: the Concept of Place in Contemporary Markets,* edited by Sherry, J. F. NTC Business Books, Chicago, IL.

McAlexander, J. H., Schouten, J. W., & Koenig, H. F. (2002) "Building brand community". *Journal of Marketing,* vol. 66, no. 1, pp. 38–54.

McWilliam, G. (2000) "Building stronger brands through online communities". *Sloan Management Review,* Spring, pp. 43–54.

Morsing, M. & Oswald, D. (2006) "Novo Nordisk A/S: integrating sustainability into business practice", in *Corporate Social Responsibility: Reconciling Managerial Strategies Towards the 21st Century,* edited by Kakabadse, A. & Morsing, M. Palgrave MacMillan, New York, NY.

Muñiz, A. M. & O'Guinn, T. C. (2001) "Brand communities". *Journal of Consumer Research,* vol. 27, no. 4, pp. 412–432.

Ring, P. S. & Van de Ven, A. H. (1994) "Developmental processes of cooperative interorganizational relationships". *Academy of Management Review,* vol. 19, no. 1, pp. 90–118

Schouten, J. W. & McAlexander, J. H. (1995) "Subcultures of consumption: an ethnography of the new bikers". *Journal of Consumer Research,* vol. 22, no. 1, pp. 43–61.

Thorson, E., Duffy, M., & Schumann, D. W. (2007) "The Internet waits for no one", in *Internet Advertising,* edited by Schumann, D. W. & Thorson, E. Lawrence Erlbaum Associates, Publishers, Mahwah, NJ.

Turner, J. W., Grube, J. A., & Meyers, J. (2001) "Developing an optimal match within online communities: an exploration of CMC support communities and traditional support". *Journal of Communication*, vol. 51, no. 2, pp. 231–251.

von Hippel, E. (2005) *Democratizing Innovation*. The MIT Press, Cambridge, UK.

Wang, Y. & Fesenmaier, D. R. (2003) "Assessing motivation of contribution in online communities: an empirical investigation of an online travel community". *Electronic Markets*, vol. 13, no. 1, pp. 33–45.

Wang, Y. & Fesenmaier, D. R. (2004) "Modelling participation in an online travel community". *Journal of Travel Research*, vol. 42, no. 3, pp. 261–270.

Wenger, E. (2000) "Communities of practice and social learning systems". *Organization*, vol. 7, no. 2, pp. 225–246.

Wenger, E. & Snyder, W. M. (2000) "Communities of practice: the organizational frontier". *Harvard Business Review*, January–February, pp. 139–145.

Williams, R. L. & Cothrel, J. (2000) "Four smart ways to Run online communities". *Sloan Management Review*, Summer, pp. 81–91.

16

Co-developing New Products with Customers

Emanuela Prandelli & Gianmario Verona

Introduction

In a context where customer intelligence, customer equity, and customer relation-ship management are considered the current management mantras, nurturing customer relationships has become a priority for most organizations that want to gain and sustain competitive advantage in modern, global economies. While a large number of consumer goods firms adopt a relational approach in their marketing practices, the adoption of a collaborative approach in the new product development process is still not so widespread. Indeed, firms have for years been used to keeping their innovation laboratories "closed"; therefore, open innovation represents something radically new with respect to their intellectual property rights approach (Chesbrough, 2003). In addition to that, the involvement of customers in a firm's innovation policy represents a conceptual leap, especially in technology markets where innovation policies have historically been driven by the R&D labs (Christensen, 1997).

Notwithstanding these conceptual barriers, in this chapter we intend to tackle the challenge that modern multinational corporations have to deal with. We will focus on two emerging patterns that characterize innovation in the knowledge economy: (a) the increasing openness of the innovation process owing particularly to the role of information and communication technologies (ICTs);[1] (b) the emerging role of customers as co-creators of innovation. The underlying theme of our chapter is that ICTs have created the problem – an increasing need for continuous innovation in a context where information is transparent, competitors are just one click away, and product life cycles are shrinking. However, ICTs also provide the solution – enabling new forms of value co-creation with customers and an efficient way to harness distributed competences. While customer interaction has always been important in new product development, the widespread deployment of ICTs has greatly enhanced the ability of firms to engage with customers in the product innovation process. By creating virtual customer environments, firms can tap into customer knowledge through an ongoing dialogue. The Internet, for instance, enhances the ability of firms to engage customers in collaborative innovation in several ways. It allows firms to transform episodic and one-way customer interactions into a persistent dialogue with customers. Through the creation of virtual customer communities, it allows firms to tap into the social dimension of customer knowledge shared among groups of customers with shared interests. And it extends the reach and the scope of the firm's customer interactions through the use of independent third parties to reach non-customers – competitors' customers or prospective customers.

Firms can use a variety of mechanisms to facilitate collaborative innovation in virtual environments. These mechanisms differ in terms of the stage of the new product development process for which they are most useful, and the nature of the customer interactions they enable.

In order to highlight their contributing role to the process of innovation and their potential, we present detailed anecdotes to show how best-practice firms are using these mechanisms to improve the speed, cost, and quality of their new product development process. More particularly, the remainder of the chapter is structured as follows. We provide an overview of the literature in which we discuss various conceptualizations of customer knowledge and customer involvement in marketing. Then, we highlight key patterns in technology marketing that enhance direct

---

[1] In this chapter, with the concept of ICTs we intend to include all the new tools that have been available after the advent of the Internet and, more particularly, those that refer to the web, the Web 2.0 (the new interactive applications related to Wikis, social networking, etc.), and all forms of convergence between telecommunications and TV.

collaboration with individual customers, communities of customers, and virtual knowledge brokers. We conclude our contribution with a discussion of the theoretical significance of web-based collaborative innovation and its implications for companies seeking customer value-added partners through their virtual interfaces. To this purpose the case of Ducati Motor is discussed in-depth.

The relevance of customer involvement in the innovation process

Collaboration has become an established way of doing business with suppliers, channel partners, and complementors. However, with a few notable exceptions, working directly with customers to co-create value remains a radical notion. As consumers have become increasingly empowered and demanding, marketing scholars have preached the benefits of customer relationship management – essentially an "inside-out" approach to retaining customers that is based on the misguided notion that the company is the arbiter of the relationship and the customer plays a passive role. In today's connected world, however, collaborative marketing – the valuable process of partnering with the end-user to maximize value – is the goal. Actually, firms have always sought to build deeper customer connections to make their marketing, and especially the innovation process, more effective. Several contributions highlight different stages in the evolution of the relationship between a firm and its customers in the context of supporting and catalysing new product development activities.

At the simplest level of the firm–customer interaction, customers play the role of passive receptors of the firm's innovation activities. The key idea at this stage is to improve the fit between the firm's offerings and customer needs by surveying customers and importing customer understanding into the firm. Firms need to listen to their customers by developing a market orientation, because market knowledge plays a strategic role in supporting their competitive advantage, improving new product development processes (e.g. Dougherty, 1992). Market sensing ability and internal organization are seen as key factors driving innovation success (Verona, 1999), along with effective R&D and manufacturing routines (Hayes, Wheelwright, & Clark, 1988). Firms try to understand the expressed desires of their customers, called the "voice of the customer" (Hauser & Clausing, 1988), usually through focus groups, customer surveys, and research techniques like concept testing and conjoint analysis (Leonard & Rayport, 1997). According to

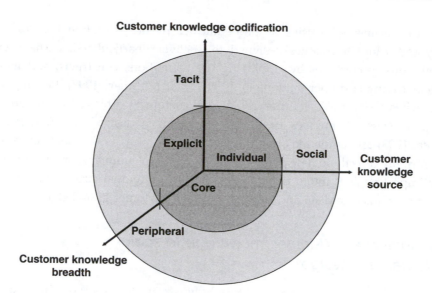

Figure 16.1 Three expanding dimensions for customer knowledge absorption

this perspective, the firm–customer relationship tends to be a one-way import of explicit knowledge from individual customers already included in the company's customer base. Actually, customer knowledge plays a broader role in marketing, and customer knowledge absorption activities can be extended across three different dimensions (see Figure 16.1).

From explicit customer knowledge to tacit customer knowledge

When customers are viewed as passive recipients of the company's value proposition, the firm cannot fully understand customer knowledge assets developed within their specific contexts of experience. At the next level, firms have attempted to involve customers more deeply in their marketing process by developing two-way learning relationships with individual customers. More specifically, research in the service marketing field proved that customers can play the role of partial employees (e.g. Bowen, 1986). Such two-way learning relationships enable the firm to create customized offerings for specific target segments, greatly increasing their satisfaction (Leonard-Barton, 1995). To support this two-way process, the firm's research toolkit has to expand dramatically, to include newer techniques aimed at discovering unarticulated needs through direct customer observation and interaction. For example, firms can observe customers within their native surroundings (Leonard & Rayport, 1997), engage in dialogue and work closely with lead users (Tabrizi & Walleigh, 1997), conduct market experiments by using a "probe and learn" process (Hamel & Prahalad, 1994) and adopt techniques designed to uncover unarticulated, perhaps even unconscious, preferences by employing the metaphors, constructs, and mental models driving customer thinking and behaviour (Zaltman, 1997). Pushing such approaches a step further, firms can involve customers directly in their product design process. Techniques based on participatory design (e.g. Anderson & Crocca, 1993) and empathic design (Leonard & Rayport, 1997) enable customers to contribute directly to new product development. In summary, one-way knowledge import evolves into a richer dialogue with individual customers, allowing firms to tap into the deep and rich store of tacit customer knowledge.

From individual customer knowledge to social customer knowledge

Following the above-mentioned approach, however, an important dimension of customer knowledge still remains untapped. This is the social knowledge that develops through the interactions that customers have with each other, to develop a social identity and recognize themselves as members of specific social categories, on a contextual basis. It is a crucial dimension of customer knowledge to improve the firm's marketing activities, particularly in industries characterized by rapid and uncertain changes in customer preferences. Recently, a new awareness about the relevance of social knowledge has emerged. Some authors have introduced notions such as communitas (Arnould & Price, 1993) or community (Wenger, 1998) to describe the social and emotional phenomena in consumption. These authors suggest that customers choose specific products on the basis not only of their usage value but also of their linkage value, i.e. on the basis of their potential for stating customer identification with a specific social group. Hence, any consumption experience needs to be analysed within a social context in order to be deeply understood. The techniques that have been most commonly employed to analyse the influence of the social dimension on consumption behaviour range from the traditional workshop based on focus groups, where the main challenge is dealing with groupthinking phenomena, to anthropology and ethnography, with their emphasis on cool hunting (Leonard & Swap, 1999). Especially in the latter case, the main idea is that "people within a culture have procedures for making sense" (Feldman, 1995, p. 8). Hence, the key object of the analysis is the bundle of verbal and behavioural mechanisms through which a specific group of customers builds up social meaning. Participant observation, i.e. observation of customer activities directly sharing their experiences in real time, is the most popular method for this purpose. Techniques based on role playing have been effectively used as well in order to grasp tacit knowledge emerging at a collective level.

From core customer knowledge to peripheral customer knowledge

Firms can also benefit from intermediaries or knowledge brokers that collect customer-generated knowledge from a broader set of contexts and from different vantage points (Hargadon, 1998). Through direct channels of communication, companies may not be able to reach the right customers, because their interactions and perspectives tend to be limited to the markets they already serve, with all the risks of myopia that Christensen and Bower (1996) point out. In fact, in spite of the Internet's promise of global access, an individual company rarely interacts with prospects, competitors' customers, and non-adopters in emerging markets. It has a limited reach in its network of learning relationships. This is a particular problem for companies looking to expand beyond their current markets and products. Further, companies suffer from the lack of neutrality: customers often feel that the information they get directly from the company is biased or reflects a vested interest. They are much more likely to trust a third party that seeks to understand their preferences and opinions of products, brands, and manufacturers. Thirdly, companies can engage in dialogue with their customers in a limited number of contexts. Customers tend to visit a company's website when they are well on the way to making a purchase decision, or after they have already made one. As a result, companies can also find it difficult to reach people at the right time, because customers tend to interact with them at relatively late stages of the decision-making process. Knowledge brokers can connect with a broader base of customers than the firm's own customers, in contexts that are very different from the narrow context of product purchasing, and in domains that extend beyond the firm's immediate product and service offerings. On the spatial dimension, they enable companies to engage different kinds and larger numbers of customers and prospects. On the temporal dimension, they allow companies to hear from customers at earlier stages of the decision process. They also allow companies to obtain customer knowledge that is not constrained by the company's mental models or biases (Sawhney, Prandelli, & Verona, 2003). Therefore, they help individual firms to listen to more diverse and unusual voices, accessing customer knowledge that is not only both individual and social, explicit and tacit, but also not constrained by the firm's mental models or biases. By improving the "peripheral vision" of firms, these mediators help firms to escape from the tyranny of their served markets and their core customer knowledge (Hamel & Prahalad, 1994).

The role of the web in supporting collaboration with customers

The web presents several unique properties that not only make customer knowledge absorption easier and cheaper but also make it possible actively to involve customers in the firm's marketing and innovation activities. Web-based tools can simplify the activities of customer knowledge absorption by making it easier to manage systematic interactions with a select group of customers, even broader than regular customers, at a low cost. The Internet enables the creation of virtual customer environments – platforms for collaboration that allow firms to tap into customer knowledge through an ongoing dialogue (Sawhney & Prandelli, 2000).

The following properties of virtual environments empowered by ICTs are those that the current literature ascribes as antecedents of customer collaboration in innovation.

- *Reach – allowing firms to reach beyond current customers, markets, and geography.* The Internet is an open, cost-effective, and easy-to-use network relative to previous networks, such as electronic data interchange (EDI), that were proprietary and therefore costly to join or access (Afuah, 2003). These properties make the Internet a global medium with unprecedented reach, substantially increasing the number of relationships that every individual player can manage without any geographic constraints (Craincross, 1997). The Internet provides people with a vast amount of information, regardless of their location or time zone, lowering the search costs for finding exactly what they want or whom they want. In this way, the Internet facilitates extended connectivity, which is crucial for tapping into distributed competencies (Andal-Ancion, Cartwright, & Yip, 2003). It influences how organizations – and even customers – coordinate their activities, communicate, and collaborate to reduce costs and enhance the effectiveness of the firm's communications with customers and partners (Afuah & Tucci, 2000).

- *Interactivity – permitting true collaborative work instead of merely "knowledge import".* Virtual environments break the age-old trade-off between richness and reach (Evans & Wurster, 1999). In the physical world, communicating (and absorbing) rich information requires physical proximity or dedicated channels, while sharing information with a large audience requires compromises in the quality of information. Therefore, the number and the quality of relationships that any player can develop in the physical world are limited by this reach–richness trade-off. In virtual environments, it is possible to go beyond this trade-off and create two-way relationships with a large number of players without compromising on the richness of the same relationships. On the web, companies can richly interact with a huge number of customers on a systematic basis, in this way supporting true collaboration.

- *Scalability – allowing firms to connect with thousands of customers.* Positive network externalities create incentives to extend the number of connections enacted by the individual player. On the supply side, the incremental cost to reach any new customer progressively tends to decrease because of the predominance of fixed costs compared with variable costs (Shapiro & Varian, 1998). On the other side of the network, consumers find more value in a network as the number of users of the network increases. According to the so-called Metcalfe's law, the value of a network increases in proportion to the square of the number of people using it. So the first competitor to achieve a critical mass of customers can potentially achieve dominance (Downes & Mui, 1998). As a consequence, when a company has reached the critical mass of connections, these tend to increase further in a virtuous cycle. Of course, the threshold level has a limit up to which the value of the network may slope downwards because of the negative effects of a very large network – which include saturation, contamination, and cacophony; still, the threshold level of a virtual network is far greater than that of a physical network (McAfee & Oliveau, 2002).

- *Persistence – ongoing engagement instead of episodic interactions.* Virtual environments push industries to become more global: boundaries between industries tend to blur on the web (Prahalad & Ramaswamy, 2004); at the same time, the division of innovative labour tends to develop across geographies (Linder, Jarvenpaa, & Davenport, 2003). The joint effect is that it is much less likely to find all the competences needed to support innovation within the same organization. The Internet can be used to coordinate activities and information-sharing between otherwise disconnected pools of knowledge and competences on a systematic and global basis, at a lower cost than in traditional, offline environments (Afuah, 2003; Porter, 2001). Hence, virtual environments create the need for engaging an increasing number of players on a systematic basis (because of more diverse competencies needed), and at the same time they provide the solution (owing to low-cost coordination mechanisms and opportunities for sharing the innovative labour on a global and continuous basis).

- *Speed – reduced latency in the "sense-and-respond" cycle – real-time results.* The Internet has a powerful effect in increasing the flexibility of the network, making it possible not only to involve different partners at different times but also to transform weak relations into strong relations, and vice versa, depending on the complexity of the knowledge that needs to be transferred. Real-time, two-way, and low-cost communication makes it easy to consolidate specific customer relationships on a contingent basis through ad hoc virtual communities and online conversations (e.g. Hagel & Singer, 1999). As a consequence, the individual player can benefit from high plasticity in the organization of their connections with different actors, on a very dynamic basis and with low costs of conversion, once the platform of interaction has been created.

- *Peer-to-peer – allowing access to customer-generated social knowledge.* As we already said, the web also vastly augments the firm's capacity to tap into the social dimension of customer knowledge, by enabling the creation of virtual communities of consumption to collect and analyse knowledge that develops through spontaneous conversations among customers. Customers self-select themselves on the basis of the focused interests promoted by specific communities. This self-selection means that customers are highly involved and motivated to share knowledge with other customers and community managers, making their contribution both richer and less expensive than in the offline world. The phenomenon of word-of-mouth epitomizes it. However, offline no tools are available for companies, except focus groups, to make accessible social customer knowledge. Online, virtual communities make it possible systematically to leverage social customer knowledge, for the first time monitoring "word-of-mouse" phenomena (Reichheld & Schefter, 2000).

- *Indirect ties – allowing access to the partners' partners' knowledge.* While direct ties play a key role in determining the network access, indirect ties are also useful, because firms learn not only from the knowledge of their partners but also from the knowledge of their partners' partners (e.g. Ahuja, 2000). The Internet also serves as an important tool for generating indirect ties. It is a low-cost open platform (e.g. Ruefli, Whinston, & Wiggins, 2001): anyone anywhere can connect to it and contribute to the public discussion. Therefore, it is easy to access the knowledge of partners once-removed from direct partners (Afuah,

2003), as well as the knowledge of customers' customers. The Internet positively impacts on the number of indirect ties that firms can develop because it allows them to access electronic archives and virtual communities of a partner's partners, absorb this already codified and digitized knowledge, and recombine it in new ways. Virtual environments also influence structural autonomy – the network property of having "relationships free of structural holes at their own end and rich in structural holes at the other end" (Burt, 1992, p. 45). As we discussed earlier, firms are finding it increasingly difficult to gather all the competences needed to support innovation. The Internet can be used to coordinate activities and information-sharing between otherwise disconnected pools of knowledge and competences on a global basis and at a lower cost than in traditional, offline environments (Afuah, 2003; Porter, 2001).

In conclusion, as the above properties highlight, ICT allows for a continuous and rich dialogue with a huge number of customers at a very low cost. Therefore, it makes the one-way customer knowledge import and dialogue with individual customers more efficient and effective. The Internet also vastly augments the firm's capacity to tap into the social dimension of customer knowledge, by enabling the creation of virtual communities of consumption to collect and analyse knowledge that develops through spontaneous conversations among customers. Finally, on the web peripheral knowledge can be more easily grasped, especially by independent third parties who act as knowledge brokers by filling structural holes between individual customers and communities of customers on one side, and specific firms on the other side.

Collaborative innovation

We propose that the above-mentioned unique characteristics of the web allow the firm to evolve from a perspective centred on interaction with customers to a perspective focused on active collaboration with customers intended as partners in value creation (Prandelli, Sawhney, & Verona, 2006). The differences between the former and the latter are quite relevant. In the first case, the interaction is the locus of economic value extraction and markets are considered as forums for value exchange. The main competitive issue for the individual firm relies on better understanding customers in order to create a superior value proposition *for* them. On the other hand, when we move towards a perspective centred on firm–customer collaboration, the interaction becomes the locus of co-creation of value and value extraction, and markets are forums for co-creation of experiences (Prahalad & Ramaswamy, 2004). The main competitive issue for the firm is to create value propositions *with* its customers: the firm and its customer collaborate in co-creating value and then compete in extracting value (Sawhney, Verona, & Prandelli, 2005).

Virtual environments can leverage two main drivers in enhancing opportunities for collaborative marketing, and the literature has recently begun to explore them (see Table 16.1 for a review).

Firstly, the web empowers customers across marketing activities. In virtual environments, customers have the opportunity to define what information they want and what product they are interested in, and hence they have the chance to increase their control over any exchange process, pushing companies to change their information policies in dealing with them from opaqueness to transparency. The balance of power between the company and the customer is shifting towards equilibrium and the boundaries between them are blurring (Berthon, Holbrook, & Hulbert, 2000). Specifically, customers have the possibility to *self-inform*, as they can research products and issues on their own without relying on experts (e.g. on the medical websites WebMD.com and MedlinePlus. com). According to the "Internet efficiency view", in digital environments, where product information is separated from the physical product, customers are fully informed about processes and all available alternatives, reducing opportunities of profit for retailers (Bakos, 1997; Brynjolfsson & Smith, 2000). Hence, they can *self-compare* product features and prices side by side from competing manufacturers with a few clicks of a mouse (e.g. on the websites PriceGrabber.com and DealTime.com). Customers can also monitor reputations of manufacturers to assure themselves of product and service quality, enacting a sort of *self-police* approach (consider, for instance, eBay.com and BizRate.com). Finally, they can *self-organize*, creating or joining communities of interest or conducting conversations on products, interests, lifestyles, or issues to share their experiences (e.g. iVillage.com and Experts-Exchange.com), and *self-advise*, providing feedback for their peers on the basis of their experiences with products and manufacturers (e.g. Amazon.com, PlanetFeedback.com, Epinions.com, and Ciao.com). Extreme applications of these tools can even enable customers to boycott companies whose behaviour they consider explicitly against their own interests.

Table 16.1 Review of the literature on collaborative marketing

Effect enabled by the web	Activities extended to customers	Influential contributions from literature
Customer empowerment	Self-information	Ariely (2000)
		Berthon, Holbrook, & Hulbert (2000)
		Haubl & Trifts (2000)
		Yadav (2000)
	Self-comparison	Bakos (1997)
		Brynjolfsson & Smith (1999)
		Lynch & Ariely (2000)
		Maes (1999)
		Sviokla (1998)
	Self-organization	Armstrong & Hagel (1996)
		Granitz & Ward (1996)
		Kozinets (1999)
		Rheingold (1993)
	Self-advice	Constant, Sproull, & Kiesler (1996)
		Gerhoff & West (1998)
		Hanson (2000)
		Kanstan (1997)
		Shardanand & Maes (1995)
Customer involvement	Collaborative segmentation	Kozinets (1999)
		Sawhney & Prandelli (2000)
	Collaborative positioning and branding	Barwise (1997)
		Holland & Baker (2001)
		McWilliam (2000)
	Collaborative generation of value propositions	Dahan & Hauser (2002)
		Urban (2000)
	Collaborative selection of value propositions	Burke, Rangaswamy, & Gupta (2001)
		Prelec (2000)
	Collaborative design of value propositions	Sawhney & Prandelli (2000)
		Thomke & von Hippel (2002)
		von Hippel (2001)
		von Hippel & Katz (2002)
	Collaborative development of value propositions	Constant, Sproull, & Kiesler, (1996)
		Iansiti & MacCormack (1997)
		Kollock (1999)
		Lakhani & von Hippel (2000)
		von Hippel (2001)

(*Continued*)

Table 16.1   Continued

Effect enabled by the web	Activities extended to customers	Influential contributions from literature
	Collaborative testing of value propositions	Dahan & Srinivasan (2000) Thomke (1998) Urban, Weinberg, & Hauser (1996)
	Collaborative pricing	Carr (1999) Dolan & Moon (2000) Kambil & Agraval (2001)
	Collaborative support	Mathwick (2002) Muniz & O'Guinn (2001) Sproull & Kiesler (1991) Wellman & Gulia (1999)
	Collaborative communication	Jurvetson (2000) Kenny & Marshall (2000) Hennig-Thurau et al. (2004) Reichheld & Schefter (2000)

However, the most radical novelty in firm–customer relationships introduced by the web is not related to customer empowerment but to direct *customer involvement* in marketing and new product development activities through ad hoc virtual interfaces. This is the second driver of collaborative marketing and innovation in digital environments (Prandelli, Verona, & Raccagni, 2006). Customers can be involved in a process of joint definition of their cluster of belonging, enacting a process of *collaborative segmentation* (e.g. on the website for snowboard fans SnowBoarding.com). *Collaborative positioning and branding* becomes possible, to the extent that customers can define together with the company the values associated with its brand and contribute to making them evolve in time (Barwise, 1997), as happens, for instance, through the huge virtual club and the mini websites purposefully managed by Diesel (Verona & Prandelli, 2002). In this way, direct customer involvement helps to build stronger brands through the appropriate usage of virtual communities (McWilliam, 2000). This means that customer participation fundamentally changes the manner in which brands are developed: producers no longer create an image for a brand and pass it on to the consumer; instead, the producer and consumer interactively create brands through joint participation in digital settings (Holland & Baker, 2001).

Going a step further, customers can participate in a process of *collaborative generation* of value propositions, contributing to the enhancement of company creativity through their own competences, matured in their own contexts of experience (as on the websites created by mass-market companies, such as Procter & Gamble, Kraft, and Ben & Jerry's). In the search for successful new product ideas, the aim is to reduce uncertainty by identifying customers' preferences and interacting directly with them to absorb various potential stimuli that could open up new paths (Dahan & Hauser, 2002). New value proposition generation can also considerably benefit from virtual communities of customers. By encouraging direct and iterative communication in the online community, these groups generate knowledge regarding consumption shared at the social level, which is difficult to grasp using other research tools (Urban, 2000). When firms solicit ideas from customers, it is essential for them to establish clear rules regarding intellectual property rights (Thurow, 1997) and to create appropriate financial or social incentives for customers to share their creativity and expertise. Well-designed incentives can remarkably improve customer-based idea generation (Toubia, 2004). For instance, motorcycle companies such as Aprilia encourage direct customer participation by offering rewards such as spare parts for their motorcycles. Reward mechanisms can be introduced for the most competent customers to compete with each other in solving specific innovation problems. These mechanisms can include financial remuneration, which can be significant in some cases. For instance, the Innocentive.com site originally created by Eli Lilly provides reward mechanisms for the generation of new concepts in several industries, ranging from plastics to mass-market consumer goods that can reach $1 000 000.

Customers can then *collaborate in selecting* the offering ideas more likely to have success on the market (consider, for instance, the joint process of new concept car selection enacted by Conceptlabvolvo.com). Virtual reality gives innovative companies the opportunity to develop different product concepts in great detail, thus allowing consumers to compare individual product features and select the most convincing concept. This also makes it possible to increase response flexibility and possible changes in market and technology, thereby reducing product development time (Iansiti, 1995), promoting the processes of learning from low-cost mistakes (Thomke, 1998), and preventing the information collected at the beginning of the product development cycle from becoming outdated (Eisenhardt and Tabrizi, 1995). Virtual focus groups can also be proficiently used to this purpose (Burke, Rangaswamy, & Gupta, 2001). The so-called "information pump" (Prelec, 2000) is based on virtual focus groups where participants are asked to express their opinions about new product concepts in order to identify the most successful ones. The aim is to make an objective evaluation of the quality and internal coherence of the participants' opinions, which are evaluated by an impartial expert as well as by other participants. In order to ensure this method functions efficiently, information must be updated in real time, and an appropriate system of incentives should be created for participants. This method is particularly useful, as it makes it possible objectively to classify the opinions of individual participants regarding new product concepts, and it allows for the evaluation of the quality and reliability of each respondent (Dahan & Hauser, 2002).

Increasing even further their level of involvement, customers can take part in activities of *collaborative design*, either embracing user toolkits for product design (as on the Dell website) or co-designing the offering together with the company or other customers (as promoted on the Peugeot websites). User toolkits are merely coordinated sets of user-friendly tools for the configuration of new products that allow users to self-develop innovations (Thomke & von Hippel, 2002). These toolkits usually support specific projects within a specific product category. Within this domain, the user is free to innovate, develop customized products through mechanisms of repeated trial and error, and even suggest new patents for the finished product. In this way, the user can create a preliminary design, simulate its development and prototyping, evaluate how the product will function when used, and proceed to systematically improving it until he or she is satisfied with the final version (von Hippel & Katz, 2002). User toolkits for innovation provide users with true design freedom, as opposed to merely choosing from lists of options provided by mass customization. They can even be used to get customer suggestions on patents for finished products. A broad range of industries has begun to introduce these applications. For instance, in the software industry, it has been widely demonstrated that it is useful to promote consumer involvement in the co-definition of products by allowing users to download beta versions and asking them to identify possible bugs (MacCormack, Verganti, & Iansiti, 2001). Customer-driven, web-based toolkits to support innovation processes have also been successfully developed in the industries of computer circuits, plastics, and consumer goods (Thomke & von Hippel, 2002). User design mechanisms can also be applied by ad hoc virtual cross-functional teams created by companies rather than by the larger virtual communities of product users, often stimulated to participate in ad hoc design contests (Sawhney & Prandelli, 2000).

Similarly, customers can play a key role in *collaborative development* of the same offerings. Users can contribute, both individually and through participation in virtual communities, to the final offering realization, leveraging their specific knowledge and skills. Such an activity tends to be diffused, especially when it is related to products characterized by digital content (Iansiti & MacCormack, 1997), which often support customer collaboration in the offering development through the adoption of open-source mechanisms (good examples are provided by the HP Partner Program within the HP website, the Nokia Forum, and the Jini Community developed by Sun Microsystems). In fact, open-source mechanisms have expanded into many different industries (for instance, sportswear) where systematic new product development is essential (von Hippel, 2001). Specifically, open-source mechanisms support communities that are completely run by and for the users and allow them to exchange opinions on specific products that are initially mainly technical (Constant, Sproull, & Kiesler, 1996) but can lead to direct collaboration in the creation of new products and services (von Hippel, 2001). In these systems, each user does not necessarily develop the needed product or service alone – as in the individual application of the toolkits for user innovation – but can benefit from the innovative suggestions freely made by the other users. In the typical case of software products, this means that each user can obtain a copy free of charge and can legally study its source code and modify and distribute it to others without any remuneration (Lakhani & von Hippel, 2000). Regardless of the specific industry considered, the reason these kinds of distributed innovation mechanism are so successful is that they enhance the reputation of each user, who concretely contributes to the final output, and promote a reciprocal relationship in the creation of the final product. Moreover, the sense of responsibility towards the group and the awareness of the significant impact on the community often represent important stimuli to those who are qualified and want to participate (Kollock, 1999).

Customers can also help the company in *collaborative testing* and debugging of its new products, as proposed on many websites developed by video game and software companies (consider, for instance, the intense activities of collaborative testing deployed to catalyse the development of Navigator 3.0). New technologies such as rapid prototyping, simulation, and combinatorial methods make it possible to generate and test different product versions (Thomke, 1998). Web-based tools further enhance this approach by exploiting the potential of virtual reality, three-dimensional images, and animation to generate low-cost virtual prototypes that are fairly close to the quality and completeness of the physical one (Dahan & Srinivasan, 2000). The web thus makes it possible simultaneously to test different product configurations (virtual product testing) as well as different market situations, that is, different marketing mixes to complement the supply (virtual market testing) in order to choose the best solution with the direct collaboration of the end-users. Consumers can view and evaluate detailed descriptions of each prototype, which are integrated with virtual tours around and even inside the product. In this way, all the product components can be seen before consumers make their final evaluation. As in the idea selection stage, consumers can modify, at least in part, some product features by choosing some predefined modular attributes in order to identify the price–attribute combination that best satisfies their individual need. For instance, Google beta-tests its new ideas in the Google Labs section of its website. Web-based beta-testing is very common in the software, e-commerce, and video game industries.

After the new offering has been defined, on-the-web customers can quote prices to sellers instead of being "price-takers" and contribute to defining the most appropriate price for new offerings, participating in a process of *collaborative pricing* that is very common on websites such as eBay.com, PriceLine.com, and FreeMarkets.com. Recently the Radjohead Band made a similar application in their own web site, allowing users to freely set the price for their own music in digital format.

Finally, *collaborative support* can be pursued in virtual environments: customers can resolve problems on their own by searching knowledge bases and providing mutual advice through discussion forums (as on the websites Remotecentral.com and Treocentral.com, and in the section HP OpenView Support of the HP website). The reciprocal trust catalyses the exchange of experiences and mutual support, and the exchange of information enhances member relationships (Sproull & Kiesler, 1991).

Following a similar logic, *collaborative communication* can also be strongly enhanced by the web. Customers can take part in viral marketing programmes (Jurvetson, 2000), transforming themselves into advocates and even testimonials for the company. For instance, Mercedes has encouraged the owners of its products to submit snapshots of themselves next to their vehicle, in order to show the true spirit of the fan. On the same track, Mazda and Conde Nast have partnered to create a contest whereby contestants can submit photos representative of their interpretation of Mazda's "Zoom-Zoom" slogan, while Procter & Gamble, with the initiative "Pantene Protagonist", has launched a similar competition for its shampoo (Prandelli, Sawhney, & Verona, 2008). In fact, users can even turn into veritable proselytes of the company's products, as in the well-known Apple experience, made even stronger through the ipodlounge. com site, where customers congregate to show the world what they would like the next iPod to do and to look like. Owing to the reliability of the information source, these forms of "word-of-mouse" (Reichheld & Schefter, 2000) can enhance product and brand exposure at a very low cost and enhance final trust. For instance, leveraging the over 50 international virtual communities of Lego fans, as well as Bricklink.com – the "unofficial LEGO (R) marketplace" created by the same customers in order to trade their own products and projects – the company has been able largely to consolidate its image. Going a step further, in 2002 Lego even tried to present a new product – the "Santa Fe Super Chief" – just to its best 250 fanatics, selected through their participation in virtual communities. Without relying on any other commercial investments, Lego was able to sell the first 10 000 pieces of the above-mentioned new product in 2 weeks, just leveraging its customers' word-of-mouse (Antorini, 2005).

High costs of contact and personalization made all the above-mentioned collaborative activities unfeasible on a broad and systematic basis in traditional physical environments. In digital settings, such activities can be deployed by both the individual company and independent third parties which play a knowledge brokerage role for multiple business customers, enlarging the scope of customer knowledge absorption for each individual player (Verona, Prandelli, & Sawhney, 2006).

Figure 16.2 summarizes the contribution of web-based tools in order both to enhance customer integration and to favour a process of customer competence leverage.

A company application of collaborative innovation: the case of Ducati Motor

In the motorcycle industry, companies create a competitive advantage not only on the basis of technical product superiority but also on the basis of their ability to interact with their customers and create deep customer relationships across the entire life cycle of ownership. Motorcycles are a lifestyle-intensive product, so

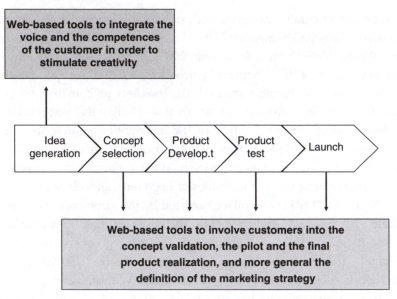

Figure 16.2 Web-based tools along the new product development process

motorcycle companies need to foster a sense of community among their customers in addition to offering innovative product features.

Ducati Motor, a manufacturer of motorcycles headquartered in Italy, was quick to realize the potential for using the Internet to engage customers in its new product development efforts (Prandelli, Sawhney, & Verona, 2008). The company set up a web division and a dedicated website – www.ducati.com – in early 2000, inspired by the Internet sales of the MH900evolution, a limited-production motorcycle. Within 30 minutes, the entire year's production was sold out, making Ducati a leading international e-commerce player. Since then, Ducati has evolved its site to create a robust virtual customer community that had almost 200 000 registered users by the end of 2006. Ducati considers the community of fans to be a major asset of the company, and it strives to use the Internet to enhance the "fan experience". A community function has actually replaced the traditional marketing department. The community function is closely connected with product development, and the fan involvement in the community directly influences all the company's innovation activities.

First of all, virtual communities play a key role in helping the company to explore new product concepts. Ducati has promoted and managed ad hoc online forums and chats for over 3 years to harness a strong sense of community among Ducati fans. The most popular discussion is about products and the biking experience. These conversations are highly relevant for Ducati's better understanding of customer needs and for the company to gain insights into new products and services. Ducati also realized that a significant number of its fans spend their leisure time not only riding their bikes but also maintaining and personalizing their bikes. As a result, Ducati fans have deep technical knowledge that they are eager to share with other fans. To support such knowledge-sharing, the company has created the "Tech Café", a forum for exchanging technical knowledge. In this virtual environment, fans can share their projects for customizing motorcycles, provide suggestions to improve Ducati's next-generation products, and even post their own mechanical and technical designs, with suggestions for innovations in aesthetic attributes as well as mechanical functions. In the Customer Service area of the website, individual bikers can self-signal their technical competencies and solve mechanical problems posted by other Ducati fans. These technical forums help Ducati to benefit from spontaneous customer knowledge-sharing, and help the company to glean suggestions for improving its marketing, engineering, and customer support.

Of course, the emerging ideas do not necessarily represent the preferences of the broader market for Ducati products. To validate its insights, Ducati uses online customer surveys which help in quantifying customer preferences. The company gets extraordinary response rates, often in excess of 25%. For instance, on 20 October 2003, three new concepts of Ducati SportClassic were presented simultaneously at the Tokyo International Motorshow and online with a mini site from which it was possible to access an ad hoc survey. The purpose was to understand the interest of the public in the motorcycles in order to decide whether and which one to put into production; in fact, no engineering components had yet been developed at that time. Almost 15 000 answers were collected in 5 days, and more than 96% of them recommended the production of all three models. In total, over 310 000 people visited the SportClassic site, and more than 16 000 took part in the survey, expressing enthusiasm and interest in Ducati SportClassic. As a consequence, the company decided to put all three models into production, and to launch them on the market sequentially, so that the Paul Smart 1000 Limited Edition was released first (November 2005), followed by the Sport 1000 (March 2006) and then the GT 1000 (September 2006).

Virtual communities come, then, to play an important role also at the product design and market testing stages. For instance, in early 2001, the community managers of Ducati.com identified a group of customers on its website who had particularly strong relationships with the company. They decided to transform these customers into active partners, involving them in virtual teams that cooperate with professionals from R&D, Product Management, and Design of Ducati Motors. These virtual teams of customers work with the company's engineers to define attributes and technical features for the "next bike". Through this mechanism, Ducati recognizes opinion leadership and provides recognition for members within its customer community. Contests are also used in order to enhance and reward customer involvement. For instance, in 2002 the company created a competition called "Design Your Dream Ducati", where fans were challenged to interpret in any form their "Dream Ducati". The response rate was incredibly high, and the winning projects were selected by a team involving, among others, the CEO, the Chief Manager of the Design Department, the Creative Director, and some journalists. Hence, this event was also an occasion to involve the traditional R&D department directly in online activities in the light of the ongoing dotcom integration.

More broadly, all new product designs are reviewed and tested with a huge sample of customers. Within the virtual community, current and future Ducati bike owners discuss and review proposed product modifications that can be tested online in the form of virtual prototypes. They can even vote to reject proposed modifications. They can also personalize products to their preferences, and can ask Ducati technicians for suggestions on personalizing their bikes to their preferences.

Forums also help Ducati to enhance customer loyalty, because its fans are more motivated to buy products they helped to create. Ducati's CEO has mandated the involvement of all the company's product engineers in customer relationship management activities. They are required periodically to interview selected Ducati owners from the company's online database of registered fans – adding a physical dimension to the online interaction.

Being deeply aware about the possibilities of the web, in March 2006, the CEO Federico Minoli started his own blog – called "Desmoblog" – within Ducati.com. This is the first corporate blog in the motorcycle industry worldwide. It has been created without any form of censorship, and it has been used to improve new product development and launch on the final market. For instance, in the spirit of "opening the gates of the factory", some months before the launch of the new motorcycle Hypermotard, in May 2007, Minoli started to post a series of comments directly involving the customers in the final stages of the product development process. An example of this series of comments is a video clip on YouTube, the purpose of which was to bring the fans "behind the scenes of the Research & Development department to see first hand where the Hypermotard is today, to see how things are being put into place, and to hear the impressions of the test riders who have ridden the bike" (Federico Minoli, Desmoblog, 14 February 2007).

Ducati also attempts to go beyond its customer base in an effort to gather ideas from as broad an audience as possible. Ducati community managers monitor relevant forums and bulletin boards hosted on independent websites, such as the community of American Ducati fans hosted on Yahoo!. Ducati community managers take part in these forums, sometimes identifying themselves and remaining anonymous at other times, depending on the nature of the topics and the sensitivity of the audience to privacy concerns. Ducati managers also monitor vertical portals created for bikers, including Motorcyclist.com and Motoride.com, micro sites that aggregate specific segments of interest to Ducati's – such as women bikers, the fastest-growing demographic group in motorcycling – as well as other communities that have life style associations with the Ducati brand. Through these diverse "listening posts", Ducati tries to ensure that it expands its peripheral vision beyond its own customers, and beyond the customers it can reach directly by itself.

Conclusion

In this chapter we have highlighted that a peculiar form of the broader notion of open innovation (Chesbrough, 2003), that is, collaborative innovation in which customers are involved to co-create products with firms across the new product development process, represents a new strategy for firms that intend to make their customer strategy real. While contributions in recent years have highlighted a general attempt by managers to address new customer knowledge dimensions that can be more valuable for innovation purposes (that is, tacit versus explicit, social versus individual, and peripheral versus core), it is particularly owing to the contribution of ICTs and Web 2.0 applications that firms can finally aim at capturing and absorbing customer knowledge in new ways. The cross-industry anecdotes provided in the "Collaborative innovation" section and the cases included in the section concerning Ducati Motor's application of collaborative innovation are, to our understanding, a nice exemplification of these emerging opportunities. If virtual environments support the evolution of customer–firm relationships from interaction to collaboration across all marketing, and especially innovation activities, some key questions still remain open. Hence, of the many research issues that can be pursued in this area, we do believe that the most pressing one is related to the need for empirically testing the impact of the usage of such tools in order to improve the efficiency and the effectiveness of the product development process. A promising future direction for research concerns the specific role of the organizational side of collaborative marketing and innovation, looking at the implications for the design of the most effective social integration mechanisms in order to support an authentic cooperative environment.

From a managerial viewpoint, clear implications emerge for the design of virtual environments supporting collaborative marketing and innovation activities. All the web-based tools that we have described in this chapter are – or at least should be – synergic and complementary. Moreover, they can mutually self-support each other. As a consequence, they have to be used simultaneously as part of an integrated innovation strategy, rather than being conceived as independent "silos" for engaging in a dialogue with customers. Every company should try to combine several mechanisms within an integrated portfolio in order to assure success to its web-based collaborative innovation process. Hence, simply through the balanced implementation of different mechanisms, a company can enable a truly multichannel platform to support its collaborative innovation activities effectively.

In any case, it is quite intuitive that deep collaboration even with a few customers online can be quite effective and stand alone in enhancing creativity and generating new stimuli by leading users. However, these then, of course, need to be verified on a broader basis of customers, representative of the entire company's target market. The validation of such stimuli can rely exclusively on the web only in those cases where the entire target market is well represented online – cf. software or video game users. In all other cases, digital technologies can be more properly used to integrate, rather than replace, traditional market research tools. This appears to be fundamental in order to allow the company to take actions that are not biased by those web users typically more oriented towards experimentation compared with the rest of the mass market that is not yet present online.

References

Afuah, A. (2003) "Redefining firm boundaries in the face of the Internet: are firms really shrinking?". *Academy of Management Review*, vol. 28, no. 1, pp. 34–53.

Afuah, A. & Tucci, C. (2000) *Internet Business Models and Strategies*. McGraw-Hill, New York, NY.

Ahuja, G. (2000) "Collaboration networks, structural holes, and innovation: a longitudinal study". *Administrative Science Quarterly*, vol. 45, pp. 425–455.

Andal-Ancion, A., Cartwright, P. A., & Yip, G. S. (2003) "The digital transformation of traditional businesses". *MIT Sloan Management Review*, Summer, pp. 34–41.

Anderson, W. L. & Crocca, W. T. (1993) "Engineering practice and co-development of product prototypes". *Communications of the ACM*, vol. 36, no. 4, pp. 49–56.

Antorini, Y. M. (2005) "Analysis of the adult fans of Lego user's group". *Paper presented at the MIT User Group Conference*, Sloan Management School, Boston, MA.

Arnould, E. J. & Price, L. L. (1993) "River magic: extraordinary experience and the extended service encounter". *Journal of Consumer Research*, vol. 20, pp. 24–45.

Bakos, Y. (1997) "Reducing buyer search cost: implications for electronic marketplaces". *Management Science*, vol. 43, no. 12, 1676–1692.

Barwise, P. (1997) "Brands in a digital world". *Journal of Brand Management*, vol. 4, no. 4, pp. 220–223.

Berthon, P., Holbrook, M. B., & Hulbert, J. M. (2000) "Beyond market orientation: a conceptualization of market evolution". *Journal of Interactive Marketing*, vol. 14, no. 3, pp. 50–66.

Bowen, D. E. (1986) "Managing customers as human resources in service organizations". *Human Resource Management*, vol. 25, no. 3, pp. 371–383.

Brynjolfsson, E. & Smith, M. D. (2000) "Frictionless commerce? A comparison of Internet and conventional retailers". *Management Science*, vol. 46, no. 4, pp. 563–585.

Burke, R. R., Rangaswamy, A., & Gupta, S. (2001) "Rethinking market research in the digital world", in *Digital Marketing*, edited by Wind, J. & Mahajan, V. Wiley, New York, NY, pp. 226–255.

Burt, R. S. (1992) *Structural Holes: the Social Structure of Competition*. Harvard Business School Press, Boston, MA.

Chesbrough, H. (2003) *Open Innovation: the New Imperative for Creating and Profiting from Technology*. Harvard Business School Press, Boston, MA.

Christensen, C. M. (1997) *The Innovator's Dilemma*. Harvard Business School Press, Boston, MA.

Christensen, C. M. & Bower, J. L. (1996) "Customer power, strategic investment, and the failure of leading firms". *Strategic Management Journal*, vol. 17, pp. 197–218.

Constant, D., Sproull, L., & Kiesler, S. (1996) "The kindness of strangers: the usefulness of electronic weak ties for technical advice". *Organization Science*, vol. 7, no. 2, pp. 119–135.

Craincross, F. (1997) *The Death of Distance: How the Communication Revolution will Change our Lives*. Harvard Business School Press, Boston, MA.

Dahan, E. & Hauser, J. (2002) "Product development – managing a dispersed process", in *Handbook of Marketing*, edited by Weitz, B. & Wensley, R. Sage, New York, NY, pp. 179–222.

Dahan, E. & Srinivasan, V. (2000) "The predictive power of Internet-based product concept testing using virtual depiction and animation". *Journal of Product Innovation Management*, vol. 17, March, pp. 99–109.

Dougherty, D. (1992) "Interpretative barriers to successful product innovation in large firms". *Organization Science*, vol. 3, pp. 179–202.

Downes, L. & Mui, C. (1998) *Unleashing the Killer App: Digital Strategies for Market Dominance*. Harvard Business School Press, Boston, MA.

Eisenhardt, K. M. & Tabrizi, B. N. (1995) "Accelerating adaptive processes: product innovation in the global computer industry". *Administrative Science Quarterly*, vol. 40, no. 1, pp. 84–110.

Evans, P. & Wurster, T. (1999) *Blown to Bits. How the New Economics of Information Transforms Strategy*. Harvard Business School Press, Boston, MA.

Feldman, M. (1995) *Strategies for Interpreting Qualitative Data*. Sage Publications, Thousand Oaks, CA.

Hagel, J. & Singer, M. (1999) *Net Worth. Shaping Markets when Customers Make the Rules*. Harvard Business School Press, Boston, MA.

Hamel, G. & Prahalad, C. (1994) *Competing for the Future*. Harvard Business School Press, Boston, MA.

Hargadon, A. B. (1998) "Firms as knowledge brokers: lessons in pursuing continuous innovation". *California Management Review*, vol. 40, no. 3, pp. 209–227.

Hauser, J. R. & Clausing, D. (1988) "The House of Quality". *Harvard Business Review*, May–June, pp. 63–73.

Hayes, R. H., Wheelwright, S., & Clark, K. (1988) *Dynamic Manufacturing. Creating the Learning Organization*. The Free Press, New York, NY.

Holland, J. & Baker, S. M. (2001) "Customer participation in creating site brand loyalty". *Journal of Interactive Marketing*, vol. 15, no. 4, pp. 34–44.

Iansiti, M. (1995) "Technology integration: managing technological evolution in a complex environment". *Research Policy*, vol. 24, pp. 521–542.

Iansiti, M. & MacCormack, A. (1997) "Developing products on Internet time". *Harvard Business Review*, September–October, pp. 108–117.

Jurvetson, S. (2000) "Turning customers into a sales force". *Business2.0*, March.

Kollock, P. (1999) "The economies of online cooperation: gifts and public goods in computer communities", in *Communities in Cyberspace*, edited by Smith, M. & Kollock, P. Routledge, London, UK, pp. 3–25.

Lakhani, K. & von Hippel, E. (2000) "How open source software works: free user-to-user assistance". MIT Sloan School of Management Working Paper no. 4117.

Leonard, D. & Rayport, J. F. (1997) "Spark innovation through empathic design". *Harvard Business Review*, November–December, pp. 102–113.

Leonard, D. & Swap, W. (1999) *When Sparks Fly. Igniting Creativity in Groups*. Harvard Business School Press, Boston, MA.

Leonard-Barton, D. (1995) *Wellsprings of Knowledge. Building and Sustaining the Sources of Innovation*. Harvard Business School Press, Boston, MA.

Linder, J. C., Jarvenpaa, S. L., & Davenport, T. H. (2003) "Toward an innovation sourcing strategy". *MIT Sloan Management Review*, vol. 44, no. 4, pp. 43–49.

MacCormack, A., Verganti, R., & Iansiti, M. (2001) "Developing products on Internet time: the anatomy of a flexible development process". *Management Science*, vol. 47, no. 1, pp. 133–150.

McAfee, A. & Oliveau, F. X. (2002) "Confronting the limits of networks". *MIT Sloan Management Review*, vol. 43, pp. 85–87.

McWilliam, G. (2000) "Building stronger brands through online communities". *Sloan Management Review*, vol. 41, Spring, pp. 43–54.

Porter, M. E. (2001) "Strategy and the Internet". *Harvard Business Review*, vol. 79, no. 3, pp. 63–79.

Prahalad, C. K. & Ramaswamy, V. (2004) "Co-creation experiences: the new practice in value creation". *Journal of Interactive Marketing*, vol. 18, no. 3, pp. 5–14.

Prandelli, E., Sawhney, M., & Verona, G. (2006) "The emerging organizational models of distributed innovation: towards a taxonomy", in *The Future of Knowledge Management*, edited by Renzl, B., Matzler, K., & Hinterhuber, H. Palgrave, New York, NY, pp. 137–160.

Prandelli, E., Sawhney, M., & Verona, G. (2008) *Collaborating with Customers to Innovate: Conceiving and Marketing Products in the Network Age*. Edward Elgar, Cheltenham, UK.

Prandelli, E., Verona, G., & Raccagni, D. (2006) "Diffusion of web-based product innovation". *California Management Review*, vol. 40, no. 4, Summer, pp. 109–135.

Prelec, D. (2000) *The Information Pump*. Center for Innovation in Product Development. MIT Press, Cambridge, MA.

Reichheld, F. & Schefter, P. (2000) "E-loyalty". *Harvard Business Review*, July–August, pp. 105–113.

Ruefli, T. W., Whinston, A., & Wiggins, R. R. (2001) "The digital technological environment", in *Digital Marketing*, edited by Wind, J. & Mahajan, V. Wiley, New York, NY, pp. 26–58.

Sawhney, M. & Prandelli, E. (2000) "Communities of creation: managing distributed innovation in turbulent markets". *California Management Review*, vol. 42, no. 4, pp. 24–54.

Sawhney, M., Prandelli, E., & Verona, G. (2003) "The power of innomediation". *MIT Sloan Management Review*, vol. 44, no. 2, Winter, pp. 77–82.

Sawhney, M., Verona, G., & Prandelli, E. (2005) "Collaborating to create: the Internet as a platform for customer engagement in product innovation". *Journal of Interactive Marketing*, vol. 19, no. 4, pp. 4–17.

Shapiro, C. & Varian, H. L. (1998) *Information Rules. A Strategic Guide to the Network Economy*. Harvard Business School Press, Boston, MA.

Sproull, L. & Kiesler, S. (1991) *Connections. New Ways of Working in the Networked Organization*. MIT Press, Cambridge, MA.

Tabrizi, B. & Walleigh, R. (1997) "Defining next generation products: an inside look". *Harvard Business Review*, vol. 75, no. 6, pp. 116–124.

Thomke, S. H. (1998) "Managing experimentation in the design of new products". *Management Science*, vol. 44, no. 6, pp. 743–762.

Thomke, S. & von Hippel, E. (2002) "Customers as innovators: a new way to create value". *Harvard Business Review*, vol. 80, no. 4, pp. 74–81.

Thurow, L. C. (1997) "Needed: a new system of intellectual property rights". *Harvard Business Review*, September–October, pp. 94–103.

Toubia, O. (2004) "Idea generation, creativity, and incentives". Massachusetts Institute of Technology Working Paper, January.

Urban, G. L. (2000) "Listening in to customer dialogues on the web". Center for Innovation in Product Development Working Paper. MIT Press, Cambridge, MA.

Urban, G., Weinberg, B., & Hauser, J. (1996) "Premarket forecasting of really-new products". *Journal of Marketing*, vol. 60, pp. 47–60.

Verona, G. (1999) "A resource-based view of product development". *Academy of Management Review*, vol. 24, no. 1, pp. 132–142.

Verona, G. & Prandelli, E. (2002) "A dynamic model of customer loyalty to sustain competitive advantage on the web". *European Management Journal*, vol. 20, no. 3, pp. 299–309.

Verona, G., Prandelli, E., & Sawhney, M. (2006) "Innovation and virtual environments: towards virtual knowledge brokers". *Organization Studies*, vol. 27, no. 6, pp. 765–788.

von Hippel, E. (2001) "Innovation by user communities: learning from open-source software". *MIT Sloan Management Review*, vol. 42, no. 4, pp. 82–86.

von Hippel, E. & Katz, R. (2002) "Shifting innovation to users via toolkits". *Management Science*, vol. 48, no. 7, pp. 821–833.

Wenger, E. (1998) *Communities of Practice: Learning, Meaning, and Identity*. Cambridge University Press, Cambridge, UK.

Zaltman, G. (1997) "Rethinking market research: putting people back". *Journal of Marketing Research*, vol. XXXIV, November, pp. 424–437.

17

Consumers' Participation in Market Co-creation: How Gay Consumers Impact on Marketing Strategies through Consumer Society

Stefano Podestà & Luca M. Visconti

Introducing market co-creation and politics

The bond between innovation and markets can be viewed in various ways. Nonetheless, the topic has long been dominated by an almost univocal interpretative paradigm that enforces the leading role of companies in the strategic creation of markets. Far from contesting firms' momentum in market innovation, we wish there to be a better understanding of the role that consumers, both individually and in their social aggregations, play in transforming markets and social arenas.

From a theoretical perspective, we detect three main phases in addressing the role of consumers in market innovation: (i) the subject–object interpretative framework; (ii) the user-dominated paradigm of innovation; and (iii) the subject–subject logic. Firstly, the traditional *subject–object* framework has long been in favour. In this perspective, although the company holds the main role in directing market innovation, the customer's importance is developed in terms of "customer orientation". As such, consumers constitute a key constraint to companies and remain the final link of the productive and transactional chain. Therefore, customers are basically framed as passive agents who lack subjective agency. The *user-dominated* paradigm of innovation represents the second stage and largely benefits from Eric von Hippel's work. In the course of his 30-year research on innovation, this author has questioned the subject–object view, suggesting a more participative role for customers in product and service design. Von Hippel has long argued that customers are the source not only of unsatisfied needs but also of potential solutions and innovative ideas (i.e. what he defines as the "contained in need information": von Hippel, 1977, p. 64). Consequently, consumers cease to be mere constraints to companies and acquire fresh legitimation as eventual resources. In fact, the extent to which companies are able to pick up hints from their customers, using them to elaborate new product/service concepts, conditions their capability to outsource part of the innovation activities, and part of the related costs as well. More recently, a *subject–subject* paradigm of marketer–customer exchanges has come to life. Through the epistemological lens of the service-dominant logic, Vargo and Lusch (2004) claim a crucial role for the intangible assets exchanged between and across companies and consumers. Within this frame, the authors underline co-creation as a central feature of the relationship connecting companies to their customers. However, we need to wait for Peñaloza and Venkatesh's contribution to get a deeper sense of the way meanings are constructed in market exchanges. These authors suggest that, in postmodern markets, "value in exchange" is overtaken by "value in use". In so doing, they unpack customers' creative skills in generating value and meaning both in product/service exchange and in use, and conclude that markets are social constructs where the cultural and political authority of meanings can be fully appreciated (Peñaloza & Venkatesh, 2006, p. 305).

From an empirical perspective, this chapter contextualizes to gay consumers the topic of consumer agency in market co-construction. Gay consumers actually offer a rich field for the investigation of the way in which individuals and groups navigate consumption in order to transform market and social contexts. The archetypical mainstream–minority dynamics and the gay subculture document a variety of forms of market innovation that occur both in the interaction between gay consumers and companies and additionally across the exchanges between gay and heterosexual consumers. By enlightening this double-rail line, we develop managerial implications in terms of: how companies can target gay consumers; how gay consumers can lead the symbolic transformation of markets; how heterosexual consumers on their own can change the meaning and the positioning of gay iconic brands and products over time. The chapter intends to discuss: (i) how the gay subculture fosters the market creativity of gay consumers; (ii) the way in which gay consumers can lead market changes by exerting pressures and manifesting agency over companies; and (iii) the market confrontation between gay and straight consumers operating along consumption crossover dynamics.

Compared with the previous chapters in this book, this chapter therefore has three main distinctive features. Firstly, it accounts for the role of *consumer agency and subjectivity* (for an extensive analysis, see also Chapter 12), both as individual consumers and as members of social aggregations (in this work, the heterosexual mainstream and the gay minority). In so doing, we update the prosumer tenet (Kotler, 1986; Toffler, 1980) to the topic of market innovation and to the issue of mainstream–minority dialogues. By including the role of customers in this interplay, we hope to complement the understanding of strategic market creation.

Secondly, we go beyond the sole marketer–consumer horizon by questioning the potential for innovation generated by the *consumer society* (i.e. the consumer–consumer dimension). By consumer society we mean the discursive activities performed by various consumers, here heterosexual and gay consumers interacting in the market milieu. We suggest that market transformation can additionally be originated by the market and social cross-talks occurring at the consumer level. Such exchanges may be both collaborative and oppositional, but they are always endowed with innovative power. We show how gay consumers can symbolically appropriate certain brands and products so as to transform them into gay icons. Similarly, we also document the opposite path by which gay icons are transferred into the heterosexual realm by means of imitation and straight contestation. These market activities carried out by active consumers impact upon companies' strategies and performances, and thus stimulate the ongoing re-elaboration of their supply system and market behaviours.

Thirdly, this chapter acknowledges *the role of markets in innovating sociopolitical equilibria,* and vice versa. We suggest that markets can be innovated while mirroring gay people's quest for more fair and equal sociopolitical conditions (Peñaloza, 1996). We share the assumption that markets not only are *generated* by marketer–consumer interaction but are also *generative* in the way they affect marketers and consumers' choices. In this light, strategic market creation can be further investigated by studying "what markets do and how people use them and are used in them" (Peñaloza & Venkatesh, 2006, p. 312). In this way, we detect potential for the innovation of companies to arise from communication campaigns and supply strategies effectively contrasting gay stereotypes or supporting legitimation of gay people beyond market boundaries. For example, when targeting the gay market, companies may decide to position their ads in main-stream media and foster a neutral (e.g. L'Oréal), or even positive, representation of gay individuals (e.g. Ikea, Budweiser, etc.). They may additionally agree to sponsor gay events and political crusades (e.g. Absolut Vodka with the American association Gay and Lesbian Alliance Against Defamation (GLAAD), Citroën with the Italian gay pride movement, etc.), as well as to disclose diversity management programmes applied to their employers (e.g. American Express, Ernst & Young, etc.). As such, we explore how the consumption sphere mirrors the regular exchanges between heterosexuals and gay people and documents how products are exploitable not only as depositories of meaning (Baudrillard, 1968; McCracken, 1986) but also as active providers of meaning (Arnould & Thompson, 2005; Holt, 1997) to challenge or confirm the economic, political, and social order. In the presence of an increasingly hypercommodified society (Slater, 1997), products are actually powerful tools in relation to the current social debate on mainstream–minority interconnections and market creation. In this framework, we picture identities as a fluid, participative, and discursive asset (Lindridge, Hogg, & Shah, 2004; Thompson & Haytko, 1997) that constantly deals with meaning attribution, sharing, and even opposition. In fact, gay consumers are not only, or necessarily, compliant with mainstream and companies' requirements; they can decide to fight to gain greater freedom, civil rights, and satisfaction. Gay consumers are therefore agents of market transformation: they help create new market opportunities (Chasin, 2000; Lukenbill, 1999; Tréguer & Segati, 2003) while challenging crystallized market and social structures.

Below, we illustrate the connection between the gay subculture and gay people's attributed capability of trendsetting, which acquires particular relevance for the topic of strategic market creation. We explore possible rationales for gay people's trendsetting skills and locate this quality within the consumer–company inter-play. We then move to the heart of our discussion by disentangling the impact of gay consumers on companies' market innovation. By means of a dynamic taxonomy of gay consumptions, we discuss gay consumers' transformative power embedded in contestation and symbolic appropriation praxes. We then introduce the topic of consumer–consumer oppositional dynamics and the impact this has on market changes, in particular via consumption crossover. Finally, we conclude by reconsidering the previously listed topics in search of implications to orient managers in the praxis of market innovation.

Sources and features of gay creativity

Gay people are publicly described as trendsetters. This collectively held belief belongs to the same rich set of stereotypes depicting gay males as wealthy, fashionable, stylish, single, and effeminate (Badgett, 1995, 2001; Wardlow, 1996). Challenging or confirming gay stereotypes is far beyond our goals. Nonetheless, the frequently recorded connection between homosexuality and creativity deserves to be better understood if we want to disentangle the roots of market creation from the gay perspective.

However, gay creativity is not only a matter of stereotyping: some industries are dominated by gay creativity, including fashion, design, architecture, and other artistic fields. At the same time, gay creativity also pertains to peculiar ways of approaching consumption (Keating & McLoughlin, 2005; Sender, 2004) that, drawing on the camp subculture (Kates, 2001, 2004), transform consumer objects into "divine" expressions of taste. In this section we examine closely the origins of gay innovation and evaluate its distinctive features.

The existential roots of gay creativity

Gay people's propensity to innovation has two main explanations (Visconti, 2008). Firstly, we address the maturation of gay creativity as a side effect of the coming-out experience (i.e. "existential explanations"), which depicts the life stages gay people have to pass through in order to identify, accept, and socially manifest their sexual orientation. Moreover, the coming-out path is embedded in sociopolitical, cultural, and institutional contexts, which additionally account for gay creativity. As such, at a second level we mainly look at the idiosyncratic values pertaining to the camp subculture (i.e. "subcultural explanations"). Considering life experiences, the emergence of gay identity stimulates creativity in three ways: (i) through self-reflexivity;

(ii) through the defensive stance adopted to overcome social disapproval; and (iii) through the attempt to overcome dissatisfaction with the present.

Self-reflexivity is the individual or collective capability to think and narrate the self that leads to states of superior self-consciousness. Typically, self-reflexivity is stimulated when (minority) identities are questioned and made socially problematic (e.g. with migrants, women, gay men and women, etc.). As members of a socially stigmatized subgroup, gay people generally present reflexivity and can eventually show political agency when struggling for their sense of self (Kates, 2002). Self-reflexivity is instrumental in the capability to keep the balance between the heterosexual and the gay cultures, and can result in the constant training of innovative skills to move across the two worlds: *"This sensitivity is probably caused by the consciousness of one's homosexuality, which stimulates the process of self-identification. I think it's more or less the same for everyone. And this kind of introspective experience is very formative and leads us to question reality. We have a much deeper relationship with reality thanks to the work we've been doing on ourselves"* (Paolo, 40-year-old gay architect).

At a second level, many gay people describe themselves as potential preys in the postmodern jungle. In spite of homosexuality becoming increasingly acceptable, it still represents a controversial aspect of identity and leaves the door open to occasional attacks by extreme fringes of the cultural mainstream. Paradoxically, the fact that these attacks are not the rule but a creeping risk lurking in the folds of everyday life increases the uncertainty of gay people and their need to be vigilant. Again, we observe a positive effect of this condition on sensitivity and reactivity of gay people: *"I think gays are more creative thanks to the need to constantly develop their ability to adapt and defend themselves. This state of alert inevitably stimulates your sensors because you need to learn to watch the world with the utmost attention. It originates from the need to defend ourselves and then it produces a new capability. Our skills for quick adaptation may also become a creative capability, since you can get inspired by almost anything ... This is probably the only good effect of being persecuted. You perceive more than others. You hear more than others. I believe this is why gays are so good at grasping changes and setting trends"* (Marco, 48-year-old gay architect). Consequently, the state of distrust affecting gay life is a powerful spur towards anticipation and innovation.

To conclude, social segregation, economic marginalization, legislative gaps, religious contestation but also market isolation (e.g. owing to the lack of proper offers or to misrepresentations) may all favour the dissatisfaction of gay people with the present. Such dissatisfaction fuels gay creativity in the form of transformative strategies to construct sounder bases for the future: *"Like any other group feeling uneasy with its present conditions, gays try – at least – to project their hopes into the future. Therefore, they try to set trends in which they can be the leading players"* (Gerry, 29-year-old gay engineer).

The subcultural roots of gay creativity

A second set of explanations about the origins of gay creativity pertains to the specific features of the gay subculture. This short overview of camp cultural meanings is again functional to a deeper understating of the relationship linking gay consumers to market innovation. In detail, we discuss: (i) the quest of gay people for freedom; (ii) egotism; and (iii) the search for distinctiveness.

Freedom acquires multiple facets within the gay community. Overall, gay people describe themselves as unchained individuals who define, frame, and deploy sexual identities free from castrating heterosexual models. Moving from this general remark, freedom is manifested in the contestation of religious and cultural anathemas, and can occasionally assume visibility during gay rituals (e.g. Gay Pride, Sydney's Mardi Gras, or Halloween). In similar contexts, freedom is combined with pride and transgression in order to challenge the sociocultural cage imposed by the heterosexual others (Foucault, 1977; Kates, 2002; Rinallo, 2006). At the same time, freedom also entails the fluid capacity of gay people to cut across gender representations. Gender (in)flexibility (Kates, 2002) implies gay people's functional deployment of both femininity and masculinity. Femininity is typically used in order to question the heterosexual chains, while masculinity is used to arouse sexual/affective interest from other members of the gay community. When protesting against limiting gendered rules, gay people innovate social roles and market opportunities (e.g. through trash and camp consumption).

Egotism relates to gay people's narcissism which is documented by their investment in personal endowments to face the strong competition within their community. In addition, egotism is engendered by other external factors, including the legislative vacuum in terms of same-sex couples' rights. Fulfilling personal needs is therefore quite a recurrent trait of the gay social profile. In addition, several gay icons (e.g. Paris Hilton, Cher, or Britney Spears) and consumption preferences (e.g. fashion items, clubbing, and drugs) represent an overcelebration of hedonism and lightness, as a probable antidote against the negative experience of social segregation and/or as a form of protest against the Catholic, normalizing, and restrained models of life. However, self-centredness can foster the adoption of personal and potentially disrupting ways of interpreting the world and the market. In this light, innovation and egotism reveal their nature as interconnected constructs.

Finally, distinctiveness mainly pertains to consumption both within and beyond the boundaries of the gay subgroup. Looking at the heterosexual/gay market dialogue, gay consumers constantly modify their consumption patterns to mark the difference from straight consumers. In recent years, metrosexuality (Flocker, 2003) has progressively led to the heterosexual adoption of some gay brands or consumption styles. Gay consumers have reacted to the blurring of consumption boundaries and invested in the rejuvenation of their consumption to keep up with such transformations. Within the gay subculture, distinctiveness is additionally valuable, since it constitutes a competitive differential in terms of seductiveness: *"I believe homosexuals always try to step out of the group. They need to keep changing to avoid the risk of being homologated"* (Beppe, 41-year-old gay broker). In these terms, distinctiveness relates to a capital of individual resources (Arnould & Thompson, 2005), which ultimately spawns a continuous and fast transformation of market trends.

Paradoxical features of gay creativity: ephemerality and trendsetting

In the previous discussion, we have documented the roots of gay creativity and concluded that gay consumers can be considered empowered agents of market change. In this subsection we wish to highlight how gay creativity and innovation are paradoxical features, as gay people are contextually trendsetters while showing strong focalization on the present. We conclude that gay people are creative and innovative, but also characterized by high rates of ephemerality.

Gay people's lack of project orientation is the result of a composite set of forces, including the already mentioned legislative gaps, social ostracism towards the gay subculture, market segregation, and the hypercelebration of youth by gay people within their community. Nowadays, youth and freshness are values per se, regardless of sexual orientation. Nonetheless, they assume specific meaning when looking at the gay world. In fact, youth is an icon of the uncontaminated age, far from the experience of gay people's social isolation, market marginalization, and sexual promiscuity, which some gay people collapse into the idea of *pasteurization* (i.e. the process of experiencing sorrow and corruption). Overall, these cultural, political, normative, and market forces combine to crystallize the representation of gay people's future as a sterile, empty, and mysterious land. Scary and conflictual, the future is progressively left aside, whereas the present is appropriated as the sole domain available to gay people.

In this way, gay people's "caged present" and creativity are the two sides of the same coin. Reconciling the paradoxical coexistence of these two features is possible when observing how *gay people combine innovation with ephemerality*. Gay men do not invest in long-lasting market innovations; on the contrary, they participate in the elaboration of short-lived market trends. Gay innovation therefore contains the seeds of its own termination and is best appreciated by fully acknowledging its mortality. In this light, gay people's innovations are like beautiful butterflies: colourful, dreamlike, impalpable, but also condemned to a short life. We argue that it is not by chance that gay men dominate some market fields of creativity such as the fashion design industry, in which trends are generated and die every 6 months. The constant rejuvenation of gay creativity has several explanations. Firstly, the art of transformation is very much a part of the gay subculture. Secondly, gay identity is fluid and transformative because of gay people's double-belonging to the heterosexual and to the gay cultures. Finally, by constantly playing on their ability to innovate, gay people maintain their competitive advantage in relation to their straight counterparts. Gay creativity therefore essentially recalls the spectacular and vanishing character of a fireworks display.

To sum up, this chapter explores the co-creation of markets by means of consumers' exchanges with companies and other consumers. Given our focalization on gay consumers, we have moved from a deep exploration of the rationales and the peculiar traits of gay creativity and innovation. In the following section we confine our discussion to the consumption sphere, and illustrate how gay consumers lead market changes by means of contestation and symbolic appropriation. We start with a synthetic review of the existing literature on gay marketing and gay consumption, and then quickly move on to our interpretative model of consumer market creation, in which four praxes of market innovation are listed and critically contrasted.

The transformative power of gay consumption

The making of gay marketing

Framed as a non-brand-focused community (Kates, 2002), the gay market has been frequently described as a gold mine (Kates, 1998; Lukenbill, 1999), a myth (Badgett, 2001), a new marketing frontier (Tréguer & Segati, 2003), a way out of the closet (Bowes, 1996), and even a strategic arena for accommodating gay people and heterosexuals within the society (Chasin, 2000; Peñaloza, 1996). In particular, thus far scholars have researched areas such as the processes of (gay) identity formation (Kates, 1998, 2002), the social construction of barriers and the constant redefinition of cultural spaces (Bowes, 1996), gay servicescapes (Haslop, Hill, & Schmidt, 1998), consumers' signalling acts to mark membership and separation (Lukenbill, 1999) and companies' entry strategies into the gay market (Kates, 2004; Tréguer & Segati, 2003).

From a theoretical point of view, this work mainly refers to three streams in the literature: (1) the CCT (Consumer Culture Theory) approach (Arnould & Thompson, 2005), which provides the interpretative framework to describe marketplace subcultures and heterosexual/gay dynamics; (2) the consumer agency stream, which suggests we should acknowledge the increasing consumer subjectivity and participation in social movements (Vargo & Lusch, 2004; Witkovski, 2004) and therefore adds understanding of gay consumers' political exploitation of consumer goods; and (3) the gay studies (Chasin, 2000; Kates, 1998, 1999; Lukenbill, 1999; Sender, 2004), which largely address the topic of how "diverse" sexual orientation impacts upon market behaviours.

In this study, we concentrate on the gay market. Marketing scholars have documented gay people's high rates of internal variation and the pervasive impact of homosexual orientation on consumption behaviours (Kates, 2002) as well as on the social and political dynamics linking gay people, straight people, and businesses (Chasin 2000; Freitas, Kaiser, & Hammidi, 1996). Given the multifaceted structure of gay identity (Lukenbill, 1999; Wardlow, 1996), gay people typically present alternating identities as they experience the paradox of contemporaneously identifying themselves with the gay and the heterosexual cultures. Gay consumers are therefore both in-groups and out-groups. This sense of multiple belonging is mirrored by consumption behaviours, as we will better illustrate in the following discussion, in which we show how gay consumers are able to combine idiosyncratic consumption with products and brands from the undifferentiated, mainstream market. In addition, we will also describe processes of symbolic appropriation and the dynamics of imitation and consumption crossover enacted by heterosexual consumers.

In so doing, we show that, in spite of the relevance of gay consumers in contemporary socioeconomic settings, they still experience discrimination at numerous market levels. With reference to company strategies and praxes, marketing deficiencies reveal their insidious nature, since the dearth of available products and services targeted to GLBT (Gays, Lesbians, Bisexuals, and Transgenders) (e.g. suitable insurance plans, gay holidays and resorts, etc.) can be read as further confirmation of gay people's alleged invisibility and stigmatization (Walters & Moore, 2002). In addition, companies' communication campaigns help (de)construct stereotypes about gay consumers (for an extensive review, see www.commercialcloset.com). As such, market (co)creation largely contributes to shaping the gay–heterosexual relationship. From a business point of view, acknowledging the existence of the GLBT market, providing a consistent offer in terms of products and services, or advertising to this minority audience, all represent instruments of market creation. At the same time, this has an impact on the way gay people are socially perceived both within and beyond the gay community. In fact, stereotypes, power relations, and social acceptability are closely linked to companies' market choices and to the way they transform gay people's and straight people's experience of the marketplace.

Consumer co-creation of markets: contestation, symbolic appropriation, and cross-consumption

Gay consumption is a sophisticated example of market innovation nurtured by the dialectic relationship between companies and gay customers, as well as between gay people and heterosexuals. In fact, gay consumption documents innovative ways of autonomous appropriation of already existing products, which are infused with camp meanings and deployed in ways that build a strong sense of community. On the other hand, straight people participate in this market confrontation when consuming brands and products symbolically attributable to the gay minority, and when they help challenge market/social barriers through consumption behaviours.

Relying on previous classification of gay and straight consumption categories (Visconti, 2008), we show *how gay consumers innovate the market through direct interaction with companies*. In detail, we document two main strategies of market creation: (i) "contestation" and (ii) "symbolic appropriation". We also address a further source of market change, represented by the *exchanges occurring between gay people and heterosexuals within the consumer society*. In the latter situation, we comment on strategies of "crossover consumption" as further forms of market transformation.

Gay/straight consumption categories are classified by means of two dimensions (Colacchio & Mastrangelo, 2006; Visconti, 2008): (i) the rate of product gayness, which marks the distance between "typically gay" versus "non-gay" patterns of consumption; and (ii) the agency expressed by consumers in product deployment separating "adaptive" from "proactive" market behaviours. By crossing these dimensions, four typologies of products and brands are defined (see Table 17.1): (i) "functional products", that is, goods strongly tailored to gay consumers' idiosyncratic needs; (ii) "symbolic products", iconically appropriated by gay consumers (the so-called gay marker goods and gay marker brands) (Kates, 2002); (iii) "affluence products" representing areas of consumption crossover between gay/straight consumers; and (iv) "generic products" indicating the neutral set of products not implicated in current gendered discourse. In particular, we argue that functional and symbolic products tangibly result from gay consumers' contestation and appropriation praxes. In parallel, we assume that affluence products document gay/straight crossover consumption.

Contestation originates from the existence of gay consumers' distinctive market needs. When we think in terms of products and services, such as gay travel, specific bank and insurance accounts, gay clubs and cruising areas, gay Internet websites and chat-lines, or gay pornography, we easily define consumption spheres exclusively consumed by gay people. As such, functional products are not appropriable by straight people, because they would not gain any functional and/or symbolic reward from their exploitation. To quote just a few examples, Outtravel (www.outtravel.it) is a company organizing gay cruises and other exclusive holidays. Turning our attention to the vast offer available on the web, we can mention gay chat-lines (e.g. www.dlist.com), dating sites (e.g. www.gay.com), and e-media (e.g. www.gaytv.com). Similarly, it is worth mentioning Visa's Rainbow Endowment project, funded through Rainbow card subscriptions and use, and committed to promoting the health and social integration of GLBT

Table 17.1 Trajectories of consumer market co-creation

Strategies of market creation	Firm-driven innovation	Contestation	Symbolic appropriation	Consumption crossover
Product implicated	Generic products	Functional products	Symbolic products	Affluence products
Product characteristics	- Low gayness - Adaptive market behaviour	- High gayness - Adaptive market behaviour	- High gayness - Proactive market behaviour	- Low gayness - Proactive market behaviour
Examples	- All products and brands not belonging to the other categories	- Gay insurance - Gay travels - Gay clubs - Gay porno - Gay websites	- Gay marker goods (e.g. toiletries, fashion, design) - Gay marker brands (e.g. Gucci, Prada, Gaultier, Mini, Absolut Vodka, Levi's etc.)	- Cosmetics - Fashion - Design - Arts
Main target	- Straight consumers	- Gay consumers	- Both	- Both
Main adopters	- Both	- Gay consumers only	- Gay consumers mainly	- Straight consumers mainly
Main market creator	- Companies	- Gay consumers	- Gay consumers	- Straight consumers
Power-keepers	- Companies	- Gay consumers - Companies	- Gay consumers	- Straight consumers
Main outcomes	Pros: - High potential Cons: - Mainstream logic	Pros: - Legitimation - Satisfaction Cons: - Segregation	Pros: - Community - Distinctiveness Cons: - Separation	Pros: - Diffusion - Exchange Cons: - Loss of uniqueness
Trajectories of change	- Towards symbolic products	- Back to generic products	- Towards affluence products	- Back to generic products

(Continued)

Table 17.1   Continued

Strategies of market creation	Firm-driven innovation	Contestation	Symbolic appropriation	Consumption crossover
Managerial implications	- Push innovation	- Pull innovation - Niche marketing - Diversification - Strategic caution	- Pull innovation - Advertising - Packaging - Place - Event marketing	- Pull innovation - Advertising - Product placement

(www.rainbowcard.com). In all these cases, gay consumers deploy their agency in order to acquire market visibility, eventually read by companies in terms of market potential.

The strategies of market contestation are endorsed by lobbying activities and pressures on mass media. They also generate contradictory effects, as they combine the crystallization of market and social boundaries with the gay market and social legitimation as well as with the opportunity of receiving a highly tailored market offer (Kates, 1999, 2004). In other words, by restricting gay identity to the sole homosexual side, contestation generates ad hoc forms of market supply, which can be seen as market ghettoes and an eventual evidence of gay consumers' marginality or difference. The paradoxical impact of functional products (i.e. legitimation *and* segregation of the gay community) largely confirms the socialization of consumption along confrontation between gay people and companies. In fact, companies' supply strategies and consumers' market accommodation generate effects far beyond the economic sphere, as they fuel the social representation of gay people and the definition of their acceptability. At the same time, and in spite of its political significance, we cannot forget that this category of products is not superfluous because it reveals a set of needs idiosyncratic (and frequently crucial) to the gay community that deserve proper market solutions.

From the company's point of view, among the examples previously listed we find two main categories of companies. On the one hand, we have firms pursuing niche market strategies (e.g. Outtravel, D-list, Gay.com, etc.), which aim to meet the exclusive needs of gay consumers. On the other hand, we also find companies diversifying their targets (e.g. Visa, American Express, etc.), which face the risk of losing their traditional customers when openly addressing the gay market. In this light, we consider functional products as promising fields principally to companies that are newcomers, and thus start with targeting the gay community. By means of consistent market strategies – including supply customization, explicit advertising, and sponsoring of gay crusades – these companies can acquire legitimation within the gay subculture and benefit from gay consumers' trust and loyalty (Kates, 2004). By contrast, diversified companies have to be more cautious when entering the gay market. They need to estimate the risk they run with reference to their mainstream market; contextually, they have to evaluate if gay customers can ever interpret them as reliable partners according to their brand image, past history, and market resources. Consequently, these companies generally use communication in more ambiguous ways, and can even decide to enter the gay market under completely new brands.

Symbolic appropriation takes place when gay consumers actively select and adopt tangible artefacts (e.g. specific products) or intangible artefacts (e.g certain brands) through which they express, confirm, or challenge their socialized identities. Symbolic products are the result of this process of appropriation and represent the vivid evidence of consumption deployment as the mediator of gay identity (Keating & McLoughlin, 2005, p. 146). Therefore, they represent an effective tool to enhance gay people's sense of belonging and mutual identification. At the same time, they can be interpreted as an expression of gay power when providing gay people with market and social distinctiveness.

From the managerial point of view, gay people's praxes of symbolic appropriation give rise to two questions: (i) the detection of product categories most frequently appropriated by gay consumers; and (ii) the way meanings are transferred into symbolic products and brands. With reference to product/brand selection, the list of industries mainly involved in the process of symbolic appropriation is strongly tied to the very roots of the camp subculture. Overbeautification, celebration of change, gender inflexibility, or narcissism all provide fertile soil for the major attention gay consumers generally devote to product categories such as toiletries and cosmetics, fashion garments and jewellery, home design, beauty centres and gyms, but also clubs, alcoholic drinks, and health food. Further, we also explain how brands and products are admitted to the gay Olympus by means of processes of meaning attribution. Why are brands like Gucci, Dior, Gaultier, Cavalli, DSquared, Coca Cola, Alessi, BMW, Mini, Bang & Olufsen – to quote but a few – considered to be gay friendly? Empirical evidence shows two complementary processes of meaning infusion. On the one hand, companies may actively look for legitimation among gay consumers (Kates, 2004). For example, in Italy, Citroën Pluriel has gained gay consumers' attention by sponsoring gay prides and involving Dolce & Gabbana in the design of the car. Similarly, Absolut Vodka is a worldwide gay-friendly brand because of its long-time support of the gay crusade. On the other hand, gay consumers may also enact their agency by selecting specific products or brands that are progressively imbued with gay meaning. Typically, gay consumers are more likely to select products and brands already having a few of the following features (Visconti, 2008): (i) luxury and exclusivity, which challenge the negative associations of the idea of minority (i.e. through luxury, the limited number of individuals possessing a given product are no longer interpreted as a marginal minority but as a "lucky few" group); (ii) originality, which appeals to gay consumers' trendsetting aspect; (iii) ambiguity, which mirrors gender (in)flexibility and stimulates the "gaydar" (i.e. the gay radar used to detect other gay people); (iv) kitsch, which goes hand in hand with the principle of transgression; (v) revenge, which relates to their struggle to achieve full social acceptance and recognition; and (vi) seductiveness, sustaining the idea of products/brands as allies in the perennial search for beauty and youth.

Consequently, we argue that companies operating in industries having a certain "gay closeness" (e.g. toiletries, fashion, health food, etc.) will better benefit from the opportunities generated by gay consumers' symbolic appropriation. Secondly, we additionally suggest that companies can actively stimulate symbolic appropriation by means of advertising campaigns, product placement strategies, interventions on the product design and packaging, store experience, etc. By listing product characteristics that mainly impact gay consumers' appropriation, we also identify the key managerial drivers to support companies' strategies fostering symbolic appropriation.

Finally, we direct attention to the level of consumer society and thus to the confrontation between straight and gay people. *Consumption crossover* (Grier, Brumbaugh, & Thornton, 2006) throws light on the most intensely dialectic area of gay/heterosexual consumption. In detail, the "commodification of symbolic, gay cultural artefacts" (Keating & McLoughlin, 2005, p. 147) opens the way to the adoption of gay consumption patterns by heterosexuals. Under the impact of the "metrosexualization" of contemporary societies (Flocker, 2003; Rinallo, 2006), straight men are increasingly mimicking gay consumptions, in particular by expropriating gay marker goods and brands. By means of imitation, heterosexuals are reshaping the set of gay symbolic products and contextually challenging the social boundaries separating gay and straight people. A prime example is provided by Dolce & Gabbana. As a matter of fact, the brand was originally identified as a gay icon under the impact of the two designers' manifest coming-out (Domenico Dolce and Stefano Gabbana publicly admitted being a couple). Strategies of product placement (e.g. the adoption of the D&G style by fetish stars like Madonna), coupled with provocative messages challenging Catholic ethics, boosted gay consumers' attachment to the brand. However, over time the company started targeting the mainstream market to the extent that straight consumers have positively accepted D&G products as emblems of glamour and seduction, drawing on the widespread stereotype of the fashionable gay man. At the same time, product placement shifted from gay icons to mainstream symbols, including especially some popular football players. Today, many gay consumers consider D&G as a mass brand that no longer pertains to the key values of the gay subculture.

Looking at the way consumption crossover impacts upon heterosexuals' market acculturation, we observe how, through affluence products and brands, straight consumers filter some cultural traits out of the dominated gay subculture. Overall, consumption crossover implies that market acculturation operates also at the level of the dominating group (in this case, heterosexual consumers), which progressively acquires selected consumption habits pertaining to its marginal counter-part. In this way, consumption crossover not only helps modify group boundaries but also additionally rearranges power relationships to the advantage of gay consumers.

If we look for explanations of how gay consumptions are spread across straight consumers, three groups of rationales can be listed. Firstly, gay people have been depicted as trendsetters, and this tenet has progressively been institutionalized. This implies that they are path-breaking agents, not necessarily confined within their own community. Gay consumers also play on their ability to create market trends, since this can be considered as an expression of superiority, and a powerful tool used to improve – or even subvert – their socially dominated position. Secondly, we observe several agents of contamination that promote the circulation of gay cultural meanings: the media, especially advertising, have been targeting gay people, making them more visible and legitimating them in market and social terms. In addition, women also help disseminate certain gay consumption habits: influenced by their gay friends, they often induce their partners/brothers to imitate gay aesthetics and buy/consume specific products and brands (e.g. cosmetics, perfume, clothing, and so on). Finally, straight people may also try to erode gay people's competitive edge (created by the existence of symbolic products) by means of consumption crossover (i.e. they "consume" their rivals). However, this differential cannot be fully eliminated, as the gay subculture is partially inalienable. In fact, straight consumers might be able to mimic the content of gay consumption (i.e. the same products and brands), but they can hardly replicate gay meanings, which are definitely rooted in the camp subculture of consumption (Kates, 2001). In this light, consumption crossover is an expression of "keeping while giving" (Weiner, 1992) and the confirmation of gay people's partially inalienable wealth.

Recalling managerial implications, the praxis of cross-consumption does not offer immediate suggestions for marketing strategies, as it entails dynamics mainly involving gay and straight consumers. In other words, cross-consumption originates within the consumer society and only indirectly impacts upon companies' strategies. Nonetheless, we can figure out a few insights for companies aiming to ride the waves of straight consumption of gay symbolic goods and brands. In particular, we suggest companies may deploy product placement when using gay endorsers to advertise their product to the mainstream market. By enforcing the idea of gay consumers as trendsetters, companies can dissimulate their real intent of eventually reaching the heterosexual target. The impact of gay endorsers on heterosexual consumers will probably be sounder for industries where gay consumers are publicly attributed greater creativity and taste. Similarly, firms can also exploit below-the-line communications, such as events where gay consumers are deployable as product-endorsers.

Finally, generic products are a quiescent, neutral land characterized by low product gayness and adaptive consumption behaviours. These goods constitute the large majority of the daily consumption of both gay and straight consumers and do not convey any meaning in relation to sexual orientation. As such, this category of brands and products is the field where consumers' and companies' agency can be fully expressed. Gay consumers can draw on generic products to generate new symbolic forms of consumption. At the same time, companies can adopt proactive market strategies to increase the gay-friendliness of their products and brands. Recently, for example, the AEG Company has been beckoning to the gay consumer target through an advertising campaign promoting the new combo line of dryers and washing machines. In the ad, the sleeves of two men's shirts are holding hands, as the pay-off recites *"Made for one another"*. The literal sense of this campaign describes the perfect integration of dryer and washing machine, while the meta-message ironically exploits gay codes. As such, generic products represent the new frontier of the forthcoming firm-driven strategies of market creation.

Implications and concluding remarks

This chapter is intended as a complement to the analysis of market creation solely from the company point of view. Relying on the theoretical contributions of CCT and *consumer agency*, in the previous discussion we have talked about the active role of gay and straight consumers in creating markets as a side effect of their negotiations with the consumer society and companies. By illustrating how gay consumers may use products to cope with social discrimination and marginalization, we have endorsed the idea of consumption as the mediator of identity. By infusing meanings into consumption artefacts ("consuming as integration"), gay and straight consumers deploy objects and brands so as to mark their membership of social groupings ("consuming as classification") (Holt, 1995). To sum up, we detect areas of subjectivity both for gay and heterosexual consumers. Gay consumers show active intervention whenever they: (i) fight to obtain additional functional products (i.e. contestation); (ii) transform generic products into symbolic ones (i.e. appropriation); and (iii) reject symbolic products. In a parallel manner, straight consumers manifest their agency in market creation whenever they: (i) contrast the supply of functional products (e.g. by boycotting companies openly targeting the gay community); and (ii) imitate gay consumers' symbolic consumption (i.e. cross-consumption).

Reconsidering the *role of companies*, we conclude that they find opportunities to generate market innovation while interacting with gay and straight consumers, and while observing their interplay at consumer society level. In particular, we detect promising areas of market creation along the praxes of contestation and symbolic appropriation, where companies are more directly involved by gay consumers. Additionally, companies can also deploy consumption crossover to reposition their products and brands by infusing them with gay meanings valuable to straight consumers. As such, we comment here upon the rough potential of generic, functional, symbolic, and affluence products from the perspective of companies aiming to innovate their markets through stable interaction with current and prospective consumers. Consequently, we conclude that, although mutually exclusive, these four product/brand categories are not rigid and can change over time under the impact of the interaction between consumers and companies (see Table 17.1).

Functional products probably constitute the most unchangeable set of products and services. We have documented the idiosyncratic essence of these products as rooted in needs that exclusively pertain to the gay market. For this reason, consumers and companies cannot easily transform the content of this category. In particular, we consider two main options provoking a change in the content of gay functional products. Firstly, companies may acknowledge certain unmet needs manifested by gay customers through contestation praxes. In this case, innovation is customer driven but operated through companies, and terminates in the addition of new, specific products or services targeted at the gay market (e.g. consider the first gay tour-guide "Spartacus", the first gay media, etc.). By contrast, functional products can be transformed under the impact of institutional changes that eliminate previously existing gay peculiar needs. For example, gay insurance policies or bank services tailored to gay couples make sense only in contexts lacking norms to protect and regulate the rights of same-sex couples. This means that legislative and institutional shocks may lead to the termination of given functional products and their transformation into generic ones (e.g. gay insurance policies will be replaced by generic policies). In this way, the stock of functional products is exposed both to possible extensions (through companies' tailored offers) and reductions (under institutional shocks).

When we turn our attention to the other three product categories (i.e. *generic, symbolic, and affluence products*), we more easily grasp the potential that companies face in terms of market creation. Generic products are accessible gold mines, as they can be symbolically changed into prospective gay marker icons. We have already shown how gay-close industries (e.g. fashion, design, etc.) and/or specific brand/product features (e.g. luxury, ambiguity, originality, etc.) help translate generic products into symbolic ones. For example, the traditional toilet paper may acquire gay appreciation by changing its usual white colour to deep pink or other fancy alternatives. Looking at real market cases, the Mini and the Volkswagen Beetle have acquired the status of gay iconic products as they respond to the gay quest for perennial youth owing to the brands' evergreen feature and the high standard of their design. Reverting our lens of analysis to affluence items, we confirm the set of opportunities companies have in fostering the adoption of gay-addicted products/brands by straight consumers. In particular, companies can effectively increase or play with the gayness of their supply so as to appeal to the mainstream market.

Conclusion

To conclude, we believe this chapter raises some issues of dramatic relevance to a variety of audiences, including marketers, scholars, and students preparing for their managerial careers. While observing the multiple ways in which gay and straight consumers impact upon market creation, we separate companies into two main categories: companies focusing on the niche gay market and companies diversifying their market offer so as to include the gay target. The first companies are much more free to select their entry strategies, and can openly work to root their brands in the gay subculture. Envisioning their managerial levers, they range from explicit advertising to functional offers, and from sponsoring of gay movements to diversity management policies directed towards their employers. On the other side, companies diversifying their targets should be more cautious in following their strategies to the gay market. In particular, they have to be convincing with gay consumers and at the same time avoid offending straight consumers. In the past, some companies have coped with this problem by using gay women when advertising to gay men. This choice was motivated by the double appeal of gay women to both gay men (who appreciate to a greater extent the homosexual decoy of companies' communications) and heterosexual men (who may be stimulated in their erotic fantasies). In addition, companies can also deploy popular but ambiguous endorsers who catch gay and straight consensus at the same time (e.g. David Beckham, Ricky Martin, etc.). They can also locate hidden gay codes in their ads, which can reward gay customers while not disturbing mainstream ones (Kates, 1999).

Overall, the chapter documents multiple directions (consumer agency and company choices) and multiple levels (consumer–company and consumer–consumer dynamics) of market creation. Further, by linking market innovation to the social reshaping of gay/straight lives, it also contributes to the stream of studies advocating "a more transformative marketing practice that is sociohistorically situated, culturally sensitive, and organic in accounting for and adapting to contemporary global, technological, and sociocultural developments" (Peñaloza and Venkatesh, 2006, p. 299).

References

Arnould, E. J. & Thompson, C. J. (2005) "Consumer Culture Theory (CCT): twenty years of research". *Journal of Consumer Research*, vol. 31, March, pp. 868–882.

Badgett, L. M. V. (1995) "The wage effects of sexual orientation discrimination". *Industrial and Labor Relations Review*, vol. 48, no. 4, pp. 726–739.

Badgett, L. M. V. (2001) *Money, Myths, and Change: the Economic Lives of Lesbians and Gay Men*. The University of Chicago Press, Chicago, IL.

Baudrillard, J. (1968) *Le Système des Objets*. Editions Gallimard, Paris, France.

Bowes, J. E. (1996) "Out of the closet and into the marketplace: meeting basic needs in the gay community", in *Gays, Lesbians, and Consumer Behavior: Theory, Practice, and Research Issues in Marketing*, edited by Wardlow, D. L. Haworth Press, New York, NY, pp. 219–244.

Chasin, A. (2000) *Selling Out: the Gay and Lesbian Movement Goes to Market*. Palgrave, New York, NY.

Colacchio, F. & Mastrangelo, D. (2006) "Nuove opportunità di marketing di nicchia per la media impresa: il segmento gay". Working paper, IULM University, Milan, Italy.

Flocker, M. (2003) *The Metrosexual Guide to Style: a Handbook for the Modern Man*. Da Capo Press, Cambridge, MA.

Foucault, M. (1977) *Discipline and Punish: the Birth of the Prison*. Tavistock, London, UK.

Freitas, A., Kaiser, S., & Hammidi, T. (1996) "Communities, commodities, cultural space, and style", in *Gays, Lesbians, and Consumer Behavior: Theory, Practice, and Research Issues in Marketing*, edited by Wardlow, D. L. Haworth Press, New York, NY, pp. 9–41.

Grier, S., Brumbaugh, A. M., & Thornton, C. (2006) "Crossover dreams: consumer responses to ethnic-oriented products". *Journal of Marketing*, vol. 70, no. 2, pp. 35–51.

Haslop, C., Hill, H., & Schmidt, R. A. (1998) "The gay lifestyle: spaces for a subculture of consumption". *Marketing Intelligence and Planning*, vol. 16, no. 5, pp. 318–326.

Holt, D. B. (1995) "How consumers consume: a typology of consumption practices". *Journal of Consumer Research*, vol. 22, June, pp. 1–16.

Holt, D. B. (1997) "Poststructuralist lifestyle analysis: conceptualizing the social patterning of consumption in postmodernity". *Journal of Consumer Research*, vol. 23, no. 4, pp. 326–350.

Kates, S. M. (1998) *Twenty Million New Customers! Understanding Gay Men's Consumer Behaviour*. The Harrington Park Press, New York, NY.

Kates, S. M. (1999) "Making the ad perfectly queer: marketing 'normality' to the gay men's community?". *Journal of Advertising*, vol. 28, no. 1, pp. 25–37.

Kates, S. M. (2001) "Camp as cultural capital: further elaboration of a consumption taste". *Advances in Consumer Research*, vol. 28, pp. 334–339.

Kates, S. M. (2002) "The protean quality of subcultural consumption: an ethnographic account of gay consumers". *Journal of Consumer Research*, vol. 29, pp. 393–398.

Kates, S. M. (2004) "The dynamics of brand legitimacy: an interpretative study in the gay men's community". *Journal of Consumer Research*, vol. 31, pp. 455–464.

Keating, A. & McLoughlin, D. (2005) "Understanding the emergence of markets: a social constructionist perspective on gay economy". *Consumption, Markets and Culture*, vol. 8, no. 2, pp. 131–152.

Kotler, P. (1986) "The prosumer movement: a new challenge for marketers". *Advances of Consumer Research*, vol. 13, no. 1, pp. 510–514.

Lindridge, A. M., Hogg, M. K., & Shah, M. (2004) "Imagined multiple worlds: how South Asian women in Britain use family and friends to navigate the 'border crossings' between household and social contexts". *Consumption, Markets and Culture*, vol. 7, no. 3, pp. 211–238.

Lukenbill, G. (1999) *Untold Millions: Secret Truths about Marketing to Gay and Lesbian Consumers*. The Harrington Park Press, New York, NY.

McCracken, G. (1986) "Culture and consumption: a theoretical account of the structure and movement of the cultural meaning of consumer goods". *Journal of Consumer Research*, vol. 13, no. 1, pp. 71–84.

Peñaloza, L. (1996) "We're here, we're queer, and we go shopping! A critical perspective on the accommodation of gays and lesbians in the US marketplace". *Journal of Homosexuality*, vol. 31, no. 1/2, pp. 9–41.

Peñaloza, L. & Venkatesh, A. (2006) "Further evolving the new dominant logic of marketing: from services to the social construction of markets". *Marketing Theory*, vol. 6, no. 3, pp. 299–316.

Rinallo, D. (2006) "Metro/fashion/tribes of men: negotiating the boundaries of men's legitimate consumption", in *Consumer Tribes: Theory, Practice and Prospects*, edited by Cova, B., Kozinets, R., & Shankar, A. Elsevier/Butterworth-Heinemann, Oxford, UK.

Sender, K. (2004) *Business, Not Politics: the Making of the Gay Marketing*. Columbia University Press, New York, NY.

Slater, D. (1997) *Consumer Culture and Modernity*. Polity Press, Cambridge, UK.

Thompson, C. J. & Haytko, D. L. (1997) "Speaking of fashion: consumers' uses of fashion discourses and the appropriation of countervailing cultural meanings". *Journal of Consumer Research*, vol. 24, no. 1, pp. 15–42.

Toffler, A. (1980) *The Third Wave*. William Morrow, New York, NY.

Tréguer, J.-P. & Segati, J.-M. (2003) *Les Nouveaux Marketings*. Dunod, Paris, France.

Vargo, S. L. & Lusch, R. F. (2004) "Evolving to a new dominant logic for marketing". *Journal of Marketing*, vol. 68, no. 1, pp. 1–17.

Visconti, L. M. (2008) "Gays' market and social behaviors in (de)constructing symbolic boundaries". *Consumption, Markets and Culture*.

von Hippel, E. A. (1977) "Has a customer already developed your next product?". *Sloan Management Review*, vol. 18, no. 2, pp. 63–74.

Walters, A. S. & Moore, L. J. (2002) "Attention all shoppers, queer customers in aisle two: investigating lesbian and gay discrimination in the marketplace". *Consumption, Markets and Culture*, vol. 5, no. 4, pp. 285–303.

Wardlow, D. L. (ed.) (1996) *Gays, Lesbians, and Consumer Behavior: Theory, Practice, and Research Issues in Marketing*. Haworth Press, New York, NY.

Weiner, A. (1992) *Inalienable Possessions: the Paradox of Keeping while Giving*. University of California Press, Berkeley, CA.

Witkovski, T. H. (2004) "Re-gendering consumer agency in mid-nineteenth-century America: a visual understanding". *Consumption, Markets and Culture*, vol. 7, no. 3, pp. 261–283.

Index